Collected Works of Northrop Frye

VOLUME 5

Northrop Frye's Late Notebooks, 1982–1990:

Architecture of the Spiritual World

Collected Works of Northrop Frye

Alvin A. Lee, General Editor

Jean O'Grady, Associate Editor

Nicholas Halmi, Assistant Editor

The Collected Edition of the Works of Northrop Frye has been planned and is being directed by an editorial committee under the aegis of Victoria University, through its Northrop Frye Centre. The purpose of the edition is to make available authoritative texts of both published and unpublished works, based on analysis and comparison of all available materials, and supported by scholarly apparatus, including annotation and introductions. The Northrop Frye Centre gratefully acknowledges financial support, through McMaster University, from the Michael G. DeGroote family.

Northrop Frye's Late Notebooks, 1982–1990:

Architecture of the Spiritual World

VOLUME 5

Edited by Robert D. Denham

For Jane,
who protected Norrie so
he could write these
notebooks.
with affection,
Bob

UNIVERSITY OF TORONTO PRESS
Toronto Buffalo London

© Victoria University, University of Toronto (notebooks) and Robert D. Denham (preface, introduction, annotation) 2000

Toronto Buffalo London

Printed in Canada

ISBN 0-8020-4751-3 (Volume 5)
ISBN 0-8020-4752-1 (Volume 6)

Printed on acid-free paper

Canadian Cataloguing in Publication Data

Frye, Northrop, 1912–1991
Northrop Frye's late notebooks, 1982–1990 : architecture of the spiritual world

(Collected works of Northrop Frye ; v. 5–6)
Includes bibliographical references and index.
ISBN 0-8020-4751-3 (v. 5)   ISBN 0-8020-4752-1 (v. 6)

1. Frye, Northrop, 1912–1991 – Notebooks, sketchbooks, etc.
I. Denham, Robert D.   II. Title.   III. Series.

PN75.F7A3 2000   801'.95'092   C99-932846-8

This volume has been published with the assistance of a grant from Victoria University.

University of Toronto Press acknowledges the financial assistance to its publishing program of the Canada Council and the Ontario Arts Council.

University of Toronto Press acknowledges the financial support for its publishing activities of the Government of Canada through the Book Publishing Industry Development Program (BPIDP).

In Memory of My Mother and My Father

Contents

Preface

Northrop Frye practised the notebook form of writing for more than fifty years. Altogether there are seventy-six holograph notebooks among the Frye papers at the Victoria University Library, all but two of which are in cloth or paper-covered books. (Two unbound notebooks were kept in loose-leaf binders.) They come in various shapes and sizes, the amount of material they contain varying from a few pages to 253 pages. The earliest notebook dates from the late 1930s, when Frye was at Oxford, and the final entries in the latest notebook were made in 1990, only a few weeks before his death. Although portions of some notebooks are drafts of Frye's various writing projects, most of the material consists of neatly laid-out paragraphs separated by blank lines (occasionally two paragraphs will constitute a single entry). The holograph notebooks contain approximately 750,000 words, excluding the drafts. In the 1970s Frye began typing some of his notes. This experiment was not in his view altogether successful (he even wrote of wanting to destroy his typed notes for *The Great Code*), but a large portion of these notes is practically identical in scope and form to the holograph notebooks. Other typed material contains summaries and occasional commentaries on books that Frye was reading. The typed notes constitute another 350,000 words.

Most of the material in the present volumes comes from the final six years of Frye's life, 1985–1990. A few of the sections in the typed notes are as early as 1982. Selections from the remaining notebooks—another six volumes of material—will be issued in due course by my coeditor, Michael Dolzani, and me. We have organized the material by chronological and/or thematic units. One volume, for example, will be devoted to Frye's early notebooks, another to his commentaries on romance, and still another to the large book that he planned to write following *Anatomy of Criticism*. There will be separate volumes of the notebooks for *Anatomy of Criticism* and *The Great Code*, and a final volume containing a selection from the typed notes.

During the summer of 1992 Dolores Signori and I catalogued and briefly annotated sixty-eight of the notebooks. Six notebooks were added to the collection in 1993. Brief descriptions of these can be found in Signori's *Guide to the Northrop Frye Papers* (Toronto: Victoria University Library, 1993), 191–4. Two additional notebooks came to the collection in 1997, having been discovered in the bedside table of Elizabeth Eedy Frye, Frye's second wife, after her death. In citing and otherwise referring to the first sixty-six holograph notebooks I follow the numbers assigned in the *Guide*: 1–10, 11a–11i, 12–29, 30a–30r, 31–41. The two unbound notebooks and the eight additional holograph notebooks, which were added to the Northrop Frye Fonds after 1991, have been numbered 42 through 51. The headnotes for the holograph notebooks give the year of accession and box number in the Northrop Frye Fonds where they are located.

Although Frye sometimes referred to the typed material as "notebooks," I have called them "notes" in these two volumes to distinguish them from the holograph notebooks. Many of the typed notes are located in files that the *Guide* describes as "miscellaneous," some files containing more than fifty discrete units of material. These files have been assigned numbers from 52 to 58. In those cases where I have not reproduced the material in a file in its entirety, having omitted typescripts not clearly related to the themes of *Words with Power* and *The Double Vision*, the first selected unit is designated by number 1 following a decimal point, as in Notes 54.1, the second unit by number 2, as in Notes 55.2, and so on. The headnotes for the typed material give the year of accession, box number, and file number in the Northrop Frye Fonds. In the present volumes "Notebook" always refers to holograph material, and "Notes" to typed material.

My goal in transcribing the notebooks has been to reproduce the text exactly as Frye wrote it, with the following exceptions. From Notebook 44 I have omitted several sentences of a personal nature that relate to someone still living. I have regularized Frye's use of the comma and period with quotations marks, following the standard North American practice, and I have italicized the words and phrases that he underlined. I have not called attention to any of the minor corrections and additions that Frye himself made on both the holograph and typed manuscripts, and I have silently corrected the few obvious typographical mistakes in the typescripts. The endnotes do, however, record the places where Frye cancelled an entry, or part of an entry, as well as those places in the typescripts where he made a substantive holograph addition. All editorial additions have been placed within square brackets. These additions include paragraph numbers, expansions of abbreviations, and an occasional uncertain reading, punctuation mark, inflection, or *sic*. I have not called attention to variants in spelling, such as "Dostoievsky" and "Dostoevsky," "Hölderlin" and "Holderlin," "center" and "centre," and the like. In order to reduce the number of endnotes, I have frequently recorded within square brackets the source of Frye's references to Biblical passages and Classical authors, as well as to works, mostly poems, where the edition is not important. When Frye himself refers to pages or to entries within a notebook, I have put the paragraph number of the reference in square brackets. Frye's own square brackets have been replaced with braces: { }.

The annotations are of the sort one would expect in such an edition. They identify (and sometimes quote from) Frye's sources and references, explain things that might not be clear, refer the reader to other passages in the notebooks, and, as indicated, explain irregular features of the manuscript. The editions cited are not necessarily those Frye used or owned. If, however, his own library did contain an annotated copy of a work that is cited, whatever the edition, I have included that information in the note. Except in a few cases this information is restricted to the secondary sources that Frye owned. As the notebooks were often the workshop out of which Frye's books were forged, the annotations also include a large number of references, of the "see" variety, to Frye's published work, especially his books. These references will enable the reader to compare the published and the notebook forms. Some notes direct the reader to see paragraphs or notes "above" and "below": these prepositions refer only to the notebook in which such directions are found. References to other notebooks, both published in the present volumes and unpublished, give the notebook and paragraph number (e.g., NB 27, par. 230). I have generally restricted cross-referenced material in other notebooks to the original citations of Frye's sources and of his own books and essays, and to those occasions where Frye himself refers to previously written entries. The first citation of a source, including Frye's own works, will be the first entry following the titles in the index.

Acknowledgments

I express my thanks to the executors of the Northrop Frye estate for permitting me to edit Frye's notebooks; to Alvin Lee, the General Editor of the Collected Works of Northrop Frye, and Jean O'Grady, the Associate Editor, for their support and guidance; to Robert Brandeis and his staff at the Victoria University Library for their generous assistance; to Christine Cable for scanning some of the typed notes to disk; to Pat Scott of the Fintel Library, Roanoke College, for her efficient handling of my many interlibrary loan requests; and to the National Endowment for the Humanities for a fellowship that provided me a year of uninterrupted time to work on the notebooks. I am grateful to Alvin Lee, Margaret Burgess, Nicholas Halmi, Jean O'Grady, and the readers of the manuscript when it was in the review process for the many corrections and additions they suggested for the annotations. Deserving special praise are Margaret Burgess for her extraordinary copy-editing skills and Nicholas Halmi for preparing the index.

My thanks to the following people who replied to my queries and whose answers, in most cases, made their way into one or more of the notes: Joseph Adamson, Edna Aizenberg, Albert C. Albriola, David R. Bains, Fernande Bassan, Walter Jackson Bate, G.E. Bentley, Jr., Geoffrey Bennington, Richard Berchan, William Blissett, David Blostein, David Scott Bockhoven, Dan Breazeale, Jerome Buckley, Eleanor Cook, Thomas Cordle, Jonathan Culler, Kerry Dean, Scott D. Denham, Michael Dolzani, Morris Eaves, Lajos R. Elkan, Joseph Esposito, Robert Essick, Angela Esterhammer, Patrick Evans, Sidney Feshbach, Richard J. Finneran, Marshall Flowers, Frank Fowke, Robert Fulford, Paul Fussell, John Gordon, David Gray, Charles Guignon, Michael Happy, Anthony J. Harding, Geoffrey Hartman, Charles Heller, John Spencer Hill, Nelson Hilton, Philip Hiscock, Walter Kelly Hood, Burkhard Henke, Heather Jackson, Karen James, Douglas Jay, John E. Jordan, Richard Jordan, Mark Kessinger, Horst Lange, Alvin Lee, Dennis Lee, Rosemary Lloyd, Simon Loekle, Maurice Luker, Jack Lynch, Chris McConnell, Gerald R. McDermott, Robert M. Maniquis, Louis Martz, Edward Mendelson, Jamie Meyers, Carolyn Murray, Melvyn New, Mervyn Nicholson, Perry Nodelman, Keith Noseworthy, James Ogier, Jean O'Grady, Morton Paley, Jeanette Panagapka, Bansi Pandit, Roger Pearson, Jaroslav Pelikan, Marc Plamondon, Tilottama Rajan, Paul Redding, Karl Reisman, Christopher Rickey, Robin Robbins, Christian Rogowski, Florinda Ruiz, Suchitra

Samanta, Jonathan Schull, John Sebolt, Lisa Sherlock, Robert E. Smith, Dale Snow, Michael Squires, Joan Stambaugh, Matthew Stewart, Owen Thomas, Ranald Thurgood, Chris R. Vanden Bossche, Greg Ulmer, Yiman Wang, Robert White, Jane Widdicombe, Robert L. Wilken, Thomas Willard, L. Pearce Williams, Gordon Wood, Glenn Wooden, Carl Woodring, Anthony Yu, and Larry Zolf.

Abbreviations

Frye's own abbreviations have been expanded in square brackets, with the following exceptions: AC (*Anatomy of Criticism*), AV (Authorized Version), c. (century), EI (*The Educated Imagination*), FS (*Fearful Symmetry*), GC (*The Great Code*), N.T. (New Testament), and WP (*Words with Power*). The abbreviations that follow are used in the endnotes.

AC	*Anatomy of Criticism: Four Essays*. Princeton, N.J.: Princeton University Press, 1957.
AV	Authorized Version
Ayre	John Ayre. *Northrop Frye: A Biography*. Toronto: Random House, 1989.
BG	*The Bush Garden: Essays on the Canadian Imagination*. Toronto: Anansi, 1971.
CP	*The Critical Path: An Essay on the Social Context of Literary Criticism*. Bloomington: Indiana University Press, 1971.
CR	*Creation and Recreation*. Toronto: University of Toronto Press, 1980.
CW	Collected Works of Northrop Frye
DG	*Divisions on a Ground: Essays on Canadian Culture*. Ed. James Polk. Toronto: Anansi, 1982.
DV	*The Double Vision: Language and Meaning in Religion*. Toronto: University of Toronto Press, 1991.
EAC	*The Eternal Act of Creation: Essays, 1979–1990*. Ed. Robert D. Denham. Bloomington: Indiana University Press, 1993.
EI	*The Educated Imagination*. Bloomington: Indiana University Press, 1964.

Erdman	*The Complete Poetry and Prose of William Blake.* Ed. David Erdman. Rev. ed. Berkeley: University of California Press, 1982.
FI	*Fables of Identity: Studies in Poetic Mythology.* New York: Harcourt, Brace and World, 1963.
FS	*Fearful Symmetry: A Study of William Blake.* Princeton, N.J.: Princeton University Press, 1947.
FT	*Fools of Time: Studies in Shakespearean Tragedy.* Toronto: University of Toronto Press, 1967.
GC	*The Great Code: The Bible and Literature.* New York: Harcourt Brace Jovanovich, 1982.
Hughes	John Milton. *Complete Poems and Major Prose.* Ed. Merritt Y. Hughes. New York: Odyssey, 1957.
MC	*The Modern Century.* Toronto: Oxford University Press, 1967.
MD	*The Myth of Deliverance: Reflections on Shakespeare's Problem Comedies.* Toronto: University of Toronto Press, 1983.
MM	*Myth and Metaphor: Selected Essays, 1974–1988.* Ed. Robert D. Denham. Charlottesville: University Press of Virginia, 1990.
NB	Notebook
NF	Northrop Frye
NFC	*Northrop Frye in Conversation.* Ed. David Cayley. Concord, Ont.: Anansi, 1992.
NFCL	*Northrop Frye on Culture and Literature: A Collection of Review Essays.* Ed. Robert D. Denham. Chicago: University of Chicago Press, 1978.
NFF	Northrop Frye Fonds
NFL	Northrop Frye Library (the books in Frye's personal library, now in the Victoria University Library)
NFR	*Northrop Frye on Religion: Excluding "The Great Code" and "Words with Power."* Ed. Alvin A. Lee and Jean O'Grady. Toronto: University of Toronto Press, 2000.
NFS	*Northrop Frye on Shakespeare.* Ed. Robert Sandler. Markham, Ont.: Fitzhenry and Whiteside, 1986.
NP	*A Natural Perspective: The Development of Shakespearean Comedy and Romance.* New York: Columbia University Press, 1965.
NUS	*No Uncertain Sounds.* Toronto: Chartres Books, 1988.
OE	*On Education.* Markham, Ont.: Fitzhenry and Whiteside, 1988.

RE   *The Return of Eden: Five Essays on Milton's Epics.* Toronto:
          University of Toronto Press, 1965.
RSV   Revised Standard Version
RW   *Reading the World: Selected Writings, 1935–1976.* Ed. Robert D.
          Denham. New York: Peter Lang, 1990.
SE   *Northrop Frye's Student Essays, 1932–1938.* Ed. Robert D.
          Denham. Toronto: University of Toronto Press, 1997.
SeS   *The Secular Scripture: A Study of the Structure of Romance.*
          Cambridge, Mass.: Harvard University Press, 1976.
SM   *Spiritus Mundi: Essays on Literature, Myth, and Society.*
          Bloomington: Indiana University Press, 1976.
SR   *A Study of English Romanticism.* New York: Random House,
          1968.
StS   *The Stubborn Structure: Essays on Criticism and Society.* Ithaca,
          N.Y.: Cornell University Press, 1970.
TS   Typescript
TSE   *T.S. Eliot.* Edinburgh: Oliver and Boyd, 1963.
WGS   *A World in a Grain of Sand: Twenty-Two Interviews with
          Northrop Frye.* Ed. Robert D. Denham. New York: Peter Lang,
          1991.
WP   *Words with Power: Being a Second Study of "The Bible and
          Literature."* New York: Harcourt Brace Jovanovich, 1990.
WTC   *The Well-Tempered Critic.* Bloomington: Indiana University
          Press, 1963.

Introduction

I

The notebook, from Leonardo to Camus, is an established genre, its species as varied as those of other genres. Some notebooks, such as Coleridge's, move in the direction of the diary and the confession: they not only chronicle the events of the writer's daily life but probe the hopes and fears of the psyche as well. While Frye's notebooks do contain material that will be of considerable interest to his biographers, their form is altogether different from the diaries he kept in the 1940s and 1950s, and their intent is neither to record his personal life nor to explore his own psyche. The notebooks are first and foremost the workshop out of which Frye created his books. After *Anatomy of Criticism* Frye produced books at the rate of about one per year, giving the impression perhaps that writing for him was a facile enterprise. But the process was anything but that for his four major books. *Fearful Symmetry* (1947) and the *Anatomy* (1957) were each more than ten years in the making; *The Great Code* (1982) was begun more than a decade before it appeared; and *Words with Power* (1990), as Frye notes in the introduction to *The Great Code*, was "in active preparation" in the early 1980s.[1] The hammering out of *Words with Power* was, therefore, no less laborious a process than that required for Frye's other major books, and the notebooks in the present two volumes provide an extraordinary record of that process.

These volumes contain four large units of material (Notebooks 27, 44, and 50 and Notes 52) that relate primarily to *Words with Power*: these units constitute about eighty-five per cent of the present edition. These are followed by two sets of typed notes (Notes 53 and 54.1) for *The Double Vision*: they originated with Frye's lectures at Emmanuel College, presented in May 1990 and published posthumously. The first of these contains his ideas for the three lectures at Emmanuel; the second is for the fourth chapter of *The Double Vision*, a chapter he wrote before he submitted the book for publication. Finally, there are six brief units of material (holograph and typed) (54.2, 46, 47, 48, 11h, and 55.1) containing speculations on, among other things, both *Words with Power* and *The Double Vision.* While the focus of the entries in all of the notebooks is on Frye's book project at the time, he continually, like the Wife of Bath, wanders by the way, composing entries on scores of topics that have no obvious connection to the project at hand. An entry will be triggered by a detective story he is reading, a newspaper article, a lecture or sermon he has to prepare, a Latin quotation, a glance at the books on his shelves, a quotation he remembers, a letter received, a memory from a trip, and occasional personal reflections—thoughts about his own status as a critic, about the difficulties of writing, about the bankruptcy of contemporary criticism.

It is clear that Frye wrote in more than one notebook at any given time. He kept some of his notebooks in his office at Victoria College, but most of them were discovered at his Clifton Road home. Although no records were kept to indicate which notebooks were found in which location, my hunch is that Frye composed some entries in his Victoria office and others at home. But he may well have written in two or more notebooks at his home, picking up whichever happened to be handy, whether upstairs at his writing table or downstairs in his sitting room.[2] Writing, in any case, was, if not an obsession for Frye, as essential a part of his life as eating and sleeping. Frye wrote because he could do no other, and the process was not always liberating. "I know from experience," he writes, "and I've read the statement often enough, that if one could turn off the incessant chatter in one's psyche one would be well on the way to freedom. In all my life I've never known an instant of real silence."[3] Several times Frye expresses a deep desire for the apophatic and contemplative life, or at least for certain moments when he could "turn off the chatter in [his] mind, which is making more noise than a punk rock band ('drunken monkey,' the Hindus call it) and relax into the divine knowledge of us which is one of the things meant by a cloud of unknowing."[4] More than forty years before the period of the late notebooks, Frye ruefully wondered "what it would really be like to get one's mind completely clear of the swirl of mental currents. It would be like walking across the Red Sea to the Promised Land, with walls of water standing up on each side."[5] The fact that Frye was never really able to turn off the "drunken monkey" is what accounts for both the sheer mass of material in the late notebooks and the constant repetition of ideas, hunches, insights, poetic passages, and illustrations. Still, Frye approached the discipline of note-making with Benedictine zeal: "working at what one can do is a sacrament," he writes at the beginning of Notebook 44. Or again, "My whole life is words: nothing is of value in life except finding verbal formulations that make sense."[6]

The disadvantage of reproducing the notebooks in their entirety is obvious: life is short, and some of the notebook entries are much more engaging and more central to understanding Frye's mind than others. But the assumption behind the project called the "*Collected* Works of Northrop Frye" is that it is important for readers to have reliable texts for the whole of Frye, and so be enabled to decide which parts of his works are of interest or use to them, or are necessary to an overall understanding of his life and works. Beyond that purpose, however, the advantages of having an unabridged record of the late notebooks outweigh the disadvantages of their bulk. With the notebooks, the process is as important as the product, one form of which we already have: the books that resulted. Frye, like Hegel, is on a monumental quest. The quest is not toward absolute knowledge, as he says several times,[7] but toward absolute vision. Its goal is a vision beyond both the kerygmatic and the poetic, a form of vision that Frye characterizes in dozens of ways, but most revealingly as interpenetration. The late notebooks are a kind of labyrinth that Frye is both building and trying to extricate himself from: he sometimes ascends to moments of pure illumination; he sometimes descends into the dark abyss; he often gets lost in the maze; he is beleaguered by false starts and dead ends; he is haunted by a multitude of ghosts that keep flashing across his inward eye, which is clearly not the bliss of solitude. He describes the quest as a purgatorial journey:

My whole conscious life has been purgatorial, a constant circling around the same thing, like a vine going up an elm. I note that I'm repeating even things from earlier pages of this notebook. And "purgatorial" is only a vague hope: maybe I'm not really going up to a final apocalyptic vision but just going in circles, like a senile old man who thinks the two-hundredth repetition of the same old story is new. Perhaps the end is the choking of the host. Well, when it's vertigo to look down and despair to look up, one can only keep going. But there again I'm assuming an up and a down, and assuming I'm going somewhere. Actually I keep revolving around the same place until I've brought off a verbal formulation that I like.[8]

The depth and complexity of Frye's purgatorial journey could be only dimly perceived in a selection of the notebooks.

Notebooks are generally a private form of writing, and Frye certainly never entertained any notion of publishing them himself. "I don't need to unscramble that silly parenthesis: I'm not publishing this," he says at one point, reminding himself that he need not worry himself with stylistic propriety.[9] And in the course of a series of poignant entries following the death of his first wife, he remarks, "It's a good thing this notebook is not for publication, because everyone else would be bored by my recurring to Helen."[10] But there is a difference between the absence of an intent on Frye's part to use the notebooks for anything other than his own writing projects and the knowledge, which he seems clearly to have had, that the notebooks would some day be published. The very fact that we have seventy-six notebooks, along with the files of typed notes he preserved, provides some evidence of Frye's awareness that these documents would someday be read by others. He appears to have considered this form of his writing as of a different order from the countless reams of manuscripts, including thousands of pages of holograph and typed drafts, that he consigned to the dustbin. Moreover, while the notebooks occasionally contain a laconic entry, a hasty jotting, an outline, almost all of the paragraphs are syntactically complete units. They are not the polished prose of Frye's published work, but they do reveal a genuine concern for the rhetorical unit that can stand by itself. Such care in the construction of the prose would hardly seem required if Frye were writing only for himself. In addition, the notebooks are rather meticulously laid out, their pages numbered and each entry separated from the next by a blank line. Frye even revised his notebooks, correcting mistakes, inserting an omitted word here and there, and cancelling some of the repeated passages.

But the clearest clue to what I believe was Frye's awareness of the probable eventual disposition of the notebooks is his sense of an audience. When Frye writes, "See the title of my *Festschrift*," or, "See my notes on *The Ivory Tower*," he is providing instructions to an implied reader. When he feels guilty about a particularly vulgar outburst and later rewrites it in "a more polite way," he does so for the sake of an eventual reader. When he says, "I have very few religious books, & those

I have stress the mystics,"[11] he is certainly not writing to remind himself about the nature of his own library. When he identifies his own allusions, he is not providing the gloss for his own sake. There would be no reason for Frye to tell himself what he writes in the Coda of the present edition or what he records in this entry: "It doesn't matter how often I'm mentioned by other critics: I form part of the subtext of every critic worth reading."[12] There would be no reason for Frye to say to himself, "I've written a paper on Stevens as a variation-writer."[13] Hundreds of passages such as these betray Frye's consciousness of a reader other than himself.

II

Frye's late notebooks are the record of a religious quest, and in the course of that quest he writes here and there about the intent of the process. He speaks, for example, of the relation between his obsessive note-taking and the books that eventually emerge: "All my life I've had the notebook obsession manifested by what I'm doing at this moment. Writing in notebooks seems to help clarify my mind about the books I write, which are actually notebook entries arranged in a continuous form. At least, I've always told myself they were that."[14] In the same notebook Frye refers to the discontinuous form of his entries as aphorisms: "I keep notebooks because all my writing is a translation into a narrative sequence of things that come to me aphoristically. The aphorisms in turn are preceded by 'inspirations' or potentially verbal *Gestalten*. So 'inspiration' is essentially a snarled sequence."[15] While the notebook entries are ordinarily not as brief as an aphorism (they contain about seventy-five words on average), they do consist on the whole of discontinuous reflections. But, as "snarled sequence" suggests, the entries are by no means unrelated to each other. Frye will often devote a succession of paragraphs to a single topic,[16] and he frequently refers to previous sections of the notebook in which he is writing at the time and occasionally to other notebooks.

Frye puts "inspiration" in quotation marks because the actual genesis of the notebook entries is often somewhat mysterious. "I think in cores or aphorisms, as these notebooks indicate, and all the *labor* in my writing comes from trying to find verbal formulas to connect them. I have to wait for the cores to emerge: they seem to be born and not made."[17] In one of his notebooks for *Anatomy of Criticism*, he speaks of these aphorisms as auditory epiphanies: they are, he says, "involuntarily acquired" and have "something to do with listening for a Word, the ear being the involuntary sense."[18] If the birth of the aphorisms comes from things "heard," the connections among them come from things "seen." Realizing the potential of a "verbal *Gestalten*" or a pattern of continuous argument, Frye says, has something to do "with the spread-out performance of the eye."[19] But, as the notebooks unequivocally reveal, the pattern of continuity is never achieved without a mighty struggle: once Frye got hold of the building-blocks, "the spread-out performance" was never necessary or even predictable. In his words, "Continuity, in writing as in physics, is probabilistic, and every sequence is a choice among possibilities. Inevitable sequence is illusory."[20] The sequence that Frye eventually achieved in his published work came only after revisions of numerous drafts, sometimes as many as eight or nine revisions. Some of the chapters in *Words with Power* were, in their early form, as long as a hundred pages, so Frye's revisions involved a great deal of cutting.[21] He would typically type three or four drafts himself before giving them, often with holograph additions and corrections, to his secretary Jane Widdicombe to type or enter on a word processor.[22] Once he received the draft back, he would revise again, and this process would be repeated as many as five times. But the notebooks themselves are by no means drafts: they reveal a stage of Frye's writing before, sometimes years before, he began even to work on a first draft.

Frye was obviously an intuitive thinker. In Notebook 11f he says, "In my speeches I often speak of earlier moments of intensity. They were usually not moments of intensity, but only look so when I remember them. In a sense, therefore, I'm simply lying."[23] A half-dozen of these moments, nevertheless, were important enough for Frye to continue to refer to them: an experience in high school when the albatross of Methodist fundamentalism fell from his neck, an illumination about Spengler during the summer of 1931 in Edmonton, a sudden intuition about Blake during his second year at Emmanuel College, a vision of the shape that *Fearful Symmetry* would finally take, and two epiphanies referred to more than twenty times in the notebooks—one in Seattle during the summer of 1951 and the other "a few years later" on St. Clair Avenue in Toronto.[24] Frye refers to these moments variously as intuitions, epiphanies, illuminations, and enlightenments. They were experiences of unity—experiences, as he says, "of things fitting together" in a momentary flash of insight.[25] Such experiences are best described, not as mystical or even religious, but as visionary or spiritual. "Above the soul," Frye writes,

> is the spirit, and when the "body" makes contact with that, man possesses for an instant a spiritual body, in which he moves into a world of life and light and understanding that seemed miraculous to him before, as well as totally unreal. This world is usually called "timeless," which is a beggary of language: there ought to be some such word as "timeful" to express a present moment that includes immense vistas of past and future. I myself have spent the greater part of seventy-eight years in writing out the implications of insights that occupied at most only a few seconds of all that time.[26]

These insights are an important part of Frye's visionary poetics, but they should be distinguished from what Frye calls the aphoristic "cores" that he sets down in the notebooks. The latter, which he often refers to as "hunches," are essentially discontinuous. They are not epiphanic wholes, but epiphanic parts which, Frye hopes, will find their proper whole. Frye's epiphanies may be involuntarily acquired, but scores of them, once they have made their appearance, recur with regularity throughout the notebooks. The intuitions get repeated, reformulated, and refined, as Frye returns to his "repetitive & endlessly recycled thoughts" in his search for the proper verbal formula to build what he calls his "palaces of criticism."[27]

III

If Frye is an intuitive thinker, he is also a schematic one. It would be misleading to think of what he calls "the spread-out performance"—his effort to arrive at a continuous argument—as occurring only when he began to organize his aphorisms for a first draft. The deductive framework for Frye is always prior. While it is true that he thinks "in cores or aphorisms," it is no less true that he thinks geometrically, and such thinking is a feature of Frye's mental life that was with him from the beginning. Even in his student days he could hardly put pen to paper without a diagram in his head. He refers to his own work as possessed by "a mandala vision," the mandala being "a projection of the way one sees."[28] In Frye's grammar of the imagination the mental diagrams are what provide the syntax or ordering principle for the aphorisms. Or, to borrow another pair of Frye's terms, while the aphorisms belong to *mythos*, or experience in time, "the spread-out performance" is a matter of *dianoia*, or representation in space. "I have proceeded deductively," Frye announced in *Anatomy of Criticism*,[29] and thirty years later he is still proceeding deductively. "In the next few days," he writes with no sense of irony, "I must do a blitz on this infernal book, get its main construction lines blocked out, & then start reading."[30] Or again, "I've got stuck in my noddle the two names Prometheus and Hermes, and am beginning to feel that, apparently just for reasons of symmetry, there must be a second cycle incorporating the bulk of the imagery of modern poetry that doesn't get into the Eros-Adonis cycle. I'm putting it in the strongest terms a hostile critic would apply: because I've got a pretty pattern to apply, the facts have simply got to conform to it, and naturally with that attitude I'll succeed sooner or later." And then Frye adds, "You can't be original unless you work with hunches and treat them exactly as a paranoiac would do. Of course I find what I want to find in the texts themselves: what else does the double meaning of 'invention' mean?"[31] This is the typical Frygian approach: first, to set up the organizing framework and then to look around for the myths and metaphors to give body to the structure.

The defining feature of the present notebooks is, in fact, Frye's continuous effort to develop the organizing pattern for *Words with Power* and *The Double Vision*. The doggedness with which Frye pursues various schema for the conceptual framework of *Words with Power* is obvious even in the first of the late notebooks. One early formulation comes from the phases of revelation in chapter 5 of *The Great Code*. Another is a series of dialogues between word and spirit. But the most prominent scheme meets us early in the first notebook of the present edition, paragraph 13 of Notebook 27—what Frye calls the "HEAP scheme," the acronym for Hermes, Eros, Adonis, and Prometheus. Frye is devoted almost to the point of obsession to exploring the metaphorical and thematic implications of these four gods. They are, he says following Blake, "the spectres of the dead" because they have no concentering vision, and Frye sets out like a questing knight to discover such a vision for them, the four quadrants of which will be, when the code is finally deciphered, Hermes Unsealed, Eros Regained, Adonis Revived, and Prometheus Unbound. Each of the four gods represents a cluster of numerous thematic associations: the number of entries dedicated to the HEAP cycle in all of the notebooks exceeds eight hundred, and in the late notebooks Frye devotes almost three hundred separate paragraphs to one or more of these "spectres of the dead," or, what he calls, borrowing Emily Dickinson's phrase, "our confiscated gods."[32] The four gods are also called "emblems" and "informing presences," and they eventually become, in the second part of *Words with Power*, "variations on a theme."

The four gods had been a part of Frye's consciousness from an early age. His interest in the Adonis archetype can be traced all the way back to his undergraduate reading of Frazer, Prometheus to his reading of Shelley, Eros and Hermes to his reading of Plato.[33] Adonis, Prometheus, and Eros figure importantly in his account of the Orc cycle in *Fearful Symmetry*, and these three also make their way into *Anatomy of Criticism*. Hermes is the odd god out, so to speak, during the years Frye was writing the *Anatomy*. He does speak of Hermes' role as the angel-messenger or Covering Cherub in one of the important notebooks during the decade between *Fearful Symmetry* and the *Anatomy*, but this role is not connected with the archetypes of the other three gods. It is not until Notebook 7 (late 1940s–early 1950s) that we get a spatial representation of the gods as a cycle of archetypes, with Orpheus now joining Eros, Adonis, and Prometheus as the fourth god, Frye locating them as cardinal points on a circular diagram with horizontal and vertical axes. This diagram was one of the many components of what Frye called the "Great Doodle." In his diagrammatic way of representing the HEAP cycle, the gods eventually took their places within the quadrants, rather than at the cardinal points. By the 1980s Frye's mental diagram of the cycle tended to take the shape shown in figure 1. The HEAP scheme remained in a state of flux for a number of years: it "keeps reforming & dissolving," as Frye says in Notebook 44.[34] He experiments with several additional sequences: AEHP, PEAH, HAPE, HPAE, EAHP and EAPH,[35] before finally settling on the order Hermes, Eros, Adonis, and Prometheus. These archetypes—what the four gods represent apocalyptically as well as demonically—help direct and give shape to the last four chapters of *Words with Power*, which is clearly the more creative and dynamic half of the book. What, then, do the four "spectres of the dead" represent for Frye? The question cannot be answered in a word. The four gods, as already said, are slippery categories, and the associations that the gods trigger in Frye's mind are long-standing and part of what he himself calls his "dizzily complex constructs."[36] But table 1 will perhaps provide readers a kind of map for making their way through the themes and analogues that Frye attaches to the spectres in the late notebooks, the

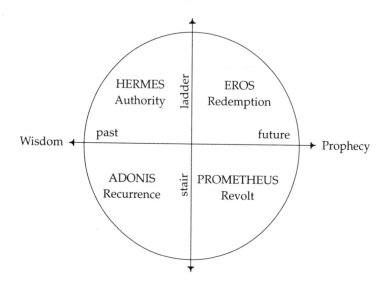

Figure 1

awakening of which the last half of *Words with Power* is designed to achieve.

One striking difference between the late notebooks and *Words with Power* is that the HEAP cycle, so prominent in the former, practically disappears in the latter. Adonis makes only a cameo appearance, Hermes remains completely offstage, and Eros and Prometheus have only minor roles at best. The primary reason for this is that Frye, who conceived the four gods as each occupying the quadrant of a cyclical diagram, decided, in one of his late revisions of the book, to abandon the cycle as his fundamental organizing image and to replace it with the *axis mundi*. Ascent and descent along a vertical axis become the primary structural metaphor of Frye's "variations on a theme." But he cannot completely abandon the four gods with whom he has had such a longstanding and intimate relation, and all four do, in fact, come on stage toward the beginning of the final chapter of *Words with Power*. "Each of our axial surveys," Frye writes, referring to the mountain, garden, cave, and furnace archetypes,

may be linked to a god or informing presence: the presiding deity of the ladder of higher wisdom, outlined in the fifth chapter, is Hermes the psychopomp; of the ladder of higher love, Eros; of the descent and return theme of lower love (i.e., fertility), Adonis. Our present hero of lower wisdom is Prometheus, the Titan who created man, in some accounts, and the defier of the gods, who overthrew (or reduced to absurdity) the cult of sacrifice, and brought to man the fire that made his civilization possible.[37]

IV

As for the rhetoric of the notebooks, one can naturally detect features of Frye's style on every page: the wit, the koan-like utterances that capture some paradox, the attention to the shape of the periodic sentence, the grace and elegance of the prose, the ironic tone. But the difference between Frye's notebook entries and his published work will be apparent to readers as well, for here Frye is wearing everything on his sleeve. He feels no need for the detachment that was almost always a feature of what he presented to the public, no need to create that sense of assurance that comes with a distanced academic presence. It is true that Frye insisted for many years that the antithesis between the scholarly and unscholarly, between the personal and impersonal, was an antithesis that needed to be transcended. Still, the reader will recognize immediately that the voice in these notebooks is not Frye's public voice. There is, on the one hand, the direct expression of belief. Frye's own beliefs were, of course, implicit in all his writing, from *Fearful Symmetry* on. But in the notebooks they are explicit: one could compile from these entries what would amount to a confession of faith. On the other hand, at the level simply of diction, Frye's not infrequent use of coarse and indecent language may surprise, even confound, some readers. Most will doubtless discover, however, that Frye's four-letter words are used fairly innocently, serving him as a kind of shorthand for referring to sex, which is of course one of his "primary concerns," to the male and female principles in Genesis 1 and 2 that are really the starting point of the mountain and garden archetypes, and to bodily functions. Still, Frye's language often deflates the most sober of reflections. Thus, while there is not so much as a whisper of the mock-heroic in these notebooks, there is a good measure of the Swiftian burlesque, which is one of the ways that Frye, never without a sense of irony, brings his soaring speculations back down to earth.

If we cannot always with assurance follow the sequence of the arguments in Frye's published work or always understand clearly why one

TABLE 1
The Spectres of the Dead: Variations on a Theme

	Hermes	Eros	Adonis	Prometheus
Axis Mundi Image	Mountain—higher wisdom	Garden—higher love	Cave—lower love	Furnace—lower wisdom
Awakened Spectre	Hermes Unsealed (Gospel)	Eros Regained (Wisdom)	Adonis Revived (Prophecy)	Prometheus Unbound (Law)
Phases of Revelation	Creation, Law	Gospel & Participating Apocalypse	Prophecy & Participating Apocalypse	Exodus, Wisdom
Word Manifestation/ Spirit Response	Law/Wisdom	Panoramic Apocalypse/ Participating Apocalypse	Prophecy/Gospel	Creation/Exodus
Cosmological Principle	Authority	Polarity	Cycle	Revolt
Object of Epiphany	Logos	Spirit	Logos	Spirit
Narrative Direction	Tragic	Comic	Tragic	Comic
Feminine Aspect	Mother (Juno)	White & red bride (Magdalen)	Black Bride	Sister (Athene)
Blakean Analogue	Tharmas [or Urizen] (*natura naturata* world)	Urizen [or Tharmas] (world of cycles)	Orc (world of cyclical revolt)	Los [or Urthona] (world of titanic revolt)
Biblical Analogue	Authority	Redemption	Renewal	Revolt
Primary Concern	Freedom (play) or construction	Sex	Food (place of seed)	Shelter (construction) or freedom of action & thought
Primary Element	Descent to water	Ascent in air	Descent to earth	Ascent in fire
Epiphanic Principle	Logos	Spirit	Logos	Spirit
Colour	Indigo	Green	Blue	Yellow

TABLE 1 (concluded)

	Hermes	Eros	Adonis	Prometheus
Associated images & themes	Ark, way (path), the occult, dream worlds, systole-diastole movement, Grail legend, "everlasting gospel," Atlantis, tower & winding-stair patterns	Fire, radical spur, reversal in time, courtly love, *naturata naturans*, source in Plato & Ovid, Eve-as-garden, Song of Songs, centre, Bruno brother struggles	Seed, conservative spur, cycle of time, Graves / Frazer themes (dying-god sequence), Rabelaisian themes, sacrifice, Sabbath contemplation, circumference, white goddess pattern, Spenglerian cycle	Fire-seed, fire in fennel stalk, technology, education (forethought), Albion-Finnegan figure, communication, utopias, trickster, drunken-boat pattern, network (De Quincey), Blake & Shelley
Eliot's Four Quartets Analogy	*Burnt Norton*	*Little Gidding*	*East Coker*	*The Dry Salvages*
Analogues of Modern Consciousness	Heidegger	Freud	Nietzsche	Marx
Verbal Cosmos of Literary History	Pre-Romantic hierarchy	Romantic reversal	Pre-Romantic hierarchy	Romantic reversal
Temporal Analogue	Past	Future	Past	Future

paragraph follows the next, we nevertheless have the impression that *he* knew where he was going. But this confident sense of direction is often absent from the notebooks. "God knows," he writes at one point, "I know how much of this is blither: it makes unrewarding reading for the most part. But I have to do it: it doesn't clarify my mind so much as lead to some point of clarification that (I hope) gets into the book. Hansel & Gretel's trail of crumbs." Or again, when speculating on the relation between the dialogues of word and spirit and the four levels of meaning, Frye remarks, "I don't know if this is anything but bald and arbitrary schematism." Or still again, "I'm again at the point in the book where I wonder if I know what the hell I'm talking about."[38] Remarks such as these are sprinkled throughout the notebooks, and there are entries in which Frye begins to explore an idea but, by the time he gets to the end of the paragraph, forgets the point he was going to make. Over and over we are confronted with a self that is human, all-too-human. There is nothing particularly surprising in this: writing for Frye was a discovery procedure, and we should not expect that every aphorism that came to him should issue in a "verbal *Gestalten*." In this respect Frye's notebooks are like Nietzsche's own book of aphorisms, *Human All-too-Human*, an exercise in free thinking; and free thought, by definition, is under no obligation always to issue in certitude. The personality of the writer is revealed too in the occasional intemperate epithets ("fool," "idiot," and the like) that Frye hurls at himself for overlooking the obvious or for a lapse in memory, and in the self-deprecating remarks ("By the standards of conventional scholarship, *The Great Code* was a silly and sloppy book").[39]

I have indicated that the notebooks do not really belong to the genre of the diary or personal journal. But from time to time Frye does move away from direct speculations about *Words with Power* and other writing projects. He occasionally worries, for example, about his status and reputation. He sometimes takes swipes at other critics (e.g., Frank Kermode and Terry Eagleton, Francis Sparshott),[40] something Frye almost never did in his published work: only on the rarest of occasions would he even politely mention a critic or detractor by name. But the most personal of all the entries, as well as the most poignant, are motivated by the death of Frye's wife Helen in Cairns, Australia. About one-fifth of the way through Notebook 44 Frye announces that Helen, his wife of forty-nine years, has died. For the next eight entries he writes of his grief and of his love for her, of his hope to see her in the invisible world across death, of his desire for her peace, of her apotheosis into sainthood.[41] Helen's presence continues to be felt through the remainder of the notebook.[42] Frye expresses the guilt he has about having taken her on the long trip to Australia, and he even entertains the notion that this decision was tantamount to murder. But as his guilt begins to wane, Helen emerges as his Court of Love mistress—his Laura or Beatrice.[43] And as the distance from her death increases, he can write,

> The Helen I now love is someone whose human faults & frailties count for *nothing*: the word "forgiveness" I shrink from, because it implies that I'm in a superior position. I think (with Keats) that life may be purgatorial in shape, only I'd call it a vale of spirit (not soul) making. I think of her as someone for whom the full human potential is now able to emerge. Perhaps my love and the affection so many had for her helped to do that for her, being the same kind of thing that the R.C.'s [Roman Catholics], with their mania for institutionalizing everything, identify with masses & prayers for the dead. If so, then she's an angel, not to be worshipped, according to the N.T., but an emancipated fellow-creature.[44]

Frye even sees *Words with Power* becoming "a memorial to my lost love," a book that must be "worthy of God and of Helen," a new Word born to them, and Notebook 44 ends with his declaring Helen to be an angel.[45]

The death of Helen affected Frye deeply, and it helps, I think, to account for the prominence of death as a theme in those parts of the notebooks written after August 1986. One has only to compare the relatively few entries about death in Notebook 27, which dates from 1985, to such entries in the subsequent notebooks, where death becomes a major theme. It is a major theme in *Words with Power* as well. Frye writes often about death not merely as a theme in literature and religion but as an apprehension in his own consciousness: he is clearly anxious about his own death, worries whether he will live to see his various projects completed, and speculates about, as he puts it, "life across death."[46] This is one of the few cases in the notebooks where we see an event in Frye's life helping to determine the direction of his writing in both the notebooks and his published work.

V

The late notebooks provide a fairly full account of what Frye was reading during the last five years of his life. With a dozen or so exceptions (e.g.,

Dante, Rabelais, Henry James, Charlotte Brontë, Virginia Woolf, E.M. Forster) his reading did not centre on literature: with his prodigious memory, he already had a formidable grasp of the literary tradition anyway. But there are writers he devotes substantial attention to in the notebooks who are left behind in *Words with Power*. The significance that the French symbolists, for example, had for Frye—Rimbaud and Laforgue and especially Mallarmé—is not apparent in his published work. Mallarmé enters Frye's argument in *Words with Power* six times: in the late notebooks he appears in sixty-nine entries, mostly in connection with Frye's fascination with *Igitur, Cantique de Saint-Jean, Un Coup de Dés*, and Mallarmé's letters to Henri Cazalis. Frye is attracted to Mallarmé because, like Blake, he has the imagination of a religious visionary. (At one point Frye refers to "the pan-literary universe which only three people understand: Blake, Mallarmé, and myself.")[47] He is a poet, writes Frye, "who will take me through the third great crisis of the birth of the spirit out of the depth of fallen spirits," who sometimes talks "as though literature was a 'substitute' for religion," who sees the pure poem as a symbol of "something transcendent," who "tries to sink himself in myth & metaphor so completely that the kerygmatic will speak through," and who believes "there really is some kind of resurrection by faith in myth."[48]

With all the attention given to Mallarmé one naturally wonders why he was never the subject of an essay by Frye or why he is used in the published work only for an occasional illustration. But this points to one of the features of the notebooks—the material they contain that was never developed in Frye's books and essays. If Mallarmé and the HEAP scheme disappear into the background in *Words with Power*, so do a number of other topics we encounter in the notebooks, topics which Frye seems utterly committed to exploring but which we know almost nothing about from his published work. The long list of such topics, some of which Frye even plans to write essays on, would include Schelling's philosophy of mythology and revelation, De Quincey's network image from "The English Mail-Coach," "fairies and elementals," the American Romantics, the Vedic myth of Hiranyagarbha (especially the seed of fire in the midst of the waters), and Poe ("the greatest literary genius this side of Blake").[49]

When Frye says that the few religious books he has focus on the mystics,[50] he is referring to Eckhart and Boehme and Joachim of Fiore, or Floris, writers who appear with regularity in the notebooks. He is perhaps also referring to certain Eastern texts. Before completing his work on *Fearful Symmetry*, Frye had flirted with the East. Large portions of Notebook 3, written in 1946, are devoted to his reading of the *Lankavatara Sutra*, to his speculations on the bardo state in *The Tibetan Book of the Dead*, and to Patanjali's *Yoga-Sutra*. He even sets out to follow Patanjali's eightfold path, devoting a number of pages of the notebook "to codify[ing] a program of spiritual life" for himself.[51] Frye's published work provides only the scantest evidence of his interest in things Eastern. But in the late notebooks we find him speculating on such things as the *I Ching*, the yin–yang balance of Taoism, the *Rig Veda*, Jnana yoga, the *Avatamsaka Sutra*, and Gopi Krishna's *Kundalini* ("a book that impressed me").[52]

Some of Frye's reading is, if not altogether odd, at least surprising—books such as Merezhkovsky's *Atlantis/Europe* and Maureen Duffy's *Erotic World of Fairie*. Frye admits that Merezhkovsky comes "close to a lot of the von Daniken mythology," but then, he adds, "yesterday's kook book becomes tomorrow's standard text."[53] There are in the notebooks, as one might expect, a number of Frye's old chestnuts—books such as Graves's *The White Goddess*, Frances Yates's studies in hermeticism, the mythical speculations of Gertrude Rachel Levy, Huxley's *Perennial Philosophy*, Carroll's Alice books, the novels of Bulwer-Lytton and Rider Haggard. But some readers will no doubt think it strange that Frye would even be curious about such books as Michael Baigent's *The Holy Blood and the Holy Grail*, Robert Anton Wilson's *The Cosmic Trigger*, Marilyn Ferguson's *The Aquarian Conspiracy*, Itzhak Bentov's *Stalking the Wild Pendulum*, and A.E. Waite's *Quest of the Golden Stairs*, *The Pictorial Key to the Tarot*, and *The Holy Grail*—"kook books" all. It would be difficult to imagine Frye citing such esoterica in *Words with Power*, but he does justify his interest in such writers as Waite, who is only "superficially off-putting":[54]

I've been reading Loomis and A.E. Waite on the Grail. Loomis often seems to me an erudite ass: he keeps applying standards of coherence and consistency to twelfth-century poets that might apply to Anthony Trollope. Waite seems equally erudite and not an ass. But I imagine Grail scholars would find Loomis useful and Waite expendable, because Waite isn't looking for anything that would interest them. It's quite possible that what Waite is looking for particularly doesn't exist—secret traditions, words of power, an esoteric authority higher than that of the Catholic Church—and yet the *kind* of thing he's looking for is so infinitely more important than Loomis' trivial games of descent from Irish sources where things get buggered up because the poets couldn't distinguish cors meaning body from cors meaning horn. Things like this show me that I have a real function as a critic, pointing out that what Loomis does has been done and is dead, whereas what Waite does, even when mistaken, has hardly begun and is very much alive.[55]

The notebooks also reveal Frye's attraction to neo-natural theology, represented by his interest in Erwin Schrödinger and David Bohm, the latter of whose theories on the implicate order do get cited in *The Double Vision*. But from reading such recognized physicists Frye moved in the direction of "pop-science" writers, as he calls them.[56] These include Lyall Watson and "the Tao of Physics people": Fritjof Capra, Rudy Rucker, and Ken Wilber. Frye's reading does not always take such a curious course, and his published work provides no hints of his interest in New Age science. As one might expect, Frye devotes a substantial amount of energy in the notebooks to engaging the great speculative minds in the Western tradition. Heraclitus, Plato, and Aristotle are the Classical philosophers to whom he most often recurs. Among modern discursive thinkers Hegel is his great hero, though he admires the *Phenomenology of Spirit* as an Odyssean quest, not as an introduction to Hegel's system: "If Hegel had written his Phenomenology in *mythos*-language instead of in *logos*-language a lot of my work would be done for me."[57] Frye keeps returning to Kant's idea of "purposiveness without purpose" in the *Critique of Judgment*. He spars with Kierkegaard, wrestles with Nietzsche, engages Freud and Marx throughout, argues with Jung, assimilates Lacan's "alienated *moi*" into his own system, finds Samuel Butler captivating and the "chain-thinking" in Berkeley's *Siris* compelling, debates with Julian Jaynes about his theory of the bicameral mind, draws on Huizinga's *Homo Ludens*, and worries repeatedly about Derrida (because of his attack on the Logos) and Bultmann (because of his attack on myth). The index reveals just how extensive and wide-ranging the dialogue is that Frye carries on with the intellectual tradition—its philosophers (e.g., Schopenhauer), its mythographers (e.g., Eliade), its theologians (e.g., Tillich, Buber, Barth), its literary critics (e.g., Bloom, Bakhtin).

A number of the writers to whom Frye devotes attention in the late notebooks—Samuel Butler, James Joyce, Thomas More, William Blake, Baldassare Castiglione, William Morris—became the subject of essays he produced during the late 1980s. These essays eventually made their way into *Myth and Metaphor*, along with several other essays Frye wrote in the late 1980s, such as "The Dialectic of Belief and Vision," for which the notebooks were also the workshop.

VI

Almost thirty-five years ago I picked up *Anatomy of Criticism*, read it, and realized I was in the presence of an extraordinary mind. For a number of years I was convinced that this was the central work in the Frye canon, even though in the 1960s the canon was not all that large. I was attracted to, among other things, the *Anatomy's* schematic ingenuity, its power as a teaching manual, and, as I had come under the sway of the New Criticism, its claims for the autonomy of both literature and criticism. Had I come to Frye by way of *Fearful Symmetry*, I suspect that my view of his work would have been different. In any case, as I have followed the contours of Frye's career, I have become more and more convinced that what is fundamental to his work is not so much the principles outlined in the *Anatomy*, though that is surely a book that will remain with us, but the principles we find in those books that serve as the bookends of his career, *Fearful Symmetry* at the beginning and fifty years later the two Bible books and *The Double Vision*. I have had a developing intuition that the central feature of the superstructure Frye built is its religious base. There are hints in the *Anatomy* (in Frye's account of anagogy, for example) that he takes spiritual vision seriously, but no one, I think, would argue on the basis of that book that such vision is central. My feeling about the essentially religious foundations of Frye's work has been strengthened during the six years I have been pondering the late notebooks, which, incidentally, begin with an entry on original sin and, 3,684 entries later, end with one on the Sabbath vision. The notebooks, as I have already indicated, are, beyond the obvious practical function they had for Frye, a record of his religious quest.

I will not repeat what I have said elsewhere about such a view,[58] but it does deserve a brief comment. To begin with a few passages from the notebooks where Frye remarks on the *telos* of his own undertaking:

Any biography, including Ayre's, would say that I dropped preaching for academic life: that's the opposite of what my spiritual biography would say, that I fled into academia for refuge and have ever since tried to peek out into the congregation and make a preacher of myself.[59]

For a long time I've been preoccupied by the theme of the reality of the spiritual world, including its substantial reality.[60]

I'm an architect of the spiritual world.[61]

Art is not simply an identity of illusion and reality, but a counter-illusion: its world is a material world, but the material of an intelligible spiritual world. . . . the dialectic of belief and vision is the path I have to go down now.[62]

I've been called a mystic as well as a myth critic, because some people think that's an even more contemptuous term. If myth is really mythos, story or plot, then mysticism is being initiated in the mysteries.[63]

I've been using the Bible to help me get to a plane of metaphor beyond hypothesis.[64]

I'm no evangelist or revivalist preacher, but I'd like to help out in a trend to make religion interesting and attractive to many people of good will who will have nothing to do with it now.[65]

I'm still in search of a genuinely "charitable" vision of spirit that can unite everybody.[66]

Frye's religious vision is firmly rooted in the Protestant Christian tradition and in the prophetic vision of William Blake, for whom the "Everlasting Gospel" was the gospel of love. But Frye's religious views are often expressed unconventionally. He eschews all theological doctrines, systems, and institutions. When he does resort to theological language, it is almost always in the context of an event or an experience, such as the Incarnation, the Resurrection, the Crucifixion, the Apocalypse, and he understands such events or experiences, as the notebooks clearly reveal, in terms of myth and metaphor. His view of religion is, therefore, what he calls counterlogical and counterhistorical. While his views locate themselves in the Christian tradition, they are nevertheless often idiosyncratic. But that gives him little pause:

I haven't the least objection to having it said that my religion is essentially my own creation. I feel that it must be that way because my understanding of anything is finite; but I think the position I do hold is one that enables me to crawl a little farther and discover a bit more. Faced with a Jew, a Moslem, a Catholic, an atheistic humanist, I should not deny for a second that they also have positions from which to advance. All this is very elementary: one assumption I've so far left aside. I am what I am because of certain historical events: the Protestant Reformation, the Anglican settlement, the Methodist movement, the transfer of religious energies to the New World. Hence if I express a tolerance that grants to any position the capacity of moving nearer whatever truth is, I am also annihilating history, assuming that all religious theory and practice today begins in a kind of apocalypse in which past history has exhausted its significance as such. The nineteenth-century obsession with conversion, mainly from Protestant to Catholic positions, was a desperate effort to keep history continuous: I think it no longer works, if it ever did.[67]

What Frye calls vision often leans in the direction of mysticism, something that in the intense moment of recognition lies on "the other side of consciousness."[68] In such moments, Frye writes, "what's below consciousness, traditionally called the body, may suddenly fuse with what's above consciousness, or spirit. These are the moments of inspiration, insight, intuition, enlightenment, whatever: no matter what they're called or what their context is, they invariably by-pass ordinary consciousness."[69] One of the functions of the critic is not simply to translate poetic language into another, lesser language, but "to establish the relations of poetry with its wider verbal context. A different kind of activity is suggested at that point. The awareness of language may begin with the awareness of ordinary consciousness, but it soon becomes clear that language is a means of intensifying consciousness, lifting us into a new dimension of being altogether."[70] This intensifying or expanding of consciousness is sounded as a refrain throughout the notebooks.

The first chapters of both *The Great Code* and *Words with Power* seek to outline a theory of language that will account for how a sacred text, such as the Bible, which is fundamentally a complex tissue of myths and metaphors, goes beyond the poetic. In *The Great Code* he defines this meta-step as kerygma. In *Words with Power*, it is the mythical and imaginative mode which always gets excluded from ideology, a mode presided over by, in Frye's curious locution for the gods, "the non-human personal." Kerygma and the relation of identity captured by metaphor are the terms Frye sometimes uses in the notebooks to capture the ultimate aim of the poetic. At other times he wants to press even farther to a "kerygmatic breakthrough."[71] This is a state of being that goes beyond what he calls in both Bible books the panoramic apocalypse. The movement beyond kerygma and metaphor is a movement from Word to Spirit. In Frye's words,

the panoramic apocalypse, the thematic stasis, the myth as dianoia or
picture, represents the end of experience as knowledge. It's normally as far
as literature can go, and the dianoia it reaches is a design of hypothetical
metaphor. To move on to the seventh phase of participating apocalypse one
has to move back to existential metaphor, and let the preceding narrative
structure one's life. To do this is to repeat the incarnation, the Word becoming flesh. When the Word's mythos is complete it discarnates, & we attach
ourselves to the Spirit that works by metaphor.[72]

This is what faith means for Frye. Throughout the notebooks he keeps
returning to Hebrews 11:1 almost to the point of fixation, trying to
translate into his own terms the meaning of *elenchos* and *hypostasis* and
the relation between them.[73] "The Dialectic of Belief and Vision" includes the most fully developed of his several commentaries on the
passage.[74] But the notebooks also contain some extraordinary entries on
faith, including the following: "Faith is the recurring sense of revelation,
i.e., an existential reality beyond the hypothetical [poetic]. This revelation is the vision of a "new" creation—new to us, that is. Such a faith, if
attained, redeems and justifies all literature."[75] The vision about which
Frye speaks is the interpenetrating universe of symbol and spirit.

The paradox of interpenetration is the verbal formula Frye most often
calls upon in the notebooks to define his vision of the new creation and
the participating apocalypse. The idea of interpenetration, which, as
Frye records in his notebooks, he first encountered in Whitehead,
Spengler, and the Mahayana sutras, is used in several different contexts,
but the most frequent is a religious one. "The Holy Spirit," he writes,
"who, being everywhere at once, is the pure principle of interpenetration."[76] Frye associates interpenetration with anagogy, apocalypse, spiritual intercourse, the vision of plenitude, the everlasting gospel, and the
Incarnation. It is finally one of Frye's many efforts to define metaphorical
literalism, which is based on the principle of identity (x equals y), to get
beyond subject–object categories, to push language as far as it can go in
its struggle to explore the ineffable silence that surrounds, even helps to
define, the religious experience.[77]

VII

Frye carried on this exploration until the very end, never able to give his
pen a moment's rest. Even before he had completed *Words with Power*, he
had begun to lay plans for his next books. One is what he calls his Utopia

book, a book he sees emerging from the themes of creative ascent in the last chapter of *Words with Power*. It would be a book focusing on social models and on education, issues Frye had already treated in four essays from the 1980s (on More, Butler, Castiglione, and Morris). These essays, in fact, would provide the core of the book,[78] which, Frye speculates, might even turn into one of the volumes of his ogdoad project. Because references to this project appear occasionally in the late notebooks, it deserves a word of explanation.

The ogdoad was an eight-book vision that Frye used as a kind of road map for his life's work. As with all of his organizing patterns, the ogdoad was never a rigid outline, but it did correspond to the chief divisions in Frye's conceptual universe over the years. Throughout the notebooks he repeatedly uses a code to refer to the eight books he planned to write. The original plan was actually eight concerti that Frye dreamed of writing—a dream he had at age nine. At about the same time, after reading Scott's novels, he imagined writing a sequence of historical novels, and after he had made his way through Dickens and Thackeray, this modulated into "a sequence of eight definitive novels." When Frye was fourteen, each of these novels acquired a one-word descriptive name, and these names, along with their hieratic forms, remained with Frye over the years, appearing hundreds of times in his notebooks as a shorthand designation for his books, both those completed and those anticipated. In the 1940s the eight books were reduced to what Frye called his Pentateuch, but they expanded shortly after that into the eight once again. Frye himself provides several keys to the ways that the ogdoad shaped his preoccupations over the years. In one of them he says,

Suddenly, & simultaneously with the final & complete conversion to criticism, my old adolescent dream of eight masterpieces rose up again and hit me finally and irresistibly. Blake became Liberal, the study of drama Tragicomedy, the philosophical book, now a study of prose fiction, became Anticlimax, Numbers became Rencontre, Deuteronomy Mirage, & three others took nebulous shape. For several years I dithered, doodled, dawdled, dreamed & dallied. It was silly to let an adolescent pipe-dream haunt me like that: on the other hand, it did correspond to some major divisions in my actual thinking. So I kept on with it. When I finished the Blake, it became zero instead of one, & its place was taken by a study of epic. In my notes the initial letters of the eight books were cut down to hieratic forms: L for Liberal; ⅂ for Tragicomedy; Λ for Anticlimax; Λ̷ for Rencontre; V for Mirage; ⊢ for Paradox; ⊥ for Ignoramus; T for Twilight.[79]

TABLE 2
The Ogdoad

The Eight Novels	The Pentateuch: An Intermediate Scheme (1940s)	Later Permutations (following 1940s)	The Hieratic Code	The 1970s Permutations & Blakean Analogues (cycle of the first four books begins again)	The Final Variation
Liberal: a satire; witty comedy of manners	Genesis: on Blake	**Liberal**: Blake; after 1947 this became a study of epic	⌐	**Liberal**: the Bible book; Urthona	*Fearful Symmetry*
Tragicomedy: a panoramic novel; complex plot; many characters	Exodus: a study of drama, especially Shakespearean comedy	**Tragicomedy**: the study of drama; interest in plots began with Scott	⌐	**Tragicomedy**: a book on Shakespeare; or study of literary imagery; Orc	*Anatomy of Criticism*
Anticlimax: an austere & forbidding novel	Leviticus: a philosophical "summa" of modern thought	**Anticlimax**: a study of prose fiction	∧	**Anticlimax**: long book on education; or on prose forms and Utopias, education; Urizen	Essays written during time of *The Great Code*, or Shakespeare
Rencontre: a war novel	Numbers: a study of Romanticism and its after-effects	**Rencontre**: grows out of Spengler enthusiasm	∠	**Rencontre**: *Fearful Symmetry* or a rewritten version of it; or a history of English literature; Tharmas	Essays written during time of *Words with Power*, or *A Study of English Romanticism*
Mirage: undefined	Deuteronomy: on general aesthetic problems	**Mirage**	∨	**Mirage** *Anatomy of Criticism*; Enitharmon	*The Great Code*

TABLE 2 (concluded)

The Eight Novels	The Pentateuch: An Intermediate Scheme (1940s)	Later Permutations (following 1940s)	The Hieratic Code	The 1970s Permutations & Blakean Analogues (cycle of the first four books begins again)	The Final Variation
Paradox: a dizzily complex novel		**Paradox**	⊢	**Paradox** "The Third Book" Vala	*Words and Power*
Ignoramus: the profoundest ("because I was an agnostic by then & had started to read Hardy")		[seldom appears in notebooks]	⊥	**Ignoramus** Ahania	A volume of essays on Canadian literature; Utopia book
Twilight: subtitled "Valedictory": "my *Tempest*," "the work of my old age"		[seldom appears in notebooks]	⊤ ⌐ or ⌐	**Twilight** Enion	A volume of essays, or *The Critical Path*; an anagogic book of aphorisms; *Century Meditations*

Throughout the 1970s and 1980s the scheme continued to change, but Frye never abandoned it. Some of the principal features of the ogdoad are summarized in table 2. As this bald summary reveals, the various parts of the ogdoad changed over the years, and by the time we come to Frye's late notebooks, the ogdoad undergoes two additional transformations. The first of these results from Frye's study of the Bible having become two separate volumes. On the first page of Notebook 47 we are confronted with a rather cryptic list of hieratic codes and book abbreviations. Deciphering the code cannot be done with certainty, but it appears that Frye initially takes *The Great Code* and *Words with Power* to be, respectively, Anticlimax and Rencontre, thus bringing to completion the first half of the ogdoad. But then there is a second hieroglyph, where it is clear that *The Great Code* and *Words with Power* are taken to be the beginning of the second sequence of eight, Mirage and Paradox respectively. That would leave Ignoramus and Twilight to be the last two books of the entire sequence. One of these, as we know from Notebook 44, Frye intends to be the Utopia or social models book.[80] For the eighth book—Twilight—he does entertain the notion of writing a book on communication,[81] but the most intriguing proposal for the last book he plans to write is what he calls his anagogic book, a book of aphorisms.

The desire to complete a book of aphorisms emerges from a dozen or so entries in Notebooks 44 and 50. "I wonder, Frye writes, "if I could be permitted to write my *Twilight* book, not as evidence of my own alleged wisdom but as a 'next time' (Henry James) book, putting my spiritual case more forcefully yet, and addressed to still more readers."[82] The reference here is to James's *The Next Time*, the story of a writer whose work is admired by a small coterie but who is frustrated by his failure to reach a large audience. Frye even proposes several models for his anagogic book: Anatole France's *Jardin d'Épicure*, a series of learned reflections on sundry topics; Dmitry Merezhkovsky's *Atlantis/Europe*, Nietzsche's *Gaya Scienza*, Cyril Connolly's *The Unquiet Grave: A Word Cycle by Palinurus*; or the final book might be modeled, Frye muses, on Thomas Traherne's *Centuries of Meditations*. "I wouldn't want to plan such a book," Frye writes, "as a dumping ground for things I can't work in elsewhere or as a set of echoes of what I've said elsewhere." "Such a book would feature," he adds "completely uninhibited writing" and "completely uninhibited metaphor-building," and some of the entries might even be fictional.[83] Toward the end of Notebook 50, when Frye realizes that he may not live much longer, he suggests still another variation on the final book. He scribbles somewhat cryptically, "Opus Perhaps Posthumous: Working Title: Quintessence of Dust. Four Essays." And then, a dozen entries later, he adds, "Quintessence and dust; Quarks or pinpoints; Quest and Cycle: Quiet Consummation."[84] "Four Essays," the subtitle of *Anatomy of Criticism*, hints at the conventions of the anatomy as a genre, and "Quiet Consummation" was the title of a novel that he planned to write, in fact began writing, in the 1940s. He even speaks of writing a bardo novel, resurrecting another fantasy from the 1940s. For *Twilight*, then, Frye is looking for a form that will combine the creative and the critical— something aphoristic, anagogic, erudite, imaginative, even fictional.

The striking thing about Frye's last-book fantasies is their correspond-ence to the notebooks themselves. Frye himself makes the connection between the "aphoristic book" and his "notebook obsession,"[85] and the notebooks are a Promethean exercise in uninhibited writing and meta-phor-building. The notebooks in the present volumes are, of course, not *Twilight*, not the anagogic book of aphorisms that Frye dreamed about— "'my own' book of *pensées*," as he calls it.[86] But it is possible that the core of *Twilight* would have come from a selection of these late notebooks. When Frye says that *Twilight* is "ideally . . . a book to be put away in a drawer and have published after my death" and that he always thought of the final book in his ogdoad fantasy as "something perhaps not reached,"[87] possibility moves in the direction of likelihood.

The Moebius strip paradox, as I call it, that Paul can speak of "Christ in me" because Paul is a particular whole of which Christ is a part, while Christ is a universal whole of which Paul is a part, belongs with the point above. This wisdom cannot be pictured as "I am." This "Christ in me" is the opposite of "I am Christ."

The fact that there are two apocalypses explains why the panoramic one is so full of images and mad, with being or energy expended for a further end in view.

Every story begins in the middle, because it is always possible to ask "What happened before." Hence "once upon a time" means "despite this fact, I'm beginning."

I suppose I should look at Bishop Burnet's Theory of the Earth. Its late date is significant: of the two Biblical accounts of creation, he was so obsessed by the Jahwist one that he could not deal with the other. This got him into trouble: in other words clergymen (Burnet & the "Canobar" tradition) were being forcibly withdrawn from serious thinking. He seems, again like Bryant, to have been trying to work the theory of the deluge as the natural-objective counterpart of the fall.

Ps. 12:8 says that the wicked travel in a circle: the AV translation bungles it. Eliot's phrase per contra course?

1. From NFF, 1991, box 25, Notebook 27, p. 7 (courtesy of Victoria University Library).

It was, as we say, "the best thing that could have happened," that Helen should have died when she did. Why is that an event which shows the care and the mercy of God ~~like~~ the most hideous and insensate of crimes if I had taken her life instead? One of those questions so obvious that we forget ever to ask it: it's not as easy to answer as all the automatic answers that come pouring out suggest. Is there another dimension to God as scapegoat, bearing the sins of mankind? I suppose "vengeance is mine" is in a similar category.

Meanwhile, let's think about the one idea all this grief has brought me so far. I said in GC that the invisible world in the Bible was not a second order of existence, as in the Platonic tradition, but the means by which the visible world becomes visible, as the invisible act is the medium of visibility. The one really invisible world is the world across death: is that what makes us to see the seen? Is the visible world the world of faith (pistis), as in Plato, that is the elenchos of the unseen?

My suggestion that grief for the dead impedes and disturbs them may of course be the crassest and crossest of superstitions: one has to try out such things to see if they have any resonance. But grief emphasizes the pastness of the past, and so works against the mythical imagination. Helen was — that's the beginning of tears and mourning. Helen is. What she is, perhaps, is a central element in the unseen which will clarify my understanding, if such clarification is granted me. My whole and first conception may have to link with this: I'm right to pray to God, because God is the unity and totality of all this: but the perspective can reverse into millions of presences — the saints, in short. Helen would smile at the notion of being a saint, but I suspect that sanctity is something created by love, not necessarily some kind of essence ~~but a center for seeing:~~

Christ leads us through no darker rooms
Than he went through before.

2. From NFF, 1993, box 1, Notebook 44, p. 54 (courtesy of Victoria University Library).

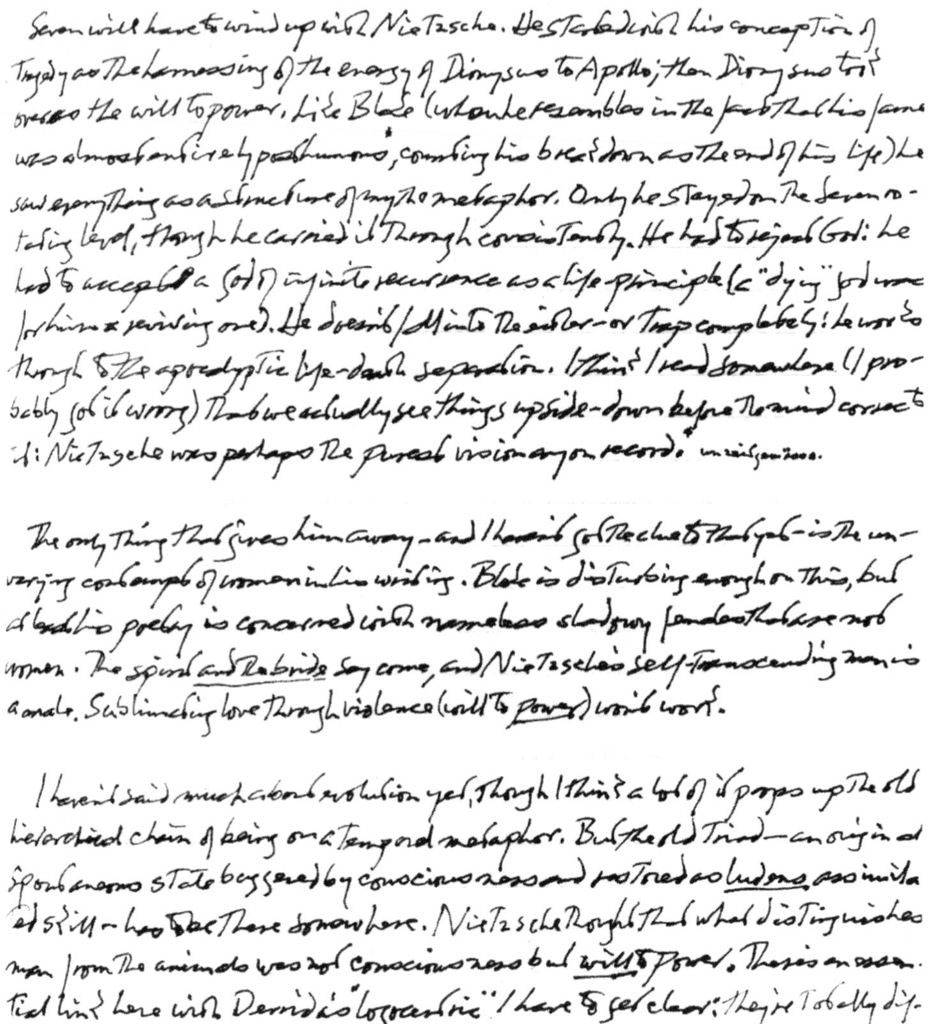

Seven will have to wind up with Nietzsche. He started with his conception of Tragedy as the harnessing of the energy of Dionysus to Apollo; then Dionysus turns over as the will to power. Like Blake (whom he resembles in the fact that his fame was almost entirely posthumous, counting his breakdown as the end of his life) he saw everything as a structure of mythic metaphor. Only he stayed on the seven rotating level, though he carried it through consistently. He had to reject God: he had to accept a god of infinite recurrence as a life-principle (a "dying" god was for him a reviving one). He doesn't fall into the sister-or-trap completely: he works through to the apocalyptic life-death separation. I think I read somewhere (I probably got it wrong) that we actually see things upside-down before the mind corrects it: Nietzsche was perhaps the purest vision on record. [illegible]

The only thing that gives him away—and I haven't got the clue to that yet—is the unvarying contempt of women in his writing. Blake is disturbing enough on this, but at least his poetry is concerned with nameless shadowy females that are not women. The spirit and the bride say come, and Nietzsche's self-transcending man is a male. Sublimating love through violence (will to power) won't work.

I haven't said much about evolution yet, though I think a lot of it props up the old hierarchical chain of being on a temporal metaphor. But the old triad—an original spontaneous state buggered by consciousness and restored as ludens assimilated skill—has its place there somewhere. Nietzsche thought that what distinguishes man from the animals was not consciousness but will to power. There's an essential link here with Derrida's "logocentric" I have to get clear: they're totally different, but seem to agree on the verbal as part of the intermediate stage.

3. From NFF, 1993, box 1, Notebook 50, p. 187 (courtesy of Victoria University Library).

4. From NFF, 1993, box 1, Notebook 46, p. 4 (courtesy of Victoria University
   Library).

Northrop Frye's Late Notebooks, 1982–1990:
Architecture of the Spiritual World

VOLUME 5

Notebook 27

This notebook comes from the time that Frye was working on Words with Power. *As we learn from the final entry, he completed the notebook on 1 January 1986. Internal evidence suggests that all the entries except those composed on New Year's Day of 1986 were written in 1985. The notebook is in the NFF, 1991, box 25.*

[1] The doctrine of original sin comes eventually to this: man is a crazy Oedipus obsessed by two desires: to murder his father God and to rape his mother Nature.[1]

[2] Myth is a story, a word originally identical with history but now distinguished from it. It's a story which is both historical and anti-historical (i.e., didn't happen). In totality it's counterhistorical: it reverses the slithering movement of time and *confronts*. The Crucifixion is a myth: whether Jesus was crucified or not, many other people were, and Jesus was in every one of them.[2] Hence the royal Crucifixion, the individual one that stands for all others, stays in front of us: this is what you are, so far as what you are is the summation of what you've done.

[3] So far I've given this the universalizing or Aristotelian context, but others are possible: in Burnt Norton a presence comes down and informs the not-quite existing present with a real existence. The movement is a Yeatsian gyre, bringing the cyclical dance of Nature down to a point.

[4] Metaphor is the statement "A is B" which carries with it the realization that A is not in the least B. It is logical & a statement of difference in

what it suppresses: it is anti-logical in what it asserts. So it's counter-logical, creating an identity, opening a current of energy between personal (subjective) and impersonal (objective) worlds.[3]

[5] I suppose Locke is the basis of descriptive theory; his primary qualities are those that can be explored by mathematics, and words are there to describe the secondary ones.[4]

[6] I once consulted the I Ching, using toothpicks instead of yarrow stalks, saying I didn't want an answer to the specific problem but general advice about what to do and be. I got, without qualification or "moving lines," the second or K'un hexagram,[5] meaning, I suppose, that I was to be a "feminine" or receptive writer.

[7] That tiresome link with McLuhan cropped up again in the paper. McLuhan would be on the Chi'en side,[6] I suppose: his ideas were, he said, "probes"—a male metaphor—without social context. He supplied the context by naive determinism: technology is alleged to create society.

[8] Wisdom is the Pisgah vision at the end of law. Prophecy is the outsider's vision, and one form of such vision is that of the child or fool (out of the mouth of babes, etc. [Matthew 21:16]). I think my own perspective has prophetic elements, and a lot of them are connected with what I can see to be neoteny.

[9] Knowledge is cyclical: the sun goes over your head; what you learn is the last thing you've learned, & you attach it to the other things you've learned; nothing is new *under* the sun.

[10] In experience you stand on the sun's orbit, which revolves below you: everything is a beginning, yet not a beginning because it's discontinuous; a time for all things. The Fool in the Tarot stands on a precipice. I wonder if this sudden emergence of the moral folly of experience out of the cycle of knowledge isn't something crucial to the book: perhaps the Eliot fire-sermon [*The Waste Land*, pt. 3] cycle top, in contrast with the Mallarmé Igitur bottom.[7]

[11] Soul is the essence of the body and escapes from the body at death. The East says it can't go anywhere except into another body. Spirit is the

substance or hypostasis of the body: it can transform the soul-body into itself.

[12] Knowledge is acquired by the individual but transmitted to a community & is fulfilled there. Experience is acquired by society but transmitted to the individual & is fulfilled there. Wisdom is thus the individual's growth out of tradition. The bee's flight is wisdom; his load of pollen knowledge. Creation is Logos as communal conscious awakening: law is Logos as tradition & cultural heritage: prophecy is communal imagination. Exodus is the individual within the social body, wisdom the spirit within the total soul; gospel the spirit within the spiritual (total) body.[8]

[13] Hermes, Prometheus, Adonis & Eros are spectres of the dead: they have no "concentering vision."[9] The Bible provides that: the four become four aspects of Logos. Exodus is the mother; Wisdom the daughter; Gospel the bride part. Apocalypse the redeemed harlot (the bride no longer a virgin). All Blake, so far. Hermes the Father (I mean Creation is), Law the teacher, Prophecy the Son, Pan. Apoc [Panoramic Apocalypse][10] the Holy Spirit, the male counterpart of the black bride.

[14] The two apocalypses are the union of the male Holy Spirit and the female who was the origin of the conception. This is the world of the Taoist balance of heaven & earth, & the Yeatsian perfect fuck.[11]

[15] So all the to-do in the Bible about the Great Whore & Co. is really Sarah's jealousy of Hagar. Hagar is all aspects of the White Goddess, Queen of Heaven, the mythical prototypes of the cruel stepmother & Goneril-Regan daughter figures, & so on. (This is a silly note.)

[16] Exodus: after a revolution everything freezes in the revolutionary mould. All cultural life depends on edging back to a pre-revolutionary situation, where Socrates & Jesus are still alive.

[17] The Law stage is Torah, instruction: hence my mythology, cosmology, & encyclopaedic points go here.

[18] All the drunken boat people either do or don't have an Atlantis.[12] Marx had one in his classless society & withered-away state; Freud

didn't have one. Jung did, but in finding it he lost the dialectic of ego and repression, so he can't replace Freud. Also, of course, Marxists, like Freudian revisionists (not the word: I mean Lacan) plunge rapturously into the dialectic for its own sake and end, & to hell with Atlantis.

[19] A contributor to George Johnston's Festschrift quotes Hans Denk [Denck] as saying that (my paraphrase) anybody confronted with an antithesis who doesn't look for a third term doesn't known his ass from the crater of Etna.[13] Protestants thought the Church would evolve into reform, but it didn't: Protestant countries became so for political reasons, & they & Catholics settled down to an adversary situation. Marx thought capitalism would evolve to Socialism, but it didn't: the two systems are just adversaries, though each has improved slightly by borrowing from its rival.[14]

[20] "I am a wise and good man" is grammatically impossible, because such predicates cannot be attached to anything beginning with "I am." Even Jesus resented being called good [Matthew 19:17]. The ego doesn't co-exist with wisdom & goodness.[15]

[21] No: Hermes is both Creation and Law, natural & social order. Prometheus is both Exodus and ("forethought") wisdom. In their feminine aspect they're the genuine mother (Juno) & sister (Athene). Adonis is both prophecy & panorama; Eros both gospel & participation. Feminine: the black bride who becomes white & red (Magdalen).

[22] If the Bible is metaphorically female, it's because redeemed man, the fourth person (or presence) of the Trinity, is metaphorically woman.[16]

[23] Trotsky is said to have remarked, of the Russian formalists of his day, that they believed that in the beginning was the Word, whereas all good Marxists were committed to "in the beginning was the deed."[17]

[24] I want to outline the major elements of mythology (authority, aspiration, cycle & polarization) and then, using Blake's Four Zoas passage, describe the fourfold dialogue of Word & Spirit in the Bible as their "concentering vision."[18] Female because it's the containing body of these dialogues.

[25] The accuser's view is that the essence of man is the sum total of the things he has done; the redeemer's view is that it is the vision of what he is trying to make of himself at any given time. The former rests on evidence and the continuity of time; the latter on discontinuity and hope (because the vision is certain to be obscured by failure or neurosis).[19]

[26] The cosmos of authority is inherently a ladder, the chain of being, and so is its reversal: I think Donne says in a sermon that even the angels, who can fly, mounted the steps of Jacob's ladder.[20]

[27] The Moebius strip paradox, as I call it, that Paul can speak of "Christ in me" because Paul is a particular whole of which Christ is a part, while Christ is a universal whole of which Paul is a part, belongs with the point above [par. 20] that wisdom cannot be predicated of "I am." Thus "Christ in me" is the opposite of "I am Christ."[21]

[28] The fact that there are two apocalypses[22] explains why the panoramic one is so full of images of work, work being energy expended for a further end in view.

[29] Every story begins in the middle, because it is always possible to ask "What happened before?" Hence "once upon a time" means "despite this fact, I'm beginning."

[30] I suppose I should look at Bishop Burnet's theory of the Earth.[23] Its late date is significant: of the two Biblical accounts of creation, he was so obsessed by the Jahwist one [Genesis 2:4–25] that he couldn't deal with the other. This got him into trouble: in other words clergymen (Bryant & the "Casaubon" tradition)[24] were being forcibly withdrawn from serious thinking. He seems, again like Bryant, to have been trying to work out a theory of the deluge as the natural-objective counterpart of the fall.

[31] Ps. 12:8 says that the wicked travel in a circle: the AV translation bungles it.[25] Eliot's prickly pear caucus-race.[26]

[32] The myth is neither historical nor anti-historical: it is counter-historical, creating a stasis in the movement of time.[27] The metaphor similarly is counter-logical, creating a stasis in the movement of causality. I

said this on the first page [par. 4]. The metaphor says "A is not B" as
clearly as it says "A is B," and from the point of view of the denial "A is
B" can be only the unit of a purely hypothetical world.[28] I've been using
the Bible to help me get to a plane of metaphor beyond hypothesis. It's
becoming clearer that the reader's reaction is the direction of that: *Paradise
Lost* is hypothetical in itself, but it's "real" (whatever that means) to me,
not because I share Milton's beliefs but because I possess his metaphors.

[33] So (as I've always known) literature passes through belief and anti-
belief to counter-belief, or what I called in the MLA paper a catharsis of
belief.[29] (Whatever Aristotle meant by catharsis, what I mean by it is
sailing through the Hercules-pillars of "is" and "is not" (I mean rather, of
course, the Symplegades)[)].[30] My position on value-judgments is a part
of this.

[34] I've often said that Hopkins would have been a very great critic if he
could have junked his anxieties, such as calling Whitman "a very great
scoundrel."[31] I think (a) it doesn't matter what Whitman was, except
when his clap-trap injures his poetry (b) Hopkins was something of an
intellectual thug himself, and *that* doesn't matter except when *his* clap-
trap invades his poetry. This is the kernel of truth in the critic-as-judge
metaphor, but a judge has a deeper responsibility than being a voice of
his time, uttering *its* clap-trap as well as its vision.

[35] Problems of belief are still with me: for all practical purposes "I
don't believe in God" and "I believe in no God" are interchangeable.
They seem to me to be very different statements, and the agnostic-atheist
distinction doesn't exhaust the difference.

[36] The vision of creation, or total intelligibility, is intolerable to man:
this is what Job was warned against, & what Faust could not "endure"
(Tragen) from the Erdgeist.[32] Man has to become a creature contemplating a fellow-creature in bits and pieces, the blind man's elephant. God
contemplating creation is the model for man "observing" the Sabbath or
Bride of God. Xy [Christianity] changed the Sabbath to the repetition of
Sunday, the original light, brighter than a thousand suns, & even one we
can't look at. This makes no sense except by thinking of Sunday as the
eighth day of *new* creation, which man has at least partly built himself,
his coral island.[33]

[37] The third word of the Bible, rendered "created" in the AV, is never employed to describe what man can also do. Hence there is no real apocalyptic vision in the O.T. where the images of human work become spiritual *and* substantial.

[38] The literal response to creation is the peculiar society, set apart from others by a distinctive mythology, God calling Abraham or Moses and forming "Israel." Israel is the pattern for what I call the verbal temenos [sacred space]: the universalizing of Israel, purging it of sectarian and racist elements, seems to me inevitable, but of course I'm not a Jew. However, "Christendom" is only a swollen Judea.

[39] The law is allegorical because it makes the Jews a type. Note that I could stress the revolutionary side of the Exodus less and concentrate more on the saving remnant, the isolated Utopia, the small group called out of Ur or Egypt. Anyway, positive law, doing what others don't, is ultimately individualizing. Wisdom understands the creation *through* the law.

[40] The prophetic or outsider's vision creates the ∪-pattern out of Israel, & thereby the inverted ∪ or cyclical vision for the world. It's only in this negative form that the Bible incorporates the cyclical vision. The Gospel response to it carries on with this theme of a subordinated cyclical vision.

[41] I suppose the whole book turns on the thesis that the spirit is substantial: it's the realizing of primary concern out of the language (Word) of primary mythology. Only the total Word can make the spirit substantial. Everything else, including Marx's critique of Hegel, is ideological. I don't want to become a conservative Hegelian, and my goal is not absolute knowledge, whatever that is, but the Word & Spirit set free by each other and united in one substance with the Other detached from Nature and identified as the Father. This doesn't subordinate the female: it wakens and emancipates her, Eros Regained in short. Jesus' establishing of the identity of the other as Father is what makes him the definitive prophet.

[42] Panoramic and participating apocalypse are related as Sailing to Byzantium is to Byzantium.[34] The former is the vision of the new crea-

tion, & gives an impression of a construct "out of" nature. It's only the latter that's the real interpenetrating vision.

[43] I must look up Victor Turner on anti-structures and the generative power of rituals.[35] The 19th c. (especially Newman) obsession with institutional continuities is second-level stuff, the sacramental analogy. Rituals that are alive have to be created out of living myths, & they have to be going in the practice-habit direction, not the repetitive direction (ruling over change).[36]

[44] Hazard Adams makes quite a bit of my footnote on mathematics, relating it to Yeats' Vision.[37] I don't know how far I can go in the "Tao of Physics" direction,[38] but Yeats did see that "Pythagoras planned it" [*The Statues*, l. 1], and that mathematics was a part of Eros Regained.

[45] I have an old note about eros and logos, creation by desire and creation by the Word.[39] It may be linked with another which quotes Huxley's *Perennial Philosophy* as saying that the soul is female and the spirit male.[40] Note that the new heaven and the new earth is the real Tao, yang & yin in perfect balance.

[46] One negative evidence of the substantiality of spirit is that spiritual enemies don't die: they always return like flies to horseshit. The power that can send them into the "deep" is a greater one than we can imagine: that's the polarizing operation at the end of the world.

[47] Auden's For the Time Being is a useful example of a Christian construct on a Schopenhauer basis, but perhaps Wagner's Parsifal, considered as the epilogue of the Ring cycle, is a better one.[41]

[48] The Exodus or liberal response includes the fragmented nature of languages and the encasing of cultural thinking within those languages. Hence the frequent missionary fallacy of "What do *you* call God?" and the like.

[49] Perhaps I've been overlooking the narrative of, first, heaven and earth locked together in a sexual union, second, an Oedipal Son or Logos pushing them apart to form the world of consciousness-creation, third, this Logos growing, like the *Begriff* in Hegel, until Heaven and Earth reach the Tao balance as Father and Spirit.[42]

[50] Literature is an art; the context of the art, the cosmology, is its code. This was what was assumed to be true of music in the 16th c. The cosmology in turn is the thematic stasis of the myth, and the myth is *the* story in which all of the others find their genesis & telos.[43] I've been here before. Note however that Blake's Orc & Urizen & the rest are not just *psychologized* gods like Jung's archetypes, because his humanity underlies Nature too. The Code is knowledge & universalized; experience comes out of poetry & the rest, which the Spirit creates.

[51] Experience takes one to the third prophetic level, which can be thaumaturgic until it renounces its magic (my Baal fable),[44] or go off the rails into insanity.

[52] If I'm right about the Word growing like the *Begriff* in Hegel [par. 49], the *Phenomenology* is an Odyssey as well as a Purgatorio climb. The Odyssey is the cycle redeemed, beginning & ending at *home*; the Purgatorio is the climb to polarization.

[53] In establishing the difference between a mythology and a cosmology, I don't see why I can't just go back to my "thematic stasis" principle, which is all right. The thematic stasis of the Messiah's quest is Jacob's ladder, and the same construct would have appeared if there had been no Bible, only Classical or Mithraic constructs. The central elements of course are the chain of being and the Ptolemaic hierarchy: I don't know if I need to reproduce all the handbooks & the familiar details.[45]

[54] Intensely anthropocentric view: herbals & lapidaries based on the principle that everything in nature contains an element relevant to human concerns, & in fact was mainly created for that purpose. "How America abounded with Beasts of Prey and noxious Animals, yet contained not in it that necessary Creature, a Horse, is very strange" (Browne, R.M. [*Religio Medici*], 22).[46] (The last three words were added in the 1643 edition.) The breakdown of this structure runs through Voltaire's Micromegas.[47] Blake was still fighting for it, but only because he held to the pre-existence of the humanity of God.

[55] I was hoping to find out something about Bruno's conception of polarity, as used by Joyce in FW [*Finnegans Wake*], but Clive Hart's book doesn't even have Bruno in the index, though Vico is all over it.[48] The ladder is the thematic stasis of the cosmoi of authority & revolt (or

aspiration); the cycle is its own thematic stasis; the polarized or apocalyptic revelation is the thematic stasis of the *quest*. Note that the quest has
two poles, just as the ladder has two directions.

[56] Speaking of FW, I don't see the Mallarmé or *symboliste* affinities: for
all the disguise & distortion there's a perfect orgy of *naming* in it: books
of the Bible, suras of the Koran, poems of Moore, catalogues of rivers &
cities, etc. I should however think of FW occasionally as *above* consciousness and pointing to what comes next, not as wholly an archaeological dig, as Joyce himself often seems to do. The dream state could be
"astral."

[57] Anyway Joyce isn't Freudian, I think: Freud has no Atlantis, no
Finnegan even: everything gets absorbed in the repression-confrontation
dialectic, just as Marxism is absorbed in its dialectic and ignores the
classless society or whatever that's its alleged goal. Connections here
with the antithetical relation of bourgeois and Marxist societies I made in
my Innis introduction.[49] But Freud's resistance to more speculative extensions of his work, like Jung's or Reich's, is much easier to understand
than, say, Einstein's to quantum physics.

[58] Ascent may be to the new: when it is, descent is the recovery of the
old that was excluded by repression, forgetting, or lack of awareness. It's
a harrowing of hell or rather limbo: a redemption of the dead, a recalling
of past to present. Similarly new formulations of myth recapture lost and
neglected implications. The Grail stories are profounder than cauldrons-
of-plenty myths, and my reading of them is profounder than they are.

[59] Metaphor starts out as magic, half creating and half perceiving, as
Wordsworth says,[50] elemental spirits, totems, local gods, & the like. The
Biblical opposition to "idolatry" involves renouncing the magic and
sublimating or internalizing the verbal metaphor. So metaphor is the
arrest of magic and of logic; myth is the arrest of history and dialectic.

[60] Re the note on p. 6 [par. 25], that we are actually the result of what
we have done (accuser's view) and potentially what we are trying to
make of ourselves (redeemer's view); we are imprisoned *by* what we
have done, but unless we have committed a major crime, like Claudius
in *Hamlet*, that doesn't bother us too much: we adjust to the steady

narrowing of our interests and abilities as we age. If we try to "make something" of ourselves, we find that we are imprisoned *in* what we are. Hamlet himself is the greatest example in literature of a titanic spirit thrashing around in the prison of what he is.

[61] Reich (I think: maybe it's Reik) calls this prison characterological armour.[51] Of course a whole culture, like an individual, gets imprisoned in this armour, which is where the authority of prophecy comes in. The prophet may be, like Hamlet, neurotic or even mad, because he's the victim of a social claustrophobia that practically all the people in that society don't feel—or rather, have repressed.

[62] Re up and down ladders on p. 15 [par. 58]: in the age of authority ascent is to the "unfallen" past, man's true inheritance, as in the *Purgatorio*. Descent was to the unknown and forbidden future, the Witch of Endor,[52] the people in the *Inferno* who know the future but not the present.[53] The post-Romantic ladder, especially after the rise of evolutionary analogies, has ascent to the new and descent reclaiming the old.

[63] The later model is closer to the rising side of Christ's quest. His death and resurrection re-established the genuine tradition of revelation, as the later Harrowing of Hell formulation of it tried to say. His ascent is recorded not so much in the Ascension as in the Transfiguration or upward metamorphosis.[54]

[64] The thematic stasis of myth is not "a" metaphor but a metaphorical diagram. The two-way ladder, which is really a double spiral, the circle; the divided line.[55] Oh, God, if I could only bring off a book establishing these as the structural principles of poetry and then showing that they're the structural principles of the Bible also.

[65] Ernest Becker's *Denial of Death*, 49, says what Otto's book on the holy is really about is the lack of courage to face the vision of creation:[56] Faust's failure with the Erdgeist.[57] That's why, like Dante with the beasts [*Inferno*, canto 1], we have to turn our backs on it and run through the whole sequence until we face it ("new" creation) in the last apocalypse.

[66] Ernest Becker in *The Denial of Death* says, following Otto Rank, that character is founded on a lie about reality, that neurosis compresses this

into an inability to unite, or to separate, depending on the kind of neurosis it is, his bit of experience.[58] The creative person, like the neurotic, creates a symbolic world, but hypothetically rather than existentially—these are my terms, not his.

[67] Well: the metaphor is the structural or positive or creative lie: it asserts something in the teeth of experience. It's not only counter-logical; it's counter-ironic, facing the irony of absurdity and "thrownness" in nature.[59]

[68] Literature is founded on the metaphor that arrests logic and the myth that arrests history: its works are objects of contemplation. (All arts aspire to the condition of painting; that's just as true as what Pater said about music.)[60] The Bible suggests that there is a structure beyond the hypothetical.

[69] Here arises the dialectic (*not* the conflict) of faith and doubt. Doubt is the recognition of the hypothetical, imaginative, literary aspect of the Bible. The "fundamental" type of belief assumes a "what's really there" quality in the text that no serious critic could accept for a moment. If such "thereness" existed, there'd be no need for churches and all sects would be *ipso facto* ridiculous. (Jews and Moslems are just as sectarian as Christians.)

[70] Faith is the recurring sense of revelation, i.e., an existential reality beyond the hypothetical. This revelation is the vision of a "new" creation—new to us, that is. Such a faith, if attained, redeems and justifies all literature.

[71] The first step of faith is neurotic, pushing its world into "another" world, & splitting man into an immortal soul and a mortal body. Here Christ, as notably in pietism, becomes a transference object, usually ending up as a mother. The second step is an antithesis between work (trying to create a "better" world) and play (cultivation with the aid of imaginative arts). The antithesis of soul & body is resolved by the spiritual body; the antithesis of work and play is resolved by the Word, which is both the working word and the literary play word.

[72] The continuity of the Creator, as something there from the original

big bang, cannot be maintained. The real Creator is also a creature, or rather, the new vision of the first conscious creature. Creation of nature raised to a second power, the synthesis of present nature and human culture. Creation embodies the workable, the achievable, and the playable or conceivable. Charity & contemplation.

[73] Reverting to something I said earlier [par. 68]: all arts aspire to the condition of painting or sculpture in the context of contemplation, where they are icons "beyond words." They aspire to the condition of music when they are an experience "beyond words," experience being what Pater was interested in. In what context do they aspire to the condition of literature? Is there a "beyond words"? Eliot certainly thought there was.[61]

[74] Nature is the symbolic Mother: she's been there from the beginning. Hence the vision of creation has to focus on a Father, and then on a *virgin* mother, a mother who can't be involved with my mother or anyone else's mother. Or Jesus' mother, for that matter—see Blake's Tirzah poem.[62]

[75] If metaphor is counter-ironic satire has a *very* positive role: Rabelais is essential to Dante as I've always said. Here we are back to the porous osmotic wall between the oracular and the funny.

[76] Dante has something he calls the *sprone* or spur:[63] I wonder if this is the function of the erotic in starting off the exuberant perception, the sense of the beautiful, sublime, heroic, & finally the divine? Perhaps there are two spurs, the other being the *social* spur, the voice of others where "conscience" starts off, wherever it ends. This would include the church, of course, and ancestral voices. Perhaps Eros is the radical spur and Adonis (chorus of women around a dying god) the conservative one.

[77] To see creation is not quite seeing God: nothing can see God except the God in us. Perhaps man can see God unharmed, but unharmed because he doesn't recognize him. (I should avoid writing notes like this: it's dangerous to start getting glib about God.)

[78] I've told my story about the priest of Baal who saw that Baal was the

True God in contrast to a God jumping around on cue to do stunts.[64] But what about the God who descends out of the whirlwind to answer Job? *That's* what Baal can't do. *Restoring* Job is an anticlimax.

[79] "Paganism" ends in the cycle of the white goddess, and the white goddess is momma, the object *we* want to fuck instead of letting the Father do it. But we're mortal, and she is the body of our death as well.[65]

[80] Metaphor arises as part of the effort to create the third knowledge of a "thou" world out of the deadlock of "I" and "It." As the first "Thou" is a sexual object, it's founded on Eros.[66]

[81] Larry Zolf has been quoted as saying that ideas are the first resort of the (political) amateur.[67] I suppose that's a repetition of the young person trying to understand his own emotions and only getting ideas about them.

[82] I wonder if Joyce is just fooling around in his references to Lévy-Bruhl or if he's calling attention to his principle that primitive thinking is metaphorical identification with the thing. (FW)[68]

[83] Such identity, *participation mystique*[69] or whatever, may be the real Word beyond words.

[84] One reason why definitive criticism is something no critic would be fool enough to think about is that every poem has a community of readers, and one reader isn't all the others too. Even if it were possible, it would not illuminate the poem but merely replace it.

[85] On one side of the metaphor is ecstatic identification, the mob frenzies of the Bacchanals, the self-hypnotism of the shaman, the hysteria of the sorcerer. Then comes the ironic distancing of the hypothetical poetic metaphor. On this level art is possessed: it doesn't take possession. But beyond this is the counter-ironic aspect of metaphor, the sense of revelation recaptured by a (spiritual) community which is what the word "gospel" is all about.

[86] The pious infantilism, or infantile pietism, that turns Jesus into a pure transference symbol ("cast thy burden upon the Lord" [Psalm

55:22]) ends by turning him into a mother ("Safe in the arms of Jesus").[70] I said that.

[87] Re the previous (but one) note: expanded consciousness is not religion, of course, but it may be the precondition for any ecumenical or everlasting-gospel religion. Note that the gospel-church begins with ecstatic phenomena (speaking in tongues), and that our own time is rich in frenzies and hysterias along with more genuine phenomena. LSD (when it's a good trip) appears to increase the intensity of the feeling of oneness with the object.

[88] The thematic stasis of metaphor is the royal metaphor; the thematic stasis of myth(ology) is the cosmology. Metaphors, I suppose, must stick together like myths: the identity-as metaphor, the class as individual, corresponds to mythology. Now if I could only figure out the relation of the Moebius paradox to that . . .[71]

[89] I've probably got the point that in the Promethean set-up we often climb to the future, so that descent themes have to do with recovering the past. I sidled into this by way of William Morris and my "prerevolutionary" idea about the artist. Also that Oscar Wilde passage about music and the intensity of experience we have without knowing we have it,[72] which makes, e.g., King Lear recognizable.

[90] Merezhkovsky's Atlantis/Europe is a good guide here:[73] yesterday's kook book is tomorrow's standard text. Incidentally, Morris' *Earthly Paradise* is set in a symbolic Atlantis.

[91] If McLuhan's principle holds up, that the content of a new medium is the form of an earlier medium, then the content of written literature is the form of oral literature.[74]

[92] The subject cannot be a subject, or live in the subject-object world of ordinary experience, until he becomes an object to himself—until there is a split within the subject. That's Lacan's *stade du miroir*, essentially: the ego also has a *moi* that's its own fighting & aggressive self.[75]

[93] Wyatt's sonnet: "My galley, chargèd with forgetfulness." It uses allegory, of course ("Drownèd is Reason," etc.), that being part of a

poet's defensive armor then. But, despite the Tottel editor, the "comparison" of love and voyaging is not allegory but analogical metaphor,
touching at points of identity (as when the "stars" of line 12 are the lady's
eyes). The sonnet is based on Petrarch's 156 in Vita [*Sonnetto in Vita*], but
it's not a translation: the climactic line 12,[76] so skilfully led up to, isn't in
Petrarch.

[94] Anyway, this conception of continuous analogical metaphor, as
something different from allegory, has to be looked into. The whole
Courtly Love convention, vis-a-vis Christianity, is an example of it.

[95] Hegel himself calls the Ph. [*Phenomenology*] a ladder (II.2.5).[77]

[96] So one of the main themes of the book has to be the modulation
from one dichotomy to the other. The old one has a "soul," immortal and
superior to the body, striving to become "good" by observing the law. In
the later one a "spirit" forms within the psyche and the whole self-
defensive ego, including the Freudian superego, collapses into Lacan's
moi, the ego that can't be transformed.

[97] When I say old & later I don't mean chronologically: one is the
invariable uniform of authority and ideology, the other the genuine
apocalyptic confrontation of spirit and the spiritless. The latter is the
"lost soul," which as I've constantly said everyone has, and should take
care it gets well lost.

[98] Forms of spiritual growth: the father-soul and the mother-body
(dying to) bring forth the spirit-child. I think this is alchemic. Odyssey
pattern: the old beggar, least likely to succeed, growing in reverse of
ordinary aging until he becomes not just master of the house but the body
of the house. Hegel's *Begriff*,[78] the infant exposed and abandoned by the
common-sense world, turning out to be the Prospero of the whole show.

[99] Kant's perverse morality: the moral act isn't moral if you like doing
it; only nasty-tasting medicines do you any good, is an extreme version
of Freud's superego-consciousness dominating a repressed unconscious.
The dialectic between them has to be linguistically structured on both
sides, as Lacan saw,[79] and as the Maslow people show when they en-
courage self-dialogue of the "top dog and underdog" type.[80]

[100] Where does the lost soul go? If I believed in reincarnation I'd have *that* answer, with the proviso that one's consciousness should not be committed to it. (It never is: if it were there'd be memories of former lives, and there isn't, except for young children in India, where it's culturally accepted).

[101] I've often said that Hegel's Ph G [*Phänomenologie des Geistes*] interests me deeply in itself, but not as a preface to Hegel's system. This is linked on my part with my feeling that Moses was the only person who ever saw the Promised Land. The system is only a Prussian Canaan.

[102] The authoritarian construct is still there in Kierkegaard's Either-Or, I think, and its model is the tragic Neigung-Pflicht conflict.[81] Freud's superego-driven consciousness with its dungeon of "repressed" impulses is the model, as I've said: observe the Sabbath or go to church or whatever—anyway, shut up and do as you're told. This is the law responded to by the prudence stage of wisdom. But as soon as wisdom develops toward spontaneity it inches toward prophecy, which means "listening" for a new speech.

[103] The Spirit is born, or reborn, from prophecy, and its enemy is Lacan's *moi*, the self-alienated ego or projected Narcissus. The *moi*, I suppose, must be the Spirit's twin brother, born at the same time and the hero of a dream world while the Spirit sleeps. The *moi* remembers everything except its spiritual heritage: if it remembered that it would vanish.

[104] The Word-Spirit dialogue is slowly assuming a spiral or ladder shape: it conceivably might work out to a counterpart of Hegel's Ph [*Phenomenology*], only in images instead of concepts, with a religion of *parable* forming its crisis. And, of course, there's the other great hope that it would follow the four levels of meaning.

[105] It seems to me that the Spirit doesn't speak by the prophets, as the Creed says,[82] but that the Spirit hears the real Word in the prophecy. Hence all the he-that-hath-ears stuff [Mark 4:9]. The crucial difference between Jesus and his prophetic predecessors is his possession of the genre of *parable*, as distinct from ecstatic vision. I've always known that the parable was the unit of a freeman's education (liberal: Milton's

Raphael) and that it was crucial in all Bible-imagination studies, but I left it out of the GC. If Job is the new Genesis, the parables are a third, the Genesis of Spirit. And of course I mustn't forget the Apocryphal parables, especially Susanna and Tobit.[83]

[106] The dialectic movement from creation to exodus is clearing. The forming of a specific mythology is the only possible response to a hidden creation. As Blake says, religion is a specific social development of the Poetic Genius [*All Religions Are One*]. In a sense a mythology negates or denies the creation, on Hegelian principles.

[107] In fact, I wonder if I couldn't boil down the whole sequence to a single chapter on the Phenomenology of the Imagination. Law negates the revolutionary element in Exodus; wisdom, once it reaches the limit of the prudential or how-I-love-the-law stage, begins to reverse the movement back to a lost spontaneity. This produces the prophetic or outsider's vision, and that negates itself again to form the spiritual community. And so on to the second or participating apocalypse, which negates the first by turning it back to the creation, the one cycle that is not a failed spiral.

[108] That should be one chapter out of the eight. Possibilities for another include (a) a history of literary Biblical forms, from *sage* [i.e., saga] through to a tremendous breakthrough in Job, then folktale from Ruth & Jonah through Susanna & Tobit, and then the second breakthrough from emblematic vision to *parable*. Parable is a literary form leading up to action, crossing S.K's either-or bridge.[84]

[109] Then (b) a history of metaphor (with myth) from ecstatic to literary, thence becoming a microcosm of language & thus leading to the conception of one consciousness, which I'm quite sure is of Christian origin. This is really my Odyssey theme, the beggar advancing to the metaphor (royal) of the house.

[110] Only I've got it stuck to (c), the authoritarian picture of the soul dominating the body. Kant's moral act that *must* go against inclination, Freud's superego-driven consciousness locking up desire in the jail of "repression"—the Urizen-Orc picture I know so well. If the father-soul stops spanking the mother-body long enough to screw her instead, the

child-spirit may get born. If it does, it grows & grows & grows into a spiritual body, the parental soul-body unit collapsing into a self-alien-ated ego, Lacan's *moi*, the twin (as above [par. 103]) tanist brother. That in its turn has to get unstuck from the up-and-down ladder.

[111] Query: would the up-down ladder section boil down to a single chapter including Hermes & Prometheus? No, it wouldn't. Stop this.

[112] The main difficulty in my writing, as I've often said, is in translat-ing discontinuous aphorisms into continuous argument. Continuity, in writing as in physics, is probabilistic, and every sequence is a choice among possibilities. Inevitable sequence is illusory, & especially so in logic, where, just as q is always followed by u, so "rigor" is always followed by "mortis."

[113] "God is God only insofar as he knows himself: {this} is a self-consciousness in man and man's knowledge of God that goes on to man's knowing himself in God." Hegel's Philosophy of History, in Kaufman, 273.[85] If I, so ignorant of Hegel, feel that I understand this better than a first-rate Hegel scholar does, I must be onto something, if I'm right. Only, of course, the real verb isn't "know."

[114] Derrida's "logocentric" doesn't seem to be what I'd call logocentric at all: it seems to begin with a transcendental signified, and the Logos as the "image" or "voice" of it. His logocentrism is a hierarchy, the thing I start with and want to turn inside out.

[115] In some ways I regret having raised the word "science" in the AC [7–8]: people think I was starting a critical-establishment move. But I wasn't thinking of academic bureaucrats: I was thinking of confused undergraduates.

[116] In any case my four-stage dialogue seems to be (1) conservative epiphany and radical response (2) both conservative (3) radical epiphany and conservative response (4) both radical. The Spirit deconstructs the Word.

[117] Jacob's ladder is the (O.T.) antitype of the Tower of Babel. Angels descend *and* ascend. In the N.T. the Word descends & the Spirit (presum-

ably) ascends after finishing his job. (The body of Mary has, like Beulah, two gates,[86] the "labyrinthine" ear where the Spirit leaves, and the womb, or virgina, as Joyce would no doubt call it.) That's the Incarnation-Nativity. At the beginning of Acts the Word ascends (antitype of Elijah) and the Spirit descends (final antitype of Babel).[87] So my notion that Jesus is the Word as prophet & the Gospel the communal response of the Spirit seems to be right.

[118] So the apocalypse begins with the release of the Word from incarnation.

[119] If Moses is the symbol of the law, & Solomon the symbol of wisdom, & Elijah the symbol of prophecy, then what corresponds to the wandering in the wilderness, the deluge, the expulsion from Eden is the division of the kingdom that reduced the tribe of Judah to an ark?

[120] There must be a final chapter on what are generally considered post-Frye developments in criticism, related to my conception of a crisis in concern. So far, everything seems to be "logocentric" except what Derrida writes and scratches out again.[88]

[121] My sequence is not "progressive" except to the degree that reading the Bible from beginning to end is a progress. All four stages are with us all the time.

[122] Metaphor eliminates space, or at least, like dream space, we're aware of space but don't know where it is. Myth eliminates time with its counter-historical confrontations. The creation myth, squeezed into a six-day week, shrinks time to a preposterous minimum—all creation myths do. Metaphor arrests space, just as myth arrests time. Here is Joseph; there is the fruitful bough: the "is" is not necessarily a logocentric assertion of identity:[89] it is rather an imperative: space, shut up.

[123] I have three key images for the book: the ladder, with its modulations of tower, mountain, spiral-gyre, and the like: the boat-ark, floating, "drunk" and directionless on the sea or, in a different form, through the wilderness, and the cave or void, the empty space where divine presence is re-established (holy of holies; Jesus' tomb; the place of the oracle). I can see a vague patterning: the ladder is the emblem of the Creation-Exodus

dialectic; the drunken boat of the law-wisdom one, the cave of the prophecy-gospel one. I probably need a fourth, but it better be good.

[124] The fourth, I think, must be the Way (all possible puns included), which is not a here-to-there direction but the reconstructed (or deconstructed, it doesn't matter which) ladder.[90]

[125] The ex-hodos was both a way and a breaking out of the way. Similarly with every prophetic withdrawal into the desert—and, naturally, with Noah. Note the contrast of Abraham & Moses stories: the emphasis is on claustrophobia in Egypt: in Chaldea on guided but free movement.

[126] Joseph (and Daniel, who repeats the Joseph story) polarizes the Jacob-ladder, moves down through a "pit" to Egypt & a prison, his coat of many colors disappearing in that winter-dream world, and organizes time into cycles. Daniel has a lion's den also. This I have, mostly.[91]

[127] If I'm old hat because I'm "logocentric," I want to know why I'm that, and not just be that because I'm ignorant of the possibility of being anything else. The N.T. certainly defines faith in logocentric terms, as a hypostasis [substance] and an elenchos [evidence][92]—the latter, it is true, only in an existential context.

[128] In metaphor, as I said, across [par. 122], we have Joseph "here" and bough "there": by identifying them in an assertion which "everybody" knows is not "real" identity we eliminate space and have only verbal space. Similarly with myth and time. The god, I said, stabilizes the metaphor: all religions lean in a subjective (Dionysian) direction, where you identify with the god through a group, or an objective one where the god remains transcendental and adored.

[129] How can one hit the exact middle where you neither do nor don't identify?

[130] The conception of the word as a servomechanism, a signifier of a signified generating it, is one I have opposed from the beginning. The signifier in turn is contradictory: that's why I find so much in the metaphor, which says it's self-contradictory.[93]

[131] When the signifier becomes a signified, it does so in relation to a reader, who absorbs the signifier function. When I said that the text was the place of the resurrection of the presence I implied, of course, that the presence had already died.[94] Each experience is different, as Paul's was from Peter's: to some it wouldn't happen at all.

[132] The identification of Jesus with the Word is too explicit to dodge, but the connection of my "Spirit" with the Holy Spirit is something I don't want to get embroiled in unless I have to. If there are two truths in Buddhism[95] there can be two in Xy [Christianity]: one denominational (gospel stage) the other a spiritual or everlasting gospel (apocalyptic stage).

[133] But if I keep my Lacan-shaped psychological revolution at the Wisdom stage I can hardly dodge it. The reader, I just said, absorbs the signifier, but not the ego-reader. The ego, born of the stade du miroir and essentially a Narcissus mirror, has to consolidate into the father-mother superego of "lost soul," and Spirit takes over, who can't say "I am a wise and good man" because the "I am" has disappeared.[96]

[134] I've just read Magliola's *Derrida on the Mend*,[97] of which I had great hopes at first, but he's just an uptight mick. At the end there's a casual remark that the scriptures are and always will be logocentric. He doesn't give a damn what happens to the Bible—all he cares about is his magibloodysterium. The old fuddy-duddies at the Council of Trent, passing one reactionary resolution after another in the spirit of the blindest panic, knocked Catholic scholars out of Biblical scholarship completely, and this was reinforced in the 19th c. by (I think) the bloody-minded old bugger Pio Nono.[98] In the 1940s there was an edict that made more sense, but irreparable damage had been done by that time.[99]

[135] Re the fact that art moves away from possession (only paintings can really be owned, & even they gravitate toward museums) and that a possessive attitude to art makes it morally impotent; cf. the speaker of [Robert Browning's] "My Last Duchess," who murders his wife because she smiles at other people but treasures her picture that smiles only at him.[100] Or rather, no living woman can be *completely* possessed, so he gets rid of her.

[136] I've mentioned how in the 19th c. religion gets identified with the find-the-true-church puzzle [par. 43]. Newman is the pattern here. I suppose S.K.'s attack on "Christendom," perhaps even Nietzsche's anti-Xn [anti-Christian] polemics, are a kind of neo-Protestantism.[101]

[137] Certainly the first page of the Bible is as logocentric as one can get. First, the transcendental signified (God, or Being). Second, the created things (beings), which are also signifiers of a second Word of God, part of Derrida's primary ecriture.[102] Third, things as signifieds of the words in the text. Fourth, the words as signifieds of the ultimate signifier, the reader, who gives meaning to the words like Adam naming the animals.

[138] The entire movement of the Bible is a gradual and finally a total reversal of this set-up. With the Incarnation the Word goes the whole way from God to the reader and enters the reader's world. He also defines the Transcendental Being as Father, as the infinite extension of ourselves through time and space. Thereby the Spirit is formed, and finally comes to be a total consciousness capable of the vision of creation.

[139] The two accounts of creation in the Bible provide us with a spectacular creation, featuring dividing and opposition, transcendental in reference, and an immanent one, featuring the permeation of life & moisture into death & dryness.

[140] The (Genesis) 1:1 to 2:3 account is the germ of the logocentric ladder; the 2:4 to 2:25 one the germ of the garden. In the first account the climax of the working word is man (presumably); in the second it's woman. Thus:

First	Second
1. Light (vs. darkness)	"Mist" in drought
2. Firmament (vs. "waters")	Man
3. Vegetation (land & sea)	Garden
4. Sun-moon-stars	River
5. Creatures of Water & Air	All animals but man
6. Land animals including man	Woman
7. Rest (archetype of Sabbath)	Naked Innocence[103]

[141] The story of the Fall is attached to the second, & is precipitated by

woman because "man" redeemed *is* woman. The alternative Fall story, Noah's flood, should really be attached to the first. Note that the fourth act substantializes the first in both accounts. In the second "man" ('dm) is combination of water ("mist," 'd) and blood (dm). He's clearly androgynous, in contrast to the later man born of woman, and probably an Adam Kadmon[104] or *archetypus gigas*.[105]

[142] The two Exodus stories of Abraham & Moses are of course linked by the Akedah [binding of Isaac]-Passover image, but are contrasted in that Abraham's exodus is free & untrammelled, with no resistance from Ur, whereas the Egypt of Israel is a prison to be burst through. Abraham's call follows the second version of creation: note the emphasis on the polarized wives. Paul of course says they're law & gospel, but Hagar is rather a white-goddess mother figure. Leah & Rachel are nearer the law-gospel poles: Sarah & Rachel bear sons at an advanced (or postponed) age.

[143] Law is the substantiating of creation, the fourth act completing the first. Wisdom revolves around not just Solomon but Solomon's bride or mistress or whatever, the playing daughter of God. Gospel of course is the Church-Bride. Blake's reversal of this symbolism needs to be taken with his point that the sexual is *not* the human.[106]

[144] So the ladder of Eros and the Garden of Adonis are clearing up. Adonis is *adonai*, the Lord; he's wounded like Christ, and is nursed by Venus like Christ in the Pieta. Now I have to think about the cave (ark) of Hermes and the whatsit of Prometheus.[107] I thought of "way" for my fourth figure, as an emancipated and apocalyptic ladder, but may have to think about fire, or perhaps even rock.

[145] The apocalyptic finale will have to take in the total-consciousness speculations of Schrodinger [Schrödinger] and (now) David Bohm.[108] I wish I could see something more in Derrida than I do: the écriture business[109] still seems to me to be crap; & the Derrida cult hysteria. But, of course, I must be wrong. I've said that the primacy of the spoken word is a literary, or rather a poetic convention: true, we say that a poet "writes" poetry, not that he speaks it, but still the meaning of the poem is being referred back to a repetition of an oral performance, like the score of music (reading here aural for oral). I must think about Biblical references to writing (e.g. the Book of Life & the names written in it).

[146] Wisdom stresses continuity, and its female connections are reflected in the female pertinacity for continuing a line. Tamar, Ruth, Lot's daughters—Rahab is said by Matthew to be Ruth's mother-in-law [1:5], and Ruth, in modern language, simply climbs into bed with Boaz. Tamar, along with Leah & Rachel, are referred to at the end of Ruth [4:11–12]. The social reversal in the Magnificat [Luke 1:46–55] & Song of Hannah [1 Samuel 2:1–10] carries on the upsurge of the spirit.[110]

[147] Whenever Eros got into the Xn trdn. [Christian tradition] (Inge has it in his book on mysticism)[111] Eros (not Cupid) is certainly a Gentile type of Christ, and Prometheus of the Spirit. Fire seems right; it's what the gyre kindles. Try to think about Abraham's furnace; fire descending to the altar (less Elijah than Chronicles), the three "children" (magi?) in Nebuchadnezzar's furnace [Daniel 3]. Blake certainly thought Los's furnaces had something. Smart on Abraham's.[112] Speaking of magi, they should have been women, as they're antitypes of the Queen of Sheba's visit to Solomon.

[148] The richness & complexity of Biblical imagery in Finnegans Wake is extraordinary. Finnegan is the dreamer; the other characters are shifting identities in the dream (i.e. the sleep of history). Finnegan never wakes, because his zodiac of mourners hold a "wake" to keep him asleep. They tout HCE as his successor (i.e. his Narcissus reflection or chief piece of self-alienated ego in the dream world). For his two sons who become three soldiers in the dream, see the Genesis pattern of two & a shadowy third— the murdered Abel, the cursed Ham, Abraham's three angels who seem to be Jehovah & two angels. Also James & John (sons of thunder) with Peter (?), Moses & Elijah with Christ. The amnesia & twins theme of romance. There's probably a microcosmic dreamer too.[113]

[149] I wish I had an atom or two of evidence for the birth of the Spirit and the consolidating of the ghostly father & mother into the self-alienated ego. Anyway, Hermes the thief, who steals cattle in infancy to make himself an ark, belongs to that section.[114] The only canonical incident of Jesus' boyhood is that he "stole" away from home to be about his "father's" business while his "real" father & mother were looking for him [Luke 2: 43–9].

[150] Tactical question: does the rest of my Washington paper,[115] the

revival of ecstatic metaphor in the sixties, the present crisis in consciousness, the interchange of reality & illusion, and the *verum factum* principle,[116] belong in the introduction? If it does, perhaps the conception of
the Bible as a total reversal of a logocentric creation principle could
follow.

[151] Thus, without losing its specific historical orientation through
Judaism and Christianity, the Bible is an archetypal model of a perennial
philosophy or everlasting gospel. At least, that's what I'd call it if I were
writing a book on religion. We really do move from creation to recreation.

[152] Well, hell, what with all the "babes & sucklings" bit in the gospels
[Matthew 21:16], the colloquy with Nicodemus [John 3], the symbolic
child in the midst of the disciples, and the exhortation to "hate" one's
father & mother [Luke 14:26] (i.e. the ghostly deposit they leave in the
psyche), I don't know how much more evidence I need. It's the poetic
side of it I want, of course: Mallarmé's *Igitur* is not exactly a suckling
babe. Of course again, Mallarmé belongs to the Annunciation stage, & is
one of those 19th c. people fascinated by John the Baptist & Salome.[117]

[153] A N.T. professor once ended a lecture course on the Gospels with:
"something happened; we don't know what." As a ringing affirmation
of faith, his trumpet was giving a somewhat uncertain sound,[118] but it
was a quite honest inference from the pseudo-historical fantasies that
make up so much of Biblical scholarship. The mythical "this happened/
couldn't have happened" presentation is a parable: here's the story;
what do you make of it? You ask, but how much of it is true? The answer
is, all of it and none of it: it's the only story you're going to get: what do
you make of it? *Verum factum.* My question is: what do the poets make of
it?

[154] On the seventh day of creation the creation became objective to
God, which confirms the cloven fiction. The second account of creation,
largely ignored except for the Fall story, shows us a spiritual God giving
life to a *natura naturans.*[119]

[155] Tactic: should *all* the Washington paper,[120] with the two concerns
and mythologies, join the first chapter? And *what* is the first chapter?
Simply an introduction plus overview?

[156] In the second creation man ('dm) follows mist: woman follows river, though I don't know of any verbal connexion. Man in the sense of human being ('dm) is a compound of fertilizing moisture ('d) and blood (dm). *Male* humans (zakar) are born from women.[121]

[157] I'm dimly beginning to see two introductory chapters, one on myth, metaphor, mythology, ideology and concern, and one on the eight phases as four Word-Spirit dialogues. The Four Zoas follow,[122] with two final chapters, one on the birth of the Spirit & the definition of the true Father & Mother, and a final one on the reversal of the logocentric vision.

[158] There are four falls in Genesis: the fall from innocence in Eden, which is explicit in the Jahwist account; the fall from the vision of creation (angel with sword); the fall of civilization (Noah's flood) & the fall of language (Babel).

[159] The four images are based on a middle-earth mythology and are of course projections: the eighth phase puts an end to that. I don't see how I can get out of my mind the notions that (a) Xn [Christian] vision supersedes Jewish law (b) the everlasting gospel of the Spirit supersedes the church. I mean, I believe these things, but beliefs are a hindrance to clear exposition.

[160] The fall of language is reversed by the reversal of the logocentric vision; the fall of civilization by the reversal of the white-goddess cycle into black bride polarity; the fall of innocence by the birth of the Spirit in the soul-body hierarchy; the fall of vision, I suppose, by these three working together.

[161] I've got the two upper-world images, the ladder & the garden, flowing beautifully out of the two accounts of Creation: I wish the two lower-world ones would cooperate better with Exodus imagery. Of course the ark appears instantly; and I shouldn't be so bound by my four images not to see the central importance of a non-human blood sacrifice in the Akedah [binding of Isaac] and the Passover. But "furnace of iron," though there, is a bit peripheral.[123]

[162] "Kairos is best in all things," says Hesiod, meaning, roughly, proportion.[124] Creation is in kairos, the *unit* of time, the timeless instant

presented in our framework. It returns as Eliot's moment neither in nor out of time in Revelation. The Hebrew equivalent is usually 'et, but a very important word to be kept in mind is mo'ed, which can mean appointed time or place, either above (Isa. 14:13) or below (Job 30:23) the earth.

[163] Shelley's cave of Demogorgon or Eternity comes from Boccaccio, whose source is Claudian on Stilicho's consulship.[125] Dylan Thomas' white giant's thigh poem ends with a reference to Fawkes fires [*In the White Giant's Thigh*, l. 160].

[164] Adam is the soul & Eve the body of the garden, so the end of the upward climb is the resurrection of the body. Some climbs are sublimated: Moses' climb up Pisgah didn't unite him with the Promised Land. Cf. my remark that St. George's vision of the distant Jerusalem identified the dragon with the space between him & it. The annihilation of space, and the coming of the interpenetrating vision, is the *klimax* of the ladder.[126]

[165] A lot of creation myths start with someone digging up a speck of earth on his fingernails from the bottom of the sea. Link with the floating-boat & emerging Atlantis imagery.

[166] So far I see only six chapters: introduction, four emblems, conclusion. It may expand. The introduction should take in my whole social-authority thesis, and the first two emblems are reasonably clear. The second half of the book ain't.

[167] I don't know if I have this: Swift's "Celia shits" poem[127] is always taken to be an uncomplicated expression of Swift's "excremental vision."[128] Well, doubtless it is: if you don't have an excremental vision you have no business trying to be a satirist, at any rate not a major one. But it's partly ridicule of the pseudo-idealism of (I think) Strephon, to whom it's never occurred that women have the same physical basis to their lives that men have.[129]

[168] Well, that's an interruption. I think I can produce a rough draft of a book fairly soon—I mean of the first half—I'm not attending. The second half may come clear in pieces, though I don't have many ideas for the conclusion different from the introduction. Total consciousness and the

disappearance of space into interpenetration is about it. What does seem right is that I should get an intelligible draft as soon as possible and then keep it around for a year or two filling in details from reading.[130]

[169] The story of the Flood immediately follows the coming of gods-descended giants. A fifth aspect of the Fall is the loss of gigantic size (and age). That's Prometheus-linked, of course.

[170] The Bible is the most logocentric book in the world, so Derrida is one of my main hurdles. But I don't think the whole answer is in the straight apocalyptic reversal of creation. That would give Derrida a substantiality he doesn't want. The nearest thing to an answer is my part-and-whole oscillation. Christ as a whole of which I am a part remains logocentric. That, probably, includes, or traditionally has included, a leap of faith into objectivity. I as a whole of which Christ is a part am in a defering [deferring]-differing world: a Promethean sense of total consciousness, or leap of faith into subjectivity, being part of that.[131]

[171] The Fall acquired the knowledge of good and evil which is the archetype of all false polarities. That's the starting-point of all hierarchic ideologies, and explains why we interpret the creation as logocentric hierarchy. The male-dominated civilization that followed was a perversion of the fact that man redeemed is woman—also that because man fell as woman, man is to be subordinated to God as woman to man.[132]

[172] The four epiphanies of the word, the (hierarchic) creation, the law, the denouncing prophet and the Judge, are all sick. They're all devils. The four responses of the Spirit, as such, are, if less sick, pretty inadequate. I don't want Israel, nor elitist wisdom, nor the church, nor a harp-playing reward in heaven. The interactions are what's important.

[173] I suppose what Derrida calls erasing the text is what I mean by eating it (Ezekiel 3).[133] Truth is aletheia,[134] the tearing of the veil of forgetfulness: it isn't simple remembrance but recognizing what we didn't know we knew, and we approach it only by circumventing ideology: what I call the pre-revolutionary manoeuver. Not just that Socrates & Jesus are still alive, but that everybody is.

[174] The priority of speech to writing in poetry, I said, is that while we

say that X "writes" poetry, not that he speaks it, the poem is being referred back to a performance. The Bible is hashed up in a way that makes this impossible: translation is only one of many factors here. You can't ask God to repeat: written words can, but "Huh? Wuzzat?" is inappropriate for God.

[175] The Exodus repeats the Deluge: it's the escape of a few (saving remnant) from a falling empire. Secular analogues are the Greece of Aeschylus & the England of Shakespeare, escaping from Persia and Spain respectively, before they too turned into empires. The archetype of the Israel within an empire is Joseph, & later Daniel.

[176] Why do we get the revelation in the Bible bass-ackwards? Because, according to Blake, the "Reactor" has to be "revealed in his system," which of course is ethnocentric.[135]

[177] It's the interaction of Word and Spirit that's important. The epiphany of the Word as Creation forms Israel, and the final cause of Israel is living in the Promised Land, or garden. Well, Moses saw that, but Israel didn't: the first generation died in the wilderness, the second got the bloody butcheries of Canaan and the anarchy of Judges. Note that all eight, so far as I can see, begin in demonic parody.

[178] However, the law, the second epiphany, generates wisdom. Wisdom is more explicitly female, the glory or Schekinah[136] of the Word, and its central symbol is the temple. Thus law and wisdom substantiate or hypostatize Creation & Exodus. And just as ladder (Creation) and garden (*telos* of Exodus) flow out of the two accounts of creation, so, perhaps, they do out of the two versions of law, the ceremonial (female and sacramental analogy) and the moral.

[179] The first two dialogues employ the images of ascent. Prophecy-gospel is based on the descent of the seed, so, although under the sign of Hermes, it includes a lot of Adonis imagery. The seed of the Word-Flesh was buried by the Spirit in the Mother's womb: it remained hidden (symbolized by our eating and drinking it) until it disappeared into a tomb. Threatened birth, of course, with ark and cave (manger). Floating on the sea (Milton's birds of calm image)[137] isn't so explicit, except for the fishing imagery.

[180] We get Lilliputians & Brobdingnagians in the lower world because the former are seed-people: note how in Eliot's WL [*The Waste Land*] we begin with demonic ego-seeds and end with a controlling and very undrunken boat. Mustard-seed in MND [*A Midsummer Night's Dream*], which incidentally becomes a giant in a gospel image.[138]

[181] Anyway, the giant begins demonically, with cannibal images. But he becomes the Albion-Finnegan who wakes up from his dream and abolishes his twin—the dreamed Narcissus ego. (Finnegan is, I think, the macrocosmic dreamer in Joyce, and he never wakes up, never abolishes his dreamed double HCE. The microcosmic dreamer is a tavern-keeper in Chapelizod, and his name may be Porter.)[139]

[182] I'm beginning to wonder about polarities. All false or ethnocentric polarities are founded on [the] good-and-evil one of Genesis, which in turn is founded on shame, or erotic repression. These are also the genuine polarities of primary concern. To move from one to the other is the Biblical quest. I wonder if all aspects of apocalyptic vision have to start by defining their opposite: the demonic (the Nobodaddy god, penal codes, hell, etc.) may be the spur or goad that starts the vision going.

[183] The Egyptian counterpart to the flood story features a drunken goddess, blood and beer.[140] Cf. Noah's wine. This has left traces in the Passover story, with its destroying angel drunk (probably) with the blood of Egyptian children, the type of the winepress-trampler in Isaiah.

[184] The soul-body dialogue in literature is always a put-down of the body (cf. Vaughan's Gethsemane one [*The Evening Watch*]), except for that wonderful poem of Marvell's that comes so close to Hamlet, the consciousness (body) feeling imprisoned *by* itself (soul) [*A Dialogue between the Soul and Body*].[141] Somebody quoted by Huxley, probably William Law, says the real trouble with man is not what he is, but that he is.[142]

[185] Ezra Pound ascribes to Erigena the phrase "omnia sunt lumina." Cf. the "great acorn of light" at the end of the Cantoes.[143]

[186] Hegel's Ph [*Phenomenology of Spirit*] is founded on the type of spiral staircase that can exist only in thought: one that starts at an apex (wrong word, of course) and expands as it goes up. Wonder if I could find this in

Shelley or elsewhere: of course there are descending narrowing movements like those in De Quincey.

[187] Man named Henry Redner in Australia has written a book called In the Beginning Was the Deed,[144] & traces it as central modern ("Faustian") heresy up to (I think) Heidegger.

[188] Man is asleep and fantasizing in the ladder, garden and seed worlds. His central activity there is *quest*, the projection of Word into Deed that enables him to go on sleeping. In the fire world he's compelled to wake up, hence the first thing he does is withdraw the quest. Paradise Regained, Prometheus Unbound, Parsifal, Tolkien, etc.

[189] The ladder world sets up a natura naturata,[145] and this ideal is followed by the law-wisdom dialogue in its progress from contract to Utopia. It's at the prophecy phase where the will takes over from the intellect, and we're pushed into (a) the third or tropological level (b) a conception of natura naturans. This all begins demonically, as usual: Calvin has the divine demonic will, and Kierkegaard sometimes presents God as an ironic trickster. Also the Church freezes up Eros by extending the incest taboo to damn near everything.

[190] Still, what the released flame of Prometheus illuminates is, among other things, the true ladder as the four phases of meaning. The flame, by the way, has to include the occult link between the living fire & the warm-blooded organism I mentioned in GC [161–2].

[191] Well, that's the story: what do you make of it? Life is a slow & laborious process of discovering that reality inheres in what we make and not in what's presented to us. To die is to be faced with the same question again. Worshippers of Satan the accuser put this in the form: well, that's what you did, now take the consequences, which usually means hell, or occasionally a heaven boring enough to be hell. I'd rather have it (because it's what I want it to be that will be decisive) in the form: well, that's it: now what? That is, the equation reality = what I make will become an absolute. If limits do not disappear, they certainly must recede greatly.

[192] I treat my four dialogues as a progressive sequence, but I doubt that that's anything more than rhetorical tactics. I don't think it's really a

hierarchical ladder: I think each stage contains all four; they're aspects of one thing.

[193] Eckhardt [Eckhart] speaks of a *Gottheit* who is nothing because he's transferred everything to God.[146] Sounds like what the God-is-dead people say about kenosis. It's the void that's the antitype of "vanity" (apocalyptic fullness, rather), the absolute spirit that's the apocalyptic contrast to hebel or mere breath. It's the silence that's the echo of speech: Eckhardt [Eckhart] associates *Gottheit* with the *resting* God of the seventh day.[147] And, of course, it's the clear light that's the apocalyptic opposite of the hell-fire that burns the fennel-stalk of the self.

[194] Perhaps the Conclusion should be, or include, a primer on how to read: i.e., reading as a technique of Jnana yoga.[148]

[195] I've got apocalyptic & demonic fire & water in GC [145–6, 161–2], but not air—I've got the spirit-hebel contrast on p. 52 [par. 193].[149] Also there's seed, the seat of new birth or of the parable of the sower vs. the "impure" seed of the first birth & the spilled seed of Onan [Genesis 38:9]. The Hymn of the Soul in the Acts of (I think) Thomas links this with a pearl at the bottom of the sea,[150] & *that* links with code messages in *Endymion* & elsewhere.

[196] I don't much like the way I seem to be following the four-element symbolism of the Eliot Quartets, although East Coker isn't about the *locus amoenus* exactly. Note that the "logocentric" ladder world is a differential one, although the significant differences are all perceived as differences of *degree*, in Ulysses' sense.[151]

[197] I have very few religious books, & those I have stress the mystics. I have great difficulty, nonetheless, in reading, say, Boehme, because mystics (less true of Boehme than of others) seem so masochistic: isn't this stuff just wonderful that we have to say we believe anyway? But now Boehme is making more sense as I move closer to light and signature symbolism. Once more, it's not that I "believe" him but that this is the kind of link between the Bible and the creative imagination that I'm looking for.

[198] The deliberate absurdity of the mental processes ascribed to God at the time of the Deluge indicates the mythical meaning: wrath is (as

I've said so often) the opposite of anger or irritation. The flood is an image of the disastrous chaos that man prefers: there won't be another God-inspired flood because God is not an avenger. Calvin was a deluge-theologian: the immense gap between a theological lawyer with his case & the powerful creative energy of Genesis, not afraid to make God look a fool—well.

[199] The knowledge of good and evil projects the struggle of brothers and its conceptions of antithesis and polarity. God appears in time (= the dream of history) in this form. Waking from time reabsorbs one's shadow-twin into oneself. Jung says it also reveals the genuine female (anima) within.[152]

[200] One centrally important feature of the Eliot Quartets is that the world of the buried spirit is *below* hell. The subway passage in *Burnt Norton* [sec. 3b] is the hell-world of *The Waste Land* and *The Hollow Men*, and we have to go deeper. That's the link between Eliot and the Romantic construct.

[201] To descend is to pass through the chattering, yelling, gibbering world of the demons of repression to the quiet Spirit below. As Eliot says, contradicting the Sibyl, it's not easy to go *all* the way down.[153] To reascend is to bind the squalling demons into a unified creative power.

[202] That's the individual or voluntary descent, which may well be an impossibility. The descent of grace, or the Holy Spirit, has to pass through the gibbering Tower of Babel and destroy it, as with that Tarot card. He comes with the opposite of Babel, the gift of tongues that only the Spirit in the depths—himself—can recognize. Abyssus abyssum invocat.[154]

[203] The whole "Nobodaddy" aspect of God, the corpse-eating ghoul in the sky worshipped by the Aztecs, the fool-God of the flood (across [par. 198]), is put there to make the wrong kind of "literal" reading impossible.[155]

[204] This conception of creative descent *through* hell and reascent through creativity is of course in Dante, and I think underlies the Comus-Tempest schematism. Also the apocalyptic-demonic polarity has to be applied to everything. I got fire & water into GC,[156] but the air of

"inspiration" vs. the hebel-breath of illusion needs more emphasis, and so no doubt does the good earth of Eden & the cursed desert of the dry places. Freedom also has a polarity: as Boehme said, there's a freedom of chaos as well as of creation.[157]

[205] I question whether it is possible to write diachronic history—that is, apart from things like Pepys' Diary. To write about history you must stand outside it, in a synchronic ambience. That means that all history has to have some mythical underpropping, "decline and fall" or whatever.

[206] I need more on primary & secondary concern. I want the Innis stuff about Reformers & Marxists settling into an adversary situation.[158] Marxism in theory transcends ideology, & some bourgeois masochists (Barthes) go along with this. But when we look at what Lenin says about religion it's clear that a counter-ideology is being set up: there's no transcendence of ideology. So my faith-ideology-secondary concern and charity-transcendence-primary concern still stands.

[207] Anyway, the religious-secular dichotomy doesn't work, except as an illusion of ideological adversaries. A "pro-religious" attitude merely keeps an "anti-religious" one in business, and vice versa. That's the real implication of my aligning revolutionary psychologies in Biblical religions and Marxism, not some bromide like "Marxism is really a religion after all" (though I've said it is in interviews).[159] Everybody knows that all religious social phenomena are inextricably bound up with "secular" elements in politics and economics. So in reverse.

[208] To call religion an illusion or communal neurosis, as Freud does,[160] says nothing either: we create all our reality out of what begins as illusion, and living under social discipline is itself a neurosis. What Freud said of religion was, in effect, precisely what Karl Krauss [Kraus] said of Freudian therapy; that it is the disease of which it professes to be the cure.[161]

[209] This dissolving of the religious/secular dichotomy would take me quite a long way. What does have to be abandoned in religion are the things that violate primary concern, like human sacrifice or persecution of "heretics." But such things are, again, inseparable from "secular"

forms of tyranny, cruelty or exploitation. A superstition is something we do without knowing why we do it; if we are faced with the question of why we do it, we must rush in to plaster it over with rationalizations.

[210] "Wait without hope or desire."[162] That's silly: nobody can do that. What's meant is: work without *projecting* hope or desire.

[211] The memory selects, rejects, rearranges, condenses and displaces. In short, it *mythicizes* our history.

[212] What there is left of the data-world is the sense that there is infinitely more to be known. I am uttering the profound truth that we do not know what we do not know.

[213] The up ladder finds heaven to be a mechanism, therefore inferior to an organism. Next it discovers that the design & function in an organism is produced by, or at least through, that organism. That makes the whole "deist" notion superfluous. Note how the devaluing of mechanism goes along with the *growth* of technology: the innocent tinkling music box cosmos of the Middle Ages is pre-technological.

[214] In King Lear, the world pointed to by the word "nothing" is below the order of nature, but not as low as the demonic world of Goneril, Regan, Cornwall, & most of Edmund.[163] Similarly, in Milton, chaos is above hell. Where does the shift come that reverses the two? Because even Eliot, in Burnt Norton, puts the way of "vacancy" lower than the subway, which is the nearest he gets to hell [ll. 93–129]. Wherever & whenever it comes, it brings a positive, non-demonic descent into literature.

[215] The old sinister descent to the world of a foreordained future, with hell below that, is all Virgil gives. The Biblical archetype is the Witch of Endor seeing "gods" ascending from below the earth.[164]

[216] Re the first entry in this notebook: perhaps creative power comes, not from simple frustration, but from the frustration of sin: from the Father who refuses to die, the Mother who renews her virginity and gets away. The tyrant or Nobodaddy Father and the white goddess hag are the ghosts of guilt feelings.

[217] This reflection was suggested by Rimbaud's *Memoire*.[165] I suppose the point of the [Rimbaud's] *Saison en enfer* is that the fall of man doesn't go deep enough; one has to plunge into, and absorb, the preceding fall of the angels (i.e. of human *spirits*, not soul-bodies).

[218] The traditional hell is the one where we're in the company of fallen angels but keep projecting as other powers, hence as torturers and executioners. Once you identify with them, and have pushed self-imprisonment to its limit, you discover that the Spirit must have the Word (alchimie du verbe).[166]

[219] Nietzsche is unintelligible except in a spiritual dimension that sees Christianity as confined to the human and projecting planes. Rimbaud's criminal > exile > seer sequence is linked to my "pre-revolutionary" point: Marxism has turned into a perverted humanism, crushing the spiritual wherever it can.

[220] Vaughan's Regeneration contrasts stones in a well "nailed to the centre" and others, evidently alive, dancing through the flood.[167] The Bateau I use begins with "haleurs" nailed to stakes by Indians and setting the boat free to "dance" (it's drunk) on its own.[168]

[221] Poe's Eureka ends with a vision of an oscillating rhythm of concentration and diffusion:[169] this recurs in Baudelaire's Spleen et Ideal[170] and elsewhere. Concentration & diffusion is central to this part.

[222] Rimbaud again: "Venus Anadyomene" is a deliberately "shocking" poem, but not obscene: no hatred is expressed for the poor creature. "Mes Petites Amoureuses" I thought obscene at first, because of the hatred ("Que je vous haïs!") and sadistic wishes to break their hips. Yet the real context of this poem is the Lettre du Voyant, in which it is included, and the letter prophesies a new age of poetry where women will have a leading part. The "amoureuses" are not girls but false Muses. He says the poem isn't part of the argument, but (a) it is (b) one can take that remark both ways.[171]

[223] The Lettre du Voyant is a manifesto of shamanism. Tom o'Bedlam is a degenerate shaman, with his horse of air; Edgar's assuming the role ("raisonné dérèglement")[172] is a link with Rimbaud. I'm sure that Rimbaud

will lead me to the link between the garden of wisdom and the drunken boat (ark) of prophecy.

[224] I am not assuming anything about Rimbaud's (religious) attitudes, merely that anyone brought up as he was could not have avoided contact with Biblical imagery in his most impressionable period, namely his childhood. There's some Shakespeare too: I think some MND [*A Midsummer Night's Dream*] allusions apart from "Bottom," and in the usual order we begin with a world cleaned off by the deluge, as in the Tempest masque. Actually his phrase is "l'idée du Déluge,"[173] which is very exact.

[225] Garden is female; wind in garden male: city is female; temple male: Except the Lord g. [god] & Crashaw's "Love's architecture is its own" [*In the Holy Nativity*, l. 47]. The temple is the body of the *way* up, the head of the phallus.

[226] De Quincey: (I don't know how much of this I have) interests me because he moves from a world of consciousness to dream, in the opposite direction from displacement. He resembles Coleridge in planning huge projects & being too dependent on subjective insights for sequence to get them off the ground.

[227] He starts with a labyrinthine consciousness, a maddeningly diffuse & digressive beginning, like a detective scanning the ground for clues. Certain labyrinth symbols loom up: the pursuit of the lost girl (Ann in COE [*Confessions of an English Opium-Eater*]); death of girl-child (Lake Poets [*Society of the Lakes*]); network of communication (Mail Coach ["The English Mail-Coach"]), or simply "non est inventas" (Murder essay ["Murder Considered as One of the Fine Arts"]).[174] Sudden focus of incident (Mail Coach & Murder) establishes a funnel through which the diffused labyrinth imagery pours. Below (Atlantis submarine imagery) is the world of dream where one identifies the source of original sin (one's Narcissistic self) and repeats the fall of man.[175] Maybe that's the detective story archetype: clue in the labyrinth leading to identity of who done it. The clue is the looming urgent symbol of dreamland, and the sudden act of violence gives trivia portentous importance. The police are a miniature Last Judgment.

[228] Just to keep the *size* of the job in mind:

The creation is the "universe" (anthropocentric view of the natural environment).

Law is social, cultural, historical conditioning.

Prophecy is creation (art and science).

Apocalypse is the final polarization of reality (new "creation").

History is the (literal) Exodus response.

Philosophy is (allegorical) Wisdom response.

The total body of imagination (Blake's Golgonooza) is the (everlasting) Gospel or tropological response.

The response to Apocalypse is the interpenetrating vision.

[229] After the Fall (i.e. the turning away from creation) the Father is lost & becomes otherness. At the Gospel stage the Otherness is recognized as Father. This stage goes along with the escape from the prison of Narcissus, the self-alienated *moi*, the Hamlet of the soliloquies. The double action culminates in the romance *cognitio*: waking from the amnesia dream and reabsorbing the projected twin. The awakened self takes over from the mechanically conditioned puppet who has been imitating him.

[230] Spiral descent: whirlpool & maelstrom: Troy dance[176] & Aeneid VI, Mallarmé's Igitur & St. John of the Cross: descent to the eternal Demogorgon (who rises in the car of the hour): Mallarmé's & Yeats's midnight: descent to Mothers in Faust: Chapel Perilous, present in *The Waste Land*.[177] But *is* this in the Bible, apart from Paul's remark that the Spirit searches the deep things of God?[178]

[231] It looks as though I should read (sometime) Abrams' NS book,[179] and investigate a story of Kafka's about a character named Gracchus.[180] Of course I'm a fool not to make more use of Kafka.

[232] But it's Mallarmé who will take me through the third great crisis of the birth of the spirit out of the depth of fallen spirits. (Victor Hugo of course saw the primary importance of the theme, but was too much in love with his own rhetoric to do more than talk about it.)

[233] Just as the ladder of Jacob has its parody in the Tower of Babel, so the garden of the Song of Songs has its parody, although I don't know that the Bible provides it. The Tower, in the first place, goes through various modulations, some pleasant (Milton's penseroso Platonist brood-

ing over what's left to him of the chain of being: elemental spirits and other spirits neither devils nor angels) and some sinister. The latter usually feature an *imprisoned* female (Rapunzel). The Hérodiade sequence begins with the Nurse's prologue, and one of Mallarmé's favorite words, *abolie*.[181]

[234] What Mallarmé was after was his own version of a Nativity Ode (note the word "n'abolira pas"[182] in the *Coup* de Dés). That's the Igitur-Coup de Dés sequence. The opposite to the Nativity at the winter solstice is the St. John summer solstice, where the woman of death with the prophet's severed head (the antitype of Judith, not impossibly of Esther with the crucified Haman) stand opposite to the infant at the Virgin's breast. A lot of 19th c. poets of course got hung up on Salome, but Mallarmé's Cantique gets it.[183]

[235] Well: Igitur's name is one thread of continuity in the descent to nothingness. Throwing dice doesn't abolish chance, but chance can be manifested by the dice throw & then kept at bay.[184] Anyway, the whole programme carries out my shift of "literal" from things to words. The descent to nothingness reduces reality ("verité") to "rien," and one is left with the creation of a fiction that is real because it is a fiction. It's Vico's *verum factum*[185] in a world without God—other than creative man, that is.

[236] This for Mallarmé is the birth of the Spirit, and is described in Resurrection terminology—and he would know that resurrection is not rebirth.

[237] The imprisoned princess in the tower and the severed head come from Poe—that Psyche Zenobia's story with all the tee-hees.[186] I looked up Yeats' King of the Great Clock Tower, but there seemed to be nothing there.[187] Even the scythe ("faux") of the Cantique is in Poe.[188] Long way from the Bible; but it's the ass end of the garden and tower cluster. I suppose females in elegant surroundings like the one in the -yx sonnet[189] also belong to the *aboli*-world—*luxe*, as he calls it: cf. the neurotic dame in *The Waste Land*.[190]

[238] Well, the next thing we know tower & garden have disappeared into the "tarn" or whatever & we're in a world of shipwrecked fragments & drunken boats. One small glimmer: the Antigone sense of the need for

burial makes the floating fragment a planted or buried seed: the garden of Adonis cunt-symbol takes root for a new life. Rimbaud's drunken boat flowers out of a seed in his childhood memory—he, Mallarmé, Shelley, were all brooders on water, repeating the Spirit birth again. Look again at Rimbaud's Beth-Saida piece [*Beth-Saïda, la piscine*].

[239] The mirror & window imagery, with or without lace curtains, is probably in Richard's book:[191] it looks damn complicated, but Mallarmé must have thought about Paul's "riddle in a mirror" a good deal. The dentelle that s'abolit is contrasted with the mandolin with its (eventually) fertile "ventre" or womb developing out of a belly of emptiness. The swan stuck in the ice turns on the word *glace* that connects ice & mirrors. In that sequence, the "luxe" world of the first recalls the Egyptian burying of everything precious in a king's tomb.[192]

[240] There really is some kind of resurrection by faith in myth in Mallarmé. One English counterpart would be Dylan Thomas' Winter's Tale. Cohn's book on Rimbaud (1973) has a footnote (p. 158) on the *noyé pensif* theme: Ferdinand's drowned father, Glaucon in *Endymion* (he says he's the "spectral father" of the poet), the *veillard* [*vieillard*] in the *Coup de Dés* who carries the *ombre juvénile* in him, and several other things.[193]

[241] The *bateau ivre* tosses as lightly as a cork: cf. the MS in a bottle of Poe (it must have been corked), de Vigny's Bouteille scyla mer, Rabelais' baqbuq, the flask in *Igitur*.[194] The message floating on the sea links with the riddle or cipher under it (*Endymion* & the inscriptions in Poe's Pym). Then to the floating ark with the baby-hero in it (especially if you add the talismans of recognition), the "shield son of Sheaf" that turns up in *Beowulf*, etc. ad-lib. The black bird in *Igitur* comes from Poe's raven, but, what with the ancestors' ashes, is a phoenix parody too. Note that Prospero wants to "drown" his book [*The Tempest*, 5.1.57].

[242] I think I can begin a fresh section with the theme of the creative descent, emphasizing de Nerval, Baudelaire, Rimbaud and Mallarmé. The non-Christian writings are especially valuable because their rejection of "belief" structures forces them to concentrate more directly on the metaphorical ones.

[243] The tradition for the creative descent, apart from Aeneid VI, is the

romance-satire one. Gerard de Nerval, who is pretty astute in such matters, mentions Apuleius along with the Vita Nuova at the beginning of *Aurélia*, & "Peregrinus" (Lucian) elsewhere.[195]

[244] The oracular dream is often associated with the vision of prophecy (subordinated as a rule) in the O.T. But no dreaming seems to occur in the N.T. except in Matthew, & there, apart from Pilate's wife's dream in 27 [vs. 19], it's confined to the first two chapters.[196] The dream of wisdom is led to the epiphany of prophecy.

[245] The word ma'lah, which means ascent or steps going up, also, in Ezra 7:9, means return from Babylon to Jerusalem.

[246] GC stopped with the decentered Bible, where every sentence, in theory, is a microcosm of the whole structure. Now if we go back to unity, we find a lot of gaps: that's where people like Frazer & Hook & Gaster jump in with their analogues. I suppose my ideas have always revolved around what I used to call the Druid analogy, i.e., the shadow-Bible constructed out of what the Bible does *not* say, a Derridean *supplement*,[197] perhaps, *my* (not Blake's) Bible of hell. The "secular scripture" was a bone thrown to this voracious mutt.

[247] The N.T. antitype of Jacob's ladder is John 1:51.

[248] The ladder-cosmos, though it had four levels of time, is essentially a spatializing metaphor: it, so to speak, annihilates space by filling it up. It is a cosmos of plenitude, with no nothingness in it. Its nature is *naturata*, with the *naturans* focus in the garden-body-cunt.

[249] According to Milton, Eden was washed away in the flood to abolish the notion of sacred space [*Paradise Lost*, bk. 11, ll. 829 ff.], transforming the place-*there* into the state-*here*. The emancipation makes the ark a *bateau ivre*, even though at that stage Noah could, as Antonio says, scape being drunk for want of wine.[198]

[250] The fire-chapter should include, first of all, Little Gidding and the two Byzantium poems. SB [*Sailing to Byzantium*] is a panoramic apocalypse: every state of the chain of being appears on fire as nature is

destroyed & the artifice of eternity replaces it. Byzantium burns from the inside. Note how intensely Heraclitean both Eliot & Yeats get when they enter the fire.[199]

[251] My ladder chapter assumes that the Renaissance continued the microcosmic thinking of the Middles Ages. I don't understand the view that it introduced an antithesis between man and cosmos.

[252] The root meaning of the Greek word *parabole* is juxtaposition. A is juxtaposed to B. If B is a different entity we have signifying or centrifugal meaning; if the same, metaphor; if A is a particular of a universal B, the first two are united.

[253] I still can't grasp Derrida's *écriture* concept.[200] One does not understand the logos by hearing it, only by speaking it and listening to what one says. Writing, to me, is essentially this action of speaking and self-listening. Reading writing leads to saying "I see what you mean."

[254] I should think about whether my four categories have both a positive analogy and a demonic parody. There must be several types of parody. Oedipus is a parody of the virgin-born, bride-rescuing, father-reconciling Messiah. Narcissus imprisoned in the mirror-world is a parody too, the Polyphemus cannibal-giant figure a Leviathan parody of the *archetypus gigas*.[201] In the third phase the empty space or Holy of Holies, the void that is the context of everything, is parodied by the nothing world of Igitur.

[255] Toute pensée émet un coup de dés, says Mallarmé.[202] Cf. Heraclitus' axiom about the child moving pieces in a board game.[203] Wyatt's sonnet, "My galley, chargèd with forgetfulness"[204] is based on the same analogical metaphor, a shipwreck enclosed by the dialectic of will and chance.

[256] It's becoming clearer that the last two stages are dominated by the alternating rhythms of contraction and expansion. That's what *Eureka* ends with. The things possibly connected with it include:
   a) the little & big people in the underworld.
   b) logocentric & differential in Derrida.
   c) choice & chance in Yeats & Mallarmé.[205] Double helix.

    d) interchange of whole & part in Paul's Christology.
    e) exchange of fire and all things in Heraclitus.[206]
    f) yang (concentrating) and yin (diffusing) rhythms.

[257] Myth contracts time: metaphor contracts space. They lead "upward" in a narrowing spiral. The masque, from Jonson to Milton, represents upward as inward.[207]

[258] g) the particular and the universal
    h) condensation and displacement in Freud.
    i) metaphor & metonomy in Jacobsen [Jakobson][208] (Lacan has h and i)
    j) systole-diastole; integral & differential (calculus or whatever)

[259] I suppose Derrida really oscillates between the logocentric and the logocircumferential. Anyway, what's the Biblical setup? I think it's polarized between the first coming of Christ in water and his second coming in fire.

[260] A book called The Looking-Glass God, by Nahum Stiskin, identifies yang with concentration & yin with diffusion.[209] (Otherwise a rather hazy book). A woman poet (Emily Dickinson) might naturally say "my business is circumference,"[210] if yin is female.

[261] In GC I talked about the shrinking of sacred space to the Holy of Holies.[211] The disappearance of that with the Antiochus-Caligula statue meant that sacred space disappeared and turned into a state of mind.[212] (Milton's destruction of Eden, which goes along with the ark.) After that we pass through a vortex that starts diffusing again.

[262] Universals are real in Thomas [Aquinas]; individuals in Duns [Scotus]. The former leads to the circumferential Christ of the apocalypse; the latter to the central hidden Christ of the Incarnation. Actually the Kingdom of Heaven is the Biblical essence of the third archetype.

[263] To go from the ladder-garden world to the ark-flame one, think of going from Ash-Wednesday to the Quartets, from The Tower to A Vision (if only Yeats had got the vision!). Note that I was first attracted to archetypal criticism by Colin Still's book on The Tempest,[213] with its central conception of the ladder of elements, a conception going back to

the pre-Socratics. Heraclitus says there's an exchange of "fire" and of "all things," as there is of "gold" for "wares."[214] That's something to chew on.

[264] Paine, *Rights of Man*: "He {Burke} is not affected by the reality of distress touching his heart, but by the showy resemblance of it striking his imagination . . . he degenerates into a composition of art, and the genuine soul of nature forsakes him." (P. 24 of the Everyman ed.).[215]

[265] For all their tedious cuteness, Lewis Carroll's Sylvie and Bruno are closer to being actual children than Alice is. Alice is a *preternatural* child, and an astonishing achievement: I know of nothing in all literature remotely like her. But she belongs to another world than the world of our seven-year-olds, though she is utterly real in her own terms.

[266] Natural-theologians used to say that evolution must be divinely guided, as it is impossible for its complicated directiveness to arise out of blind chance. The usual answer is that there is no question of "blind" chance, but of chance operating within a framework of natural law. But natural law, unlike human law, is neither an imposed commandment nor a response to one. It is simply a series of statements about how nature has been observed to behave. So the "chance within law" answer is a tautology: things happened the way they did because they happened the way they did.

[267] If natural law is anything more than that, the origin of such law is a far deeper mystery than the origin of life.

[268] Kandinsky says in his *Reminiscences* (1912) that this is the third age of the Spirit prophesied by Joachim of Floris.[216] Of course he was a theosophist. I'm interested in statements like that, of course, but one can't restrict such things to historical periods: at most they're new emphases only on something already there.

[269] Curious how *Axel's Castle* is invariably listed as a most standard text on symbolism.[217] Wilson was, at least then, a vulgar Marxist who devoted a chapter to Axel as a clay pigeon. Wilson wouldn't have known a symbol if it had bitten him in the ass.

[270] Xy [Christianity] has always stressed that man can never be more

than a creature, never can become God. That's because the formula "I could become God" is a purely linguistic one: we think of an ultimate, give a name to it, and immediately arrive there in thought (if it is thought). To renounce this is to lift the veils of the last claustrophobia. That's what Blake meant when he said that man can have no idea of anything more than man (except by a Hegelian antithesis which, this time, he can't digest).[218]

[271] Yeats may have known more Axel than I had thought: a privately printed translation of it appeared in 1925.[219] It has Yeats' soul-self dialectic, though less clear-cut: Axel shuts himself in a high lonely tower to study the Rosicrucians: the Eros-Thanatos Tristan denouement is a little like the Shadowy Waters.

[272] Axel is a grotesque & À Rebours in some respects a funny manifestation of *symbolisme*. In the latter the famous trip to England is quite intentionally funny: Das Esseintes[220] gets to the railway station & comes home. Why should he take his impulse to visit England "literally"? He doesn't have to get sick on the Channel crossing; doesn't have to choke in London fogs, doesn't have to go on eating English food. But Axel merely kills himself because he's afraid the rest of his life will be an anticlimax.

[273] In Xn [Christian] symbolism the black bride, the Virgin Mary, combines the three phases of the white-goddess cycle: she's obviously virgin & mother, & that colossal Byzantine fresco in Torcello[221] makes her a million years old, though untouched by any aging process. To contrast her with a fetish like the Venus of Willensdorf [Willendorf][222] is to realize that there are men and women in the Resurrection, though no males or females.

[274] I've read a lot of crappy books on the Grail, yet there remains a fascination with it. Christ breaks bread, says "this is my body," & the bread disappears into the disciples' guts, including Judas' (John 13). Then he takes the cup, but after the wine is drunk the cup *must* be left behind, like the mantle of Elijah. So it's a central symbol for what persists in this world as a communion with Christ.

[275] It's always been a mystery to me how the Idumean Herod[223] managed to build a temple acceptable to the Jews. In the N.T. Jesus seems to accept this temple, yet only as a type of his (risen) body.

[276] I know that when I suggested the possibility of a human primary concern that overrides all conceivable ideologies I'm flying in the face of Roland Barthes and the rest of the Holy Family. It's high time that sacred cow was turned out to pasture. By the sacred cow I mean the omnipresence of ideology, & the impossibility of ever getting past it.

[277] Someone confronted me the other day with the old chestnut about whether there was a contradiction between Paul's emphasis on faith and James' on works. Here is a question where, for once, historical scholarship is relevant. If James is what it so obviously is, a second-century sermon by a preacher who was afraid that Paul's doctrine was being simplistically misinterpreted, there's no contradiction. But if it is actually an epistle by James the brother of Jesus, it is difficult to avoid the conclusion that Christianity was a schizophrenic religion to begin with, a reform of historical Judaism kidnapped by Paul's Christ-myth.

[278] I've said elsewhere in this notebook that I'm not interested in the cliché "Marxism is really a religion after all" [par. 207], but in the fact that the religious-secular, theist-atheist antithesis doesn't make sense anymore. It restates the old business about the resemblance between Biblical & Classical myths. The paranoids said the heathen fables were all devil's parodies; the reasonable people said they were the natural man's counterpoint to revealed truth. Today there are thoughtful people in Latin America and elsewhere who realize that Christianity and Marxism sooner or later have to kiss & make up: there are paranoids in Marxism yelping about "ideological contamination" and now I see the Vatican bureaucracy has come out with a no-you-mustn't admonition to politically radical priests.[224]

[279] (The advantage of not being a Catholic is that when a coven of cardinals comes out with an asinine pronouncement I not only know they're wrong {so do many Catholics} and can say so openly {so will radical Catholics of courage and conviction} but can say so privately and to myself {very difficult for the most committed radical Catholics}).

[280] I still can't make any sense out of Derrida's assertion that metaphysics excludes writing. But of course his *écriture* includes everything that's visualizable. I have studied the metaphorical diagrams underlying some metaphysical systems, and however shallow such study may be, it's convinced me that *that* is the écriture basis of conceptual thought. In

GC I showed that the same visualizable structure, more obviously metaphorical and imagistic, informs the Bible. Hence the crucial importance
of its apocalyptic conclusion, the epopteia or vision of the Word illuminated by the Spirit "when every eye shall see him" [Revelation 1:7].

[281] That's clearing a little: the Creation is, as I've said, a mass of
écriture, but the Fall ensured that we'd interpret that only in logocentric
ways, & by a metaphysic of speaking presence. The real apocryphon in
the Bible is the table of metaphors I uncovered, & that becomes visible in
the Apocalypse, which is the renewed vision of creation.[225]

[282] Television brings a theatricalizing of the social contract. Reagan
may be a cipher as President, but as an actor acting the role of a decisive
President in a Grade B movie he's I suppose acceptable to people who
think life is a Grade B movie. The Pope, whose background is also partly
theatrical, is on a higher level but the general principle still holds. It goes
with reaction, identifying the reality with the facade. Wouldn't it be
wonderful if, just for once, it could be true that Father knows best?
Emotional debauch of father-figuring.

[283] Two things that may be connected. One is the Lamarck-Darwin
business I've mentioned before.[226] I haven't read Lamarck, but I have
read Samuel Butler. I don't think, as I say, that the transmission of
acquired characteristics is the real point at issue, even if Lamarck thought
it was. I think the point is the mechanism of mutation. With everything
so fully provided for in a genetic code, the notion of a *random* mutation
simply doesn't make sense.

[284] The other thing is the mechanism of dream imagery and hallucination. That's bound up in the Renaissance with the doctrine of elemental
spirits: I'm sure that there's a coherent & consistent theory of all this
behind MND [*A Midsummer Night's Dream*], Mercutio's Mab speech
[*Romeo and Juliet*, 1.4.53–95], *Comus*, the magic & oracular dreams in the
romances, etc. Magic is a deliberate summoning up of an object-centered
ecstatic metaphor. (Poetry starts with the subject and renounces magic.)

[285] So what do we have? First, a chapter on metaphor, myth, symbol,
primary & secondary mythology & concern, ending with the modes of
interpretation: demonic parody, Gentile analogy, Jewish type, Christian

antitype, analogies in nature and metaphysics. Second, perhaps, a summary of the Word-Spirit dialogue in the Bible. Note that (so far) I have no evidence whatever that anyone saw the Bible in this shape: it's a pure construct of my own.

[286] Third, the ladder world (which *cannot* be distinguished from the spiral world except that the spiral emphasizes temporal as well as spatial movement). Thus:

Demonic parody: Tower of Babel, ziggurats in Mesopotamia and Mexico.

Gentile analogy: the ladder of Eros in Plato

Jewish type: Jacob's ladder. (It's been suggested that the original dreamer {Israel} was an Albion-type giant: I think Blake suggests this in the Job engravings) and his stone a megalith.

Christian antitype: Acts 1 & 2 (ascent of Word & descent of Spirit). (Reverse of Incarnation: Ascent {no doubt} of Spirit after he fixes up Mary; Descent of Word).

Other analogies: the chain of being; the Ptolemaic universe; the alchemical great work; descent through angels & emanations to elemental spirits.

[287] The two stages: hearing in time, then seeing in conceptual space. Somebody telling a joke may, regrettably, begin by saying "Stop me if you've heard this one," but if you "see" the joke it's *been* told & you're confronted with the "point."[227]

[288] Similarly in the Mass the monstrance display follows the reading of the creed: in most rituals the reading of a sacred myth leads up to the ritual as the *epiphany* or showing forth of the myth, the distinctive social function of the myth gives it an existential or confronting point absent from the folktale: it starts with "this happened a long time ago" and ends with "why am I telling you this story now?" Myth moves from the past to the present. That's one reason why the profoundest treatments of myth are the latest ones.

[289] There isn't any consistent difference between the demonic parody & the Gentile analogy, I think: the demonic is whatever is believed or worshipped. Difficulties here too, of course.

[290] Frances Yates is wonderful: the combination of sober documenta-

tion and the wildest guesswork is very exhilarating. Her book on Elizabethan occultism[228] gives me another step: the descent to a world *below*
hell, from which the creative ascent comes, is linked to the theme of
creative melancholy, Durer's Saturn,[229]—melancholy link—not so much
the planetary as the mythological Saturn, thrown down to "hell" (Sandys'
rendering of Ovid's *Met.* 1.)[230] at the end of the Golden Age. Lead,
Saturn's metal, then rises to gold. Chapman's *Hymnus in Nocturn,*[231]
Burton's & Milton's pensive or creative melancholy, go on to Keats'
melancholy Hyperion themes & the *poète maudit* theme in France.[232]

[291] I'm getting slightly closer to the "logocentric" progress of the
Biblical narrative. Panoramic revelation takes the seals off the world-
book apocryphon, but is really the "logocentric" climax, revelation from
a speaking presence outside. The participating apocalypse is the thing
that reverses it by putting the logos into the reader.

[292] Also there are three phases of metaphor. Phase one, the "lunatic"
phase, is that of the Bacchantes, the shaman's journeys to upper & lower
worlds, the totemic identity with the totem, the identification stages of
mysteries and initiations. Phase two, the "lover" phase, is the ideal of
one soul created out of two bodies in the sex act. Phase three is the "poet"
phase, where metaphor passes out of the "ecstatic" stage. The progress
to a fourth phase is a recapturing of the ecstatic. In Elizabethan poetry it
was assumed that the poet started as the lover of a disdainful mistress &
was driven to poetry by frustration.

[293] Everyone who suffers for his beliefs belongs to the noble army of
martyrs. Whether the beliefs are true, false, profound or absurd is of no
importance. All martyrdom manifests the brutal & stupid human psychosis, and all martyrs are equally in the service of God. The remarks in
Religio Medici about mistaken martyrs who pass from one fire to another
make me puke.[233] As Paulina should have said in WT [*The Winter's Tale*],
it is *always* the heretic who lights the fire [2.3.115].

[294] In other words, ideology is original sin, and is not got rid of by any
dunk or sprinkle. What is not ideology is manifested by the constancy of
the martyr in the disguise of a counter-ideology. That's why his beliefs
are not important. (Would I maintain this for IRA terrorists?).

[295] I stumbled over something after all in that damn myth paper:[234] when Gilgamesh rebuffs Ishtar he ascribes qualities to her that are distinguished centuries later in the *Odyssey* as Calypso & Circe. The latter sinister magician is still going strong in Diana of the Actaeon story—in fact the whole *Metamorphoses* bit seems to be tied up with the White Goddess.

[296] Returning to p. 72 [par. 266]: there's evidently still room for argument about the possibility of life arising by chance. I know that biologists can produce almost any *variety* of Drosophila they like, but have they yet produced a new species? Is there such a thing as laboratory evolution? If not, producing endless varieties is as futile as that idiot who cut the tails off so many generations of mice to see if they'd breed tailless. The thing that impresses me is that nobody, however chance and random oriented, can describe the origin of life without conveying a sense in his language of something struggling to emerge. The struggle for existence is quite different from the struggle for persistence. That's the luck-or-cunning hurdle Samuel Butler couldn't get over, and neither can I. That and the fact that "natural law" is a tautology. Maybe I should write an essay on Butler to parallel the Morris one.[235] After all, his identification of heredity and memory is a remarkably prophetic guess in the direction of the DNA molecule.

[297] Bottom of p. 81 again [par. 292]: the third & fourth phases of metaphor correspond to the distinction between literature as being pleasurable and entertaining and as expressing a commitment. Media of the fourth phase are sacred books like the Bible where the language has to be metaphorical because no other language will do, but is no longer hypothetical.

[298] Another reason why "I am wise & good" is impossible is the comparative sting in the tail: it really means "I am wiser & better than a lot of others I could mention." See Isaiah 65:5.[236]

[299] The four principles of the mythical universe I'm trying to work out have links to Blake's Four Zoas and to the Eliot Quartets. Now comes Lyall Watson's *Lifetide* with four "prototypes," as he calls them, which he says are older & more primitive than Jung's archetypes (p. 344).[237]

[300] It is a commonplace in Canadian criticism that the English imperial tradition moved toward the conquest of space, while the French colonial one, under Catholic influence, tried to keep the emphasis on continuity in time ("je me souviens").[238] Similarly with 19th c. Britain and Ireland, Russia and Poland. My first cosmos is the naturata ladder with the naturans garden-cunt in the upper middle. Then the ladder became temporal with evolution: where is the garden of time? Time is the enemy in Spenser. Perhaps it's a peak experience or the Eliot still point. FW [*Finnegans Wake*] seems to have a Shem-time and a Shaun-space association.

[301] I wonder if the three tables of imagery in GC, apocalyptic, parody-demonic & manifest demonic,[239] shouldn't be four. The apocalyptic side has two aspects, the apocalyptic proper and the analogical. This last could include aesthetic & other analogies, but particularly the Jewish or O.T. one. It carries the sevenfold progression up to the panoramic apocalypse. Maybe it takes in the whole literary area as well, which I've often thought of as analogical.

[302] I would hope that this point would help clear up the link between metaphor and Biblical typology. The analogical type, so far as it is that, is literary or hypothetical metaphor, even if in itself it's a "real" or historical event. The second apocalypse recaptures the existential or ecstatic element in metaphor, and is the stage at which the "is" in A is B means what it says.

[303] No, the O.T. type is, as I say, part of a view of history and time: it belongs more to myth than to metaphor. The literary metaphor remains spatial. Hence Gentile & aesthetic analogies are symbolically "female": the O.T. type is the male line of descent. Time and history are symbolically "male" in this context.

[304] What I need at the moment is some link between Joyce's FW [*Finnegans Wake*] technique, where everything dissolves into a mass of allusions and the deconstruction theory. The woman who wrote the book on Joyce's "decentered" universe was clearly trying to do this, but I got nothing from her, though I'll look at it again.[240]

[305] The creation myths for the second part of the book aren't in the

Bible: they're in the Rig-Veda, especially the Hiranyagarbha one.[241] That's helpful. Some 18th c. people in effect took the deluge & ark business as a repetition of the Creation. However, my notes say there are four falls in Genesis [par. 158]: from vision (P) from innocence (J),[242] from civilization (flood) & from language (Babel).

[306] The ladder is the response to the fall of vision—it doesn't have to be a hierarchy. The garden-cunt is the response to the fall of innocence, and I think it converges on WT & T [*The Winter's Tale* and *The Tempest*] as the ladder does on the Purg-Paradiso. The seed-ark baby in bulrushes-floating saved remnant is the response to the flood. The response to the fall of language ought to be some identity of word and flame hidden in fennel-stalk, prophecy released by hot coal.

[307] I must look up Willard McCarty's reference to the fire aspect of the Exodus from the "furnace of iron":[243] evidently Eliade's *Forge & Crucible* is one. Also Janet Warner's new book on Blake's art points out that in BU [*The Book of Urizen*] Urizen is *nothing*, a "shadow," "void" & "vacuum," *before* he is matter.[244]

[308] Re the FW [*Finnegans Wake*]-deconstruction link: in FW all things & events, as I said, blur into oblique allusions to them, and practically every word has a number of "supplements" besides its surface meaning.[245] Deconstruction approaches every text in the way that Joyce approached the first drafts of his WP [*Work in Progress*], or, to put it in a different way, regards every text as a potential Finnegans Wake.

[309] Of the four falls, of the cosmos, of innocence, of civilization, & of language (flood & Babel), the first two are traditionally included in the fall of Adam, which *must* have included a fall of nature, though there's no textual evidence for one. Hence later tradition put the fall of angels before the creation, so as to have a chaos all ready when Adam fell. (A second fall of angels in Gen. 6:1–4 precedes the flood.)

[310] I've made my point often enough that under the four-level scheme all arguments about "what is natural to man?" are circular, and settled by authority. There's also the fact that the demonic world must be treated as though it were outside nature. Bunyan's pilgrim in the valley of the shadow is horrified by the blasphemies & obscenities he hears,

"for verily he thought they had preceded from his own mind."[246] Hence from Blake on the demonic as well as the divine have to be reclaimed for humanity. Nobody doubts that Christian's voices *did* proceed from his own mind, but that knowledge must go with an increase of tolerance. The reliance on whipping in education is based on the belief that the demons can be driven "out," as in the Gospels.

[311] I've said too that de Sade is just as right about "nature" as Wordsworth is: he simply points to its predatory & parasitic side.[247] But no animal acts with the *malice* that man does: that's a product of consciousness.

[312] In FW [*Finnegans Wake*] the replacing of F [Finnegan] by HCE [Humphrey Chimpden Earwicker] means that the Giant Man theme is *sous rature* and HCE is its "trace."[248] Similarly with the effacing of the Kingu myth in the Bible.[249]

[313] Well: what really happens is that in all four creation-fall myths we get traces of a central effaced theme in Genesis. All four are "revealed" (i.e. made more explicit) in the N.T. Thus:

[314] In the first, the creation of the cosmos account obscures the fight with the dragon of chaos. This is "revealed" by the references to the fall of Satan in the Gospels [Luke 10:18; John 12:31] & the War in Heaven in R [Revelation 12]. These in turn depend on such things as the "Lucifer" passage in Isaiah [chap. 14].[250]

[315] In the second, the garden & Adam-Eve account, the Kingu-Ymir-Purusha dismemberment of the giant man is obscured.[251] The "traces" begin with the Akeda [binding of Isaac] and Pesach [Passover] stories and are "revealed" in the Passion: this is the cycle of sacrifice in which father & son go on murdering each other all through history.

[316] In the third, the original City of God, of which the city of Cain is the demonic parody,[252] is restored in the New Jerusalem vision of R [Revelation] & the "house of many mansions" in the Gospels [John 14:2].

[317] In the fourth, the Creation by the Word, of which there is a trace in Genesis, is "revealed" in the opening of John. (I meant to say, "of which the Babel story is the parody.")

[318] The City of Cain was destroyed in the Flood, and survived as the seed of the ark. A second ark survived the drowning of Egypt, and became the fire-seed of the golden temple. Look up Augustine's CG [*City of God*].

[319] (Completing the top of 88 [par. 312]) I never believed the "dream-language" aspect of FW [*Finnegans Wake*], even if Joyce believed it. But as a Derridean self-supplementing speech trying to recover a differential language from the traces of a logocentric one it works well enough.[253]

[320] The cosmos-chaos myth of Tharmas converges on the Way, which may be up or down and is projected as the ladder-and-snakes game. The garden-cunt myth of Luvah wraps up the whole Oedipus business, and includes the gospel symbol of wedding. The ark-to-ark cycle of Urizenic cities and civilizations is a Hermetic sealing of mythical knowledge into a "Church." The Word-Spirit dialogue of Urthona unbinds Prometheus or forethought, the Creator of Man.

[321] The sexual fall reduced humanity to half-beings: the first Adam before Eve was what the second Adam symbolizes: all men as one man. The fall was into subjectivity: the "lapsed Soul" fell.[254]

[322] The "lapsed Soul" was a female Earth, hence Eve, who traditionally started the fall, represents the original unity of Adam with the *adamah* [dust of the ground, earth]. Adam fell because he fell with Eve. As Marvell hints, the fall was already present in the separate existence of Eve.[255]

[323] That's one of my "displacement" points, the counterpart in me of Derrida's "trace" business. Every myth is a narrative moving in time, & is consequently displaced from an original identification. In the dragon-fight creation myth the dragon is identical with his killer's father: this is eliminated in *Enuma Elish*, but is still suggested in the Vedic hymns (4.18). Indra kills Vritra the dragon and, apparently, his father Tvastr who is a kind of Indian Hephaestos. Also his mother Aditi (as later) hides him from his father. Where? Why, in her womb, of course. Indra wants out & bursts through her side.[256] (Note the explicit statement in the Christian creed: "thou didst not abhor the virgin's womb").[257]

[324] My conception of displacement is closely related to the creation myth of heaven & earth as locked in copulation, a cosmic primal scene,

until a force, usually the Son-Word, pulls them apart. Every creation myth is some form of big bang theory: the something-nothing explodes into manifestation or phenomenal existence. Boehme too.

[325] I think the Washington paper (now the Chicago paper)[258] is a quite presentable outline of an introductory chapter now. The business about ecstatic metaphor links with the psychology of peak experiences[259] that— well—peaked around that time, and that links, as in the RS [Royal Society] paper,[260] with *symbolisme* & its cult of experience. I don't know how much of the symbolon-symbolos stuff I need.

[326] There's also the link between my lover-poet lyrical thesis and Graves' White Goddess.[261] If there is a link: sexual frustration is built into the W.G. cycle, but my point is so restricted & his so portentous.

[327] Oh, God, if I could only get the Hiranyagarbha point clear:[262] the seed of fire in the midst of the waters. I'm pretty sure there's something buried in that that would clear up the whole second half of the book.

[328] A picture, where a variety of images is juxtaposed & presented to the viewer, without being, except in bad criticism, referred back to the thing they represent, is much more obviously metaphorical than anything verbal. The "is" device buggers things up in the verbal arts, although of course in the full apocalyptic vision the full "is" gets reinstated. So Pound's hieroglyphic theory of metaphor is correct,[263] as far as literature is concerned, and the is is a pseudo-predication. But there's ecstatic metaphor on the other side of literary metaphor where the is enters consciousness.

[329] The metaphor is a microcosm of language, the myth is a microcosm of narrative. A lot here to think about. In fact, I've never thought much about anything else. It leaves me with what is almost certainly the central problem of this book, & the reason for my calling GC the first part of something bigger. (I didn't work out the problem of why, for instance, the deluge myth is central to the imagination: as often happens to me, I postponed it, & find myself facing it again.)

[330] More accurately, a myth is a microcosm of mythology, and a mythology is a metaphorical vision of the cosmos. It becomes a cosmol-

ogy when it's secondary and ideological: the primary mythology is the interpenetrating universe, the everlasting gospel; it's not really a cosmology but metaphorical continuity of life.

[331] I don't know either why it's taken me thirty years to complete my most elementary diagram, the centripetal-centrifugal one. Verbal structure A belongs in the total language structure A^n, which includes pictorial & musical languages as well as verbal ones. This in turn is an intermediate structure between I, the consciousness, and B, objective nature. A^n is the reality of the *verum* factum, the supreme fiction.[264]

[332] Fiction, of course, is another one of those words that preserve the imaginary-imaginative ambiguity. I got to thinking about this because of being asked by an Italian journal to contribute to an issue on autobiography at the same time that two or three articles on the subject passed under my nose. They all begin with a lot of crap about truth & falsehood. It's always a form of fiction: see below [par. 334].

[333] What's involved here is the plus-minus pons asinorum. If I say that myth departs from truth, history and ordinary temporal experience, the inexperienced or second-rate mind instinctively says, then you mean it's a lie, or, then you're anti-historical, or, then you're being static and timeless. All such minus signs are illiterate: I mean truth plus, history plus, time plus. Truth plus emotional truth or intensity, history plus presence, time plus permanence. I suppose it's another version of the either-or vs. the both-and approach.

[334] Autobiography . . . there's the anti-narcissistic type, like Joyce's Stephen, Butler's Ernest Pontifex, and (more doubtfully) Pound's Mauberley,[265] where an author studies the continuity of his life by breaking off its earlier stage & studying it. Rousseau was one of the first to isolate the generic in his life. But "I'm going to tell the truth about myself" always means: "I'm trying to grasp the human situation better by examining elements of my own experience."[266]

[335] In teaching 19th c. thought I became aware of the highly schematic element in the thinking of, at least, Carlyle & Arnold. At Harvard in 74–5 I put on the blackboard a schematic summary of *Sartor Resartus*, and I think at one time I could have done the same for *Culture and Anarchy*.

There are also diagrams for Blake, especially the s-o [subject–object] one.[267] I wonder what the link with metaphorical cosmology is here, and whether I'm tracking down the Hiranyagarbha point.

[336] In the Blake diagram, the inner Imagination-Emanation square is the box of light, the ark of the covenant, the seed of fire, in the middle of the Spectre. Female Will cosmos, which is still the deep, the flood of Noah. Incidentally, this diagram is closely related to the emerging I-A-B one. Blake defines hell as both being shut up in desire (the pure I) and as "meer nature" (the pure B).[268]

[337] Boehme appears to be saying that as the Creative Power passes from the Fatherhood to the Sonship of God, the former, the abandoned shell of desire without any more light, turns into Lucifer.[269] Once man stops projecting gods & other numinosities on nature, B turns into a mechanism—not dead, but no longer numinous. This last isn't Boehme, of course. It's the wilderness of the dying Israel.

[338] The seed of fire is (symbolically, of course) male, & the waters around it female. How does the growth or escape of the fire bring the water to life? See Ezekiel 47, of course.[270]

[339] In Blake's MT [*Mental Traveller*] both the Boy and the Female Babe are covered with flames or at any rate untouchable. In the rebirth of the Boy there's an explicit link with Uzza and the ark (of the Lavater notes).[271] But there's no water in the MT.

[340] Maybe that's because the MT deals only with the prick and cunt cosmos where the female is *under* the male ("binds her down for his delight").[272] That's my ladder & garden complex. The other half is the female as the circumference of the male, the hermetic waters surrounding the fire-seed of Prometheus. The latter explodes and expands until the roles are reversed: the reversal can either go straight into Blake's Eden-Beulah apocalypse or back to the prick-cunt cycle. FW [*Finnegans Wake*], which is cyclic but suggests something more, has the female waters slipping away into the sea.

[341] Re the I-A-B diagram: when A faces B we have the *verum factum* cosmos, reality understood only through what we have made of it. When

A faces I, we have revelation, the raising of consciousness by providing a content for it. A facing B is opaque, and shuts out B (phenomenological view). A facing I is transparent, and lets through any number of previously unconsidered elements.

[342] Anxiety influence: the child is father of the man,[273] and a writer separating himself from his younger self is killing a father figure. Sometimes (Samuel Butler, Edmond Gosse, J.S. Mill to some extent) a father-dominated figure. Often a *new* woman enters, obliterating the mother fixation, as in Vita Nuova, &, in a very curious way, Mill again.

[343] The word Upanishad is said to be derived from "to sit near" (i.e. a guru). Shankara derives it from "a loosening or destroying."[274] Wisdom is revealed by a sage, conventionally after a great deal of nudging and prodding. This situation is a projected form of the real way of getting wisdom, i.e. through a kind of self-psychoanalysis, blowing one's torpor skull off, telling the censor to go to hell.

[344] Hence Blake's Laocoon assertions that prayer, fasting, sacrifices, etc., are aspects of creating art.[275] I don't believe that the outward ceremony is Antichrist, and neither did Blake when he needed it (he wanted an Anglican funeral service). But of course it could be perverted into idolatry like anything else.

[345] Pure art & science come from the pure will to create or know. An impure stimulus is provided by the ego's desire to become adjusted, respected or famous. It's practically impossible to do without the stimulus: Milton's "Fame is the spur" passage is very accurate.[276]

[346] Death is the *basanos* [touchstone] of life, the ultimate test or touchstone of detachment. It's also a torture to those who have misunderstood the ordeal.

[347] I am old and on the shelf now, and much that is going on I no longer understand. I'm reading Samuel Delany, an sf [science fiction] writer interested in semiotics, and he begins with a sentence from Julia Kristeva I can no more understand than I could eat a lobster with its shell on.[277] I wouldn't discourage anyone from masticating and ruminating such sentences, but I'd like to think (or perhaps only my ego would) that

my greater simplicity came from a deeper level than the labyrinth of the brain.

[348] Except that my ego has also intruded into my writing and caused me to write nonsense. My adversary has not, like Job's, written a book [Job 31:35], but he's written *in* all my books, and not always on the margins. I'd like to write one book free of the ego before I go. I also wish that my clearest intervals of thought weren't accompanied by laziness and selfishness.

[349] Schelling talks about the growth of mythology into history,[278] but he doesn't seem to have grasped that the process is a double gyre and that history develops toward myth again. There's prehistorical mythology; there's history, which is contemporary with the *literary* use of myth, and there's the post-historical mythology of the Gospels.

[350] Schelling also says, following someone called Oetinger, that corporeality (the spiritual body, distinguished from the "materiality") is the end at which God's will aims: he wants to enter & fulfill space as well as time, and the end of time would also be a universal Incarnation (a *re*incarnation, but not a cyclical one). I've expanded a bit on what I've read here, but the conception of the apocalyptic vision as universal body has always been central.

[351] If man could ever *become* God, there would be an absolute limit to his growth, which would pervert the whole operation. In what sense, then, is Christ God? By looking at him the other way, not as a man who became God, but as a God who became man. So what else is new? Only, I think, the question of what language is involved to "reveal" it. The mystic keeps running out of language. (See Jean Danielou in the *Man and Transformation* Eranos book,[279] or Gregory of Nyssa, a mystic who uses flight instead of climbing for the 3–2 progression.)[280]

[352] Why does mysticism keep running out of language? Because what Freud calls an "oceanic" feeling, one that overwhelms, cannot define itself or function by creating empty spaces around itself, by excluding and absenting.[281]

[353] Why am I blocked by this book? Because I've thought of it as a

sequel, *adding* to something I did before. *The Great Code* is not volume one of anything: like the Anatomy & the Blake, it's volume zero, the book of fuck-all, the cast-skin, the excreta of dead decades. I wish my new book could take the form of an autobiography or a "science-fiction" romance, but it probably won't: it'll be more like a "deconstruction" of GC.

[354] What I seem to have is a revised Joachimism. The first age was prehistoric mythology. In the second age history became history, science science, separating from legend & cosmology. Hence myth became literary or hypothetical. Society's culture became pluralistic, following the Word that divided like a sword. The second age is the actualizing of prophetic authority. The third age is a reintegration of culture around post-mythological metaphor, a new kind of identification. This grows out of my three stages of metaphor.[282]

[355] A reader who "accepts" or believes Milton's position cannot enter into him as profoundly as a reader who sympathizes with him on a hypothetical basis, so that he can move outside him to other positions that Milton never attained. This is part of my refusal to believe that criticism is parasitic. The entering wedge is of course coming later in time.

[356] Roland Barthes says somewhere that genuine reading starts with rereading, because on a first reading you are apt to see only your own reflection.[283] Reading thus begins with objectification and entering into that verbal object.

[357] Blake's "imagination has nothing to do with memory" is about the least helpful comment he ever made. I wish he had said, "imagination begins in reversing the current of memory." Memory progressively dematerializes images and rearranges them into a Narcissus-mirror of ourselves: imagination (as Blake meant it) goes in the opposite or presenting direction of *ut pictura poesis*.[284] In memory the metaphorical context is formed by association; in imagination it is formed by an assigned context. If not narcist, memory simply follows the conventions of tradition: this is what bothered Blake. Yeats in *A Vision* was pursuing images back into the Great Memory.

[358] Space and time. An arrangement of metaphors is a cosmology, or

metaphorical space. The ladder is the main image here. Myth or narrative introduces the element of time, & the simplest form of mythical time is the cycle. Not very new, but all my four patterns, if they exist, have narratives too: the ladder narrative is falling off & climbing back up.

[359] Matthew Arnold remarked that many things are not seen in their full reality until they are seen as beautiful.[285] Obvious, but important as showing how the notion of creation is breaking away from the notion of a history of nature.

[360] I wish I had time to do an essay on Samuel Butler, but obviously I haven't.[286] In chapter 69 of WAF [*The Way of All Flesh*] he says that life is a constant struggle to adapt to the environment & that eventually we shall have to admit the unity of the universe so completely that the distinction between subject & object will disappear.[287] In chapter 73 he says that nobody can get behind Berkeley's argument.[288] Those would be the points of reference.[289]

[361] Some critics seem to talk as though, because we can't have absolute certainty in criticism, nothing is left for us but absolute uncertainty. And we're past the bicentenary of the *Critique of Pure Reason*!

[362] Traditional Christianity is euhemeristic: it takes the myth of the Gospels as straight history. It isn't history, but it's something Vico has no provision for: a myth of a god in a demotic culture and setting. Vico never questions that his poetic myth stage is primitive, nor do most of his followers. The notion that you can have a mythical development that is not primitive and yet, unlike the Classical mythology, resists the pull into the literary, is beyond most mythographers.

[363] It is difficult to avoid the analogy of the organism when talking about verbal structures. An organism assimilates part of its environment—i.e., it eats it—and adapts to the rest. Its relation to what it eats is metaphorical & its relation to what it merely lives with is metonymic.

[364] That time is the fourth dimension of space has been a middlebrow cliché since 1905.[290] But if we look at the dimensions of experience they come in a different order. The first dimension is time, the sense of continuous identity in which all living things attempt to remain, whether

by fight or flight. Human beings have some consciousness of this sense of continuing life, but their consciousness is limited: we are continuously aware of a present moment, but cannot be fully conscious of it.

[365] The dimensions of space, beginning with length, which is the objectifying of the time consciousness, seem to take a while before the total sense of an objective world is constantly present. The sense of place, or space-*there*, seems to come first, and in earlier English space frequently means an interval of time. The chain of being is not a spatial but, so to speak, a *platial* cosmos: everything has its rightful place except what is evil.

[366] The last dimension of experience is the sense of the rhythm of mutability, the growth & decay that goes on simultaneously in time and space. The emotional emphasis is usually on growth, from tiny seed to mighty tree or whatever. The Vedic myth of Hiranyagarbha, the golden seed of fire in the midst of waters, comes through the Bible as the deluge myth with the ark, the container of all life, floating on the surface. In a larger context the spark increases until the world, once drowned in water, is burned in fire. Drunken boat & other *symboliste* clichés belong here.

[367] The formulaic improvised verse that lies closely behind the Homeric poems exists in the time dimension only if the poet does not write, because a poet who doesn't write isn't thinking of lines on a page. Once written, lines go across a page & end, & a new line starts underneath, giving us the germ of discontinuity that we call *verse*, with its overtones of turning around & starting again.[291]

[368] Epos & prose, however, achieve a new kind of continuity *down* the page in space: this continuity is broken up again in lyric, with its stanzas, and in drama, with its character-speeches.

[369] Marx is supposed to have inverted Hegel by saying that Hegel's dialectic would only make sense if it were transformed from ideology to material historical forces.[292] But capitalism has matured only to the extent that it has been subjected to socialist revisionism, and communism has matured only to the extent that it has taken on bourgeois & consumerist revisions. It looks as though Hegel were right after all, & that the real Armageddon is a verbal & dialectical one.[293] The Chinese admit this,

up to a point: Russians & Americans still refuse to do so. When a myth leads to action, the action invariably perverts the myth. (*Social* action, anyway.)

[370] Hence when society is polarized and "the only choice" is fascism or communism or whatever, those who keep saying "balls to your dilemma" represent the real humanity in us. Not in Canada, where everybody says it, but Montale in Italy or Pasternak in Russia.

[371] I suppose Sade is about as far as one can go in the Romantic glorification of natura naturans: there's nothing left of the structure or system of nature at all.

[372] Whorf's metalinguistic discoveries, suggesting that we allow the grammar of our language to structure our world, are interesting and important, but they're not decisive.[294] For example, Hebrew did not have a past-present-future tense system of verbs and Greek did, but it was Hebrew and not Greek that developed a religious vision based on a historical past and a prophetic future.

[373] The simplest way to get out of this bind of letting one's grammar structure one's world is to turn from prose to the figured language of poetry, where you have to come to terms with the opposite problem, the inadequacy of the world to meet the structuring demands of language. The "is not and yet is" side of metaphor is what's important here.

[374] My view of genuine & phony mythology closely parallels the point I got from Milton, that society can't distinguish the prophet above the law from the "heretic" or whatever below it.[295] The parallel takes me back to the GC point that for Xy [Christianity] the Bible is a work of prophecy (whereas it's primarily law or "instruction" for Judaism).[296]

[375] The first question any audience would ask is, "How do we tell the difference?" And I don't know. As long as truth is linked to correspondence, all myth, including "gospel truth," will lie. I've caught myself lying to sustain the Frye myth—nothing serious except perhaps to my own moral fibre, but I have. And I'm damned if I see any methodological difference from what the Gospel does.

[376] Dogma is a form of original sin, because it is necessarily founded on a theory of words that is necessarily wrong. That's the only kind of dogmatic statement that can be right.

[377] Position One (the "fundamentalist" position) has:

A	<	B	<	C	<	D
human consciousness		verbal structure		external world		voice or word of God

[378] Note that the presence of D doesn't eliminate C, because truth of correspondence is still assumed and B finds its meaning in what's outside it. Position Two breaks B in two, a figurative part and a descriptive part. As only B1 can apply to a creation myth, say, the latter becomes simply literary and poetic. In religion that's clearly inadequate, so if, say, a Biblical scholar is also a clergyman, he speaks one language in his articles and another in the pulpit.

[379] There's no sense in writing this book at all unless I can work out a third stage of myth beyond the poetic. What follows is a series of hunches. First, my oldest & strongest conviction. Men & women derive from earlier men & women: there's no spontaneous generation. Similarly, the works of man derive from earlier works: they're not reassembled anew in each age of culture. People resist this because they're frustrated poets and dream of being poets without conditioning parents (anxiety of influence). What's true of human beings is true of human works. I imagine that the growth of the history of science will show that what's true of the arts is true of sciences: in both, the creative process doesn't improve; the critical process does. Einstein doesn't improve on Newton as Newton, any more than any son improves on his father as father. But in the temporal dimension of critical tradition there's a transcendental element. There are practical and theoretical recreations of myth: the practical one is literature, the theoretical one the criticism of literature which has to expand into a theory of myth as a whole. At present, myth criticism is regarded as an antiquated and minor subdivision of criticism: it's actually criticism itself, as critics may come to realize after they've exhausted every conceivable variety of Trivial Pursuit.[297]

[380] Revolution means the cycle of revolution and counter-revolution. The past and the future are part of it: the continuous antithesis of defending or attacking an establishment which is Marxist fodder. This is the spatial, physico-chemical, environmental side of the picture. The biological, temporal, hereditary aspect is that of incremental tradition, the transcendent factor which in criticism is the recreation of myth from the past-future into the present. It's what is symbolized by O.T. younger-son and N.T. eldest-son incarnation in the Bible, vertical intervention from a transcendent source. The autonomy of myth is the backbone of the transcendent. In the creation myth the order of God is imitated in the work of man, so that the city & garden & sheepfold become apocalyptic symbols. The reason for associating creation with God is to provide that transcendent goal out of the cycle. So when we study the myth of a Shakespeare history play, we're studying the establishing of a real present out of the story of the past with applications to *its* future (Shakespeare's own time). Of my seven stages,[298] the wisdom one winds up the revolutionary cycle of time. That's the circle of law & Talmudic commentary, of gospel & canon law, of the Koran & the Ayatollah prescriptions. Prophecy, taken seriously, is a step forward into the literary.

[381] The cycle goes as far as wisdom in my group of seven, and wisdom copes with a text of law by rationalization and commentary. Prophecy indicates the path of human folly into inevitable disaster, and the restoration of Israel by God in a metaphorical future which is really an expanded present. Commentary on prophecy is a dialectic between the social setting & the incremental tradition, & that's what criticism of literature should follow as a model.

[382] Burke says there's a point at which those who uphold wrong principles turn into bad men.[299] That's a dangerous principle to invoke: it's the Catholic Church's anathema, which has been so overused it's completely buggered the church, and the totalitarian "objective guilt," which enables a dictator seizing power, like Stalin, to shoot every human obstacle to him without losing five minutes' sleep (except for planning how to shoot some more). Nevertheless the principle does exist.

[383] The conception of "displacement" has always been with me, but I've never worked out a technique for deriving the separate-petalled flower of the story from the tightly wrapped bud of identification. I've

had many hunches in reading fiction (Scott & Dickens particularly) and I know I've got a critical technique as precise and far more useful than "deconstruction." But I've been held back by the absence of a working principle: I can see it clearly enough, but can't yet answer the question "how can anybody else learn to see it?"

[384] Fictions exfoliate from the identities of myth, but very profound fictions recapture their ancestry. In the O.T. the relation of Ruth to Naomi suggests a Persephone-Demeter cult, but in avoiding the structure of a Canaanite myth the author goes back to a simpler convention of no priests, no temples, spirits rather than named gods, and a feeling of sympathy between man and nature.[300]

[385] Now the Church of England's in a tizzy because one of its bishops says he "doesn't believe in" the Virgin Birth.[301] The time will come when such a statement will be greeted by hoots of derision, as illiterate nonsense. But we don't yet have a post-literary theory of belief. I'd like to help formulate one, and I think I could on the basis of the hypostasis and elenchos of the Hebrews definition [Hebrews 11:1]. What have substance & proof of unseen things hoped for got to do with "believing" that in 4 B.C. an unpopped virgin gave birth? Everybody *really* knows that trying to "believe in" such things is hysteria. I've got the "literal meaning" point fairly clear, but not this. One accepts the totality of the symbolic picture, but doesn't refer the details to history. But I've got to work harder than that.

[386] Truth of correspondence ("this apple is red," "I was born in Sherbrooke") is a form of measurement. It's words assimilated to mathematics, so far as mathematics is measurement. The kind of truth expressed by an aphorism, where we are impelled to say "how profoundly true that is!", is the kind of truth that words are built for. Those are verbal probes, as McLuhan called them: they're powerful magnets picking up piles of iron. Then there's the logical or horizontal truth that comes from linking aphorisms in sequence. I'm back to my GC first chapter.

[387] Review: the emblematic image giving the dianoia of a myth is, for the creation myths, the ladder-mountain-tower axis mundi, or the world tree. The "deconstructions" of this image made by Pound, Joyce, Eliot &

Yeats help to establish the two-way nature of the ladder, in particular the autonomous urge to ascent. In these deconstructions Prometheus and Eros ascents are set free. Prometheus reverses the Priestly creation, and Eros the Jahwist one. Perhaps I've been wrong all along, and Hermes & Adonis are simply the old authoritarian descent forms.

[388] No, that just won't do: there must be forms of Hermes (Unsealed) and Adonis (Revived) that are not authoritarian and hierarchical. The ladder of degree is, probably, the ultimate form of perverted and exploiting myth, and if a reconstructed version of each isn't there the whole subject's a lot of shit. The key to understanding it is likely to be the displacement technique which I think is the real target of the "deconstruction" that just shoots aimlessly in all directions. I think I'll set myself an exercise in displacement for the Smith conference.[302] Perhaps a straight displacement (Scott, for instance) followed by a profound one (Shakespeare, say) that doesn't just displace but reconstructs the myth. There's also that Ibsen play (early) that's explicitly a displacement: perhaps a later one like WDA [*When We Dead Awaken*] could form the second stage.

[389] Anyway, one thing I have to consider is whether there are another set of two or four creation myths. Both of those I've been considering have spiral forms, and suggest expanding and contracting versions. Expanding ones includes the Hiranyagarbha one: seed of fire in waters that expands to a cosmos burning in the fire of life. Noah's flood has a seed of life (the ark) floating on top of chaos. The burning bush and the pillar of fire carry Israel through the Red Sea. This expansion from a "genetic code" is clearly linked to the old spiral-mountain image, but occupies a different context (temporal rather than spatial, though the "big bang" creation vision has both). The opposite movement, starting with destruction (flood, harvest, & especially vintage or flood of blood) and narrowing down to a saved remnant seed, is probably what Mallarmé's *Igitur* is getting at, which makes the old link with the "igitur" of Vg. [Vulgate] Gen. 2:3 so wonderfully accurate.[303] The Charybdis theme seems to reappear in the "black hole" conception of astronomy.

[390] I've said that what Pound, Yeats, Joyce & Eliot do with staircase & spiral symbolism form a series of deconstructions of the old chain of being. Deconstruction, however, is a birdshot technique: it aims at the

horizon and bags what it accidentally hits. I'd prefer to pick out a real target and aim at that: my first target is to show that the Priestly & Jahwist accounts of creation are two-way staircases, with angels ascending as well as descending. Also that the ascent of the Priestly stair first annexes the demonic to the human, then liberates Prometheus. The ascent of the Jahwist stair liberates Eros. Also Oedipus: Prometheus kills the false mother; Eros unites with the true mother—Blake says she can't be a virgin mother, but I'm not so sure.[304]

[391] Position One ("fundamentalist"): truth in the Bible is, as much as possible, truth of correspondence, where the word is subordinated to event. That's crap. Position Two (liberal or, formerly, modernist): the Bible is full of myth and most of its history is legend or *sage*, but it has an existential value in spite of it. Here, if you're both scholar & clergyman, you speak in one language in articles & another in the pulpit. Then you run into the Pastoral Epistles (epistles of straw, as Luther would say) and they tell us to abandon bebelous mythous[305] and cling to the logoi or truths of the Gospel. At this point many people succumb to the temptation to choose a captain back for Egypt, to dissolve myth back into history (i.e. the phony history we get when we pretend that the covering-up myth *is* history) and fall back on Position One. Won't do: logoi are on the other side of mythoi, even if the Timothy-Titus squad didn't know or think it. And yet one can't just go into that hazy good will world where all constructs are alike. The construct one "believes in" is a part of one's own construction too.

[392] I'm trying to circle around what I think should be the subject of my next article: what I meant by saying that the statement "I believe / I don't believe literally in the Virgin Birth," or any statement of that type, has nothing to do with orthodoxy or heresy, but is merely illiterate. That involves a study of the definition of faith in Hebrews that shifts its psychological focus away from the subject-object duality of "I believe that." And towards what?

[393] What I'm hoping to get away with is a paper on "The Dialectic of Belief and Vision."[306] That's the resolution of the "is" and the "as though" I've circled around since at least the AC. I suppose one first attacks the conventionalizing of subject and object involved in "I" (who's I?) believe "that" (what's that?).

[394] After thirty years, I'm back to page one of the Anatomy. My opposition to sociological criticism is based on the principle that mythology is prior to ideology, the set of assumptions being always derived from a prior story. The story *says* nothing, and *you* say nothing: you listen to the story. Criticism often assumes that the ideology goes all the way: that there's no point at which the literary work stops saying things & keeping open the possibility of answer. If it's obviously moving from statement to myth, well, that's because of certain social pressures the writer had to conceal as well as reveal his meaning, had to be oblique instead of direct. Nonsense: obliquity is fundamental: it's the core (psychologically, anyway) of revelation.

[395] I got to this this time by thinking about MM [*Measure for Measure*], where the abdicating Duke is an irresponsible coward for running away, a fool for not choosing Escalus rather than Angelo, and a sneak for coming back in disguise and eavesdropping. None of that matters, obviously; listen to the story & shut up. But anyone can see that Lear is a fool when he abdicates: why is the same reaction as relevant here? The Duke is a folktale trickster: we don't know why he acts that way, but it all works out in the end. We're in an area of reality somehow different from real life.

[396] I have to think very hard about what literature does when it stops saying and cuts off answering, about what revelation reveals, about what kind of reality is being explored when we're not in real life. Another old chestnut is buried here too: what's the source of the silent authority of the story? I say that literature shows forth & doesn't speak, but that's just a metaphor from eyesight. (A very powerful one, though: look at (!) Hermione coming to life.)³⁰⁷ Why does God make a deal with Satan, letting him torment Job? No answer: just look at Leviathan.

[397] The trickster is sublimated in some religions (Hinduism) into a benevolent providence. Xy [Christianity] too: Jesus comes back in disguise into the world he's made [Matthew 16; Luke 24]: the Holy Spirit, blowing where it listeth, is a trickster. In the year 1925 the Etude ran a eulogistic article of Scriabine, mainly for laughs.³⁰⁸ Result for me: a lifelong interest in Scriabine. An evangelist came to Moncton and preached against "skeptical questions" like "Who was Cain's wife?" I brooded over that until I'd ripped the whole Bible to shreds. I told that to Oliver

(of Emmanuel)[309] once, & his comment in effect was precisely as above: the Holy Spirit is a trickster.

[398] What does literature say when it's silent? I can't seem to get past this metaphor of "vision." But the basis of the vision metaphor is "I see that," which brings us to square one again. It must be something more like Jacob and the angel. Belief must be all wrong as a pseudo-rational structure overriding reason. The hypostasis of the hoped-for and the elenchos of the unseen [Hebrews 11:1] must be a hell of a lot more than that.

[399] Art is not simply an identity of illusion and reality, but a counter-illusion: its world is a material world, but the material of an intelligible spiritual world.

[400] Well, the dialectic of belief and vision is the path I have to go down now. My ideas at present are as crude as a child's mud pies. However, the metaphorical kernels of belief and vision are hearing and sight. As long as belief means, in practice, the acceptance of something heard as the Word of God, the church, or corresponding body of believers, is caught in a narrowing dialectic. Any sane person can see the wisdom of separating church & state: religion, Christian, Moslem, Jewish, Hindu, is the worst possible basis for a secular society. Buddhism persecutes less, but is probably just as shaky.

[401] The church & the world both educate, but the world does a far better job, & in modern society the relevance & value of a religion is gauged by the quality of its worldliness (i.e. its urbanity). Matthew Arnold's argument, put on a historical basis, would be something like this: originally all cultural activities were in a sense religious. To the extent that *a* religion separated itself from the rest of culture, it started heading for sectarianism. To the extent that it rejoins the total body of culture, it improves itself as well as the culture.

[402] At the same time I don't want my dialectic of belief & vision to get caught in Arnold's Hebraic-Hellenic one,[310] which is mostly horseshit. But if mythology is prior to ideology, then the arts and not philosophy are the primary analogies of religion. Even the sacraments, the tradi-tional primary analogies, are closer to the arts than to argument.

[403] The sacraments are participating arts, & so are existential and lack the quality of vision in the presented arts. ("Vision" is getting further from the metaphor of eyesight, as it would include the response to music.) That would include prayer, which I suppose is a sacrament.

[404] The fundamentalists are gaining ground partly because they have a coherent theory of meaning. It's indefensible, but it's coherent. The more reasonable attitudes of liberals are reasonable pragmatically; theoretically they're half-assed. I think my identification of literal & metaphorical meaning could be the basis for a coherent theory.

[405] Hypostasis of the hoped-for and elenchos of the unseen [Hebrews 11:1]. I wish I knew enough Greek to compare the corresponding definition of vision in an Epistle to the Athenians.

[406] And of course one hears in sequential time: the "vision" following is an act of simultaneous apprehension that's in time but really lifts one out of time as well. Is this something the [Eliot's] Quartets missed: something *very* elementary & secular?

[407] Although it's really closer to Stevens' description without place than to the Quartets: the apocalyptic flash "complete without secret arrangements of it in the mind,"[311] where the Incarnate Word is suddenly Alpha & Omega. Interesting if something so commonplace as a *Gestalt* is really the lift out of time I've been revolving around.

[408] I'm no evangelist or revivalist preacher, but I'd like to help out in a trend to make religion interesting and attractive to many people of good will who will have nothing to do with it now. The literalist view of meaning makes those who take it seriously hysterical. Before long they're saying that serious writers are wallowing in filth, that children should be spanked as often as possible, that not going to church/mass on Sunday is a mortal sin, that it offends God to call one's bum an arse, & the rest of the dreary rigmarole. I suppose the root of the hysteria is the threat of hell: I note that these people are always hailing with delight something like herpes or AIDS or, of course, any uncertainty connected with evolution or the pill. Under the law, the more religiosity, the less charity.

[409] The dirty-rags lot I have no use for either: I mean the lofty esoteric

meaning hidden under the repulsive literal one. The reality of the story, according to the esoteric people, is a moral platitude. Maurice Nicoll, *The New Man*.[312] With all my self-doubts, I think I can look into myself more concretely than such people can teach me to do. And I've always distrusted allegory.

[410] I've always felt that *sum pius Aeneas* [*Aeneid*, 1.378] was not smug but only very sad. Bunyan's Christian with his burden of sin was travelling light compared to this awful burden of virtue.

[411] I suppose there's no male equivalent symbol of the irreversibility of time corresponding to woman's loss of virginity. The White Goddess has the power to renew hers because goddesses are above time. The motive for rape may sometimes be the urge to pull the woman down into the stream of time.

[412] There aren't many issues in contemporary critical theory that I haven't raised & discussed in my own context. My distinction between prose & associative speech is an example:[313] prose is the language of écriture, & makes no sense without it. It gets influenced by associative rhythms from oral speech and by rhetorical devices from verse in oratory; but there's no prose without writing.

[413] My remark in the Stratford paper that Shakespeare was not a great poet who wrote plays, but a great dramatist who used mainly verse,[314] suggests the important critical principle of the surrender to the genius of the genre. Ancient poets appealed to Muses to write their poems for them, and the Muses were generic: you wouldn't begin a love lyric with an appeal to Clio or Urania.

[414] It seems to follow from this that poets who don't commit themselves to genres are really being their own Muses. When I complained of the monotony of the personal tone in Irving Layton, of never (except for a very few poems) getting away from the sound of the hectoring voice, this was what I meant.[315] Perhaps this is another of the denigrations of writing Derrida talks about.

[415] So many of my students want to believe that the visionary writers of the Bible "just saw" what they said they saw. That's *our* conditioning,

the acceptance of a separation of subject & object. There would have been a large subjective element in their vision. That, again, isn't something they made up themselves: that's the same conditioning. The supreme fiction, the illusion that is reality, that's the vision of existential metaphor.[316]

[416] When mythology is translated into ideology funny things happen. When the principle that the individual is metaphorically identical with its class is so translated, we get the starting point of Platonism.

[417] "I believe" means that something is absent; "I see" (a metaphor) means something is distant. To repeat the Apostles' Creed in churches, which the Apostles never heard of, can be explained, or rationalized, only by Butler's principle of analogy: "I believe as though it were present, I think."[317]

[418] I've been reading another Marxist essay by someone outside a Marxist dominated country, very anxious to dissociate himself from "vulgar Marxism." The trouble is that Lenin was a vulgar Marxist.

[419] The ideological structure of a culture provides the background for an age; the mythological structure provides the temporal & traditional dimension. Ideology is the source of secondary concerns: if I could establish the mythology-primary concern link I'd be all set.

[420] A convention may be a theme, like the cruel mistress; it may be a custom, like the 14 lines of a sonnet; when it's big enough to enclose the whole project, it's a genre. A convention is an aspect of a poem's identity, what makes it recognizable as, first, a poem, second a poem of a particular time & place. As such, it's the element of welcome or invitation to read. Sometimes, as with detective story addicts, one reads partly for the convention—well, you always do, but my old point about liking or disliking the convention itself is relevant.

[421] Everybody has a point at which he can't take a convention: pornography, for example, which sacrifices all the traditional literary conventions for a prodding of reflexes, appeals only to those who like having their reflexes prodded & don't resent it. The majority of people do like being drilled & ordered & told what to do, & pornography does

this along with reversing the context & giving the illusion of escape. That day we read no farther, as Eve said.[318]

[422] I've got things now on a cross: vertical bar historical, mythological, traditional; horizontal one ideological and contemporary (though *our* historical, & the only aspect of history ideology-soaked critics would buy). Zoa cross: the vertical bar runs from the remotest past (Urthona) into the present & future (Urizen); the horizontal one from a conservative establishment-accepting role to a resistance one (Orc). To follow that up I'd have to show both tendencies at work in a given age, often in the same writer. Also the angles: I've made the point often enough that conservative & radical are terms belonging to critical use, not to authorial intention.

[423] The use of criticism to denigrate criticism, and eventually literature itself: the feeling that if we root criticism deeply enough in phenomenology or whatnot we can turn literature into a document of something else. I said this 30 years ago,[319] & its only increased since. My real beef, of course, is the relation of myth to primary concern.

[424] I suppose where deconstruction comes in is the fact that every work of literature both attacks & defends its establishment. As I've said, the adversary situation in ideology remains: the Marxist attempt to end it failed.

[425] I've said too that there are anxieties inherent in every social context of every writer. Bloom's type certainly exists, but it arises from the lack of clear tradition in the vertical bar.[320] For Gerard Manley Hopkins, the religious position he took was certainly an anxiety to him, but the only way he could attach himself to the vertical bar of deep originality.

[426] Why was I so fascinated by Frazer? Because he linked mythology with anxiety about the food supply—a primary concern. Why am I fascinated by *The White Goddess*, a wrong-headed book in many ways? Because it links mythology with sexual anxiety, a primary concern. Why did I get so fascinated by that sybil G.R. Levy?[321] Because she linked mythology to shelter & buildings, a primary concern. Food, sex, shelter, *are* the primary concerns, all grouped around God the Father & Nature the Mother.

[427] I wonder about my passion for detective stories: I read a Freudian article once that I thought was right on target about it, & promptly forgot what it said. Too close for comfort, maybe. Survival and its opposite, murder, are also primary concerns.

[428] Is ultimate concern a primary concern? I think not. No one can live a day without being concerned with food: anybody can live all his life without being concerned about God. In my table of metaphors, animal & vegetable are food, mineral shelter (for living & dead) & direction, the human itself sexual. The superhuman categories have to do with leisure, concern for survival (of death), intelligence (a need according to me), and vision.

[429] An archetype is a *sign* of a convention, an indication (because recurrent) of origin and tradition. Many archetypes are deconstructions of previous ones, like the Joyce-Pound-Eliot-Yeats ladder ones.

[430] The archetypes of work, the humanized form of nature, are relatively clear in my mind. Understanding the human level itself means understanding the fall as sexual consciousness (sex in the head)[322] that leads to domination and the crazy-Oedipus syndrome of my first note in this book. Blake's Female Will, Freudian sex and repression, the white-goddess & black bride complex, feminist criticism which stops its legalistic dust-raising sweeping stage, & even Jung, whose biggest & most totally unintelligible book is called Mysterium Conjunctionis, are all involved here. Of course sexual emancipation doesn't mean the mindless fucking that goes on in America today: that's just a counter-obsession.

[431] On the other side of that, Paradise is leisure without the narcotic disintegration of it that's inevitable under our present repressive sexuality. (It's actually a manic-depressive seesaw of repression and expression, like sado-masochism.)

[432] In this world all power leads to the abuse of power: the angels symbolize the released conscious powers of intellect & imagination. I suppose yoga techniques move in this direction: anybody who completely achieved Patanjali's agenda[323] would be an angel. Note that a lot of people, from Heraclitus to Blake, have identified man's guardian angel with his own essential genius.

[433] Romanticism was the deconstruction of the chain of being. Its polarized conservatism and radicalism both worked in that direction.

[434] I am still bewildered by the betrayal of criticism that turns all literature into an alphabet soup in which one can never find the crucial letters Alpha & Omega. That's why I've turned to the Bible, which simultaneously constructs & deconstructs (a) metaphor (b) holistic form. My main reason for thinking this a betrayal is my conception of primary concern.

[435] The paradise level is Blake's Beulah, where a lot of people are sleeping but a lot awake too—see "Regeneration" (Vaughan's poem).[324] The gods—*not* God—walk in the garden, and are the Magi & the spirits of the elements.

[436] Looking at a row of books by Carlos Castaneda, I note that the early ones are labelled "non-fiction" & the later ones "fiction," although there is no generic difference between them. Doubtless an interesting story behind that, but not one to illuminate genre criticism.[325] Zen & the Art of Motorcycle Maintenance is a confession-anatomy form also labelled "non-fiction," though the author's preface emphasizes its fictional form.[326] People are stupid.

[437] In writing about the Book of Ruth I said there were fixed story-types about women, but these types are more closely interconnected than I thought.[327] In the levirate-marriage story of Tamar the heroine is accused of being a harlot, and condemned to be burnt. That brings the redeemed harlot theme into the story. The redeemer is the go'el, which gives the translation of go'el as redeemer in Job much more point [Job 19:25].

[438] The bride from the strange land is black (S.S. [Song of Songs]), foreign (Ps. 45), or a Moabitess (Ruth). This merges with the theme of the heroine with a stain on her which is eventually annihilated. Cf. the jealousy of Joseph theme: Blake would say that virginity is a stain.[328]

[439] In late-birth stories there's a displacement of the original birth-of-hero story: the old mother, because the birth is miraculous, is really getting screwed by the Lord, even if the husband is allowed to do his best.[329]

[440] The Esther-Judith pattern still baffles me. Of course it's revolution of God's people against a tyrant (Haman rather than the Persian king), so it links with the people-female and ruler-male complex. This pattern actually does enter history in the story of Joan of Arc, and of course the Song of Hannah & Magnificat themes come into it.[330]

[441] The dialectic of belief and vision starts with the contrast in emphasis between the scholastic & the mystical, Calvinism and Anabaptist-Quakerism, Talmudism & Kabbalism. One emphasis listens to the doctrine unfold itself; the other sees the (apocalyptic) pattern. One has to be constantly aware of the metaphors of "hearing" and "seeing": they're not metaphorical in ritual, but they are everywhere else.

[442] I wonder if the vision side of this can be identified with hope. As Emily Dickinson said, hope is based on a fiction:[331] as Stevens said (and I hope he said this to the end) reality is a created fiction.[332]

[443] That last allusion is to the rumor, or fact, that Wallace Stevens called for the last rites of the R.C. church on his deathbed & then said "now I'm in the fold." Many people, even though of Catholic background, felt betrayed by this. The point is the ideological horizontal bar: Stevens made a soft & sentimental move toward the pole of acceptance, instead of staying in the middle with his own poetic authority intact.[333] If such a move underlies the poetry, as it did with Hopkins, it's simply a fact we take account of: with Stevens, as with Rimbaud, it means nothing linked to the poetry. Yeats is buried in a Church of Ireland cemetery; Blake was buried in Bunhill Fields but asked for an Anglican funeral. Blake & Yeats don't seem to me to be repudiating their poetic authority; Stevens, like Chaucer & perhaps Shakespeare ("dyed a Papist") do.[334]

[444] Primary faith without vision creates hysteria: one sees that in the staring eye, the forced extroversion, the over-confident tones. In the introverts it leads to the "crisis of faith" that's so fashionable, and eventually this "faith" disappears. Catholics perhaps have less trouble—or used to, anyway—because for them faith is essentially what runs the sacramental machinery, and that provides a continuity of action that takes the heat off the speculative mind. But the *history* of the Catholic Church certainly reveals the hysteria there.

[445] The religious perspective is essential to the study of literature: some people resent this because they cannot think of religion as anything but an ideology to be either believed or disbelieved. Then there are all the students who tell me that they can't take the "dogma" but feel that there's something about religion that's real. When I define this something as mythology, a created fiction (tautology, really), just as the world described in Genesis 1 is a created fiction to God, they get confused.

[446] A plurality of ideologies is a good thing if it prevents one from becoming tyrannical. Perhaps the most effective element in democracy is its conception of the co-existence of ideologies. This is linked to the notion I got from Matthew Arnold, that the world at its best (urbanity) educates better than the church. The "pure gospel" is the aspect of Christianity that relates to primary concern.

[447] Once again, why is Venus excluded from the *Tempest* masque? Shakespeare can't be saying that you can have a happy and fruitful marriage without sexual love. I think he's saying that the vision of renewal & fertility must be achieved first. Prospero's prudish anxieties are those of a Magus, but the general picture is of a rebirth of myth preceding the birth of a brave new world. Towards that world Prospero takes the attitude of Simeon: nunc dimittis.[335]

[448] I think I'm moving toward a re-absorption of Derrida, though on a much bigger scale than my re-absorption of Lacan. I think écriture is the valley of dry bones in the desert, & that creative reading articulates the bones and restores to them the faculty of direct speech. The direct speech has to be the "full word," containing all possible deconstructions, but it's Elijah added to Moses.[336] This is my "kerygma" point approached from the opposite direction. Moses-law is belief; Elijah-prophecy is vision. Jesus didn't write, but he was written about, & the process recreates him. Derrida's instinct in going to Rousseau as pre-eminently the man who writes about himself was sound, but it makes his case one of special pleading.

[449] My point about the hysteria of literalism seems to go in a "demythologizing" direction, but of course it doesn't: that just turns everything into ideology and confirms the hysteria it begins by trying to remove.

[450] The Classical 18th c. phase of literature seems to me an extraordinary tour de force, a literature totally dominated by ideology and quite happy about it. The German early Romantic disputes over allegory & symbol were quite right: allegory was what Classicism was, the subordinating of literature to canons derived from secondary concern. The secret was the mythological "sun king" ace kicker held by Louis XIV: if Stalin had had the slightest trace of that he might have got away with his own ideological kidnap.

[451] Of course there are cultural factors in such an ideology that I haven't thought about yet. Aesthetic factors of the type that get into the conception "Augustan," for instance. Still, one issue is that Pope & Swift were close to the centre of a small society, & you can't repeat the silly argument of Carlyle's *Past & Present*, applying leadership in a monastery to leadership in an empire of hundreds of millions. Stalin would doubtless have been pleased to hear someone say "the proper study of mankind is man"[337] with real conviction. But the immense superiority of democracy to Marxism lies in its understanding of the mutual interdependence of conflicting ideologies: Swift & Pope were Tory intellectuals in a Whig ethos, just as Byron & Shelley were left-wing Whigs in a growing imperialist ethos. When does this sense of necessary opposition begin? Perhaps with the Bishops' and Geneva Bibles, coming together in the AV.

[452] Or perhaps with the king's two bodies, which become the Parliament's two bodies after 1642. The public body is the party entrusted with government; the private one is the opposition & its "shadow cabinet." Intellectuals usually cluster around an opposition, partly because it's the locus of the mythological & symbolic, not the executive. See Mill's essay on Coleridge.[338] Incidentally, the Hal plays, H41, H42 and H5 [*Henry IV, Part I* and *Part II*, and *Henry V*], show Prince Hal putting on an act that stretches the king's two bodies thesis as far as it will go.

[453] I seem to be shocking the local religious community with my notion that "demythologizing" is a doctrine of Antichrist—well, anyway, of W.H. Auden's Herod.[339] Essentially it means "up with ideology," which is why Barth is so tolerant about Bultmann. But of course it's supposed to mean "up with fact & down with fantasy." I have a lot of thinking to do about the paradox that in religion there's no such thing as

a fact. The fact is annihilated by the myth. It's Theseus' two worlds of apprehension & comprehension again:[340] fact as fact is incorporated in historical & parallel syntheses: fact that's really experience disappears & is reborn as experience. Fact is the grain of wheat that is buried and "dies" [John 12:24]—incidentally, what a violation of fact the word "die" is!

[454] Originally the king's two bodies in Parliament were the Lords & the Commoners, where the associations of public-executive & private-cultural opposition were largely reversed.

[455] The first (later) account of creation is natura naturata, the kernel concern being shelter, hence ladders and cities & temples grow out of it. Architecture, therefore all the arts, grow out of it too. Food & sex & perhaps survival grow out of the natura naturans of Eden. Priestly creation creates the objectively symbolic; Jahwist the subjectively symbolic.

[456] Some verses in the Bible seem designed to drive the attentive reader out of his mind. One is Genesis 2:19, where God brings beasts & birds to the "adam" "to see what he would call them." Why should curiosity about such a thing be ascribed to God?[341] Another koan, even tougher, is Mark 8:14–21.[342] Considering the size of the bibliography of commentary on the Gospels, it seems an extraordinary consensus, though a purely negative one, that they all dodge the same difficulties.

[457] Well: the contrast of naturata & naturans creation accounts in Genesis recurs in Paul's telling the law-obsessed Romans that the law is fulfilled by the gospel, & then the eros-obsessed Corinthians that the gospel fulfils love. Perhaps too the contrast between Matthew's nativity of wizards (later kings), house and gold, and Luke's pastoral nativity of shepherds under the stars. That's apart from the pastoral myths and their contrast with the urban symbolism built around Jerusalem (they're sometimes brought together, as at the end of the 23rd Psalm[)]. At a certain point the temple pulls up its roots and becomes a tent.

[458] I keep wondering why there's such extraordinary magic attached, in Kabbalism and elsewhere, to the Hebrew "alphabet," which is really just a consonantal syllabary. It seems to go with the veneration of écriture,

and not just because only the consonants are written down. There seems to be an unexpressed feeling that the *silent* word, of moving lips and tongue and the like, is the real communication: the actual sounds produced are variable (e.g., Jehovah for Yahweh, Moloch for melek).

[459] So the old legend that writing was invented at Mt. Sinai has some truth. I have to watch my kerygma thesis: the more stentorian the proclamation, the further it gets from the real whispered evocation in the mind. Note that Paul's effective work was done through written "epistles," in contrast to the Athens passage in Acts [17:15–22]. One could certainly overstate such a thesis, but something is there: it brings me back to what I've thought about so often: Jesus the transfigured Word between the secretarial Moses & the illiterate Elijah.

[460] My conception of the literary metaphor as the place of the valley of dry bones, brought to life by recapturing the existential identity suggested but not asserted in it, seems to me a very powerful one.[343] After all, it was there from my beginning as a reader of Blake: when Blake spoke of seeing the world in a grain of sand he wasn't talking about hypothetical statements.[344] And it certainly does something for the whole Eucharist bit.

[461] Some of my later articles, again, are on literature as potentially a technique of meditation. The work as a whole is the seed to be swallowed in the poet's earth: what emerges is the decentralized possession. Works of art are wholes; pills are round.

[462] Also I'd like to outline a theory of the arts, and of such things as painting as the art of the unborn world, in connection with naturata creation. Music as the divergence of vowels from the alphabet.

[463] I must modify my "what are you going to do about it?" thesis (p. 41 [par. 153] and elsewhere). You're not in a position to do anything about a parable until it's become a part of your faith or lifestyle, until it's a metabolized story. I suppose this is what the Sufi & Shah Idries people[345] would say if they could find somebody capable of saying it.

[464] Anxiety over the frustration of primary concern is the reason, or one reason, why ideology corrupts myth so quickly. Nearly all mythol-

ogy expresses this anxiety. The fall story in Genesis has much more sardonic counterparts in Mesopotamia earlier—nothing new here, but the anxiety in myth should be noted. The gods are an aristocracy who do as they like, hence the revolutionary-tribal element in the O.T.

[465] I'm giving up the "science" bit in AC:[346] it's impossible to explain to this generation of critics what I mean. I never did have the analogy of the physical sciences in mind: the model was always social science, man studying himself. What I thought of was a merging of criticism with semiotics and linguistics. When critics keep saying that there can't be a science of criticism, what they're really saying is "I can't and won't write this kind of criticism," and I can't say they're wrong because I can't & won't write it myself. People will write it some day, and I thought it might be a good thing to alert the critics of the 50's to the ultimate end of what they were actually doing. But if it's just a prophecy with no present practical use, the hell with it.

[466] What would a society genuinely based on mythology and primary concern be like? Well, that involves the nature of the contract myth & the Utopian vision—except that all the Utopias we have are ideological. For primary concern, the real outlaws would be the criminals, i.e., the people who violate primary concern by murdering, slandering, stealing & raping. The latter half of the ten commandments. For an ideology the worst "criminals" are always ideological opponents, political prisoners. The people who got burned alive were heretics, coiners & witches, those who threatened or were thought to threaten the monopolies of power of priests, kings & males. "Thou shalt not commit adultery" means, for primary concern, "thou shalt not rape or seduce," because the motive for rape is not sexual but sadistic, a desire to hurt and humiliate. For ideology, of course, adultery means going outside the marriage contract.

[467] The revelation in the Bible is that of the spiritual world, i.e., a table of metaphors. It is not a cosmology: cosmology is the projecting of the spiritually creative on the objective "creation." It (cosmology) means the transfer from mythology to ideology. The Trinity of Antichrist is the false Father, the contract in the past, the false Word, the cosmology of the present, and the false Spirit, the Messianic kingdom of the future.

[468] There must be a dialectical opposition at each stage, of the type

Blake saw in the fire-cloud opposition in the Exodus.[347] The Everlasting Gospel opposes the apostolic succession. The latter is devoted to continuity in time, the former to the liberating of the Spirit. Superstition is founded on the continuity in time, as the etymology of the word indicates. It's founded also on the obliterating of the dialectic. It was superstitious for Vico's giants to think that thunder was the voice of God,[348] but at the baptism of Christ some heard the voice of God and some heard thunder.[349]

[469] I must be careful not to suggest that there ever was a Golden Age of pure mythology and primary concern. Also the third stage of metaphor, the literary and purely hypothetical stage, shouldn't be regarded negatively as a dehydrated or buried-seed stage. Its totality, as an ultimate liberation of prophecy, is the thing to stress.

[470] Romance always involves amnesia and identical twins. Amnesia in the Bible begins with the deluge, the destruction of the "memory" of an age of pure mythology (in quotes because it wasn't in the past). Also the Red Sea crossing. Jesus and Christ are identical twins, in the proper sense of identical, i.e., the same person.

[471] This latter theme has Abram > Abraham and Jacob > Israel for its O.T. types. There, the two names also seem to have the whole-and-part duality that I've ascribed to Christ.

[472] The Book of the Father. Mythology as a part of primary concern. Its relation to ideology. Its metaphorical structure. The three phases of metaphor. The projection of cosmology. The two creation myths: artificial-titanic and sexual-erotic. The projection of contract and the double meaning of law.

[473] The Book of the Word (Son). The stabilizing of myth in wisdom. Mutability Cantoes. The function of literature as the (a) recreation and (b) recovery of mythical kernels in ideology. The conflict in the minds of poets; their authority; their conflicts with ideologies. The theory of the arts as liberated prophecy. The classless society of culture as the everlasting gospel. The projection of the future kingdom: analogies of evolution. The deconstructions of cosmology starting with Vico.

[474] The Book of the Spirit. The two apocalypses and the interchange of wholes and parts. Grand coda of Eros Regained, Adonis Revived, Prometheus Unbound, and Hermes Unsealed.

[475] Naturally these four have been with me from first speculations. Perhaps they're the recoveries of the primary concerns of sex, food, structure (shelter) and freedom (play).

[476] The second part is about the dialectic of "conservative" and "liberal" tendencies, construction & deconstruction, wisdom and prophecy, the cultural tribe (saving remnant) and the empire, the social revolutionary millennial gospel and the imaginative recreation (Exodus & prophecy). Its centre of gravity is the Romantic movement.

[477] The second twist on my Ruth paper,[350] which sweeps up the whole female theme in the Bible, goes under "sex" & Adonis. I suppose each concern has an anxiety attached to it. Graves' white goddess is the anxiety of the black bride; human sacrifice, including tragic heroism in war (Hector & Achilles) is the anxiety of fertility. The anxiety of play is penal activity, which is what most work is. Both capitalist & Marxist ideology touted the work ethic. The arts are play, but players must be workers, according to this ideology, otherwise they're idlers and a threat to something or other.

[478] The first judgment by water & the last by fire: Jesus' baptism by John in water & his conveying the (fiery) Holy Spirit to the disciples. Moses as an infant found in the water: Elijah ascending in a chariot of fire. The deluge myth corresponds to the amnesia of romance: Blake speaks of a deluge of forgotten remembrances [*Jerusalem*, pl. 32, l. 16]. The identical twin theme I've noted one form of, but in the Xn [Christian] view of the O.T. Christ is the dreaming identity behind Moses & David & the rest of them.

[479] Identification by food expands into Eucharist symbolism, which dramatizes the whole-and-part paradox. Identification by sex leads to the mythical raptures & beatific visions of the saints as well as things like Donne's Extasie. Identification by shelter leads to expanding the conception of shelter to include the solidarity of society. Identification by play

would lead to such things as Yeats' dancer-dance image[351]—also to all the business about living *as* the body of one's art. Even Montaigne said his book was consubstantial with himself.[352]

[480] Why aren't clothes a primary concern? I suppose they have shelter, sexual and play links. In the Bible their original function was to conceal the genitals after the loss of innocence.

[481] Such things as the educational contract go in Part Two, as making up the conservative aspect of wisdom (mostly). Castiglione, *Emile* and Anti-Duhring.[353]

[482] Very tentative for the first part:
1. Primary & secondary concern; mythology and ideology; literature recreation & recovery of myth.
2. Existential & hypothetical metaphor; narrowed & expanded identity.
3. Creation & its projection into cosmology. The two Genesis accounts.
4. Contracts & Utopias: summary of the four primary concerns: the myth of fall and rise.

[483] Equally (at least) tentative for the second part:
5. Wisdom and its deconstructions.
6. The authority of the arts
7. Millennial & apocalyptic prophecy (gospel).
8. The two apocalypses: the metaphors of the senses.

[484] I think of Part One as background for Western culture down to Shakespeare, of Part Two as Milton-to-Romanticism, of Part Three as playing the field. But how avoid repetition? I suppose I'd better get it down: the four primary concerns, sex, food, shelter & play are Orc, Tharmas, Urizen & Urthona. Tharmas is a shepherd, Urizen an architect, Urthona a musician, Orc is—well, ὄρχειζ [testicles]. When I get to this stage I go on yattering and doodling forever, and I have to choke it off. Oh well: Urthona's the ear, Urizen eye; taste, smell & touch are strung along the Orc-Tharmas axis.

[485] Mythology, being a product of concern, cannot conflict with science. Only cosmology does that, & then only in an ideological context. I

must get it very clear that the table of metaphors in Revelation is the only genuinely mythological cosmology there is: the others are hierarchies.

[486] My whole conscious life has been purgatorial, a constant circling around the same thing, like a vine going up an elm. I note that I'm repeating even things from earlier pages of this notebook. And "purgatorial" is only a vague hope: maybe I'm not really going up to a final apocalyptic vision but just going in circles, like a senile old man who thinks the two-hundredth repetition of the same old story is new. Perhaps the end is the choking of the host. Well, when it's vertigo to look down and despair to look up, one can only keep going. But there again I'm assuming an up and a down, and assuming I'm going somewhere. Actually I keep revolving around the same place until I've brought off a verbal formulation that I like.

[487] I'm trying to distinguish a millennial vision, which is social & geared to the future (this is what humanity could do if it really tried) from an apocalyptic one, the individual confronted with a present reality he has only to step into. The social vision is approximate freedom, & ends in releasing the individual. The individual who is released, however (a) has to go back to society like a Bodhisattva (b) face his own future of death.

[488] October is my month of performance. For my Sesqui sermon[354] I'll try to find something in Paul that expresses the whole-part interchange. Then apply that to the university. The student qua student is a part of the whole: whatever he studies is the center of all knowledge. The alumnus is a whole, an individual, of which the university education he's had is part. University is connected with universe, that staggering anthropomorphism by which the whole of everything "turns around" us. The illiterate pre-Homeric bards worked in a single dimension: with writing we come to the end of a line and "turn back"; so is "verse" born.

[489] The spiritual life is also a "turning back" to be reborn of water and the spirit. And of course "conversion," with its many analogies in other religions: I think paravritti[355] is the Buddhist one. What's that phrase Carlyle quoted? "Je demande l'arrêt des coquins et des laches."[356]

[490] I must look up Origen & Clement: from what I remember, the

Greeks kept a strong sense of mythology: it was the Romans who sold
out totally to ideology.

[491] If God is a Father, he's the source of our life, life in this context
being probably consciousness. The father impregnates and withdraws:
the embryo has no evidence that he exists; he has evidence only of a
mother. How do you know a father? Get born.

[492] Two: existential metaphor solves the problem: why does culture
not make us morally any better? It also guides us from there into the
question of art as meditation. What do we meditate on? On the mythical
vision (that metaphor again) the work presents.

[493] Why am I obsessed with detective stories? As I've said earlier [par.
427], I've completely forgotten the Freudian explanation I came across
recently. In my own terms (which wouldn't of course exclude Freud) a
really top-flight detective story has two levels of meaning throughout.
Every sentence, every fact given, may be potentially a "clue": it has its
surface meaning in the narrative, and its teleological meaning as a part of
what you "see" in the final cognitio. Also, of course, the descent of the
police as a Last Judgment symbol, searching for the guilt that's in everyone, and the scapegoat as the primal anxiety symbol.

[494] The lost soul has no fear of death. No hope can have no fear, as the
poet says.[357] While there's life there's hope, and life in this context still
rejects nothingness, annihilation, as alien. No life (when life is identified
with anything individual or organic) is immortal. I don't think much of
reincarnation, the prolonging of individual identity, though it may happen sometimes with dying children. The fear of hell is the screen fear, so
to speak, covering our deeper fear of annihilation. Hell is ideological
crap; nothingness is the true myth.

[495] Back to detective stories: how many hundreds of them end with a
confrontation between detective & murderer, the latter's boasting supplying the cognitio, the former eventually foiling the latter's attempt to
kill him. Michael "disputing" with Satan over the body of Moses. As I
said to Jay, non omnis Moriarty.[358]

[496] In the detective story, I said, there's a steady counterpoint of

surface meaning & teleological meaning. Similarly in a Shakespeare play: there's a steady rain of narrative & the feeling that all the repetitions are building up to a final & total picture of the myth. As a picture, of course, the myth is dianoia.

[497] Hopkins' overthought & underthought[359] relate to this. What the process is at bottom is what Derrida's deconstruction really is: the removal of the ideological surface from the palimpsest to get down to the mythological vision. Eliot's burglar's dog-meat image[360] means the ideology often deceives the careless reader or listener, who doesn't bother looking for the myth.

[498] So the panoramic apocalypse, the thematic stasis, the myth as dianoia or picture, represents the end of experience as knowledge. It's normally as far as literature can go, and the dianoia it reaches is a design of hypothetical metaphor. To move on to the seventh phase of participating apocalypse one has to move back to existential metaphor, and let the preceding narrative structure one's life. To do this is to repeat the incarnation, the Word becoming flesh. When the Word's mythos is complete it discarnates, & we attach ourselves to the Spirit that works by metaphor.

[499] I've said that tragedy suggests its own repetition to the audience, and I haven't yet got the role of *ritual* clear in repeating and epiphanizing a myth.

[500] The worst governments are those with double ideologies, where a political doctrine is backed by a religious one, as in Iran. Israel is better, but I'd hate to live even there. But South Africa's apartheid is buttressed by a remarkably dismal Dutch Reformed creed, and fifty years ago the word "Christian" in the name of a political party meant "Roman Catholic Fascist."

[501] Ritual is not really different from mythology: it's a part of it. It's through ritual, I think, that drama and lyric evolve out of the one-dimensional epos drone of narrative. Ritual is primarily the dramatization of myth, but lyric is the form of hymns (the Psalms, the Pindaric odes). The conception of epiphany covers both drama and lyric. In later drama there are two levels of epiphany: the whole drama is one, and the anagnorisis in it is a more intensely focussed one.

[502] Back to square one: a mythos is a story with a social function. The social function is ideology; the shape of the story, which assimilates it to folktales and other direct ancestors of literature, is the "true" myth, at least for my interests. The "meaning" of the "true" myth is its context in mythology.

[503] The Book of the Father sets out the background theory and the structure of the Bible as far as the law. The Book of the Son sets out Biblical structure through to apocalypse and the history-of-ideas skeleton behind Romanticism. It is possible that *all* the major works of literature discussed belong to the Book of the Spirit. Eros R [Regained] could take in all my survival-of-Eros stuff and the white-goddess-black-bride business along with the women-in-the-Bible model. Adonis R [Revived] could deal with the whole Eucharist (food) complex; Prometheus U [Unbound] with the ladder-tower stuff; Hermes perhaps with metamorphosis from the Mutability Cantoes to Yeats. That won't quite work in that form.

[504] All the structural principles of literature point in one direction to the Bible & in the other direction to the total myth—what I used to call the Druid analogy. Could that be the relation of Book Two to Book Three? And if the four in the Spirit Book are on a Zoas cross, is there a similar cross in the first part? Myth, metaphor, contract, Utopia. Doodle, doodle. Six, by the way, should be A Conspectus of Arts in Society: authority's in One.

[505] Food themes in the Bible:
Adam & Eve lived on tree-fruits before the Fall; afterwards he tills the ground from whence he was taken. The economy is partly ranching (Abel) & partly farming (Cain). Noah's sacrifice of animals, which evidently feeds God. Miraculous provision of manna, quails, and water in the desert. Frequent famines under the monarchy, and human sacrifices at the barley harvest. Passover (the primary blood-offering), harvest & vintage sacrificial festivals. Famine is aggravated by locust-plagues & the like. Samson & the Philistine crops.
Jesus repeats the miraculous feeding of the multitudes: contrast between O.T. physical types and the spiritual bread & water of life. The Cana wedding & the symbolism of "new wine." Blood & water of the spirit. Institution of the Eucharist: O taste & see that the Lord is good

(Psalm 34). Note how, as the structure becomes increasingly spiritualized, the primitive Frazerian formula of eating the God-Man's body gets re-captured. (This is part of the regular dialectic of myth.) The sacramental analogy and the final invitation in Revelation to drink of the water of life.[361]

The Frazer theme is closely connected with the dragon-killing image: leviathan becomes food for the chosen people. In eating the external environment becomes internalized: hence the massacres of Israel's treading of the winepress and the harvest & vintage of the nations in Revelation (13?)[362] are a type of the disappearance of man into the body of God.

[506] I suppose excretion is inevitably part of the eating process in symbolism, as it is in life. Of course the apocalyptic separation of heaven and hell is the ultimate shit: I suppose after that the reproductive and excretory processes get separated. Hell is a place of shit from Dante to Pound. The assimilation of the two processes symbolizes the pre-apocalyptic mixture of life and death.[363] I find it hard to believe that the man who wrote the first three chapters of Revelation could also have written the rest of the book, but the imagery fits: Laodicea makes God puke[364] because its lukewarmness suggests the urgency of getting heaven and hell separated.

[507] The deluge is polarized between building the ark & collecting all the animals to put inside it (the undisplaced ark is Noah's body) and the holocaust of animals to feed God afterwards. After God says "man, that's good," he tells Noah he can have them all back for his own food [Genesis 7–8]. That's meat: Noah can safely be left to discover wine for himself.

[508] We never get myth free of anxiety, and therefore of ideology. That's why the legal metaphor of trial and judgment runs right through the Bible from beginning to end. Of course there's the crucial distinction between crime and sin: that's part of the argument of Job, who's innocent of crime but can hardly be sinless.[365]

[509] Similarly, Jesus was without crime, though considered the worst of criminals by society. But he can't have been sinless: that's a sterile conception. You can't live in the devil's world without making friends with the mammon of unrighteousness. Even in Job the presence of Satan in God's court is tolerable. If Jesus were sinless he'd have been discarnate.

The Crucifixion convicts the entire world of sin, but Christ takes responsibility for the sin. The Virgin Mary can't have been sinless in that context either: that, I gather, is why St. Thomas Aquinas denied the Immaculate Conception.

[510] Saying that even Jesus couldn't have been totally sinless when incarnate is what Paul says: nobody can completely observe the law. The O.T. keeps sin & crime parallel: the sins are *ritual* offenses, breaking the first five commandments. In the N.T. crime is a by-product of sin. The punishment of crime is always symbolically death: being stuck in a prison isn't death, but it's burial. Curious how often burial precedes death: the nursing homes we put the aged and senile into have invisible welcoming inscriptions saying "Come now, time you were dead."

[511] Trying to reduce the beautiful to the functional is the moral anxiety of the ideologue, just as trying to reduce sexual love to potentially "fruitful" marriage is. The formula I picked up from the Critique of Judgment, "purposiveness without purpose," puts the emphasis on *structure*, not function.[366]

[512] God, another ten pages still to go:[367] I'll never live to fill another notebook at this rate.

[513] The moralist, of course, wants to create as many categories of crime as he can, and reduce sin to crime wherever possible. Hence the importance of the redeemed harlot story that's smuggled into John 8. Making adultery a crime is usually a part of the anxiety of male domination, as in Moslem countries, & so is part of the sado-sexual set-up. Here I have to walk carefully and without guidance, because even Blake couldn't get rid of dominant-male anxieties. He saw them in Milton, but remains largely unaware of the overtones of phrases like "the disobedient female" in himself [*Jerusalem*, pl. 69, l. 38].

[514] The first acts of creation, light & firmament, interrupt the Spirit brooding on the waters: they manifest the indignant Son pushing the naughty father away from fucking the still naughtier mother. (Note I Enoch on upper & lower waters as male & female.)[368] Enuma elish is displaced too, but not quite as far.[369] Note too the greater antiquity of the mother: trees were created before sun & moon & stars. The vegetable world is the primordial female, the sky the primordial male, & between

them they create all the animals, including man. This is influence or separation fucking, & according to Wisdom its powers are wholesome and free from death.³⁷⁰

[515] In the second account, Adam is made from the female *adamah* [dust of the ground, earth], and Eve, the spiritual (i.e. conscious) female springs from him. The fall resulted from a conspiracy between Eve & the subtle serpent, who replaces the concealed dragon of the first account. The upshot was the serpent-and-tree domination of the white-goddess cycle, turning Adam into the Adonis figure manifested in Abel. The adamah was under a curse until after the flood, so the flood must have something to do with the breaking of the cycle.³⁷¹

[516] In *The Tempest* there's Sycorax, a Tiamat figure, & the three goddesses created by Prospero as a kind of halo for Miranda.³⁷² One of them is the rainbow, and I think they're post-diluvian. And they'll have nothing to do with Venus and her white-goddess cycle.

[517] The reason why detectives in detective stories are so preternaturally intelligent is that they're angels. Guardian angels of society; avenging angels for the murderer. Everyone is guilty of something, so all the major characters are suspects.

[518] I've often noticed that great novelists, from Jane Austen to Henry James, are conventional to the verge of prissiness. There are many reasons for this: one is that novelists deal directly with people under ideology. The ideology is usually shaped by both the author and his public. Novelists who are aware of another perspective (myth) are rare: Dickens is one.

[519] The fourth category of concern, "play," has two aspects at least. One is liberty, which is ultimately an individual concern, as real liberty can be experienced only by the individual. The other is equality, a primarily social concern much closer to ideology. Equality has its centre of gravity in the category of law, as equality before the law is the root of all equality. Liberty has its centre in wisdom, the law permeating the individual: the ultimate expression of wisdom as play is in GC.³⁷³

[520] Fraternity, which I've stressed so much, has its centre in exodus or revolution: revolutionaries call each other comrades. A revolution, or at

least the Biblical one, is tribal, and it settles in the top rank of society when the counter-revolutionary establishment appears, as it inevitably does. Arnold's term for the aristocracy, "barbarians," points to the tribal.[374] Besides aristocracies, there are priesthoods and sacerdotal tribal groups of "brothers" and "sisters." Another fraternal development is the guild or craft or caste, the tribal in terms of social function. The fact that every tribal group is or appears to be potentially conspiratorial accounts for certain aspects of anti-Semitism, the Jews being scapegoats for the Nazis who could project their own tribalism on them. Similarly with the "illuminati" and freemason scapegoat myths.[375] Sparta is the archetype of the tribal: the efforts to graft Athenian ideals on it, which extend from Plato to Castiglione and beyond, are bound to fail.

[521] The myth of creation has, as its ideological aspect, the chain of being hierarchy. Wisdom in its higher reaches moves back to recapture the rationale of creation, as in Proverbs 7 and 8. It understands creation as divine play, which is imitated by man in the arts.

[522] The primary myth of sex is the existential metaphor of union in one body, Donne's ecstasy. Their (the lovers') separation into two bodies repeats, oddly, the creation of Eve from the body of the adam.[376] Similarly in Marvell's garden: the primary food-and-sex union with Nature is ended by the creation of Eve. The pure myth is that of consciousness united with the body of Nature: two sexes in humanity indicates the split in consciousness that develops self-consciousness. With ideology, all sex becomes sex in the head.[377]

[523] The ideology of sex begins with the concern for reproduction, more particularly of males who are to be sacrificed as soldiers or priests. Hence the later-birth themes of Isaac (also associated with sacrifice), Samuel (the priesthood) and perhaps Cain, the first killer, and therefore the first "hero" or warrior. What develops from this is the anxiety of continuity, which is repeated in wisdom. Prophecy is the final form of the divine interruption into precedent and primogeniture. The late or miraculous births of John the Baptist and Jesus, the last prophets, show this clearly.

[524] I've often mentioned how artists and writers form schools and groups & issue manifestoes, but as they get more authority they indi-

vidualize and the groups disintegrate. This dialectic repeats the Exodus-Law > Wisdom one and also the prophecy > gospel one. Prophecy voices a social concern even if the prophet has emerged from a school of prophets: the Gospel individualizes prophecy just as wisdom individualizes law. There is no group wisdom, though the wise must recognize each other: there is no church except in the mutual recognition of those who respond to prophecy. I'm getting away from my track here: I'm thinking of the analogy (only it's more than that) of prophecy & the arts. I suppose that puts the individualized gospel in the hands of critics: not much of a prospect.

[525] Try to figure out the reason for the contrast between two types of myth. The bride from the strange land is the theme of Ruth and SS [Song of Songs], which seems remarkable considering Jewish xenophobia and the end of Ezra-Nehemiah [Ezra 10; Nehemiah 13:23–7]. But they adjusted to it on the proviso that the bride (Psalm 45) totally but totally forgets all her previous sub-Jewish life.[378] I suppose the archetype here must be Israel, conceived as the female chosen by God, making her way from Egypt to the Promised Land. The other theme, which isn't Biblical, is the male lover going in search of the imperilled female, as in the St. George-Perseus and Prince Charming stories. Solveig[379] too. This is the Eliot Figlia archetype.[380]

[526] And yet the gospels are all about the shepherd searching for the lost sheep, which in the table of metaphors is the bridegroom searching for the bride in dangerous places (i.e. the world of incarnation, the belly of the leviathan). So the centrifugal, proselytizing Christian development is the opposite of the O.T. one, with its central sacred place. But in Coronation of the Virgin pictures, which of course are post-Biblical iconography, the head of the creature world has come from that world to the home of Christ.[381] (In the logic of metaphor, the Virgin is only Christ's mother in the lower world of incarnation: in the post-apocalyptic separated heaven she's both bride and daughter.) Incidentally, did Job's three new daughters proceed from a second wife? Clearly they did, unless the Blakean theme of the absence of a mother in the spiritual world goes all the way and we're back to the original adam with Eve inside him.

[527] Re the dropped reference to Eliot [par. 525]: curious how the early

poems revolve around the figure of a male descending steps and abandoning a female who's usually a kind of complementary existence. In Portrait of a Lady she's an aging spinster, in Prufrock the "you" of the love song, in Gerontion an even more shadowy "you."[382] Sweeney & his hysterical girl friend; the old nurse or whatever in the Cooking Egg; the climb to the Virgin in Ash Wednesday; the elusive parental figures in Burnt Norton: a lot of it's prefabricated crap, but there's no mistaking the recovery of the daughter in Marina, the *Pericles* reversal of *Lear*.

[528] In the primary concern of shelter the mother is everywhere, because shelter is connected with the embryonic life. The paleolithic cave-drawings are embryonic;[383] so are the megalithic temples and the Jewish cunt-shaped temple with its veil over the secret place. All this is pure Blake, of course. Play, in contrast, is the release from the shelter, the activity of those who are born. So the shelter-play concern is a Yeatsian double gyre, and also the oscillation I've mentioned so often between the happiness of withdrawing and the happiness of belonging (individual & social).

[529] The food-sex concern is another double gyre: food is a separation ending in union; sex is a union followed by separation. The separation aspect of eating is excretion, & in sex we use the excretory organs for union. In the shelter-play gyre the embryo is, like food, within another body, and separation is the beginning of (play) life. So all the primary concerns oscillate between assimilating and separating. The artist assimilates the content of nature into form, then releases his work to the public. The shelter-embryo link is the source of my hunch that painting is an embryonic art, the art of the unborn world.

[530] There ought to be a division of ideologies or secondary concerns too. The ideological descendant of play is the work ethic, activity of a more or less penal type for its own sake. Genuine work is, of course, a preliminary of play.

[531] Or perhaps there's a distinction corresponding to my parody and manifest demonic. Work (penal) is parody; leisure, in the sense of gentlemen just buggering around, is the manifest form.

[532] The ideological parody of shelter (which goes on in the embryonic

brain of Urizen imprisoned within the skull) is the tomb of the dead God-Man (the pyramids) or the temple of the invisible god, who may or may not descend to screw his bride on the top storey.

[533] The concern of sex descends to the notion that sex isn't play but work, i.e., activity with another end in view of producing children. What I call the exploiting of the genital machinery is the manifest demonic form—whoring, that is. Naturally in whoring other forms of exploitation are involved too. I've said elsewhere that males who are potential sacrificial objects for war or priesthood are preferred [par. 523]. Close your eyes and think of England, dear: that's ideological fucking.

[534] The concern of food descends to the Frazer archetype of eating & drinking the God-Man. That I think is the parody form, the manifest form being the invisible God who snuffs up the smoke of animals when he can't get humans. Later he adds harvests & vintage to his diet. And none shall appear before me empty [Exodus 34:20].

[535] I suppose all these concerns finally consolidate into a concern for money. One stores up or spends money—sexual metaphors: one invests it & lives on its increase—crop metaphors; one buys possessions with it—food metaphors; or has a good time with it (play metaphors).[384] Misers think only of sheltering it—not themselves until after, which is the sacrificial mentality.

[536] The whole-part paradox goes under identity as (the individual with the whole a part of him) and with (individual as part of the greater whole). In other words, in Chapter Two.

[537] The reaction of the fall to creation produced the two major anxieties of place and time that form the themes of Ulysses' two languages in TC [*Troilus and Cressida*, 1.3.55–184]. Place means finding your allotted level in the hierarchy, neither up there nor down there, though constantly aware of their influence on you & your responsibility to them. Time is the anxiety of continuity projected into the future. These go in Chapter Three. The Sermon on the Mount takes an extremely dim view of both: we are urged to take no thought for the morrow and it's clear that the lilies in the field don't worry about their place in the chain of being. I suppose the whole social set-up down to Rousseau rested on the

assumption that the class structure of society was a replication of the chain of being. This is part of the pun on "law" that I keep falling over.[385]

[538] Another possible text for the October sermon[386] is Genesis 2:19. It is suggested that God, after creating animals third, brought them to Adam "to see what he would call them." God takes a friendly interest in man's struggles to control his environment with words. Curiosity too: there's no question here of "omniscience." The adam is repeating the act of creation by the word: the passage speaks only of names, but the adam is already creating a mythological envelope around himself. We don't meet language of that kind of innocence in the Bible until we hit the discourses of Jesus in the synoptic gospels. See p. 132 [par. 456].

[539] Shelter & construction: painting as an embryonic art I have. I've also often spoken of the way that technology creates introversion. The dark movie theatres & bedrooms[,] dark except for the ghostly flickering television tube, the counterpart to the skull with its rain of pictures and sounds.

[540] Time is specifically the enemy of sex: Marvell's Coy Mistress, the lemans & paramours of the Gardens of Adonis, and of course many poems of Donne. Thus the fall, which was primarily a fall of sex, brought the sense of time and the anxiety of continuity (with its past and future projections) into the world. Meditation (see the Fifth Walk of Rousseau's reveries) first turns off the sound, then the moving pictures, and when they're gone the kernel of play is left, energy without alienation.

[541] A lot of things are still a haze, but the essence of the book should be the dialectic of Word and Spirit: the particular revelation in the Bible expanded and supplemented by the universal revelation of literature. I see two chapters at the beginning with relative clarity: I should, as I've covered the ground half a dozen times. One is on myth, ideology and concern; the other is on metaphor and identity.

[542] Then Genesis & Exodus: creation projected as cosmology & the tribal or saving remnant revolution. This revolves around the Promethean and Urizenic concern for what I call shelter, but is really the concern for *place*. Then the law-wisdom concern (Urthona & Hermes) which is the concern for freedom, or what I call play. Then the prophecy-gospel

sexual concern for union oscillating with independence. The Eros-Orc area, where the whole-and-part paradox comes into focus. Finally the food concern, which ends in the apocalyptic vision of a spiritual body. Tharmas-Adonis.[387] Of course all concerns are united in the apocalypse, just as all anxieties are generated by the fall: food in the tilling of the (cursed) ground, sex in the coming of shame, shelter in the deluge myth (the wanderer with no home or place) and play in the fall of language. All of this sounds unconvincing even to me: but I hope and pray that some aspects of genuine insight are there, and that the Spirit will guide me through the Word. So on New Year's Day, 1986, I finish the notebook I filled in the wrong direction.

Notebook 44

Most of this notebook was written during the time Frye was working on Words with Power, *the earliest entries dating from about 1986 and the latest from a month or so before his death in January 1991. The last forty-nine entries were written after Frye had completed the manuscript for* Words with Power, *and some of these entries relate to material in* The Double Vision. *The notebook is located the NFF, 1993, box 1.*

[1] Orare est laborare.[1] Working at what one can do is a sacrament.

[2] I visualize a book in two parts and eight chapters. The first part would be called something like "The Primary Verbal Structures."
   Chapter One: Mythology, Ideology and Concern.
   Chapter Two: Metaphor and Identity.
   Chapter Three: Structures of Accommodation.
      (Creation, Law, Prophecy, Revelation).
   Chapter Four: Structures of Response.
      (Exodus, Wisdom, Gospel, Enlightenment).

[3] One:[2] Myths are stories with a specific social function. The function is the growing point of an ideology, which develops toward thesis language and is transmitted by philosophers, theologians, legislators, etc.

[4] The story element in myth (*mythos*) links it to folktales. The function of literature is to recreate the myth behind the ideology. All poets are affected by the ideologies of their time, but criticism discovers layers of

meaning (Hopkins' underthought and overthought,[3] Derrida's deconstruction) distinguishing the two.

[5] His contact with myth is the basis for the poet's authority. But poets don't know that, and they often adopt very foolish ideologies as part of their resistance.

[6] I think mythology expresses the primary human concerns, and ideology the secondary and derivative ones. It seems to me at the moment that the primary concerns have four main kernels: food, sex, shelter and play.[4] Food expands into a concern with bodily identity; shelter into construction and creation; play is the free energy that work is aimed at.

[7] The language of ideology, being thesis-language, contains its own opposite. Ideology functions properly in a tolerance that tries to contain the opposite. Dogmas that exclude the opposite are pernicious. The worst are those that back up political dogma with a religious or quasi-religious one.

[8] Religion may be an "ultimate" concern, as Tillich says:[5] it can't be a primary one.[6] We can't live a day without being concerned about food, but we can live all our lives without being concerned about God, impoverished as such a life would be.

[9] Faith being a secondary concern, faith and doubt interpenetrate. "There is a God" already contains the statement "there is no God." Dogma, accepting one and forbidding the other, creates hysteria, as it disturbs an imaginary social consensus to admit the opposite.

[10] We've reached several ideological deadlocks in history. Communism in my youth (the depression period) was widely assumed to be both more efficient and morally superior compared to capitalism. But capitalism didn't evolve into communism: the two systems settled down into an adversary relation in which they could improve themselves only by borrowing features from each other. The Reformation produced a similar deadlock.[7]

[11] The hysteria of dogmatism results from asserting that the mind is

unified when it's actually divided. The next stage is pathological, projecting the minority voice on someone else. Thus the Jew became the scapegoat for the voice inside the Nazi that kept saying "this racism is a lot of crap, and you know it." Faith made wholly ideological, and separated from primary concerns, turns into anxiety. Some of this of course is fairly harmless.

[12] Three: I'd originally thought of calling this chapter "Creation and Cosmology." Myth is not a proto-science, and can't conflict with science because it doesn't make pseudo-scientific statements. But when myth, under ideological influence, expands into cosmology, the situation is very different. Then, we do have to decide whether the earth goes round the sun or vice versa. As with gods no longer believed in, a refuted cosmology becomes a purely poetic structure.

[13] In Genesis there are two creation myths, one explicitly and the other implicitly divided into seven phases. Thus:

	Priestly[8]	Jahwist[9]
1.	Light	"Mist" in dry ground.
2.	Firmament in waters	Body of the adam
3.	Land & sea; vegetation	Garden
4.	Heavenly "lights."	Waters (four rivers).
5.	Creatures of water & air	Animals & birds
6.	Land animals, including humans	Creation of woman
7.	Day of rest	State of innocence.[10]

[14] On the fourth day light expands into "lights" in P, and in J the fourth act expands "mist" into four rivers. In J human beings are in quite a different category from anything else: Kabbalists & others assumed that the original adam was androgynous, because a male body assumes a female one already in existence.[11]

[15] The P account stresses division and discrimination: land from sea, light from darkness. In short, it's a vision of *natura naturata*, the kernel of the conception of nature as a structure or system.[12]

[16] Two proto-myths are enfolded in the P account: one, as is generally recognized, is the myth of creation as the killing of the dragon of chaos. This is alluded to in the Psalms & prophets.[13] The other is the myth of the

son standing straight up to push apart his naughty fucking parents. Here the "firmament" separates two "waters" (male and female according to Enoch).[14]

[17] There is no full story attached to P in Genesis, but eventually it becomes clear that there is one: the titanic revolt of angelic forces turning demonic. This hardly gets explored before the Romantic movement.

[18] The J account, with its gardens and rivers and emphasis on human sexuality, is a vision of *natura naturans*. The adam combines the mist ('d) and blood (dm). The creation of Eve is the creation of sexual man (humanity). Eve initiates the fall, i.e. man falls as sexual being: hence man must be redeemed by women (the Virgin in Catholic thought). The earthly paradise is a vision in which all four concerns merge. Food is abundant; sex is accessible; shelter needs no construct; play is there from the start, not reached after work. It's therefore primarily a vision of regenerated nature.

[19] The two myths of creation don't give us a history of how the order of nature came into being—that is, they're not pseudo-scientific competitors of such conceptions as evolution and the DNA molecule. When I speak of four major concerns I'm halfway into ideology already: the earthly paradise, as I've just said, combines them all. Where religion & science can still get together is on the conception of the objective world as an "unfolding" of an "enfolded" or unborn order, which is beyond time and space as we experience them. David Bohm's book, *Wholeness and the Implicate Order*,[15] has something on this. I suppose this is what I reach in HSU.[16]

[20] The primitive verbal basis of myth is the kind of pre-Homeric ethos which is improvised on formulaic units by an illiterate bard who, because he is illiterate, isn't thinking of lines on a page. Writing creates the "turn" from one line to another preserved in the word "verse."[17] (Note that prose, the purest form of written expression, reestablishes endlessness.) It's through *ritual* that the fragmented forms, lyric & drama, crystallize from epos.

[21] Exodus is a social response, and consolidates law; wisdom is an individual response, and consolidates prophecy; gospel is both social

and individual, and consolidates the everlasting gospel, revelation, the panoramic apocalypse, the vision of plenitude, the totality of metaphor and universal interpenetration. The final step, where all duality is erased, is the recreation of the world in its original form.

[22] The fact that the gospel is both social & individual makes it particularly the area of the alternation of whole and part perspectives. Christ is the whole man of whom we are all parts: I am a whole individual of whom "Christ in me" [Galatians 2:20] is obviously a part.

[23] I'm naturally interested in the rapprochement of religion and science, but the Tao of Physics people seem to grab something denatured and out of its cultural context from Taoism or Zen or Vedanta.[18] I think cultural specifics like exodus and gospel mean something, and I want to use them.

[24] These people (David Bohm, Karl Pribram) also talk about dismantling the ego-centered thinker.[19] What interests me here is the old chestnut about criticism as a parasitic activity. Perhaps criticism is the opposite of parasitism: it tries to be a transparent medium for the poets, many of whom are in the "egotistical sublime" area.[20] For some writers, at least, the ego may be a necessary spark plug to get the engine turning over. But the egocentric critic (Leavis) is apt to be a judging critic, perverting the whole operation.[21]

[25] Well, I've certainly said a good deal about the way the ego buggers up the creative insight, in, for instance, Yeats and Whitman. The present critical scene is typical of what the scrambling of egos produced: a sense of infinite complications where you'd have to master (note that word) five hundred books before you could even get started.

[26] It's doubtless my own ego that wonders why critics didn't feel more called to order by the piece I did for the PMLA centenary.[22]

[27] As ideology is built into mythology, I can't call it a degeneration. Still, take this from Angelus ad Virginem:
   Quomodo conciperem
   Cum virum non cognovi?   (Gospel).
   Qualiter infringerem
   Quod firma mente vovi?   (Priest crap).[23]

Perhaps it's just Nonconformist prejudice, but I don't believe the gospels stress the virginity of any woman except Mary, and what they stress about her is pregnancy. The gospels (synoptic, anyway) are an amazing purification of myth, but nothing is flawless in this world: certainly not the documents of revelation.

[28] It's ironic that Marxism, which tried to define ideology as the rationalizings of non-Marxists, should have turned into the one movement of our day that absolutizes ideology.

[29] Structures of concern can't be rationalized: the incest taboo isn't based on any intuitive knowledge of what inbreeding results in: and the horror of sodomy, beyond the fact that ass-fucking is a dirty business, is not because it's "unnatural" but because it's a parody of Jesus with his male beloved disciple, his "don't touch me" as his last words to a woman,[24] and his (or somebody's) insistence that his mother was a virgin and his father not his father.

[30] *Two* is metaphor, taken in two contexts. Metaphor, because it's a statement of identity, goes in two directions. First, it's the central and typical figure of speech. If you take out the "is" and reduce it to straight juxtaposition, it becomes the kernel of all centripetal apprehensions of words and of the "literary" aspect of all words whatever.[25]

[31] The other direction starts off with the hearing in time followed by seeing in space business. We hear a joke and then we "see" it.[26] We read the Bible and then see the apocalypse, a total body of interpenetrating metaphors. Not a cosmology, though cosmologies descend from it.

[32] A literary metaphor is hypothetical only: this was as far as I got with the AC set up. But Theseus' lunatic & lover are behind the poet, suggesting an existential identity beyond the literary kind. The relation of the existential lover and the hypothetical identity of the metaphor is deeply involved in poetry (Donne's Canonization and Extasie). Theseus is trying to keep it all within the orbit of his authority, hence "lunatic," but mystical identity above time and space is what's involved.[27]

[33] It follows, of course, that every work of literature is a meditative focus. One can develop the hypothetical seed of metaphor into another dimension. This is a very long shot so far: I've always thought of identifi-

cation *with the literature*, putting yourself in place of the hero, as the depth of absurd immaturity; clearly I mean something else.

[34] The Major Verbal Structures:
   1. Structures of Concern.
   2. Structures of Identity.
   3. Structures of Accommodation.
   4. Structures of Response.

[35] Myths of primary concern are close to wish-fulfilments. Anxieties resulting from the frustration or uncertainty make up nine-tenths of mythical activity. Anxiety about food produces human sacrifices, for example. Anxiety is different, though it may develop, from inhibition. The inhibition about eating in deference to time, eating *then*, when it's "time" to eat, instead of now, has a lot to do with the development of consciousness, as the mind organizes the reflexes of the body.

[36] Myth is the unfolding of the enfolded metaphor; criticism tries to reverse the process and reconstitute the original "undisplaced" form. But narrative, being sequential, has to be strung out along a temporal framework, after which it tries to indicate its "enfolded" shape, as with the epic that begins in the "middle" (*hamothen*)[28] and then indicates a cyclical form.

[37] The Holy Blood and the Holy Grail[29] is an extraordinary piece of Romantic Esauism, a counter-myth of Jesus as the returning rightful heir. I'm not shocked by the suggestion that Jesus had a physical wife & children, but his "blood line" would have got mixed in average humanity pretty damn soon. It's just one more guess about the historical Jesus, derived from Gospels that don't care about the historical Jesus.[30]

[38] What the book did for me was clarify the prophet-gospel connection. As man, Jesus was of the line of prophets, Moses & Elijah. The gospel is the response to his prophecy in the form of deifying him.[31] A successful Melchizedek priest-king would have been merely another deified Caesar: anything but a spiritual king would have annihilated the prophet. And a purely human prophet, of course, would have had no power to *save*: only myth can do that. And so gospel leads on to objectified apocalypse: the vision of what has been saved.

[39] AC demonstrated that realism was a "displacement" of a mythical structure [*AC*, 136–8, 155–6, 178]. For this book I'll think in terms of "unfolding." A myth, in its turn, is the unfolding or temporal sequentializing of a metaphor, and a metaphor is the unfolding of an identity into two or more bodies. At that point one organizing conception of the book, enfolding and unfolding, merges with the other, the interchange of whole and part.

[40] The *Gestalt* of a complex metaphor is the closest we can get to the sense of the integrity of a verbal structure. Integrity is not, or doesn't commit one to, a cult of holism. I have an integrity, as long as I'm alive, that I won't have after I'm dead. But it doesn't follow that, with my deafness, fallen arches, burpy stomach and limp prick, I'm a "perfect whole." The critic looks for the inner integrity which is also the vitality of the literary work. At the top level—Dante, Shakespearean romance—this includes a very high degree of wholeness in the imagery. But the wholeness isn't an end in itself: it just leads more readily to higher levels.

[41] On the literal level the literary work is withdrawn from its context: on the allegorical level its context is verbal but non-literary; on the tropological level it's where I try to put it, in the AC & elsewhere, in its literary context; on the anagogic it's reached the level of interpenetration.[32]

[42] The undergraduate of a university is a part of a whole; the alumnus is a whole of which his university experience is part. Closer to the Christ paradox of Paul is Adam & Eve before the fall, when they were part of Eden; for regenerate man Eden is a state of mind within him. That's the "swallowing" business I fell over in Milton & applied to the relation of literature to experience.[33]

[43] One reason why the response to creation is exodus is that a revolutionary society is a created or made society. Other civilizations seem to have just grown, like Topsy.[34]

[44] Criticism approaches a literary work which is a metaphor-cluster made explicit. Why do we need the critic? Because there's so much implicit in the metaphor-cluster that he didn't make explicit. Mainly, of course, the relation of context, to other cultures of words. "Deconstruction" is such a dreary negative word for all this.

[45] The part-whole shift of perspective takes off from the metaphorical kernel of food. What surrounds us is "uneaten," unassimilated, the Leviathan who's eaten us. That's why we're invited to drink at the end of the apocalypse.[35] And while I suppose all four concerns are enfolded & unfolded, play seems the most direct one: we work to acquire the skill to play.

[46] I suppose the unfolding of a life is play, really. The unfolding metaphor would accommodate Spengler, with his culture-organisms developing from a seed he can only express by a symbol: in fact every phenomenon peculiar to a culture is a symbol of it.[36]

[47] Structures of accommodation are objectified, presented *as though* they were objective. Structures of response, whether individual or communal, are presented as though they were subjective. (The social is not a true object.) Only in the participating apocalypse does this duality disappear. Shelter kernel, maybe, which develops into construction and technology, objects that are extensions of a subject. That would leave metaphorical identity as the unfolding of the sex kernel.

[48] Wisdom in the Bible is an outgrowth of Torah, instruction, the completion of the knowledge of good and evil in its genuine form. Biblical wisdom is not just wisdom, not the wisdom of Egypt or Sumeria, any more than its Yahweh is Ptah or Enki.[37] It has affinities, of course, but not to the point of blurring its identity. That's why Hebrew wisdom develops dialectically into prophecy, which again is Biblical prophecy, not Zoroaster or Tiresias prophecy. All religions are one, not alike: a metaphorical unity of different things, not a bundle of similarities. In that sense there is no "perennial philosophy": that's a collection, at best, of denatured techniques of concentration.[38] As doctrine, it's platitude: moral maxims that have no application. What there is, luckily, is a perennial struggle.

[49] One thing that HBHG book[39] did for me was start me thinking about the vividness and integrity of mythical history, e.g., the British history that revolves around Arthur. When I picked it up I thought oh God: not *another* book about Cathars and Templars and Grail romances and Freemasons and Rosicrucians. It was, but it was better than most such books because it was hitched onto an Antichrist figure.

[50] So far I've considered only the negative Antichrist, in Blake's terms, the deified Caesar who's only Caligula or Nero dead. I've not thought seriously about the *contrary* Christ, the Herrnmoral [*Herrenmoral*] Nietzchean Antichrist of the "bloodline."[40] Such a Christ would be as Nietzsche saw, a Dionysus, a dying and reviving god, not a god of resurrection. Margaret Murray's horned god[41] would be another form of such a figure: it didn't exist as the centre of an actual cult, I should think, but as an informing myth it would have great power. That is, there wasn't any horned god on one dimension of reality, but the witch-hunting torturers had one in their minds, in whose name they were committing their atrocities, & who responded to them from the women they tortured.

[51] In Blake, as I understand it, contraries combine, and when they do the negation is defined as that. What would this antithetical Christ (in Yeats's sense)[42] be when finally separated from its brutal and murky parodies, a negation that justifies all terror and cruelty and is rationalized by occult faith? A continuously dying and reviving figure at work in the world: perhaps the Holy Spirit that continues to speak by the prophets and is *not* a captive of the Church.

[52] The principle of contrary and negation might extend to the knowledge of good and evil, which again I've been considering a pure negation. The phrasing of Isaiah in his great Emmanuel prophecy shows that this is not necessarily so [Isaiah 7:14–16]. The knowledge of good and evil can also be the basis for Torah, instruction, knowledge especially of law.

[53] I've said many times that man is born lost in a forest. If he is obsessed by the thereness of the forest, he stays lost and goes in circles; if he assumes the forest is not there, he keeps bumping into trees. The wise man looks for the invisible line between the is and the is not which is the way *through* [GC, 124]. The street in the city, the highway in the desert, the pathway of the planets through the labyrinth of the stars, are parallel forms—see the title of my *Festschrift*.[43] Note how Yeats' Dialogue of Self & Soul splits between a soul who seeks the not-there and a self who returns to the there, and accepts, like Nietzsche, going in circles as a heroic occupation.[44]

[54] Similarly, it's in the third or hypothetical or literary phase of myth

that a myth can become a *model*, a hypothetical being that neither is nor is not.

[55] The P account of creation is Promethean, stressing forethought, construction, and discrimination. The J account is Erotic, with its climax the sexualizing of humanity. It is this aspect of creation that is recreated in the Song of Songs, just as the Promethean aspect is recreated in the rebuilding of the temple.

[56] If I'm on solid enough ground here, then the archetypal Adonis myth is the story of Noah and the deluge: death and rebirth through a saving remnant, the "antithetical" Christ as the Holy Spirit brooding on the water and eventually establishing an agricultural cycle and discovering wine. This ties up the cycle of water-to-water, in Graves' phrase, that I assimilated to the "ark" symbolism in the O.T.—well, the new also.[45]

[57] Now into bog again: the Hermes myth is the polluting and cleansing of the temple. Hermes Unsealed is the veil of the temple torn, the ark of the covenant opened in heaven, the metaphorical identifying of the temple with the body of Christ. So the theme starts with the Tower of Babel, I suppose.[46]

[58] But I have an uneasy suspicion that I'm making the same oversimplified mistake I made in FS and GC: establishing the polarizing of the apocalyptic and demonic and not paying enough attention (a) to the contraries (b) to the analogy of Generation identified by Christianity with the Old Testament.

[59] In dreams a house usually means the body, and the polluted temple is pure dream (Ezekiel 8:12).[47] The actualized temple is a building, an inanimate object: the temple comes to life (through death) as the risen body of Christ. The imagery is parallel to the Pygmalion-Winter's Tale myth of a statue coming to life. Note that in Ezekiel the vision of the polluted temple follows on the tremendous opening vision of the chariot-Word, the animate machine of wheels that can go where it likes all over the world [Ezekiel 1] (the four Zoas as evangelists, in this context).

[60] So now I'm wondering if mythology and ideology aren't contraries, the clash of which precipitates the persecuting ideology. In that case

mythology and ideology would be the gospels of the "Devils" and "Angels" of MHH [*The Marriage of Heaven and Hell*]. But an ideology that was a "contrary" would itself possess a sub-contrary: the antithesis contained in the thesis. Similarly, there's a subcontrary in myth: the phony class-ascendancy myth.

[61] Between Genesis 2:3 and 2:4 commentary has decided that there's a lacuna: the story of the fall that fits the P account, the revolt of the angels and the fall of demonic (titanic) powers. This insertion makes the role of the serpent in the *human* fall of Adam and Eve more intelligible. Hence *Paradise Lost*. The hell the devils fall into is in some contexts nothingness: hence I think the suggestion that Mallarmé's Igitur refers to Genesis 2:3 is imaginatively correct.[48] In any case the real demonic is pre-human.

[62] *The Turn of the Screw* is placed in an Edenic setting with preternatural children. Quint & Jessel are the "evil" forces dragging them backward; the governess is the "angel" pulling them forward into experience, equally destructive & menacing. The fairy-tale setting gives us the withdrawn master who won't & can't be bothered about anything. One can oversimplify the story by reading Q & J as objective haunting evil spirits, or by reading everything as the governess's neurotic projections, who creates the evil she thinks she fears. Notice what a high opinion of her the man has who reads her story to the group. And Miles *was* kicked out of school: it's not simple neurosis.[49]

[63] I've often noticed how stories with a strong mythical (plot) emphasis are placed in a framework, or are assumed to be told to the writer, or discovered by him in a drawer, etc. Look up that Storm story, where there are four or five wrappings.[50] It's as though we were supposed to dig for the story underneath the ideological surface: a model of what "deconstruction" ought to be.

[64] I started AC with nothing but a hunch about the contrast between centripetal and centrifugal meaning. The former is (as I've expanded it) metaphorical; the latter is usually called referential meaning. What I discovered was that there are two stages of referential meaning, the first one being to the meaning in the context of literature as a whole "outside" the individual work, the second to the verbal tagging of natural & objective data symbolized by the dictionary.

[65] Evidently Gadamer's book is one of the places I should look for the concern of play; it's a link between two of my sources, *Homo Ludens* and the *Critique of Judgment*.[51] And I shouldn't overlook the connection between value-judgments and the defence of ideology. Bruno's polarity has two aspects: the antithetical opposition of two halves of the same thing, and the final separation of life and death. Vico's repetition in different modes (displacement).[52]

[66] Comedy with its concealed gimmick: cf. Jonah & its "failed" prophecy. Job and the repetition of his daughters. Note Blake's Plate 20, where the whole Job story is frozen in a thematic snapshot, followed by the "new creation"; Plate 21 as the wakened form of Plate 1.[53]

[67] Note the significance of the frozen plot (*Waiting For Godot*) as a kind of parody of the Gestalt of the metaphor-cluster. It's not really frozen: as everyone knows, WG is wonderfully effective drama—but it employs that convention. Its temporal dimension is in the "waiting for": it's leading us up to a post-play event that doesn't take place. Something similar in HJ's [Henry James's] *Beast in the Jungle*.[54]

[68] In my two stages of referential meaning the first suggests not a monomyth but a holomyth: a map of the whole country. Looking up a place on that map isn't "pigeonholing," but trying to find a context for it. I think the Bible provides at least a survey of a holomyth. I must find out why the Marxists (Walter Benjamin) regard myth as a dragon of oppression to be slain by some ideological knight.[55]

[69] Vico's principle of repetition in different modes means that descent from a mythical model often has nothing to do with source, except by accident.[56]

[70] The big hurdle is knowing what literature to use for examples of the E-A-P-H [Eros-Adonis-Prometheus-Hermes] part. If I were following my nose, I'd be reading Henry James, and wishing to God I'd not only read more of him, but remembered more of what I did read. I've always had the greatest difficulty figuring out what the hell was going on, at the most superficial level. So The Awkward Age and The Sacred Fount & a lot of others just went up the spout.[57]

[71] The reason for this last note is this: Henry James has certain recurrent, almost obsessive themes. One (Portrait of a Lady, etc.) is the sunken Atlantis theme: fresh innocent *and wealthy* American girl goes to Europe, turns down all the decent offers she gets, marries some very dubious count de Spoons character, buggers up her whole life, that's all for now, kiddies. Another (What Maisie Knew, etc.) is the clairvoyant observer theme, often a child. Sees all, knows all, tells all, does bugger-all. But the one that fascinates me is The Sense of the Past theme, where somebody meets himself in a different time (SP itself) or in a parallel world (Jolly Corner) or meets the nothingness which is the essence of himself (Beast in the Jungle).58

[72] As for the TS [*The Turn of the Screw*] itself, it reminds me of an ironic (but still Blakean) reading of the "Good and Evil Angels" picture of Blake. You'd have only to assume that the child the "good" angel (the governess) snatches is dead on arrival. Otherwise the children are in a kind of Eden with the knowledge of good & evil destroying them.59

[73] I think instead of separate chapters on accommodation and response, which won't work, I need a single continuous argument on "The Dialectic of Revelation."

[74] The statement that Adam & Eve were naked and unadorned was too much for the commentary-stuffers. In the History of the Rechabites (II, 457) we're told "But we are naked not as you suppose, for we are covered with a covering of glory; and we do not show each other the private parts of our bodies." (The next sentence says this was true of Adam & Eve before the fall.)60

[75] How primary are my primary concerns? Note that they all have an individual reference. Is power primary, as Adler thinks,61 or, as I think, is it a secondary concern, nearly all of it anxiety, and derived from sex? My mentor here is not so much Freud as Milton, in his vision of the pre-Fall appetite for food & sex turning into passions of lust and greed that spread over all society.62 What about the concern of service? That's part of the work ethic, I suppose, and so is a secondary form of the play concern. It's the individual alone who can experience the satisfactions of food and sex and shelter and free activity, and the individual alone

who experiences the frustrations and anxieties created by their absence.

[76] The reversal of the four-level universe at the time of Romanticism is the *culbute* or primary upthrust stage of a revolution, which preserves the resurrection core in revolution, before the other meaning of "revolution" begins to operate.[63]

[77] Myth, being a sequential movement in time, is displaced from the metaphor cluster, the form in which we see it at the end. Similarly, the great reshapers of myths are not so much the poets as the sequential thinkers, Rousseau, Marx, Freud, Darwin. The poets themselves, I suppose, must be reshaping the metaphor cluster.

[78] The reason why there are two aspects of the apocalypse is the shift of perspective from part-of-whole to whole-with-part and back again. That should tie up the individual business, and still leave room for the objective and accommodating aspects of revelation.

[79] So many dreary disputes in 20th c. French literature where we have non-Marxist writers saying they just want to be apolitical and neutral, with the Marxists telling them that "neutral" statements are just as political ones. Of course they are. They're the other half of the Marxist ideology, and just as essential to it.

[80] I think I'd better start an article on "The Dialectic of Revelation," and see whether it belongs as chapter 3 & 4 of an 8–chapter book or not. It's beginning to look as though there were two dialectics, one descending from the P creation & more or less what I've got in GC,[64] and one descending from the J account & including the Four Zoas: Ruth & the Song of Songs, Jonah, the Isaiah & Ezekiel theophanies, the infancy narratives (of Samuel & Samson as well as Jesus). The latter is the literary Bible properly speaking; the former the ideological Bible. Although both take in both sides of the Word-Spirit dialogue, there's a strong lean toward the objective & accommodated in the P one & toward the subjective & responsive in the J one. One descends the ladder; the other ascends. (Writing notes before I know what I'm talking about makes for unintelligible and useless reference, but I'm close to something, I think.)

[81] I'm at the age to reread books I've forgotten: when an undergraduate F.H. Anderson told us to read Havelock Ellis' Dance of Life, & I read it with interest, but picking up a second-hand copy in a bookstore, I found I'd totally forgotten it, yet its spattery encyclopaedic style has certainly influenced my idiom, & it begins by saying that the fundamental arts are dancing & building (my freedom & shelter concerns). A footnote includes the sexual concern (mating dances of birds).[65] (Unfortunately the stinker who sold the shop the book has razored out five pages, so I'll have to find another copy {I won't keep a mutilated book on my shelves}).

[82] The close relation between dancing and sex comes out in the dancing figure of the Song of Songs, and of course the food concern is not only in the hortus conclusus, fons signatus verse[66] (and possibly the "garden of cunts" one)[67] but in the fertility-land attributes of the Bride. Ruth has the fertility theme in the harvest imagery and the son born late to "Naomi": also sex & shelter are linked for a woman (cf. the phrase *femme couverte*): cf. the cloak of Boaz spread over Ruth.[68]

[83] Confucius is often quoted as saying that if he had his way he'd begin by regulating music & ceremony. I understand the ceremony part: it's the assumption, which is thought of as magic but may not be altogether, & incidentally a notion the Taoists have too, that ceremony imitates & thereby harmonizes heaven & earth.[69] But I don't believe Confucius ever said "regulate music": if he did he shouldn't of. "Regulate by music" would make sense, & would put him in the class of Plato and others who talked as though they understood what music was all about. Except that Plato certainly did want to "regulate music," which means he knew nothing except his own obsessions.[70]

[84] Two remarks to be squeezed into the Shakespeare:[71] (1) Edgar's Poor Tom act is a prophetic (shamanic) act, hence it's involuntary and compulsive and inspired, whatever the conscious Edgar (who's rather an ass) thinks it is. (2) The final scene of WT [*A Winter's Tale*] is pure opsis: the words don't mean anything except as chorus comment or incantation: I suppose that's linked with magic as "art." It isn't what's said in T [*The Tempest*] but what's existentially done, & in WT there's the greatest contrast between the yatter about the offstage recognition of Perdita and the pure ritual of Hermione's revival.

[85] Also: King Lear is an anti-revenge play: the defeat of Cordelia's army, the failure of Lear to carry out his threats of revenge; the whole play is dominated by the theme of "no cause." A lot of people think the play is atheistic because God doesn't avenge anything. The "rarer action" in T [The Tempest] is (but check) in virtue than in vengeance,[72] virtue meaning strength as well. These are things that occur to me after lectures, but after the book is in the hands of the printers—silly when we have word processors that can do anything we have to lock everything up in the iron cage of a 19th c. linotype. Society still desperately holding on to its product.[73]

[86] Martin Esslin, The Theatre of the Absurd: "Any really fundamental analysis of reality as perceived by man leads to the recognition that any attempt at communicating what we perceive and feel consists of the dissection of a momentary, simultaneous intuition of a complex of perceptions into a *sequence* of atomized concepts structured in time within a sentence, or sequence of sentences."[74] Bloody words and woolly, but my 1 > 2 point.[75]

[87] I'm beginning to get some sense of the sequential dialectic of revelation, and am now looking for a series of epiphanic points, culminating in the apocalyptic vision itself. I'm still floundering. Job & Jonah seem to me to derive from the P creation, both being epiphanic parables of the Exodus. Ruth and the S.S. [Song of Songs] derive from the J creation,[76] and the S.S. in particular seems an epiphany of the renewed creation. Incidentally, all stages of the dialectic have a sexual aspect. The Exodus response to Creation is a human society made into the Bride of the Creator—note the liturgical association of S.S. & the Passover. The Wisdom response to Law is the Sophia-playing child of Proverbs, followed by the virtuous-woman epilogue. The deifying of Christ as the response to prophecy turns on the Virgin Birth, the rescue of the Bride, and the total celibacy of the incarnate Word. The apocalypse is the merging of Jerusalem the Bride with Christ the Temple.[77]

[88] According to Marvin Pope's commentary on the S.S., the Targum postulates a series of ten songs, covering the whole Biblical sequence, of which S.S. is the ninth. The first is Adam's song about the Sabbath, Psalm 92, which makes no sense whatever, except that the Psalm does mention the Sabbath; the tenth is referred to in Isaiah 30:29. Origen reduces these

to six. Pope's authority, Raphael Loewe, thinks Milton was aware of the ten-song schema in planning the proem to Paradise Lost. Origen's introduction to S.S., which Milton did know, lists the six as Exodus 15, Deuteronomy 32, Judges 5, II Samuel 22 [also Psalm 18], Isaiah 5, & the SS. Num. 21:17 and Josh. 10:12 are the Targum's 10.[78]

[89] Of course ideally (see the GC [78]) every verse in the Bible is an epiphany of the whole scheme. But there do seem to be poetic & metaphorical foci. The food concern is in the contract with Noah that goes with removing the curse on the ground ("eat anything"), along with the promise of regular seed-time & harvest & Noah's discovery of wine [Genesis 9:1–21]. The Exodus brings manna, quails and water [Exodus 16:11–15], wisdom has bread & wine to offer [Proverbs 9:5]; the Gospel has the Eucharist [Mark 14:22–5; Matthew 26:26–9; Luke 22:14–20]; the Apocalypse the tree & water of life [Revelation 22:14–17]. Miraculous provision of food recurs with Jesus (O.T. type is Elijah fed by the ravens) [1 Kings 17:6]. Building: the P creation; the ark (covenant); the temple; the seven pillars of wisdom; the spiritual temple as body and the new Jerusalem.[79]

[90] Re the S.S. [Song of Songs]: mythology says: "all major concerns are metaphorically linked, so there's no difficulty about a later poet (St. John of the Cross, e.g.) using its very dubious & explicit sexual images as metaphors for a concern that is not primarily sexual at all."[80] Ideology has two contrary views: (a) "this poem looks as though it were about sexual love, but it couldn't be that and still be in the Bible, so what it really means is," etc. etc. Or (b) "this poem is so clearly sexual that St. John's attempt to refine it into mysticism is a grotesque misunderstanding of it."

[91] Again, mythology notes features in the poem reminding us of fertility-cult imagery, of realistic expressions of sexual love, of ritual marriages between king & queen or their surrogates, etc. These are all features indicating the literary context of the poem. Ideology builds up "the cultic interpretation," "the naturalistic interpretation," & so on & so on.

[92] The Bible avoids ideological language, or dialectic; but its mythical material does tend to become allegorical & exemplary. Hence Chapter 3 is a descent of myth, made possible mainly by the P creation story, into

the ideological world & out again. At the law stage the ideology becomes theocratic; the gospel urges obedience to secular power to keep the spiritual community free for the apocalypse. What I'm looking for now is a chapter on the mythology of the Bible to supplement the dialectical ideology, which is now relatively clear in my mind. Then I can go on to the ideological cosmos and the mythical revolt against it.

[93] I'm told that the structure of the Anatomy is impressive but futile, because it would make every other critic a Gauleiter of Frye.[81] People don't realize that I'm building temples to—well, "the gods" will do. There's an outer court for casual tourists, an inner court for those who want to stay for communion (incidentally, the rewards of doing so are very considerable). But I've left a space where neither they nor I belong. It's not a tower of Babel: that tries to reach something above itself: I want to contain what, with a shift of perspective, contains it. Why am I so respected and yet so isolated? Is it only because I take criticism more seriously than any other living critic?

[94] The containing of the container is the Aristotelian theory of the relation of art to nature. This stops at a literal inside-outside shift.

[95] In mythological criticism, e.g. of the Song of Songs, the primary concerns of sex, play, shelter & food tend to be central & the more allegorical readings peripheral. What keeps them central? In literary criticism, the practice of poets. But what about St. John of the Cross? What he makes is a modulation from existential sex metaphor (M_2) to existential expanding of consciousness metaphor (M_1).

[96] The four major concerns are food, sex, *work* and play. Work in its Ruskin-Morris sense of creative act, in contrast to Carlyle's "drudgery," which is alienated work, with nothing in it for the worker's own benefit. I got "shelter" from a very early stage I should have outgrown, although construction, as symbolized by architecture, is an essential component of work.[82]

[97] It seems more natural to begin with myth & concern rather than with metaphor & identity.[83] But it's involved with this whole "writing" nonsense. As soon as you "see" a joke it's written, in some sense or other:

what you hear up to that point is unintelligible except as sound, hence the musical metaphors. And every narrative is a displacement of a metaphorical diagram, much as the 5th Symphony is a displacement of the tonality of C minor. When one applies such a conception to *Sartor Resartus*, say, one can make the link with my deconstruction as an attempt to get past ideology to myth.

[98] Work, if I'm right, is the basis of *contract*; play of *Utopia*, though we can't have one without the other. Food & sex get down to the apocalyptic-demonic patterns. The development of food imagery goes through the image of eating leviathan after the Messiah comes: before that the leviathan eats us (Jeremiah 51:34–6). The sexual side of this is the bride from the foreign land, the reverse form of the Jezebel Whore.

[99] The opening sentence of AC said I attached no particular importance to the construct *qua* construct.[84] I think I've got past that now, and that it's only by means of such dizzily complex constructs that one can ever get anything substantial out of criticism. Those who appear not to have such a construct, like Johnson, are attached to an ideology: those who do often don't get it worked out, like Coleridge.

[100] Hearing is uncritical, seeing critical: illegitimate rhetoric tries to minimize or circumvent the critical response & proceed directly to action. All rhetoric tries to subordinate it: that's why it's so difficult not to feel a certain bullying tone even in the Bible.

[101] I used to say that the Reformation ideology leaned to the past and Marxism to the future: but maybe all ideologies lean to the past in the end. Marxists are a lot hazier about the future socialist society than about the horrors of "revisionism," or escaping the weight of the sacred texts. Jews, too, with their future Messiah.

[102] "Dialogue": an overworked buzzword referring to the interpenetrating of opposites in ideology.

[103] I'm wrong about religion as an ultimate but not a primary concern.[85] Where did I come from and where am I going are primary concerns, even if we don't believe there are any answers. But if only the

social institution answers, the answer is ideological only. Maybe that *is* something we learn about only from literature, but God, the digging & burrowing to get at it!

[104] Science qua science is neither mythology nor ideology. The questions the pre-Socratics asked were scientific questions. What is the world made of? Is there a primary substance from which the others are derived? What really are the stars? Are there such things as atoms? Mythology had only absurd answers, & Plato's ideological pseudo-answers had not yet come on the scene. But that's where the view of myth as simply "false statement" comes from. (Except, of course, in the domain of historical fact, where the conception of "legend" intervenes.)

[105] I shouldn't have to say that I am not postulating a golden age of pure myth with no admixture of ideology; but because of the extraordinary adherence of some readers to such inferences, I do have to say it. Such an age is like the Garden of Eden, not a description of anything that happened in the past, but a postulate that makes what follows more intelligible. That raises the question of the function of postulated myths, which will bear thinking.

[106] The Bible is soaked in ideology from beginning to end: that's what's symbolized by the great trial metaphor that runs from God's contract with the adam to the Last Judgment, where Christ appears in the quite impossible role, for him, of a judge ("who made me a judge and a divider over you?") [Luke 12:14].

[107] I seem to be now in a more fertile & receptive state, more ready to respond to suggestions from what I read in literature. I've spoken of wanting to do an essay on Samuel Butler, for many reasons (Jerry's Festschrift, my own 4k course, etc.)[86] I dislike him & often find him a bore, because he's a milder version of what I so detest in Wyndham Lewis. He isn't as consistently perverted or petty-minded as Lewis, but he has something of Lewis' quality of writing from a primary motivation of envy. Miss Savage & he agree solemnly that *Middlemarch* is a very bad novel, & so through most writers.[87] Even when he expresses admiration there's an underlying current of "Oh, sure, but don't forget how important *I* am." His cult of Handel is not an exception, because it's merely a device for depreciating other music. In theory, I don't care what a writer

is *like*: in practice, some types put me off. It's part of his inability to know where paradox stops, like his paradox that when it comes to intelligence, nature loves a vacuum if it's inside the skull.[88]

[108] If there's no real difference between creation & criticism, I have as much right to build palaces of criticism as Milton had to write epic poems. My whole and part interchange works here too: inside the Anatomy, everyone is a disciple & to some degree a captive of Frye— every writer has a captive audience—but surely one can finish the book & then do as one likes, with something of me inside him. If he doesn't have something of me inside him, he won't, at this time of history, have anything of much use to say as a critic.

[109] The Buddhists keep saying, with tremendous and unending pro- lixity, that the subject-object duality is horseshit. Okay, it's horseshit: what's so infernally difficult about it? The fact that it's so difficult to overcome derives from the fact that the metaphorical kernel of subject & object is the contrast of life & death. The person for whom *that's* disap- peared really is a sage.

[110] I'm beginning to feel that the schematic structure of the Anatomy is a key to a much larger principle. People don't have to remain door- keepers in it forever, as in Psalm 23: they can go out to build palaces of their own. I suspect also that the key to philosophy is the exact opposite of what philosophers do now. It's the study of the great historical sys- tems, each of them a palace and a museum, that's genuine philosophy. At a certain point they interpenetrate into a house of many mansions, a new Jerusalem of verbal possibilities, but that's a tremendous state of enlightenment.   .

[111] I keep coming back to Henry James, wondering if there isn't some- thing in the later work relevant to me. (Some earlier work, too: the story Madame de Mauves shows the American female victim in the role of Courtly Love mistress.) What Maisie Knew, first, is not a story of what Maisie knew: it's told by an omniscient narrator who restricts his omni- science to her, but observes Maisie observing, besides telling us a great deal about what we need to know and the child doesn't & can't know. The Sacred Fount is about a lunatic who projects a vampire situation on some actual people he meets: no novelist would work that way, so what

he's doing is not an allegory but a parody of the imaginative process. But look at what's said about Maisie: "it was to be the fate of this patient little girl to see much more than she at first understood, but also even at first to understand much more than any little girl, however patient, had perhaps ever understood before."[89] So she's an archetype, like Alice in Wonderland.[90]

[112] Henry James' pansy mannerisms and distilled snobbery don't put me off as much as Butler's inverted snobbery about the upper class: the latter, however disguised as parody, is the real pain in the ass. Because that's the Englishness I had to put up with when I was principal.[91]

[113] Henry James again: the comedy of the occult. He starts with variations on the America-Europe split, as I've said. His New Comedy ballet-like plots suggest a kind of puppet-play, with the power of money as the puppeteer. *The Jolly Corner*, again, is a pioneering treatment of the science-fiction theme of parallel worlds, and *The Sense of the Past* explores this more fully. *The Beast in the Jungle* is similarly a pioneering treatment of the "Angst reveals Nothing" theme: the story of how to lose one's soul. This last is an outgrowth of the industrious-and-idle-apprentice theme, which is usually linked with the practice of the arts. *Roderick Hudson* is based on this *topos* (recently parodied in *Amadeus*):[92] the nut in *The Madonna of the Future* is losing the equivalent of his soul. Balzac's nut at least worked on his delusion.[93] Note the word "future": the sense of the future, like the sense of the past, confirms the subject-object split. The hero of SP [*The Sense of the Past*] doesn't really make that mistake.

[114] I suppose *The Sacred Fount* really deals with the idea I got from Pynchon: that art is a form of creative paranoia, which counteracts the real paranoia that starts wars and buggers nature.[94] Jean Blackall links it with Ludwig of Bavaria, who had two qualities in common with Hitler: an admiration for Wagner and a paranoid interest in architecture.[95] The latter of course is part of the Ozymandias mentality of all tyrants[96]—the Tower of Babel complex—and Wagner is the clearest example in culture of art as harnessed paranoia. The narrator of SF [*The Sacred Fount*] is "crazy," as the woman says, but he's a searching parody of the creative process.

[115] Why is earth a middle earth in all mythology? Because of the

psychological > cosmological correspondence. The lower world is the unconscious, the surface world the waking consciousness, the upper world the superconscious. I've said that cosmologies are, though literary in origin, ideological in intent (because hierarchical), so they conflict with science as pure mythology doesn't, & disappear. That seems to remove the objective aspect of myth, leaving only the psychological aspect, the kingdom of Jung. What doesn't disappear, I suppose, is the social hierarchical structure that projected the cosmology in the first place, the kingdom of Marx and Freud.

[116] Berkeley's tar-water is a late & grotesque example of the essence-of-tree imagery, used in anointing. Only it's of course an elixir (drinking of the water of life) image as well. He warns against taking the analogy between circulating sap & circulating blood too seriously, but his book is built on it. "The quantity of life is to be estimated, not merely by the duration, but also from the intenseness of living." —Berkeley, *Siris*.[97] Motto for HJ [Henry James] as well. "The air, which seems the receptacle as well as source of all sublunary forms, the great mass or chaos which imparts & receives them."[98] So air, the primest of primary concerns, is K'un.[99] Next it's a "common seminary,"[100] or Garden of Adonis. (Berkeley realizes it's not an element, but a mixture or chaos.) Obviously fire, which is both "genial" and destructive,[101] is the male principle.

[117] Freud & Marx are the thinkers who demonstrated the hierarchical & exploiting element in psychological & social setups (cosmological is the ghost of the social and the projection of the psychological.)

[118] I think there are two degrees of hierarchy. Underneath the Freud-Marx one is another that Freud didn't see & Marx didn't care about, the hierarchy of man on top of woman. The true symbolic relation, male as central and female as circumferential, then comes to light. The woman poet's business is circumference, as Emily Dickinson said.[102] There are two perversions of this: one is Blake's Female Will, which keeps man an embryo,[103] the other is the male will, which tries to expand into and dominate the circumference. Berkeley says too that "all speech concerning the soul . . . is metaphorical."[104]

[119] HJ [Henry James]: *The Golden Bowl* is an initiation story: the gim-crack phony virginity of the heroine's father-fixation is what the golden

bowl with its crack symbolizes. Here for once the Count de Spoons is a genuine European & not, like most of them, an American gone to seed, although his name is Amerigo. *The Ivory Tower* seems to have its common vulgar meaning: Graham Fielder, who is, in post-Jamesian vocabulary, a wimp and a nerd, is artificially isolated from society by being left a lot of money. He has no idea what to do with it, as he has no idea what to do with himself, so he hands it over to a friend to look after, & the friend gyps him. The result of this life without affairs program is Angst or vacancy: I don't see how even HJ could have filled up ten books with so empty a chronicle. However, it's a convincing enough study of the limits of individuality. The Marxists are so hysterically anxious to attach cultural & social conditioning to everything and everybody that they tend to ignore the whole *laboratory* aspect of modern fiction: the individual withdrawn from a social context and studied by himself in those things that only the individual can experience.

[120] HJ [Henry James], like Eliot & Joyce (& not impossibly Yeats) was obsessed by a form he had no aptitude for—stage drama. In the IT [*The Ivory Tower*] he does for each book what WMK [*What Maisie Knew*] & The *Awkward Age* do for the whole volume: plant a single character in the middle & see everything through his or her eyes. This is the *Ring & the Book* scheme, the drama turned inside out and decentralized.[105]

[121] Ideology subordinates the individual to the march of dialectic, whatever the hell dialectic it subscribes to. Mythology, which tends to feature gods, is closer to the combination of individual and archetype that's the normal unit of fiction.

[122] In the next few days I must do a blitz on this infernal book, get its main construction lines blocked out, & then start reading. I think that writers who move from "naturalism" to ironic myth are a good place to start, notably Strindberg, Ibsen & Henry James. Melville for a separate project I have in mind.[106] The HEAP [Hermes, Eros, Adonis, Prometheus] scheme keeps reforming & dissolving: the E & P are clear enough, the other two not. Keep wondering if HJ's occult stories don't go in the H direction. P is focussed on the ladder-scale chain of being, *social* hierarchy, all universes of degree, & takes off from the P creation narrative. E also has a ladder, thanks to Plato, takes off from the J narrative, & is based on sexual hierarchy. God is "male" because nature is "female":

inclusive language is superstitious nonsense, taking a metaphorical structure to be real. The sexual fall not only put man on top of woman, it also turned God into a sky-god on top of a cursed (for a time) Mother Earth. Adam is the threefold sexual male, to use Blake's language; the adam is fourfold humanity.[107]

[123] The question of play, of it's not really happening, is inseparable from all cultural development. In an Aztec ritual a man is flayed alive & the priest puts on his skin.[108] Spring festival, you see: put off the old man & put on the new, reviving what's dead in a new form. O.K., but if you were to watch such a rite being performed, the beauty & appropriateness of the symbolism is not what would strike you most forcibly. Here as everywhere the literal-minded is the bloody-minded. The only thing we can take literally in the gospels is the Crucifixion.

[124] Berkeley's *Siris* is chain-thinking, but less hierarchic than the chain of being.[109] He transforms air & fire into principles rather like those of yin & yang in Chinese mythology, then distinguishes the hidden fire that pervades all things & is the spirit of life from its epiphany or manifestation as light.[110] (The latter is caused by the entry of fire into air: epiphanies depend on sexual processes, evidently.) I must stop reading at random so much, but note the figure of the inner circumference full of eyes (207), the FW [*Finnegans Wake*] top sawyer figure (241), the remarkable anticipation of Samuel Butler (257), and the conception of "laws" of nature as a grammar (252).[111]

[125] I think Michael's right & my Ottawa paper on ladders is a good one.[112] Only *it* takes in, besides Acts 1 & 2, Milton's PR [*Paradise Regained*] climax on the pinnacle and various other Babel tumbles like Ibsen's *Master Builder* (a source of FW [*Finnegans Wake*]). Rosmersholm ends with falling into a whirlpool or millrace—Poe's maelstrom, also Norwegian. Seems to me there's a fall off a mountain in WDA [*When We Dead Awaken*]. Poe is fascinated by the figure: look at that extraordinary image in *Eureka* of the whirling man on top of Mt. Etna. Strindberg's *Keys of Heaven* ends with Babel and Jacob's ladder.[113]

[126] The progression from the ideological anxiety to the assured craftsmanship of mythology can be seen very clearly in the writers who went from "naturalism," or simply realism, in the mid-to-later nineteenth

century into mythical and symbolic patterns. Strindberg & Ibsen are
obvious examples in drama: Bernard Shaw's failure to develop such a
late period is part of a larger failure. Henry James, of course, and (someone I don't know well) Hauptmann. Often, as in Ibsen, the naturalistic
period follows an earlier one that the final period recaptures. The most
dramatic and extreme example of this in English literature is Milton.
Allowing for the immense difference in cultural context, Shakespeare
shows the same development in his "romance" period. Joyce, of course,
pulling in his resources from *Dubliners* through *PA* [*A Portrait of the Artist
as a Young Man*] & *Ulysses* to FW [*Finnegans Wake*].

[127] I doubt that I can explain this wholly on my "primary concern"
thesis, but I must look at a book, *Natural Symbols*, by Mary Douglas, that
looks relevant.[114] Such late periods are often described as leading into a
private world, but that's balls. Interest in story-telling technique for its
own sake, the "academic interest" I noted in Shakespearean romance
and compared to Bach's *Art of Fugue* [*NP*, 8], certainly enters into it, and
fits an emphasis on centripetal & metaphorical structure. It's an aspect of
the principle that myth & folktale, because of their formal similarities,
eventually combine as ideology separates out by finding its own dialectical language. It normally means a writer well enough established, socially and technically, to be less preoccupied with anxieties. Also not a
"retreat" but an increasing interest in what only the individual can
experience (not that there is any such thing as a social experience, except
in group hysterias & the like).

[128] Secondary myths are spawned from an anxious ideology that wants
to eliminate the other half of itself. When Frank Kermode gives anti-
Semitism as an example of a myth,[115] he is (a) expressing a very common
prejudice against all myth (b) defining the kind of myth that's spawned
by a hysterically one-sided ideology. Such one-sided ideological myths
are really mob creations, and a mob *must* project the suppressed other
side of its cliché on a scapegoat figure.

[129] The central symbol, the golden bowl, the white horses of
Rosmersholm, the tin drum, is metonymy, or perhaps almost synecdoche.[116] It *stands for* the whole metaphorical complex, and makes it clear
that there *is* such a complex. As writers get older & more concentrated,

they tend increasingly to use such a "symbol" to represent the thematic stasis of what they're saying.

[130] Later Ibsen should be added to the imaginative deconstruction of ladders, towers, mountains. *The Master Builder,* an influence on FW [*Finnegans Wake*], is almost a wheel-of-fortune allegory; the other egotistical monsters, Borkman and Rubek, climb a mountain to commit suicide. Incidentally, in WDA [*When We Dead Awaken*] the sculptor's former model & mistress, Irene, makes a comment suggesting that for her transfiguration is a far higher achievement than resurrection. I've got Rosmersholm's millrace & white horse elsewhere [pars. 125, 129]: here as in WDA there's the communion in death image we meet at the end of The Mill on the Floss. I need more theory to connect these examples: otherwise it's just archetype-spotting.[117]

[131] Chapter Three should take seriously my conception of the narrative of the Bible as a definitive myth. The Creation myth in its two forms, and the sexual symbolism in the Fall, I have, more or less. Exodus should be linked to the deluge as its repetition, & the cyclical and dialectical aspects of "revolution" both brought out. Law should pick up my sin and crime thesis, & wisdom my conception of work as creative act & play as release of energy, including the mental energy of contemplation. That repeats the work-and-rest rhythm of creation. The end of wisdom, the child with the skipping rope, is spontaneity or unconscious knowledge.[118] Prophecy is the embryonic word that eventually becomes the word within the Word, or divine child born of the mother & the Spirit, the *puer aeternus* of the Jungians and the Hiranyagarbha or golden egg of the new creation.[119]

[132] Chapter Four then deals with the apocalyptic metaphorical cluster, concentrating on the key images, garden, ladder-tower-mountain, way, etc. The four forms of primary concern are doubtless the organizing principle. After that it gets hazier. The most natural next step, I should think, would be the descent from the P creation myth to the ideology of four levels, and the deconstruction of this after the Romantic movement. That would naturally take one to the structure of patriarchal authority into which the J narrative descended. After that there's nothing left but the end of ideological dialectic in the life-death antithesis. This has its

two forms, the Adonis form of resurrection & the Hermes form of trans-figuration. The unsealing of Hermes is also the unsealing of the Alpha-Omega book, the alphabet of forms.

[133] According to Western traditions, God made the world from nothing; according to Eastern ones, nothingness is still its content.

[134] I've said that the literal-minded is the bloody-minded [par. 123]: note that this kind of literalism—eating the body & drinking the blood of a God-man to get his divinity, for example—recurs in the most surrealistic & hallucinatory forms of writing, as in the brothel scene of *Ulysses* [chap. 15] & in the later plays of Strindberg.

[135] Laforgue, according to his translator, said, or spoke of "lightning flashes of identity between subject and object—the attribute of genius." That and the paragraph in Butler's WAF [*The Way of All Flesh*] are two source-points—if I can find the phrase in Laforgue.[120]

[136] They say that Stonehenge & the Great Pyramid show immensely sophisticated astronomy & mathematics. That's out of my orbit: patterns normally become more schematic & comprehensive as culture matures. Their greatest point of elaboration is just before they're about to be pushed out of science or history. Also, the point about archetypes is not that they're built into the human mind, but that they are communicable through recognition. The primary area of communication is conscious: it isn't a case of deep calling to deep [Psalm 42:7]. If half the world uses an archetype & the other half doesn't, it's clear that it can mean something to that other half. The mystique of the unconscious has bedevilled myth critics. If you find fragments of a huge myth in primitive times, the process that put it all together is most likely to be in Shakespeare or Wagner or someone producing a waking dream for conscious minds [Plato, *Sophist*, 266c].

[137] Such a writer would actualize what is potential in the archaic mythology. People resist this, because a poet's consciousness may get self-conscious, turn coy or cute and go in for archetype-spotting. The poet (modern) is in the position of a medieval dog hitched to a mandrake root: it doesn't matter so much if he goes mad, but the root he's pulling is not just his own tail.

[138] My objections to Jung are not to him but to my being called Jungian: I'm not much interested in alchemy and I don't want *literature* to be turned into a psychological allegory of individuation. On the other hand, once I move back from literary to existential metaphor I'll come very close to it.

[139] The idea of using Henry James, either in a separate paper or as illustrative material, continues to attract me. Perhaps "Time & Identity in HJ" is better than the comedy of the occult title. I'm thinking of things like *The Awkward Age*, where Nanda *is* her grandmother reborn almost "literally." Incidentally we're told that the grandmother was a throwback to an earlier age yet—very nearly the SP [*The Spoils of Poynton*, 1897] era.[121]

[140] He so often says that "germs" or seeds of themes (dianoia) expand until they cover an immense 400-page novel.[122] He doesn't say much about the *generic* changes that result from this. The enfolded form *before* writing the mythos, and the unfolded form *after* it, are the two *gestalten* or "écriture" pre-existing (so to speak) forms. In the Bible the double creation myth (one male {P}, the other female {J}) is the enfolded form of what's unfolded in Revelation.

[141] My note on p. 42, bottom [par. 136], defines the gospel: the emphasis is not on the built-in but the communicable. Profound unconscious feelings are certainly called up—Xy [Christianity] is far more primitive than Judaism—but, again, deep doesn't call to deep: the marketplace of waking consciousness is where these depths are realized. That's why there's no esoterics or initiates—only gospel. Except, of course, that the progress from "literal" to spiritual meaning, which is so often identified with an exoteric-esoteric movement, goes on here as elsewhere. But that's something we're told from the start by Paul.

[142] I suppose the vogue for deconstruction has to do with its Romanticism: it takes off from the Romantic conception of creation as something opposed to *the* creation.

[143] The more doctrinaire forms of Marxism (Stalin & the gang-of-four Maoists) attempt to replace mythology wholly with ideology, and, consistently with that, deny that anything transcends the human individual except the human social. I've often felt that an over-emphasis on the

social perspective, whether Marxist or not, ignores the whole "laboratory" aspect of fiction: the isolating of an individual from his social context to study those things that only the individual can experience. (Which is practically every experience *in itself*, as distinct from its similarities in others.) The question is that the mythological perspective of tradition may lead to some kind of religious transcendental, as it so often does in practice.

[144] The fussy conventionality of so many novelists goes with their ideological anxieties. My copy of *The Awkward Age* is a paperback with the back cover talking about the "vicious, immoral" society in it.[123] I don't really see that, at least compared to what vicious & immoral behavior could be like. They wash, and their sentences parse: they don't murder or rape. But then, when I read *Mansfield Park* I thought the Crawfords much higher human types than Fanny & Edmund.

[145] We can't live a day without being concerned about food: we can't live a minute without being concerned about air. That's a good reason for the centrality of all the "spirit" metaphors. If we had to eat as much as a shrew we could do nothing but eat: perhaps the incessant breathing, however automatic, is what keeps us from entering into the real "Spirit."[124]

[146] I think my ladder image, which belongs to both Prometheus & Eros, is too fundamental to fit one of the four: it comes into everything. In Acts 1 & 2 what goes up as Word (Logos) comes down as Spirit (Pneuma): it's the Heraclitus double spiral, except that we go up to unity & down to individuality and plurality.[125]

[147] The interpenetration of work and play is also the interpenetration of necessity and freedom. If we define genuine work as creative act (vs. drudgery or exploited & alienated work), what we have to do and what we want to do are the same thing.

[148] There are books on near-death experiences, but no return from actual death, so death is still a mystery, & the helpful spirits & tunnels with light at the end may be reconstructions—anyway, we can't prove they aren't. Same with dreams. All we know of dreams is what the waking mind remembers, & we can't prove it's not reconstructing. But if

so, why reconstruct in a language so different from its own? Why do we never (apparently) dream in prose sentences or explicit statements? That's connected, I think, with the mythological basis of the arts, and the fact that they can't be *finally* reduced to ideological products. (You can't "return from the dead" by definition: if you do you're not dead, even if you're as stinky as Lazarus.)

[149] Ne sutor ultra crepidam[126] is a silly motto: if you observe it all you will ever hear is "Ow! My feet!"

[150] The dream, then, expresses desire, concern, warning, quite genuinely, but always in slightly oblique language. There is only one gate of dreams, horn on one side and ivory on the other.[127] But then there's the image-cluster that generates myth & addresses the waking consciousness. The two factors affecting the content of the dream, the events of the previous day and repressions going back to early childhood, correspond to the ideological and the mythological perspectives.

[151] The Promethean vision descends from the P creation account and the vision of natura naturata as a ladder. It gets deconstructed in Rousseau, & of course Marx: wonder if Marx is a mythologist after all, the ideological anxiety being supplied by Lenin. The Eros vision descends from the J account (and Plato) and gets similarly deconstructed by Rousseau and, more effectively, Darwin. (Note that, as the metonymic symbol for the dianoia {or rather, I guess, it's synecdoche} is the ladder for Prometheus, with all its extensions, so it's the tree of life for Eros[)]. Many popular books on evolution display the process in a tree-diagram.

[152] What has to be destroyed in the Promethean vision is exploitation and alienation; in the Eros vision it's patriarchy & male supremacy. That's where Freud conspicuously fails as an Eros prophet.

[153] I think I have just the two, really: Adonis is Anteros & Thanatos also the other side of Eros; Hermes the psychopomp has a similar relation to Prometheus. Adonis & Hermes take me into the occult & beyond death worlds, which I can't ultimately shirk. Unless Hermes is the mythical basis of Promethean ideology, and Adonis the mythological basis of Eros ideology. I distrust what sound like pseudo-profundities, but maybe I'm circling around something.

[154] Food & sex interpenetrate symbolically; so do work and play. In the P creation myth work & play (leisure) are the main themes: the climax is the instituting of the Sabbath. Food & sex (eating wrong fruit & losing sexual innocence) are the main themes of the J account. The Fall started anxieties about both: cursed ground & cursed genitals.

[155] Symbolic *development* proceeds through anxieties: it's because there is a possibility of *not* getting enough food that rituals of sacrifice develop, and with them the death-and-rebirth containing pattern of symbolism. Similarly with Grail symbolism, if it's true that it develops from Celtic food vessels and the like. The anxiety of sex of course comes out in all the cruel-mistress poetry.[128]

[156] Alternation of "oceanic" merging with a totality and the individual feeling he's a whole of which the totality is a part corresponds to identity with and identity as.[129]

[157] Is Michael the only saint who is also an angel? If so, why? If not, who are the others?

[158] The P creation story, natura as naturata, has the Enoch revolt of *angels* for its demonic side,[130] as well as Satan, Lilith and the dragons of chaos. Its line goes through Job & Jonah to the Johannine Christ. The J natura naturans one has the Adam-Eve fall attached to it, & runs through the Song of Songs, Ruth, perhaps Esther (Judith belongs here as Tobit does to the other), & Susanna, to the synoptic Christ, especially Luke.

[159] The double mirror of metaphors is also a double gyre of myth. The Bible exhibits a twofold movement of a type I first discovered in *Paradise Lost* [RE, 13–14]. One way it's all causality: everything inevitably happens from its predecessor. This makes Satan the (tragic) hero of P.L., & assimilates the epic to the "divine plan of salvation" unrolled in Puritan sermons. Puritan, because Calvin is the most complete expounder of the Bible as causal sequence. The other way the Bible is a typological series of open or timeless moments, in each of which the opportunity for breaking the sequence recurs. These moments are perhaps the seals torn off the book in the Apocalypse.

[160] My question here is: could the causal sequence be associated with

my Adonis & Hermes themes? Because logically it makes Christ a continuously dying god, and sees all earthly power as led to hell by a
psychopomp, as in the end of the Odyssey & that Chinese book. So my
view would be a straight Prometheus-Eros one after all.

[161] Don't go all out for metaphor: sunset & sunrise, a fixed flat earth, rail
tracks meeting at the horizon, are primary facts of experience but still
illusions. I have, whatever Ricoeur says, a place for the referent (the "sign"
section of AC, e.g.), and it's only in the final apocalyptic vision that the
referents become equal with each other.[131] I mean identical. "Reality," like
the subconscious in Lacan, is linguistically structured,[132] being mainly a
set of fossilized human thoughts. Even the landscape is what it is because
the early settlers cut down the trees. And behind that is what ultimately
goes back to Berkeley: to be X is to be "perceived" as intelligible.[133]

[162] Interesting how some people (Rimbaud, Christopher Brennan)
break out from a religious background to explore their gifts, then existentially when they've finished writing go back into it, or do something
silly like Wallace Stevens.[134] Link with a reader's withdrawal from
Hopkins' Catholicism or Milton's Puritanism.

[163] In a recent discussion an O.T. scholar who's made a neo-funda-
mentalism out of what used to be a liberal position—i.e. we now know
about the historical background, or will after we've sifted through fifty
tons of sewage from Scoopadacrap, Turdistan. Milton & Blake didn't
have the knowledge we now have, she said. As for St. John of the Cross,
his ignorance of all the village fertility songs bit makes him ridiculous. I
found myself so close to defending Bloom's "misreading" thesis that I
wonder whether, like most post-Frye conceptions, it doesn't fit the Bible
primarily.[135]

[164] False metaphors, or units of a phony mythology, are those of
advertising, propaganda, and the superstitions exploited by both. The
man who refuses to take a blood transfusion from a black man because
he's afraid of turning into a mulatto is using a metaphor where no
metaphor should be. Being a parody-metaphor, it might pass as a joke
("Have you heard the one about the man who," etc.), if not a joke in the
best taste. Such superstitions descend from the pseudo- or proto-
observations of nature in cosmological constructions.

[165] Note how the variety of body metaphors dries up under the Cartesian pressure of regarding the body as a mechanism. The liver as the seat of passion has gone; the metaphorical "heart" remains, but anyone who, like Sibbes, wanted to publish a rather attractive set of sermons on the Song of Songs would hardly call it *Bowels Opened*.[136] Only the brain remains the subject of a dispute as to whether it's the source or the transmitter of consciousness. I think the latter: I think there is only Spirit as subject and Otherness (the source of our life, origin and destiny) united by the Word, the articulate spirit, and the intelligible guide to the Otherness, for which "Father" is a better metaphor than the "Mother" that identifies it with Nature.

[166] This sounds like the Hindu trinity in reverse: it's the "Father" who is destroyer and preserver, and Shiva appears to be the Spirit. Not that it matters so damn much when they're all the same god. But the Bible insists that the real Otherness is not nature. In the study of nature all metaphors are pernicious: as soon as the metaphor becomes inevitable we're in the religious area.

[167] Then again, as I've always known, all the grim and hateful aspects of the Father-God in traditional religion are derived from Nature, especially in her white-goddess or terrible-mother aspect.

[168] Why does the Word have to become flesh? Presumably so that mythically it can accomplish a quest, and metaphorically identify all the categories of being. In Xy [Christianity] the judgment of society & the conquest of death & hell has [have] now taken place: the identity of all being has still to come. Surely I'm doing something more than just playing around here. The Spirit is a community at first, hence a sheltering womb: individual growth is portrayed in Jesus' "father's business" episode [Luke 2:49].

[169] The terrible power of words to inflame the emotions: words, like electricity, can illuminate and kill. A metaphor can kill a man, as Wallace Stevens says [*Poetry Is a Destructive Force*, l. 15]. At present I am deeply worried about Helen,[137] for quite valid reasons. But because I have a certain facility with verbal formulas, I can talk myself into tears (perhaps ultimately into nervous collapse) at any time. Similarly in my prayers for her recovery. I see nothing wrong with such prayers—the first part of

Jesus' Gethsemane prayer is a precedent.[138] But I don't "wrestle all night" with God in prayer,[139] because if I did it would just be a rhetorical embellishment of "Do this because I want it, or feel sure I want it, very much." And God knows too much about rhetoric to be impressed by it. I suppose there's a link here with the sentimental: the self-indulgent rhetorical amplification of nostalgia or the like. If Helen died and I had to pack up all her little trinkets, even a song I regard as cheap and silly, like "Among my Souvenirs,"[140] would work on me like a psychedelic drug. What I should feel is rather "If I didn't have to do this for her, she'd have to do it for me, and I'm in better shape to do it at present." Note too that while it is very natural, if one has had a religious conditioning, to ask God for help or thank him for an upturn in fortune, he is not asked or helped in a human vacuum: the good will and skill of doctors and nurses is a highly relevant factor. And of course it's all wrong to pray for miracles, in the sense of interruptions into the order of nature. Miracles are epiphanies, not primarily favors. (Mustard seed?)[141]

[170] This is not a diary, but Helen is dead.[142] Not of cancer: she died in peace, I was told. Her Alzheimer fantasies were already turning her against me: she seemed to feel I could get her out of hospital if I only wanted to. It's better for her to go now than to go through the final Alzheimer cycles, and it was very like her to slip out of the world so unobtrusively. I know nothing: Ned's "iron door" doesn't budge a crack.[143] I think I know when she died—3.10 p.m. AEST,—but that may be an illusion.[144] But they say there are helpers, and for so gentle and pure a spirit there must be. My hunch is that grief of survivors, being so largely self-pity, distresses, perhaps even impedes, progress to a world that makes more sense. I know that she would forgive me my sins of indolence and selfishness in regard to her, and therefore God will. I hope only that she knows now that I genuinely loved her very dearly, so far as human frailty permits. God bless, protect, and keep her among his own. I hope to see her again; but perhaps that is a weak hope. Faith is the hypostasis [substance] of what is hoped for, the elenchos [evidence] of the unseen.[145] The one thing truly unseen, the world across death, may, according to my principle, be what enables us to see what is visible. I dreaded seeing her in the hospital, because she never smiled at me: she would smile at Jane,[146] but I couldn't keep the worry out of my face and tone, and I bored her. Besides, when Jane told her she was in hospital and had to get better before she could go home, she said "I can take that

from you." When I tried to say the same thing, she said "Don't be so portentous." It was the last thing she said to me, and it sounds like an oracle. Meanwhile there is Jane, a daughter sent by God instead of nature. Guardian angels take unexpected but familiar forms, as in Homer.

[171] When I speak of helpers I am, of course, thinking of the books of reports from those who have nearly died and come back. Of course nearly dying is not evidence about actual death. But then, we do not know what we dream: we know only what our waking consciousness thinks it remembers of what we have dreamt. William James speaks of dreams of writing works of immense significance that were only the silliest of jingles when he "remembered" them afterward.[147] Something in that significance was there and didn't get through. Most, perhaps all dreams, have to pass through the gates of ivory, and whatever gets through the gate of horn is literature.

[172] The creatures that turn up in seances are probably evil & mischievous ones, not the people they profess to be, whatever they know or pretend to know. Not all: the Witch of Endor seems to have evoked the genuine Samuel [1 Samuel 28:7]. But real spirits are only disturbed by this. I want Helen's feet to be kept in the way of peace. She will speak when the time comes.

[173] It was, as we say, "the best thing that could have happened," that Helen should have died when she did. Why is it that an event which shows the care and the mercy of God would be the most hideous and insensate of crimes if I had taken her life instead? One of those questions so obvious that we forget even to ask it: it's not as easy to answer as all the automatic answers that come pouring out suggest. Is it another dimension to God as scapegoat, bearing the sins of mankind? I suppose "vengeance is mine" is in a similar category.

[174] Meanwhile, let's think about the one idea all this grief has brought me so far. I said in GC that the invisible world in the Bible was not a second order of existence, as in the Platonic tradition, but the means by which the visible world becomes visible, as the invisible air is the medium of visibility [GC, 124]. The one really invisible world is the world across death: is that what makes us to see the seen? Is the visible world the world of faith (*pistis*), as in Plato, that is the *elenchos* [evidence] of the unseen?

[175] My suggestion that grief for the dead impedes and disturbs them may of course be the grossest and crassest of superstitions: one has to try out such things to see if they have any resonance. But grief emphasizes the pastness of the past, and so works against the mythical imagination. Helen was—that's the beginning of tears and mourning. Helen is. What she is, perhaps, is a central element in the unseen which will clarify my understanding, if such clarification is granted me. My whole and part conception may have a link with this. It is right to pray to God, because God is the unity and totality of all this: but the perspective can reverse into millions of presences—the saints, in short. Helen would smile at the notion of being a saint, but I suspect that sanctity is something created by love, not necessarily some kind of essence.

> Christ leads us through no darker rooms
> Than he went through before.[148]

[176] Perhaps my notion that the unseen world is the medium by which nature becomes visible (or intelligible?) is related to Yeats' remark that nothing exists except a stream of souls.[149] Only maybe he should have said "spirits": the metaphorical link between spirit and air is stronger. Does the same principle account for the fact that the Christ of the gospels is discontinuous myth and not continuous history or biography?

[177] I notice that my remarks about near-death & dreams [par. 171], which I assumed to be genuinely new, are repeated from p. 46 [par. 148]—quite recent entries. What that says about me I don't know. One thing it may say is that I feed on myself and not on others. It's conceivable that there are demonic things done unconsciously all the time, and that some day they will be brought to light. It's possible that I drove Helen into an impasse where all she could do was die. It would be morbid to accuse myself of such an act when there's no evidence for it, and when there is evidence that she was, most of the time, happy and loved me. But many Victorian husbands must have killed their wives believing sincerely that they loved them, and God knows what the psychologists of the future will know about such things. Perhaps that's really what the Sacred Fount is all about: the hero (narrator) may be as corny as you please, but he may be a Cassandra like the governess in TS [The Turn of the Screw] for all that.

[178] One thing involved here is the "what's really going on" fallacy.

What's really going on is a cluster of illusions. I don't think it's an illusion that I loved Helen, but it would certainly be an illusion to claim that I always did the best I could for her. Of course it's always an advantage to become aware that an illusion is one.

[179] Internal and external reference again: the cult of unity in Flaubert and Henry James has to do with the centripetal direction. In HJ unity of style as well as form became obsessive, leading him to rewrite his early books, producing monstrosities of holism that modern reprints generally ignore. Every so often an ideological critic (Marxist) gets a reputation for originality by writing out the ideological half of such a book. See my notes on *The Ivory Tower* and the "laboratory" aspect of fiction [par. 119]. In GC the centripetal aspect of every verbal structure is also its literary aspect [GC, 60], so that every v.s. [verbal structure] has a literary side to it—this goes in the "art of words" introduction to the second chapter.

[180] There is no morality except slave morality: *Herrnmoral* [*Herrenmoral*] is founded on the exploitation of slaves.¹⁵⁰

[181] How I hate the word "never"!

[182] [Charlotte Brontë's] *Shirley*: full of characters spouting ideologies, including naturally the author's own. Toryism, radicalism, rationalized laissez faire, the sexist ideology Charlotte Bronte knew so much about; economic miseries of Orders in Council; the understandable but mistaken tactics of the Luddites, all dated back to 1812 from the 1840's to provide the hindsight of the Chartist parallels. Other books studying these topics directly might have more & better organized information, but if written in ideological language, however detached or partisan, would have to treat all individuals as case histories. What makes *Shirley* & other works of fiction irreplaceable is the assimilation of all this to the primary concerns of food (i.e. jobs), sexual love, work & play.

[183] Hence the "vertical" or mythological tradition becomes relevant too. But just as most social criticism ignores everything really germane to the *structure* of the book, so most *Wissenschaft* criticism confines itself to clichés about Byron & Scott & the Gothic novel or whatever. That's traditional crap, corresponding to Terry Eagleton's Marxist crap: the oversimplified Toryism of Helstone & radicalism of Yorke are the proto-

types of this in the novel itself.[151] But novels are "tracts for the times" without hindsight or history.

[184] The allusiveness of literary works to each other is part of their structure, not an ornamental or display-on-a-mantelpiece or whatnot of erudition. Cultural tastes define individual, as distinct from generic character, and Caroline's preference of Chenier to Racine is an individual trait of this kind. Similarly with the use of Coriolanus as an archetype of Moore. Readers are expected to pick up, say, a sentence (find it) that echoes both Psalm 23 and Hamlet ("prophetic soul"), or to understand why the phrase "I am not mad" should be referred to both St. Paul & Racine's Berenice.[152]

[185] With such powerful anti-sexist writing in the book, why didn't it do more for "consciousness-raising" at the time? Because literature doesn't work by magic: the reader is responsible for the moral quality of what he reads: the critic should be the avant-garde reader, so if it's anyone's job it's his. But while *Shirley* was being written a venomous attack on *JE* [*Jane Eyre*] came out in the *QR* [*Quarterly Review*], written with a classbound smugness that these days has to be read to be believed.[153] (Some of its phrases are incorporated in a later chapter of *Shirley*.)[154] The writer has authority, all right, but the resistance to that authority is very powerful, & much of it takes the form of frivolous comments about lack of unity, unconvincing plot, & similar devices for dodging the critic's one job: recognizing what's there to the best of his ability.

[186] The primary literary allusions in *Shirley* are Biblical (including Bunyan), and they come to a climax in Shirley's reconstructions of two Biblical myths. Eve, for Shirley, was not the insipid Eve, as she considered her, of *Paradise Lost*, but a Titaness-Eve, a Lilith-Eve almost. This theme is evoked in a chapter called ironically "The First Bluestocking," which takes the Genesis 6:1–4 myth & develops it in a quite extraordinary way.[155]

[187] There are also the plot-symmetries, starting with the very common Victorian convention of two heroines, one dominant and the other recessive.[156] They're not sisters, but they marry brothers. Caroline goes through a point of ritual death and recognizes her mother at the end of it: Robert Moore[157] goes through a similar point and recognizes *her*. Critics shouldn't

waste time talking about whether these devices are "convincing" or not: they're just talking about the way *they'd* have written the book.

[188] The judgment & trial legal metaphor of the Bible comes from the impossibility of reshaping the past after death. My indolence all too often made life much duller for Helen than it should have been: when I realized this I tried to "make it up" to her, to reshape time into a more comfortable context for her. Death puts an end to all that: never again can I do anything for her in this world, and the fact rebounds on me as a judgment. With her Alzheimer broken will and my own spinelessness leading us both to deadlock, we were both in a sense marking time. Perhaps every death has something of divorce about it: the kind of inevitable parting of ways that is parodied by suicide. On a more cheerful side, the last "m'amour" fragment of Pound[158] reveals (though Pound may not have known it) the profundity of Blake's "emanation" conception: the objectivity one identifies with, with the woman one loves as its incarnate centre.

[189] Shirley is a well known and highly respected novel, but it is not and probably never will be as popular as *Jane Eyre*. Popularity may have an ideological link, like *Uncle Tom's Cabin*, but this is rarely primary: the usual reason for popularity is mythological, the unobscured revealing of archetypes. I've said this: I want to say it again because of the concern thesis. The Cinderella type of story dramatizes the victory of a sexual concern over a social establishment that has every appearance of being able to suppress it.

[190] Again on sources & influences: the "background" ones, like, for *Shirley*, the influence of Byron & Scott & Gothic fiction, are secondary because they're seldom mentioned in the text in any significant way. *Coriolanus*, Chenier, the quoted ballads, & Shirley's great Genesis fantasies are primary. Similarly in the ideological area: there's the more purely social factor & the autobiographical ones (Charlotte's special knowledge of the status of women, governesses, the clergy, reminiscences of Emily & Anne in the heroines, etc.)

[191] I don't know why I've spent so much time on Rimbaud and Mallarmé when it's so clearly Laforgue who has all the answers. The ego (Moi) is, he says, Galatea blinding Pygmalion (i.e. the created world

turning objective), and nobody can do anything about it. "God is dead" is a stupid formula: all Xy [Christianity] turns on how man tried to kill God and failed. But the fact that the earth is dead is a very profound one. Laforgue was also a student of Hartmann, whose book I must look up: Hartmann says the unconscious knows nothing of sin (or evil, I forget which).[159] That is, in the descent quest there's a world below the rational separating of "good" (on top) from "evil" (below). Christian in the valley of the shadow was troubled by the blasphemies and obscenities whispered in his ear, "for verily he thought they had proceeded from his own mind."[160] A modern reader would feel that verily they had, and that for the author of *Grace Abounding* it was inevitable that they should. But the story of Christian came, according to Bunyan's own metaphor, from a dream world deeper than that valley.

[192] The Hindu conception of "prana" makes the objective metaphorical link between "spirit" and air more explicit.[161] In Xy [Christianity] there's the "blood of Christ" metaphor, the antitype of the O.T. ban on feeding on the blood of animals (i.e. identifying with the objective: the blood is the life, and eating or drinking it is identifying with the natural life through killing). Some of these reflections come from reading Huxley's *Island*, an elaboration of the Dostoievsky "Dream of a Ridiculous Man" theme. Huxley is not completely free from the silliness of, say, *The Genius and the Goddess*, but still this book is a serious one, and perhaps his best.[162]

[193] In a more sensible Christian world people would move in and out of Catholic and Protestant lifestyles, instead of all this ideological crap about once-for-all baptism or conversion, always having to be either in or out of the church. Maybe that will happen when we get rid of the religious-secular antithesis, stop thinking that "Why does a God permit so much evil and suffering?" is a serious question, and start asking the question in its genuine form: "Why do *we* permit so much evil and suffering?"[163]

[194] Chapter One is myth and concern; chapter two on metaphor and identity. That's clear. Then, perhaps, a chapter on the integration of Biblical myth & metaphor, from the two accounts of creation to the table of metaphors in the Apocalypse. Or, maybe, two chapters, one on ladders and quests and the "way,"[164] and one on substances spiritual &

physical (the four elements are spiritual but only incidentally physical substances). I hope a complete rationale of "elemental spirits" can be worked out here.

[195] My old thesis that the Romantic cosmos is the earlier one stood on its head is the right one, I think,[165] & may expand thus: Hermes & Adonis represent the hierarchical, pre-18th c. aspects of the verbal cosmos; Prometheus & Eros represent the Rc. [Romantic] reversal. I don't need or want anything beyond that, I think: those two movements, stemming from the P & J aspects of creation mythology, form a Heraclitean double helix. If so, the traditional forms don't *have* to be authoritarian, however much they have been: the way up & the way down are the same.[166]

[196] To remember without being bound to the past: to anticipate without being bound to the future.

[197] Primary concerns relate to the individual and to experience, because only the individual *can* experience. They cannot be talked about, only shown forth in symbols. The symbols, in literature, are verbal: the point that literature does not talk was one of the first established in AC [4–5]. Ideological or secondary concerns have to be rationalized, because they talk about society, and the poet is expected to respond to the arguments with the appropriate symbolic resonance.

[198] How tedious is death. Death and his brother sleep.[167] Sleep for me is a series of dreams in which Helen is alive and we're talking and planning things together. Then I wake up hearing reason say "You will never see her again," without bothering to add "in this life." Reason makes the rest of me puke. Love is strong as death [Song of Songs 8:6]: now that makes sense. I take pills, of course, but a drugged stupor is not sleep. Nor is a spirit with a cremated body dead. Ay, madam, it is common.[168]

[199] The primary thing to remember about this book is that I am free. That is, free to write the kind of book I like without being tied to sequels (though, being as I think about the Bible, there will be strong connections with GC, as my preface suggests).[169]

[200] I don't believe affirmations, either my own or other people's. The motto I've chosen for the book (quique amavit cres amet)[170] represents a hope but not a faith: I can't pin down my faith so precisely. What I believe are the verbal formulas I work out that seem to make sense on their own, & seem to me something more objective than merely getting something said the way I want it said. I hope (but again it's not faith) that this is the way the Holy Spirit works in me as a writer.

[201] In what I say about *Shirley*'s assimilation to the literary tradition is all right [sic]. But the influence of the Bible (and perhaps of the *Pilgrim's Progress*, as the Protestant equivalent of Loyola in Hopkins) is *different*: that difference is one of the things my book is about.

[202] Ong's book on Hopkins has qualified the strong anti-Catholic prejudices I acquired forty years ago, when the Thomist sales pitch was being bought by everybody. (Also the crypto-Fascist political connections, which are something else.) Scotus now looks to me like an upholder of the Blakean pre-existence doctrine: the Incarnation was a primary intention of God, not primarily an effort to repair the ruins of the fall, though it became incidentally that. As Ong says, the reversing-fall thesis, when primary, makes Christ subordinate to history, and so (as he doesn't say) generates the fallacy of the historically presented Christ.[171]

[203] Since Helen's death I've felt my love for her growing increasingly beyond the contingencies of the human situation. I begin to understand more clearly what Beatrice and Laura are all about. If the relation is reciprocal there is nothing to regret beyond the inevitable mechanisms of regret.

[204] Dialectic as language and dialectic as decision: Hegel & Marx. They both breed persecution when they're pre-apocalyptic—i.e., when one element is accepted and the other condemned.

[205] The Crucifixion is the story of how man tried to kill God and failed. But as that God was man as well, it follows that wars and massacres and holocausts, apart from all their evil and horror, are simply *futile*. I don't want to make that a smug statement, but I think it's part of the picture.

[206] I want, of course, to write one more major book, concerned with the relation of religion to literature. So far the articulating of this book eludes me, though the fragments that have come clear seem to have the requisite originality. The opening is all right: there are two parts to it, myth & metaphor. The first part speaks of myth as having an ideological function, in contrast to folktale & legend, but being superseded as language by dialectical prose. The poet to this day owes his authority to the preserving of mythological language. This makes him more primitive, but prevents him (and society) from pure ideological obsession. The units of poetry are metaphors, which in literature are hypothetical only, but are attached to what I call existential metaphor, the "lunatic and lover" of Theseus' speech [*A Midsummer Night's Dream*, 5.1.7].

[207] What comes after is a haze. I've thought all my life of a metaphorical universe map, but (a) I've already set out the Biblical one in GC and (b) the materials for such a map are already in Jung, Eliade, Graves & Levy, & putting them together wouldn't say much. I'd thought too of putting my seven stages into a proclamation-and-response sequence. Creation, followed by the revolutionary formation of Israel. This engenders the second proclamation of the law, and wisdom is the individual response to that, the permeation of one's life by law. Then comes the third proclamation of prophecy, with its climax in the message of Christ. The response to that is the gospel-church one, & the apocalypse is the final merger.[172]

[208] All that's notable in this is my conception of the P and J accounts of creation as respectively encapsulating natura naturata and natura naturans. The former begets the Urizenic authority-systems descending from the top, the latter the Orc uprising movements. I've had a quadripartite scheme of Eros Regained, Adonis Revived, Prometheus Unbound and Hermes Unsealed swirling around in my noodle for a long time, and am now beginning to wonder if Adonis & Hermes don't belong on the Urizenic side of the alternating structure. The figure of the up-&-down movement is Jacob's ladder, which comes into focus (I *can't* say climax)[173] in Acts 1 & 2, with the Word ascending & the Spirit descending.

[209] Jesus of course unites the two movements: the transfiguration or metamorphosis, where he's "up" and flanked by Moses the law and Elijah the prophet, is the Jesus of authority, proclaimer of the Word. The

resurrection with its empty tomb is the complementary event. The Trans-figuration is not in John: I think the synoptics present Jesus as fulfilling the second proclamation of the law: John presents him as the Word fulfilling the Creation. It's not a Gnostic book but a counter-Gnostic gospel. Maybe what corresponds to the Tr. [Transfiguration] in John is the raising of Lazarus [11:1–45]. I know that Jairus' daughter is raised in the synoptics [Mark 5; Matthew 9], but that's really one of those "galva-nizing" miracles of the "take up thy bed and walk" type. There isn't the same emphasis as there is on the fact that Lazarus is dead, stinkingly dead.

[210] Speaking of Gnostics, I've learned from Jonas[174] & elsewhere that they really had a point, but I've never read anything Gnostic (Christian, anyway) that wasn't a billion miles from the New Testament. I've been through what's available of the Nag Hammadi stuff,[175] and it's just a gabble chorus like the mystical frogs in Aristophanes. I think, on a proportionately reduced scale, that the bulk of critical theory is a chorus of koax[176] after the Anatomy, and I want to get back to that level. One book is excepted: Julian Jaynes on the emergence of what he calls con-sciousness. That's a book I think I'll be drawing on a good deal, though with some very different emphases.[177]

[211] I wish Jaynes hadn't used negative words like "hallucination" and "breakdown" so much: like Theseus,[178] he sees only the lunatic at the beginning of the progression, and the bicameral people of today are schizophrenics. Surely the authority of the poet depends on a recon-struction of the "bicameral" situation. Jesus' mind, for example, seems to have had a "breakdown" in the opposite direction: all his consciousness was taken over by the will of the Father. And there's a much closer link between dialectical prose and his "consciousness" than he [Jaynes] ad-mits. He says it's the "song & story" of the poets that developed con-sciousness, & regards the whole soul-body dualism as a pseudo-question from the beginning. I don't think the poets developed consciousness, though they reflected its development: they're the people who, along with the prophets, keep pulling us back to the "bicameral" stage.[179]

[212] Shakespeare's kings have two bodies, a symbolic self and a physi-cal self.[180] That makes them role models for schizophrenics & "bicamerals."

[213] This book should start with the integrity of the Bible, then use literary analogues to show its relation to literature. The more usual procedure of gathering a mass of anthropological analogies & throwing them in the general direction of the Bible is interesting & useful, but not my concern. I don't care what the Fartass tribes in New Breakwind believe about the proper time for planting yams: I care about how Jacob's ladder informs Dante, Yeats, Eliot & Pound. The same thing would be true of psychological data like Jung's libido book.[181] I think the general *grammar* of mythology is something that's really been done.

[214] I've said that I have hope about another life, but I don't have faith, in the Hebrews sense of a hypostasis of hope.[182] The furthest I can get is a negative faith: I do *not* believe that those ten squalid and humiliating days in the Cairns hospital is the total end of a lovely and lovable human being. (Total for all practical purposes: Butler & others would talk about surviving in the memory of others, but miserable comforters are they all.)[183] But when people talk of recognition scenes & such I can't commit myself. She's in heaven, Catherine[184] said: but I don't know where (or what) heaven is, or whether the word "where" applies to it.

[215] All I can do is define my hope. I didn't want her to go on living her way through the Alzheimer. I don't want her back with *that*: I'm not sure that I'd even want her back in the frailty of the human condition. The Helen I now love is someone whose human faults & frailties count for *nothing*: the word "forgiveness" I shrink from, because it implies that I'm in a superior position. I think (with Keats) that life may be purgatorial in shape, only I'd call it a vale of spirit (not soul) making.[185] I think of her as someone for whom the full human potential is now able to emerge. Perhaps my love and the affection so many had for her helped to do that for her, being the same kind of thing that the R.C.'s [Roman Catholics], with their mania for institutionalizing everything, identify with masses & prayers for the dead. If so, then she's an angel, not to be worshipped, according to the N.T., but an emancipated fellow-creature. Martyrs don't necessarily believe in rewards for martyrdom, but they behave *as* though they were citizens of a bigger multidimensional world than their persecutors.

[216] Jaynes tells us about the continuity between the bicameral mind

and schizophrenia:[186] he doesn't mention the continuity between the inner gods and the subconscious: the kind of thing that makes us instinctively call the most mentally disturbed geniuses "prophetic." But I think my authoritarian four-level structure develops from objectifying or projecting the inner authority, and my ascending ladder is part of a "bicameral" recovery. And, as I say, the king's two bodies are closely linked with symbolism's two minds [par. 212].

[217] The tyrant is the man who narrows the scope of life, in other words creates a hell out of human life, agent of an anti-resurrection.

[218] Christmas, Easter, etc., are unique events assimilated to the cycle of nature. The cyclical celebration is another way of saying that the cycle (which of course has an ironic aspect) is the only way of representing what lies beyond the cycle.

[219] An otherwise rather bad and lazy book by Hans Küng on immortality says one good thing: "Purgatory is God himself."[187] A death is one's first gasp of "spirit," meeting the Lord in the "air." *Hamlet* is much in my mind now: he's a Jaynes case of a conscious being bedevilled by a bicameral voice of authority yelling for revenge, & he has all the claustrophobia of a highly intelligent man who realizes he can't realize his full potential except after death, which naturally suggests "except by death." One of the Ghost's many functions is to make clear to him the futility of suicide. One thing I missed: at the appearance in his mother's room Hamlet accepts him completely as his father [3.4.102–14]: there's no "old truepenny" in that scene.[188]

[220] If consciousness, or the "analog I"[189] didn't exist before (effectively) 800–700 B.C., then the paradoxical role of a nothingness at the heart of Being goes with a separation of subject & object. Perhaps the Locke era marks the end of this transitional phase: I'll have to get clearer the Foucault thesis that "mankind" is a 17th c. conception.[190]

[221] Anyway, the metaphor chapter should, after establishing the hypothetical nature of literary metaphor, go on to examine, first, the lover metaphor with all its paradoxes, and then the identity-with metaphor, starting with Theseus' "lunatic" and Jaynes' "hallucination." If I could

line up my GC metaphor-metonymy-simile sequence with Jaynes & Foucault it would help. Not that I'd want to claim their authority for my own quite different thesis.

[222] The two kinds of symbol in my Royal Society paper:[191] one, as I say, is metonymic; the other is typological: the ticket is a symbol that leads to the performance.[192] Thus the Exodus is a historical symbol: what it symbolizes is man's awakening from the "nightmare" of history.[193] Law is a type of the shape of the spiritual life: Butler's "analogy" argument.[194]

[223] It's a good thing this notebook is not for publication, because everyone else would be bored by my recurring to Helen. What do I want? I *don't* want the poor lamb back with her Alzheimer condition, or at all in any world she'd have to be dragged back to. I just miss her, and the miss is a blank in nature. I've accused myself of murdering her, at least to the point of understanding what Eliot was getting at in *Family Reunion*. Like Harry in that play, I have to learn to accept the Furies as Eumenides. But I find all my ideas regrouping around her in a way I can neither understand or explain. The sermon, for example, was all about her,[195] & so will this book be if I write it. She's now a C of L [Court of Love] mistress, like the dead Laura or Beatrice. I think the judgment phase may be over for me, at this stage anyway. I helped murder her, but she was, I think, happier with me than she would have been with the other men interested in her. And perhaps I love her now in a way that I couldn't have loved her before she died. I don't want her to come back to me, unless she has her reasons for doing so, but if/when I go to her it will be all right. (It's still hope, not faith. I don't even know if it's right to say "help thou my unbelief" [Mark 9:24], because that could lead to self-hypnotism. The Holy Spirit has to take charge here.) Meanwhile, some of my letters advise thinking about our happy days together: that's like advising a starving man to remember that wonderful meal he had three months back (Job 29).[196]

[224] I don't see how deconstruction techniques fit the Bible at all: you have to start with a *lisible* text by an author you can "supplement," and such a text doesn't exist. "The Word made flesh" certainly sounds like the supreme logocentric claim, but there isn't any "transcendental signified" except the Father, who disappears into the Word. So I think there

must be what Derrida doesn't allow: a polysemous structure that directs all the "deconstruction." On the other hand, the excursus on Gen. 6:1–4 in Charlotte Bronte's *Shirley*[197] is a deconstruction of it in a way that none of her other purely literary references, such as the one to *Coriolanus*[,] even approach. Incidentally, this is a quite different question from that of popularity as the direct expression of an archetype.

[225] The third chapter, I think, picks up my Royal Society paper,[198] with its distinction of typological and metonymic symbols. The former leads directly to the "remythologized universe," where ladders and ways and the like form a body of types that have then to be "spiritually discerned." At that point, I suppose, I enter the projected-authoritarian four levels and its contrary movement.

[226] The P creation myth of natura naturata is male, and the resistance to it is titanic: all rebel angels are males. The J myth is female, the woman representing the enslavement of humanity by its own anxieties, and recovering her birthright as the people of God. If I thought these feminists had anything I'd read them.

[227] I did say in my Ruth paper[199] that it was remarkable how three of the five Megilloth featured women.[200] But what Lamentations laments is the rape of the Schekinah,[201] and what Qoheleth praises is Sophia.[202] I suppose the male counterparts would include Jonah, perhaps the kernel of Job, & the servant songs in Isaiah. Esther, by the way, dramatizes the social *culbute* of Hannah's song and the Magnificat.[203]

[228] So the course of the Bible, as I've said all along, is in the first two chapters of Acts, where the corporeal Word absents himself (Ascension) by transforming himself into the incorporeal Spirit (Pentecost). This involves a democratizing or universalizing of the Son relationship: *the* Son becomes the total community of sons & daughters. O.T. types include the Moses-Joshua and the Elijah-Elisha relationships.

[229] Surely, if "deconstruction" starts with a construal text, that text prescribes a *direction* for deconstruction, otherwise you wander forever in a wilderness of words. Such a direction involves one at once in polysemy, whatever the particular steps in the verbal ladder may be. Surely too the conception of "supplement" indicates this.[204] I suppose

the traditional fears about how "dangerous" a speculation may be if it doesn't stay on the track provoked this reaction.

[230] I suppose there are really just two levels involved: the literal, which is metaphorical, and the anagogic, which is the context. My R.S. [Royal Society] symbolism paper[205] provides the conception of the symbol as ticket,[206] the embryo of a total experience. Allegorical & moral meanings taken in on the way include the philosophical context and whatever the Marxists mean by historicity.

[231] Who was Jesus' father? Apart from poor old Joseph, there are two answers: (a) God the Father (b) the Holy Spirit. Jesus' own references to his Father seem to be to (a); but if the Comforter who was to succeed him and keep his historical function going was also his father, we're in a bind that no formula about three persons in one substance really solves. Maybe this was what was worrying the Eastern Church when they rejected the "Filioque" clause.[207] The notion of a new Father fathering Jesus is the starting point of Blake's Thunderfart god, I suppose: Los is both Time and the Holy Spirit, and the coming of Jesus consolidated the "horizon" law-god[208] into Antichrist or Satan. Jung, of course, wants Mary in as a fourth person (the Holy Spirit is really female in attributes).

[232] In pre-Galileo times one knew that the earth did not move. We say now that they thought they knew that, & that the reality of the invisible forced itself on them none the less. Similarly with what I "know" about my present widower state.

[233] I've said that the poem passes into the critical reader through a process of death & absorption in a new life. This is an essential point in *Two*,[209] where the transition is made from hypothetical to existential metaphor, or actual identity with. Also in *Two* is the sense of *dianoia* as stasis: this can be a seed or germ like Henry James' suggestion (preface to *The American* particularly)[210] or mandala object of contemplation.

[234] St. Thomas distinguishes ratio from intellectus, the former being logic & the latter what we call vision.[211] It comes from the active intellect, which comes in turn from angels or other messengers of Sapientia. Meister Eckhart talks about every soul as a Virgin Mary giving birth to the Word in the soul.[212] For poets their poems are a mimesis of the Word,

just as love for Provencal & later Italian poets become[s] a mimesis of agape, and Classical myth a (positive) mimesis of Christian myth. Aucassin's hell; the Romaunt of the Rose; the possible secret (e.g. Templar) cults.

[235] The use of Classical mythology in Christian poetry made the former a positive analogy of the latter. Similarly the poets made Eros a positive analogy of Agape, and poets talking about their Muses made the writing of poems a positive analogy of Eckhart's theological doctrine of the birth of the Word in the Soul. Erich Heller (Parsifal book) on praise as intransitive verb.[213]

[236] I may be heading for the grossest kind of illusion here, but I still wonder about Helen's functioning as a Beatrice: it may be nonsense for a man of 75 to talk about a "new life," but all I want is a new book. With God all things are possible. Beatrice was mainly a creation of Dante's love; my love recreates Helen in the sense of recognizing that if a world exists that she's now in, she's an angel. Her human frailties, as I've said [par. 215], are now *nothingness*: only what she really was remains. (My own weaknesses & guilt feelings, of course, have greatly increased.) She didn't read my stuff, of course, & didn't need to, but she respected what I did very deeply. So although both of us were physically infertile for many years, perhaps another Word can still be born to us, like Isaac.

[237] Chapter Three makes a good deal of the contrast between positive and demonic or negative analogies. The former are all *types*, and types are symbols in the ticket sense.[214] Again, I suspect that symbols also move back from the hypothetical (or, perhaps, propaedeutic) to the existential—in this context the sacramental. In "primitives" there's often little if any distinction between sacred & profane, sacramental & indifferent: if my sermon is right,[215] maybe we're returning to that. Doctrinaire Marxism gives a demonic form to this.

[238] Or perhaps I'm talking here about the direction the *myth* chapter ought to be going in, & that the symbol chapter really expands into interpenetration. So far I find the Avatamsaka Sutra disappointingly unrewarding: all I have to hold on to so far is Blake's grain of sand.[216]

[239] I've wondered so often if I really do have this book in me that I'm

in danger of persuading myself I haven't. So far I visualize three parts. Part One, theory, has three chapters: myth and concern, what I have plus; metaphor and identity; symbol and (perhaps) anagogy. Part Two, on the Bible itself, *may* revolve around (a) Jacob's ladder, & the up & down movements culminating in Acts 1–2 (b) the two versions of creation & the male-female symbolism (c) the remythologized world. Part Three is about certain literary situations that flow out of these. The ladder corresponds to myth, the remythologized world to metaphor, & the sexual symbolism to anagogic symbolism. Or perhaps the up-down stuff goes in Four, the remythologized world Five, & the sequence of seven stages from creation to apocalypse in Six. Then three (perhaps four, if the HEAP [Hermes, Eros, Adonis, Prometheus] scheme is still holding up) on literature. Seven could take in all the ladder-mountain-spiral stuff, Eight the Eros paper,[217] Nine the recreation theme from Blake to Mallarmé. I suspect that such things as my *Shirley* point may have to be transferred to Part Three.

[240] I have five or six books of those Eranos essays edited by Campbell. They're all the same book really: Frau Olga Whatsername was supposed to think up a new theme each year, but she didn't.[218] There's always an essay or two that's just wind: they're Jungians, Jung being their central figure, & how Jungians do *preach*! (Jung's father was a preacher.) But occasionally there's something rewarding: a paper by Martin Buber on the O.T. *nabi* indicates a first-stage existential form for symbol as well as metaphor.[219] Jean Danielou's paper on the dove & the darkness in Byzantine thought:[220] I can get a lot of stuff out of them, as long as I discount all that crap about myths being *projected* archetypes.

[241] I wish my mind were clearer about Derrida: it's silly to make him into a sort of critical Antichrist trying to abolish incarnational texts. To me all texts are incarnational, and the climax of the entire Christian Bible, "the Word was made flesh, and dwelt among us" [John 1:14], is the most logocentric sentence ever written. My only hunch is the one I've recorded: that if you start with one text rather than another, that text prescribes a certain *direction* of comment & deconstruction & what not, and the direction reduces to a polysemous pilgrimage.[221] You can't just wander in the wilderness of words forever. A lot of post-structural stuff seem to me just irresponsible and undirected polysemy.

[242] The first chapter on myth should, I think, reject the Jungian view that a myth is a projected archetype: that's part of the fallacy that literature must grow out of something that isn't literature. The exaggerated association of myths & dreams in both Jung & Freud should be rejected too. Vico & Schelling probably get featured: Schelling for his clear perception of how myths define a culture.[222]

[243] The second chapter, on metaphor & centripetal meaning, goes into the Humboldt conception of a verbal universe as an intermediate order between subject and object.[223] When it starts to move from hypothetical to existential metaphor by way of erotic metaphor, it crosses the great either-or divide from the aesthetic to the moral, from allegorical to moral-tropological meaning. Keep criticism & the death-to-rebirth-in possession process central throughout: it's often not realized that this process takes place through an *intensifying* of criticism.[224]

[244] The third chapter, on symbolism, will probably move from the symbol as focus, the metonymic symbol like the flag, Carlyle's "extrinsic" symbol, to the symbol as type, the "token" etymology of symbol raised to the power of anagogy, symbol as ticket to performance. A symbol always has to be a symbol *of* something, & ultimately that something is the existential reality that the token admits us to.[225] Carlyle's "intrinsic" symbol is balls: there isn't such a thing.[226]

[245] Francis Huxley, p. 134, says the ideogram for Tao means, or includes, both "step" and "stop," both a "way" of movement and of thought. He compares Latin sentis, path, & sentire.[227] In the Bible the image of way or pilgrimage runs into a full stop with Jesus' "I am the way" [John 14:6]. So if I have (so far) two main sections, one on the "elements" (narrative, metaphor, symbol) and one on the structure of the Bible, the conception of *mythos* or narrative expands into the "logical" (i.e., rhetorical) progress of thought, and also into all the pilgrimage metaphors of the Bible, as well as the narrative of the Bible. This runs into a blank wall with "I am the way," just as a narrative ends with comprehensive gestalt vision. I think I see how three chapters of elements parallel three chapters on the Bible (or what I'd like to call the "crucible"), but I wonder if "symbol" doesn't logically precede metaphor, though incorporating my time-to-space introduction to the latter.

If a third section on the "precipitates," or literary "products" took shape, that would be it: nine chapters.

[246] Only I also say that there are two directions of the narrative movement. One goes in the direction of entropy; the other in the direction of expansion after arrest.

[247] I think it's Norbert Wiener, the cybernetics man, who says that communication overcomes entropy.[228] Not always: as with water & fire in the Bible, there's a dead word and a living Word. Some books are "dead things," in Milton's phrase,[229] forgotten or surviving arbitrarily in the memory: others take us in the opposite direction from death. What Derrida is attacking is the fallacy that to have a living word you have to have a living person speaking it. The living speaker is only a symbol of a creative word that keeps throwing up supplement after supplement, yet always in a specified direction.[230]

[248] And just as there is a living word and a dead word, so there are living and dead thoughts. A handful of dead hair comes out of my comb every day, yet I still have hair. A sewer of dead thoughts, verbal shit, flows through my mind constantly: I hope there are other kinds. The repetitive & endlessly recycled thoughts are part of this too. One should remember that thoughts are not just ideas: I hope, for example, that I have discovered something of the reality of love in losing Helen. That's not just a neurotic return on myself: I think I've also got a clearer notion of what Beatrice & Laura were all about.[231]

[249] Antitypos in Greek has the primary meaning of striking back, resisting, adverse. This corresponds exactly to the way that Jesus' "I am the way" deconstructs the image of journey by turning it into a solid person.[232] It occurs in Hebrews 9:24 as well as in I Peter [3:21] (typos is in Heb. 8:5, and hypodeigma, the post-Platonic form of paradeigma, in 9:23. The AV usually translates that and typos as "patterns" or "copies").

[250] The transfiguration turns up at the very end of the Purgatorio (c. 32), where it fits the metamorphosis-upward pattern. As Dante in purgatory is travelling backwards in time towards his "unborn" existence as an unfallen child of Adam, I wonder if that's a point of contact between Western & Eastern modes of thought.

[251] Kissing as the point of contact of "oral aggression," where the eating symbol meets the sexual one. "Home" as the female environment.

[252] No Biblical prophet makes the use of parables that Jesus does; but why are there no parables in John? (The *word* parable occurs once [John 10:6], but it's a different form.) The form critics talk about a "sign" source (for the miracles) and a "discourse" source.[233] The series of signs is very important. There's the sign of water, starting with the baptism & winding up, through Nicodemus' "water & the spirit," with the Samaritan woman's well and Jesus as the water of life. There's the sign of the temple, becoming the body of Jesus; the sign of the new wine; the sign of manna vs. the bread of life, of provided food with Jesus giving his flesh to eat; the sign of life (Lazarus) vs. eternal life or doxa, and so on.[234] Also, of course, the Jonah & brazen serpent types.[235]

[253] The two dragons I want to kill are Bultmann's "demythologize" and Derrida's "logocentric." The Bible is myth from Genesis to Revelation, & to demythologize it is to obliterate it. The climax of the (Christian) Bible is "The Word became flesh, and dwelt among us" [John 1:14], which is the most logocentric sentence ever written. But I must be careful to make sure I understand them & am not just saying that my views of mythos & logos are different.

[254] I have ideas about the Bible and ideas about various works of literature. But if I can't really connect them I don't have a book. What made me think I did have one? The four levels & their inversion, mainly. At present I have three parts. One: the elements, which are myth (concern), metaphor (identity) and symbol (polysemy). Two: the crucible, the narrative from creation to apocalypse: the sexual symbolism, from the initial two creation myths to the final wedding in Revelation: the remythologized world. Three, the products or precipitates: these seem to converge on Dante, Shakespeare romance, Milton & Blake, the Romantic revolution, Mallarmé & (perhaps) Laforgue, the Eliot-Yeats-Joyce complex. God, if I have a book here, help me & guide me in the writing of it: if what I have is a pretentious fantasy, guide me into something genuine as an offering to you and a memorial to my lost love, who I hope and trust is lost to me only and found by and in you, and by me again later.

[255] Recurrent numbers, seven & twelve & the like, are elements of

design only: they represent no hidden mystery or numinousness in things. Not even the trinitarian three or the Jungian four. There are twelve signs in the zodiac, but it would be equally easy to see nine or eleven or fourteen and a half. Only fractions seem so *vulgar*.

[256] A developed civilization has a plurality of connected but autonomous pursuits, of which literature is one. A primitive society has all its cultural activities closely linked to religion. Hence the ecstatic nature of dances & myths where the "let's pretend" hypothesis is swallowed up in participation. But a modern performance of *Hamlet* is not just let's pretend either, except that the audience at least is expected to distinguish fiction from fact, with enough detachment to know it's a play, and enough sensitivity not to say that it's just a play.

[257] Hänchen's commentary on John[236] has one good point: that the Messiah myth in it has the shape of an old Wisdom myth preserved in Enoch, Ecclus. [Ecclesiasticus], & elsewhere: she descends to the world, is kicked around and ignored or mocked, & finally goes back to her own world. The dialectic from female wisdom to male prophecy seems very clear here. Why a virgin birth? Because all the redeemed are *adopted* sons of God, in Xy [Christianity] in contrast to the natural descent from Abraham that JB [John the Baptist] said wouldn't help the Jews [Matthew 3:1–12]. So everybody has to be born again without entering another womb. Doesn't quite work, but the pattern of becoming a son of a Father without needing another mother is there.

[258] Luke 7:27 and Mark 1:2 conflate a return of Elijah (Malachi 3:1) with one of Moses (Exodus 23:20). Tradition of return of Moses in Deut. 18:15–19, only this is just "the prophet" (John 1:21, 6:14, 7:40). In the Temptation scene, the three proposals are each refuted by a reference to Deut.: 8:3, 6:13, 6:16. To strike Zechariah dumb for asking "how come?" precisely as Mary does is unreasonable [Luke 1:20]: the reason is a kind of commentary on the story of the birth of Isaac.

[259] I suppose the principle of deconstruction is that all "literal" meaning, in the ordinary sense, is a *projection* of a metaphorical verbal body. Examples are the "always" and "anyway" of pilgrimage or journey metaphors. What we take "literally," in this sense, is the direction of the metaphors suggested by the author, without examining further. Poetry

is language where this procedure is obviously inadequate. Every narrative is thus a selected or chosen arrangement of metaphors.

[260] When Jesus says "I am the way" [John 14:6] time stops. There is no journey through unknown country: all the disciples have to do is walk through the open door (another "I am" metaphor [John 10:9]) of the body in front of them. That is, I think, impossible before the Resurrection. Perhaps everything that happens in the gospels is not an event but a ticket to a post-Resurrection performance. Except that the spiritual reality is not so much future as an expansion of the imaginative possibilities of the present. The myth confronts: it doesn't prophesy in the sense of foretelling.

[261] The Egyptian Book of the Dead seems to be a gigantic gnosis in which the dead man recovers the powers of all the gods, partly by knowing their names, partly by having lived without what was later called mortal sin. Many affinities with yoga, especially in samyama,[237] the acquiring of the power of what one concentrates on. Patanjali speaks of the elephant's strength: perhaps the animals of Egyptian religion have a similar meaning. (In later chapters there are "books of breathings," regarded as a great secret.)[238]

[262] Magic implies mechanism: you pronounce a name and the entity designated *must* appear and do things. A primitive building a boat will use technology, but will also mutter magic spells to take care of the intangible factors. I suppose computers are the physical realization of magic, just as the television screen is the physical realization of ghosts.

[263] The role of verse in the N.T. is puzzling. Apart from the innumerable quotations from the prophets & Psalms & other poetic parts of the O.T., there are the Magnificat & Nunc Dimittis & other hymns at the beginning of Luke [1:46–55, 2:29–32], which are probably not Luke but inserted by him from another source. The opening of John is a hymn, thought to be of different origin from the John the Baptist passages, and distinguishing the eternal Logos from the man entering the time sequence, where he'd have to have a predecessor (and followers, of course) [John 1:1–18]. Philippians & Colossians contain what are said to be pre-Pauline hymns [Philippians 2:6–11; Colossians 1:15–20], but I don't see why they couldn't be Paul himself writing at a particularly high pitch of

concentration. Similarly with the charity hymn in Corinthians [1 Corinthians 13:1–13], and the passages in Ephesians thought to be a redactor getting off on his own.[239] That sounds a little like the theory that Shakespeare's plays weren't written by Shakespeare but by someone else called Shakespeare. Paul may have been capable of a good deal of stylistic variety on his own. (Within limits: he certainly *can't* have written Hebrews.)

[264] I think some 19th c. Catholics, including Newman, tried to resolve the Bible-Church dialogue by subordinating the Bible, and so making Christ a creature of history and tradition and precedent. The Church, even if all its claims are true, continues the body of Christ in time, but the eternal Logos continually confronts it, not because it is continuous, but because it doesn't change. The Egyptians saw the victory of the apocalypse in every sunrise: the mass of course repeats the whole gospel sequence every day: but a mass that swallowed the gospel would become a black mass. I'm blithering: I've forgotten my idea.

[265] By the standards of conventional scholarship, *The Great Code* was a silly and sloppy book. It was also a work of very great genius. The point is that genius is not enough. A book worthy of God and of Helen must do better than that.

[266] Stage Two is not the Exodus: it's simply history, of which the Exodus is the form.

[267] I don't think the doleful mood recorded on p. 80 [par. 254] is the final answer. It's common knowledge that religious movements are ideological, and closely parallel political & economic ones. The seminal but immensely overstated parallel of Weber between Protestantism & the work ethic is an example.[240] The other side of this is that theological structures provide diagrammatic models for political & economic programs (cf. the ideologies of the 17th c. English revolutions). I am not interested in the relation of religion and literature, where there may be any number of "either-or" contrasts and dilemmas—aporias, we knowledgeable people call them—but in the relation of the Bible & Western literature.

[268] That is, I'm interested in the Bible specifically, because it's written

in the language of literature, the language of myth, metaphor, figured speech, rhetoric, symbol & analogy. I want to make a few suggestions about what that feature in the Bible has helped to shape in our imaginative culture—I can't do without "imagination" as my central building block.

[269] For example: of the two creation myths in the Bible, one has the human fall of Adam and Eve, the other has no fall; though one was supplied later, mainly by the excluded Book of Enoch [1 Enoch 6–10]. Actually this suppressed myth organizes the Book of Job. But the N.T. hardly knew what to do with the Book of Job. I think Boehme's view of creation as a titanic drama within the divine nature accounts for his influence.[241] Schelling seems to derive from him,[242] not that I know much about Schelling, but he & Vico are the only people before Durkheim who take myth seriously. (Or is it Dilthey? I can never remember which said which).

[270] I suppose the basis of the apophatic, contemplative, "hid divinity" tradition is the implication in Paul that "we are known," that God already has total knowledge of us.[243] What you do, then, is turn off the chatter in your mind, which is making more noise than a punk rock band ("drunken monkey," the Hindus call it) and relax into the divine knowledge of us which is one of the things meant by a cloud of unknowing.[244] Not as easy to do as it sounds: I've never known an instant of *real* quiet in my mind.

[271] Jaynes' book: the purely negative terms "hallucination" and "schizophrenia" overlook the constant tradition in poets to get *past* the tyranny of consciousness and reinforce it with a driving power that may not pull us back to the "bicameral" state but certainly isn't satisfied with the linear-discursive processes of the conscious mind. Plato, as he says, adopted Theseus' lunatic-lover-poet triad;[245] there were the "Muses" in Greece & the C of L [Court of Love] mistresses; there was the Romantic conception of "imagination"; there were the symboliste efforts to abandon the ego; there was surrealism & kindred movements in this century. Christ in the gospels, notably John, is portrayed as someone in whom the "right lobe" of the brain has completely taken over: he can do nothing except what he sees the Father do. John in particular seems to be trying to force us to say: if this man wasn't what he said he was he was certainly

the most deranged lunatic on record, unless his evangelist was, & the general ambience of the story seems to rule out paranoia on so titanic a scale.

[272] Except for shape poems, concrete poems, & typographical designs, all poetry is *conventionally* oral.

[273] I'm beginning to get glimpses of the main theme of this book: a mythical approach that's on the other side of consciousness from whatever Jaynes is talking about. The first stage of this is the violation of historical fact: the "it's just a myth & didn't really happen" stage. I got some of this into GC, along with the warning that Bultmann's effort to resolve the deadlock by "demythologizing" wouldn't work.[246] But here the "imaginative" way of reading the Bible is to be coordinated with the same way of reading literature, where, in Jungian terms, not the conscious ego but the superconscious individual directs. The way the Marxists cling to "historicity," which they make practically a synonym of Marxism, indicates that history is something to be transcended, not simply opposed.

[274] The vulnerable parts of the Bible for this approach are the creation myths in Genesis, Ruth & the Song of Songs, Job, John, and of course the Apocalypse. Oh, God, I hope this is the great religio-literary revolution I've dreamed of bringing off, and isn't just one more illusion of the same old illusion.

[275] The *tohu* and *tehom* of Genesis are "demythologized" forms of Tiamat the goddess of bitter waters.[247] Note that demythologizing is simply remythologizing. The Genesis account isn't one atom more rational or factual than its predecessor. It's more accommodated to the idiom of belief, but that's all. Note too how it's the remythologizing of Jesus (harrowing of the monster hell & the like) that's the main activity of tradition.

[276] I'm concerned with the Western trdn. [tradition] in its Greek & Hebrew origins: it's only in Greece that there's a clear development from myth to dialectic, and the literary affinities are clearest in Homer & early Greece. Also, the *literary* difference between myth & ritual is that ritual initiates dramatic forms; but it was only in Greece that it developed a full

drama with new generic characteristics. Elsewhere it hardly got beyond mummer's plays. (By "new" I mean the silly criticisms of Cornford raised by—is it Pickard-Cambridge?)[248]

[277] Whatever the ultimate fate of the Jaynes thesis, it seems reasonable to assume that dialectic is the normal language of consciousness. Consciousness thinks in terms of its own dictatorship, as in Plato's Republic. The word "individual" means (I suppose) the "undividable," which is as grotesque as the word "atom," which means the unsplittable.[249] This unitary subject naturally suggests a unitary object—in other words monotheism, the direction in which Socrates (according to Plato) is obviously going in the Apology and the Phaedo, though he clearly accepted the whole polytheistic-oracular setup. The various "bicameral" myths of the poets (the god, the Muse, the mistress, Eros, imagination, the surrealist unconscious) are remarkably consistent, and point to the inadequacy of the Jaynes thesis, which is Theseus' triad again.

[278] The first chapter is myth & concerns, primary & secondary. Primary concerns are those of the individual, who alone can experience. That means I've got two kinds of individual right away: the dictatorialized Platonic type, always awake & conscious & dominated by reason, with the will wholly enlisted in its services, & a more flexible unity-with-variety type. Secondary concerns arise from the social contract, are identity-with rather than identity-as, the "with" being society.

[279] Egyptian ladder as spire: Thespis, 396 n.[250]

[280] The first big crisis in the argument is in Chapter Two, where we move from hypothetical to erotic metaphor, and from there to ecstatic metaphor. (All metaphor is revolt against totalitarian social claims.) Eros is the highway to God. The third chapter is to deal with, perhaps be called, "Symbol and Spirit." Spirit leads toward a higher mythologizing of recapitulation (Irenaeus) where what proceeded from God at creation is reabsorbed into him.[251]

[281] The old idea that all kinds of mysteries of knowledge can be extracted from myth is, in modern terms, the fact that discursive prose is verbal work, while myths, like literature, are verbal play, & consequently can be "deconstructed" endlessly. Except that in practice you have to set

up a straight polysemous path from your construal starting point. This conception of play integrates the kookiest notion of criticism into the centre of contemporary theory.

[282] Poets meet the supremacy of ideology in two ways: by allegory and by realistic "displacement." Or both, of course: Marxism demands of literature realism with an allegorical basis. "Not ideas about the thing but the thing itself"[252] is a plea for anti-realistic metaphor disguised as a call to realism.

[283] Paul says "in him we live & move & have our being" [Acts 17:28] because if he said "her" he'd be speaking of embryos. But the "in" of "in him" is a different kind of metaphor from "in her." Or at least its context is different.

[284] No code of law in Egypt, as in Mesopotamia, because the will of the divine Pharaoh was law. Will of God delayed science in Hebrew culture for the same reason. In Xy [Christianity] the arbitrariness of the will of God is qualified by the descent of the Logos. This of course was growing in Philo, & the Stoics later.

[285] Why do people call *me* "anti-historical"? I talk about myth, and it's *myth* that's anti-historical. It's the counter-historical principle, just as metaphor is the counter-logical principle. History doesn't repeat itself: history repeats myth.[253] (It's not simple repetition, though: it's not a *da capo* aria but a theme with variations.) As I've often said, you never get logic in literature: what you get is what Susanne Langer would call virtual logic, a rhetorical illusion of logic.[254] Similarly you never get history in literature: you get virtual history, history assimilated to myth.

[286] The episode in Chapter Two about assonant devices in poetry could be expanded. A sensitive Hebrew scholar can see all the flickering and dancing of puns and other assonances in the O.T.: what gets translated is a heavy lump of "sense" that has nothing of that. It's not merely verbal magic but verbal *play*. FW [*Finnegans Wake*] [now?], of course.

[287] One has to steer a course between the Carlyle great man myth and the Marxists who think the historical process is the Holy Spirit (though of course Marxist leaders are great-man cult figures too). There's some-

thing to be said for Napoleon's observation that it was Alexander & Caesar who conquered Persia and Gaul, not Macedonia or Rome.[255]

[288] Thorkild Jacobsen's book *The Treasures of Darkness*, a sensitive and imaginative book about Sumerian and Akkadian culture, if somewhat over-bemused by Otto's book on the holy, says that two themes seem to assimilate the whole pantheon of gods, the wedding song and the under-world descent.[256] That's my Eros-Adonis axis, of course, and it unites the primary concerns of life, food and sex, with its primary anxiety and ultimate concern, death, and the passage through death. I should start thinking in terms of primary anxieties: they help to show how Tillich's "ultimate concern" is also a primary one.[257]

[289] Even more interesting is his contrast of hero and heros.[258] I must look up his associations with the latter (also the word), but the hero or warrior, seeking immortality by fame after death, is a type of the hero or ruler-god, I think, unless he means somebody like Gilgamesh, who wants immortality but refuses to accept death. He has the greater vision, of course, despite its youthful limitation. I wonder if the hero isn't the destructive half of a kind of Siva force, the constructive half of it being the builder who builds temples to house the gods, walls to protect a city (Gilgamesh), boats or arks to save their families in a flood. I still don't have the deluge myth clear, or why it's regarded as unique and un-repeatable (in Mesopotamian, Egyptian and Hebrew contexts).

[290] The greatest literary genius this side of Blake is Edgar Allan Poe—that's why he's regarded as fit only for adolescents, or French poets who don't really know English. I don't apply this to the poetry, but there's no prose tale, however silly, that doesn't hit an archetype in the bullseye. The allegedly humorous story "The Spectacles," about a man so short-sighted he falls in love with his grandmother, is an example: there's even a reference to Ninon de Lenclos.[259] I've recorded elsewhere what I got out of the domain of Arnheim story.[260]

[291] People interested in myth, including me, are often described as anti-historical, statically-minded, or Platonic idealists. That transfers to the writer a quality inherent in his subject.[261] When myth absorbs history it treats historical events as a kind of chaconne or passacaglia, a sequence of episodes representing essentially the same underlying theme. The

myth, in short, dehistoricizes; that is a barbarous word, but no more so than other words beginning with "de." It's curious that Marxist critics should talk so much about historicizing, because the myth of Marxism also turns history into a sequence of illustrations of an underlying "class struggle" ground bass.

[292] In the synoptics Jesus' "teachings," which are commentaries on the Torah, serve to link up the typological structure in which he personalizes the messianic figure pointed to by that Torah. His real originality is in the parables, which suggest that his life, from infancy to the passion, is also a discontinuous sequence of parables.[262]

[293] Chapter One deals with primary concerns; Chapter Two, where everything dissolves into the Word, forms a transition to the third chapter on symbolism, which transposes primary concern into the key of ultimate concern. The *most* primary concern of all, breathing, is transformed into spirit, & the spiritual meaning of food & drink, of love, of security & shelter & the sense of home, all follow it. The transition from material to spiritual, of course, is through the *verbal*: we don't go into a Platonic intelligible world.

[294] We think of words as human inventions, and of spirit as dissolved in nature outside us. In the N.T. the Word comes from and goes back to a world of mysterious remoteness, while the spirit works from within man, taking over first the "humanistic" world of language.

[295] Is literacy a primary concern? I should say that it was, so to speak, the primary secondary concern. It's the means of participating in the social contract, & in a society like ours illiteracy is a far worse handicap than being blind or paraplegic. But in primary (="primitive") societies there is no great yearning to read or write. I wonder if Aristotle's statement that everyone wants to know is true.[263] Everybody wants to experience, and the loss of sight or hearing or sexual power is a primary loss. Not thought.

[296] Consciousness is a magician who controls the demon of the will. Like other apprentices, it gets automatic with control, & so anarchic. Blake's Spectre of Urthona. Prospero was a magician of the old school, a Magus: he controlled a spirit of the elements and then let him go.

[297] A book on the Tibetan cult of Tara speaks of ten vows a lama has to take. The last one is: "Not to slander women, for they are the sources of wisdom." The same book has a passage about the subject-object world drying up into a word or mantra I must look up.[264]

[298] I've got to the point in Chapter One of saying that poetry is primitive but that is not a derogatory statement: even "childlike" isn't, as the child is the father of the man. Primitive also means senior, as well as, of course, primary.[265] The business of poetry's not being able to take in much abstraction & the affecting of prose syntax by the centripetal power of metaphor are themes in Two. That man Davie (I think) who plugged for syntax (Articulate Energy) was, I think, wrong, or at least limited.[266] The dropping of punctuation in modern poetry indicates a contrary movement.

[299] Primary concerns are related neither to the individual nor to society: they are generic: they antedate the I-we distinction. Of course only the individual experiences: famine is a social problem, but only the individual starves. I don't want to join the down-with-Descartes chorus, but I think a return to primary concerns and its language is taking place. The language of ideology is patriarchal, too: that's another thing that's changing. But what role does the Bible have here?

[300] The legend is halfway between the nomadic folktale and the centralized myth. It is typically a story pattern associated with a particular place. There are any number of Romeo & Juliet stories, but legend says that at this very cliff or lake two such lovers hurled themselves to their death, & so it has become known as Lover's Leap falls or cliff to this day. This specializing of story corresponds to local cults, the "high places" of Jeroboam [1 Kings 12:31–2]. Later, such legends are attached to some (usually itinerant) figure, like Hercules or Elijah. Myth, on the other hand, usually attaches to a centralized figure, like Solomon or Gilgamesh, prince of Uruk.

[301] Article in the Atlantic Monthly quoting theologians, Protestant and Catholic, about the historical Jesus.[267] Now: the Gospels present a mythological Jesus, and out of that an indefinite number of historical Jesuses can be extracted. The notion that "the" historical Jesus would emerge if we only juggled and jiggled the Gospels in just the right way, is

an obsession and an illusion. Granted that the Christ-figure was dropped into time as an egg is dropped into boiling water, it remains separate from the water. One book says that the wedding of Cana was the wedding of Jesus & Mary Magdalene, & that Jesus ducked the crucifixion and escaped to Marseilles, where he begot the Merovingian kings—the Bald, the Simple, the Fool and the Fat.[268] I don't find it convincing, but I suspect that if we found "the" historical Jesus it would be so shattering an anticlimax that very little Christianity would survive it. Only a Noah-family of people willing to accept the Jesus we now have, the mythological one.

[302] The Logos-over-Mythos superstition makes us think that Jesus was a teacher with an original doctrine, who in the Synoptics illustrated that doctrine with parables. The reverse is true: Jesus was original only as a story-teller, & his doctrines are commentaries on the O.T., echoing those of contemporary rabbis. (He was also, of course, original as a healer, but I'm thinking primarily of the literary context.) If the Gospels are inspired at all, they're inspired to prevent us from probing further than that. In John the parables disappear and are replaced by dialogues or discourses of self-definition, not of teachings. Of the thousands of things John 1 means, one is that in Christ Logos and Mythos are the same thing.

[303] One element in the third or symbolism chapter is phony representative symbolism, where primary concerns are attached to one member of an ascendant class, like Burke or Marie Antoinette (I have a quotation of Paine on this in the pink notebook I can use),[269] or all the goop & poop about the cruelty of cutting Charles I's head off (that is, considering what he did, and would have done if he'd won).

[304] Marx owes his colossal status as a modern thinker to the incisiveness with which he exposes the gap between the ideology of capitalism and the primary concerns of food and shelter that it overrides. Thus he begins with "commodity" in its secondary & primary references (reminding one of Faulconbridge's speech in King John, even though "commodity" means something rather different there).[270]

[305] The golden bowl is the "symbol" of Henry James' novel. The natural images of the Bible are, when united in the body of Christ, the

symbol of spiritual vision. But James' novels have a moving narrative (mythos) as well. I think the third chapter should move from the static apocalypse vision (which may come at the end of the second, of course) to the moving narrative vision that starts with the creation myths.

[306] Myths are constructed out of personalities assimilated to nature as ordinary experience sees nature: whimsical, unpredictable, liable to tamtrums sometimes, to serenity sometimes, sometimes bursting with life, sometimes dying or dead.

[307] Further on one: ideology is different from other things expressed in discursive prose because it's apologetic and metonymic. The world can't be perfect, so the ideological structure is *put for* the ideal as the best available. Also, it's explicitly partial: whenever a religion or political or national loyalty is differentiated from another, ideology is present. That would allow for social types of primary concern, such as the desire to know.

[308] Irenaeus on recapitulatio—find out what the Greek word is. It's the "repetition" of Kierkegaard, the new heaven and earth, the restated myth.[271]

[309] The whole Leviathan-Enoch-Lilith-Lucifer-rebel angels bit as the fall of the P creation myth I think runs through Job. It may be connected with apophatic & Boehme-like speculations of the kind the Church has always been so frightened of. Of course it's the P creation that generated the chain of being, the Ptolemaic universe, & the whole cosmic elaboration of political authority. Authority myths destroy art by making God an artist & nature his art. Browne on the horse & design absurdities.[272]

[310] Boehme with his doctrine of Nothing wanting to be Something is somebody I'll have to look at again, though he infuriates me.[273] With an apophatic God, I suppose, you just turn off the noise & listen to his knowledge of you. But a real grasp of the Priestly fall would bring out a tragic pattern that just isn't there now. The Russians (Berdyaev, Dostoievsky, Solovyov, Tolstoy, Merejkowsky) seem to know something about this. Schelling too, who's one of my central myth people.

[311] Jesus' use of the Son-Father identity leading to the grotesque myth

that God is male. Isaiah 49:15; 66:13; Matt. 23:37. Note how the mythical nature of the Gospels is, so to speak, postponing Jesus until the post-Easter hindsight. Especially in John, but then Luke's climax comes in Acts 1–2. The presence of Christ is in the meeting of the gospel & the reader: they don't point to a specific person outside them, or what Derrida calls a transcendental signified.[274] John identifies Jesus with the Logos: I think the Greek history of the word Logos is at a minimum here, but he can't have been unaware of that history.[275] (Re the above: Christ was God *and* a male, but the latter only before Easter.)

[312] Wonder if my lecture on Lear as pre-Christian prophecy could be used, including the O.T. cluster that I put into F.S.[276]

[313] If we find it difficult to tell the dancer from the dance,[277] why should we destroy our vision of the gospel by trying to separate the word from the speaker of the word? All those words are coming from inside ourselves. That is, the existential metaphor is evoked by the verbal one, and we join in the play, or dance.

[314] Jesus is not "a" historical figure: he's dropped into history as an egg is into boiling water, as I said [par. 301], and essentially "the" historical Jesus is the crucified Jesus. One can understand why the Gnostics tried to insist that the crucifixion was an illusion, but nobody can buy that now. The pre-Easter Jesus answers the question: "Can a revolt against Roman power succeed?"

[315] The answer is no, and the pre-Easter Jesus sums up the history of Israel, which is a history of "historical" failure.

[316] The first Eve was taken from the body of adam, in contrast to the world we know, which is the world of mother nature, where all new life, male or female, is born from a female mother. The second Eve was (in whatever "sense," spiritual or other) born from the Holy Spirit, and so to speak, isolated the "feminine" aspect of that Spirit. The simplest solution to my present question is: the real Gospel is not the Word simply, but the Word fertilizing the (female) spirit in the reader. That's clearly too simple, I think.

[317] Everything exclusive about Xy [Christianity] is pre-Easter; the spir-

itual or post-Easter sense is the everlasting gospel, which is "true" for those within it and intelligible, or rather interpenetrative, to (with?) those who are not. (It's really the post-Pentecost sense.)

[318] When logos established its supremacy over mythos, mythos was deprived of its ideological function. It then had to split into two parts: literary or hypothetical myth, and myth declared to be true, which meant myth with a "transcendental signified," as Derrida calls it. As that, it could be recreated as literature, but anxiety insisted on a "literal" or external basis. Hence what I call the Goethe (or rather Faust) fallacy: in the beginning God did something, and the words tell us what he did.[278] The same tendency is followed today by the jigglers and jugglers of the gospel narratives.

[319] Every one of the standard figures of speech, except the metaphor, draws attention to the fact that it's "just" a figure. The simile has its reassuring "like," the oxymoron draws attention to its self-contradiction; the hyperbole to its excess; the synecdoche to its deficiency; the metonymy to its "signified." Only the metaphor says "This is {not}." Juxtaposition of two images suggests identity, whether asserted by "is" or not; the fact that there are two images to be juxtaposed suggests the "is not" counterpoint.[279]

[320] The first chapter, which is reasonably clear now, is the Book of the Father. I don't know why, but symmetry demands that it must be. The reason why symmetry is right, as it assuredly is, will doubtless become clearer later. The metaphor chapter is about the Logos, following up the great intuition that John finds mythos & logos identical in Christ. The third chapter, on the Spirit, shows how the Spirit builds reality out of what begins as illusion, while the reality "out there" fades away into illusion. The whole in part, part in whole interchange is I think the climax of Two. At this rate, if Mallarmé really belongs in Three, maybe that's the book. But then there's the two creation myths, the up-down ladder, and—maybe the whole-part interchange is part of *Six*, for God's sake.

[321] Ideological statements deny what they say, and so can affirm by denying. When Rilke says his angels aren't Christian he's also saying that they damn well are.[280] Similarly with Mallarmé's "scarecrow" God.[281]

[322] Yes, the first chapter is about the Father: its closing cadences include the remarks on *Shirley*[282] which bring in two points: it's a corruption of the text of the Bible to assume that patriarchal ideology is anything but one more ideological corruption; two, that it's a grotesque superstition to think of God (apart from the Incarnation) as a male being. If he were, he'd *have* to have a female counterpart.

[323] There is no such thing as "literal meaning" except in historical and descriptive writing. Faust, as I say, follows the whole Christian tradition in saying "in the beginning was the act."[283] That introduces the "transcendental signified" into the Bible: in the beginning God did something, and the words are servomechanisms telling us what he did. The opening words of John, which mean exactly what they say, are there to warn us against looking for things outside the Bible that the Bible points to.[284] I don't know whether it's only Faust or Goethe himself who's being stupid here: I've always suspected it was Goethe.

[324] So that leaves only allegorical, tropological and anagogic. I used to call "literal meaning" allegorical, which is true, but of course real allegory is typology, and I wrote about that in GC, which has its faults, but I think if revised could be a very great book. The present book is tropological. It's concerned with figures of speech; it's moral and answers the question *quid agas*?[285] (the answer is: restore primary concerns to their primary place.[)] Also, apart from the Trinity, which seems to be organizing the book, everything seems to be running in threes.

[325] That means that an anagogic book to follow this one is a theoretical possibility, and here's a letter from my old student Merv Nicholson[286] urging me to write just such a book. Before I was out of my teens I'd thought that Anatole France's *Jardin d'Epicure* was in form the kind of book I'd like to write[287] (no, later than my teens). Later (much later) I read Merejkowski's book on Atlantis,[288] and thought that would be a model if the main subject were less crackpot. (Also, I'd want the Anatole-France-type book written by somebody (maybe me) with a real brain, not that languid goo in his noodle). But I suppose Nietzsche, especially the *Gaya Scienza*, would be the real model.

[326] So the anagogic book would be aphoristic, obviously, and all my

life I've had the notebook obsession manifested by what I'm doing at this moment. Writing in notebooks seems to help clarify my mind about the books I write, which are actually notebook entries arranged in a continuous form. At least, I've always told myself they were that. For GC I tried a different experiment: typing notes. They started off in the regular way, but before long I realized that I was just draining the "drunken monkey" babble of the so-called conscious mind off my skull. It didn't really work: I want to destroy those notes. The aphorism book is the "Twilight" of my ogdoad fantasy,[289] always thought of in my "seven or eight" terms as something perhaps not reached.

[327] I'm not wise enough to write a wise book (wisdom soon gets beyond words anyway) nor learned enough for an erudite book. What I might have is the rhetorical craftsmanship that's more relevant to such a job than either. Of course, it would mean living longer.

[328] The present book is recapitulating the bigger scheme. Chapter One, quite clear in my mind now, junks the literal level with its transcendental signified. Chapter Two reaches the climax of identity in a retake of GC's table identifying every category of being with the body of Christ [GC, 166–7]. Chapter Three, on the Spirit, is about *verum factum*: the spirit creates reality out of illusion, and reduces the pseudo-reality that's "there" *to* illusion. (Up to a point: some of it's there.)[290]

[329] Chapter Four begins with the two Genesis accounts, & extracts from them the three Miltonic levels of order: order, disorder (Adam & Israel) & perverted order. That can be applied to the Exodus to explain the O.T. identification of leviathan-monsters with foreign rulers: the revolutionary basis, in short. What Exodus eventually works out to is: the demonic can be simply suffered (hell) or recovered to become a titanic power in man's service. The Egyptians had wisdom & the Israelites looted it. Then we go on to law, and the illegitimate pun on law as analogical action ("types," as Xy [Christianity] says) and law as recurring natural process (return to the P creation myth).

[330] Re the bottom of p. 101 [pars. 326–7]: if Kundalini[291] woke up in my balls and shot all the way to the thousand-petalled lotus or whatever the hell in my noodle, I'd doubtless be a far better visionary, but I wouldn't necessarily be a better writer, any more than I'd be a better

pianist. Those things are separate crafts. The distinction may not work with sacred books, which makes things tougher for theory.

[331] Morris Eaves wants me to write an updated Polemical Introduction to this book: I don't know that I have that much command of the whole critical scene. He seems to feel that the post-structurals have control of the Comp. Lit. scene but that what's in central vogue now in English is a neo-historical movement, with strong Marxist affinities, trying to identify the mythical as a special case of the ideological. He spoke of being an examiner of a "whiz kid" who'd written something about death, mostly Kleist in substance, Heidegger in method—and felt she was really following the funeral cortege of Paul de Man.[292]

[332] I've said that Homeric criticism is back to a Homer who is not a man but a metaphor for the fact that we read *Iliad* & *Odyssey* as unities [*GC*, 206]. The fragments joined together postulated an editor, & this editor grew in genius until he practically became the poet—in fact did so become. In O.T. csm. [criticism] too the 4-documents plus editorial redactor have grown to the point where the ed. redact. has got to be so superb a genius that we'll soon be back to a new Moses.[293] (There's the legend about Ezra, but so far as I know nobody believes it, and what we have of Ezra doesn't look like so colossal a writer.)[294] The Art of Biblical Narrative[295] my ass: there's no such thing as Biblical narrative: there's only the Bible's narrative with a lot of sub-narratives. Similarly, there's no such thing as (except for convenience) "a" myth: there's only a mythology-grouping to which certain sub-mythical episodes are attached.

[333] The main point of Chapter Two is, I suppose, that the Hebrew Bible is written (Derrida is, I understand, a Sephardic Jew) but that the Christian Bible is also enclosed in a presence.

[334] Mircea Eliade's book on yoga says Oriental religions simply refuse to discuss the equivalent of the Biblical fall myth. The question "how did we get into this state of ignorance?" they refuse to discuss: it's beyond human capacity to discuss it.[296] The fall in the Bible may be part of its revolutionary simplification: everything *has* to have some explanation. But I wonder if the Genesis story isn't deliberately trivialized: there's something so sardonic about it (as about the earlier Mesopotamian Adapa[297] and other such stories) as compared with Paul's overblown

Midrash that poor Milton had to take so seriously.[298] And, of course, the sardonic element returns in Job.

[335] Auden has Simeon say that you can't know original sin because that's what conditions the drive to knowledge in the first place.[299] If given, that knowledge would have to be part (or possibly the whole) of revelation. I say possibly the whole because I imagine revelation is a hologram: it's all contained in each part.

[336] The third chapter is still cloudy, but it may turn on this holograph issue. A symbol is a unit of which the whole is spirit, and each unit contains the whole of spirit: this is where the interchange of part and whole comes in. The soul-body complex is to spirit as embryo is to baby, as type is to antitype, as illusion is to reality (after what we call reality has vanished into illusion). This is not "dualistic," unless it is dualism to say that an embryo and a baby live in different environments. Spirit gets its name from the most primary of all primary concerns: breathing. And air is the medium for seeing and hearing.[300]

[337] In One I introduce the theme of the double heroine: this gets picked up again in the Rcsm. [Romanticism] chapter where a female Nature is either cherishing with Wordsworth or sinister with Schopenhauer (and Sade).[301]

[338] (I may have this.) When I first began to think about a book on the literary context of the Bible, the literary critics specifically interested in the Bible were few and apologetic; today they are many and confident. The number coming the other way, from Biblical scholarship to an interest in literary criticism, has increased proportionately. I am now, therefore, not a speaker of a prologue, but a member of an aging chorus.[302] Of course every scholar of senior years living in the nineteen eighties has lived through forty or fifty such revolutions even in the fields that directly concern him. This particular revolution may confirm the accuracy of my instincts thirty years ago, but does little for me now. However:

Set the word and its origin and put the maker in his place.

So counsels the Sepher Yetzirah (Book of Creation), a pioneering work of

Kabbalism that uses the letters of the Hebrew alphabet as symbols for the creative principles of the world.[303] I have taken its advice to refer to the ordering of one's own mind, and in that context have tried to follow it.

[339] Subconscious association with sounds of words in a language; in English God is good; the Son is the sun (of righteousness); the whole is holy. Similarly with other verbal patterns: "fantasy and fugue," for example, suggests creation to a musician and chaos to a psychiatrist. Not that I know what to do with these statements.

[340] Perhaps the metaphor chapter should establish the metonymic nature of all ideology: what's in charge is *put for* the ideal, because we obviously can't have the ideal.[304] We move through erotic metaphors (Eliade, I see, has an essay on androgyne symbolism)[305] to existential metaphor, or experience of identity with light or spirit, which are forms of panoramic apocalypse. Participating apocalypse comes when we enter the Word, which up to that time is an apocryphon, remove all the seals and identify with it—Ezekiel ate it [Ezekiel 3:1–3]. This is, I suppose, one of the things meant by "deconstructing" the text. Through the writing to identity with the presence. For again, just as mythos *is* logos in Christ, so presence *is* absence, or rather, the presences of Christ & reader (with the Spirit) unite in the kingdom of absence. (That phrase is Dennis Lee's.)[306]

[341] That's where my prerevolutionary point goes, also the Burke-Paine token-metonymy one. We enter a world where Jesus is still alive, a world opposite to anything "the quest for the historical Jesus" could ever reach. This direct inner deconstructing search is the "mystic" Boehme-Blake approach—at least that's a very direct kind.

[342] Dylan Thomas in the Winter's Tale puts the crisis in the line "And the bird descended."[307] The descent of the bird-spirit at the moment of birth *and* consummation *and* death is the transubstantiating moment, as in the Eastern mass, where Epiphany replaces Christmas.

[343] The Bible also has the anados of Kore[308] in the stories of Ruth, Susanna and the Shulamite. Also Hagar is (like Ruth at the beginning) a wanderer, the female counterpart of Esau (and of course Ishmael). Naomi, who descends to Moab & comes back, is a type of the Church in Rev. 12.

[344] Three stages: first, we belong before we are, & few of us find any clarification of our social context. Second, an antithesis develops in which the individual with his wants collides with what society will let him do. Third, a state in which the individual is not diminished in dignity by his social contract. This is the state of ideal democracy, where primary concerns are primary, and therefore social concerns are subordinated to individual experience.

[345] Re the Cambridge Classicists—Frazer, Cornford, Murray, Harrison—critics are lazy, and can't hold things in their minds that aren't in vogue. It's an easy step from "I forget the stuff" to "that stuff's out of date." It's a still shorter step from there to "well, it must have been discredited by somebody."

[346] In the *Eumenides* Apollo argues that the father is the only real parent, the mother being only the place where the birth happened, & he cites the birth of Athene from Zeus for confirmation.[309] Oh, God, this business of sexual symbolism is tricky to handle: like the male-female translations of yang and yin, they're distortions of a quite comprehensible metaphorical design.

[347] I've been called a (Platonic) dualist, but I'm not one, and neither was Plato. There is only one form of dualism, the Cartesian cloven fiction of subject & object, a formidable barrier to thought because our language is Cartesian. But it isn't dualism to say that an embryo and a baby live in different environmental worlds, nor to say that before and after death are also different worlds. I said that, dammit.

[348] Erich Heller remarks of such poets as Rilke that they emphasize "praise," but intransitively: they don't praise God or nature or any object.[310] The objective of praise is still in the split Cartesian world. It's what one praises *from* that counts. In the Bible that source is God, who doesn't love anything because he is love.

[349] I've just finished rereading Bulwer-Lytton's *Strange Story*, and followed it with *Ayesha* of Rider Haggard. In spite of all the kitsch and turgid Victorian rhetoric, I found them, especially the first, quite rewarding. I'd forgotten, or thought I'd forgotten, that the end of Lytton's story is set in Australia, just before the gold rush there. The hero, with his wife

dying (in an undisplaced story she would die, whether she came to life again or not), discovers some gold, but throws it away impatiently. On August 4, 1986, Jane & I were taking a bus tour around Cairns. The hospital had encouraged us not to hang around. At 3.10 p.m. I knew it had happened:[311] I was standing on a bridge over a gorge, and flung an Australian penny into it—a gesture I've never really understood: it certainly wasn't "for luck."

[350] Anyway, I went on to Haggard because the name Ayesha turns up in the final scenes.[312] (Perhaps both of them got it from Morier, the Hajji Baba man).[313] Lytton's finale, which is rather remarkable, has a shadow-figure die and get replaced by a reviving anima: there's no doubt about Jung's affinity with romance, as of Freud's with comedy.

[351] The political analogue of Freud is Marx: what's the political analogue of Jung? There isn't one really: his real goal is the individual who's moved his centre of gravity from the ego, so its political vision is a democracy in which the individual is not diminished in dignity by his social contract. The closest approach I can think of is William Morris, but he fell into left-wing hysteria, just as Carlyle, Ruskin & Burke fell into right-wing ones. (So did Jung.) Coleridge stopped at anxiety, but was heading in the same direction, and Nietzsche is closer to Adler.

[352] I'm at the stage again, I hope, at which I can use individual papers to clarify my views on this book. (It now has a working title: "Words with Power.") My next assignment is a lecture in a series associated with the name of Thomas More.[314] I see two frames of reference. One is the vague term "science fiction," which means (a) technological fantasy or hardware fiction (b) software or philosophical fiction. The former descends from Bacon's *New Atlantis*, the latter from More's Utopia (which produces either the Eutopia or the Dystopia). The other referential area is that of the four early 16th c. books that define the nature of Renaissance secular society: the prince (Machiavelli's The Prince), the courtier (Castiglione's The Courtier), the statesman (More's Utopia) and the fool (Erasmus' Praise of Folly). Note how the paradox of the courtier who uses his accomplishments to advise the prince & thereby reduces him to a justice of the peace, reappears in the contrast of Hythloday and More himself. More provides the answer that baffled Castiglione—the state modelled on the secular virtues, although Castiglione does provide the

Eros theme the others lack. Erasmus' conception of "folly" expands into
the reality-as-illusion theme. In the science fiction area, there's a very
significant link with More in R.A. Lafferty's *Past Master*.[315]

[353] Back to Chapter Two: the second stage of response is a still photo-
graph or picture of the plot, when it's mythos-language; when it's logos-
language there's a large element of diagram, which is also pictorial.
That's been there since Plato's divided line.[316] This opens up an expansion of mythos or narrative to any kind of verbal sequence, & of metaphor or juxtaposition to any kind of pattern. Then, moving back through
erotic & enthusiastic metaphor, we see that what we get into is identity
as and with—and that, of course, to the part-whole antithesis resolved by
interpenetration (Coleridge through Barfield).[317]

[354] I want to make the interchange of reality & illusion the main theme
of Three; but I wonder if I could start with the two fundamental metaphors of way (mythos-sequence) and ladder (metaphor-stasis). One is, of
course, experience, which is always unique, and the other is knowledge,
which is never the unique. So far myth & metaphor are a horizontal-
vertical, experience-knowledge, uncritical-self conscious antithesis that
has to be resolved in a space-time union. Structural knowledge isn't real
knowledge until mythos-experience fuses with it: similarly, the uncritical preliminary reading is transformed into a *way* of reading, which I
suppose is where the "spiritual sense" theme starts.

[355] The ladder is a vertical line cutting through the mythos at a point
between past-fixated wisdom and future-fixated prophecy. That's a cross
that may give me my four sections: Hermes-authority in the top,
Prometheus-revolt in the bottom; past-centered renewal (Adonis) and
future-centred redemption (Eros). Hermes is the north-west quadrant
(past & authority), Adonis south-west (past & recurrence), Prometheus
south-east (future & revolt) Eros north-east (future & redemption). This
reverses the Hermes-Adonis relationship in my traditional doodles.

[356] I'm thinking now of three chapters on myth, metaphor & symbol.
Then an intercalary chapter on the whole Bible, applying the first three
to it & incorporating the GC theses. Then the four deconstructed Bibles
and their literary infiltrations. That's 7/8 altogether. It's doubtless in the
intercalary chapter that the way & ladder imagery goes (myth & meta-

phor, respectively: perhaps the spirit is a circle enclosing the cross. Or the still point at the centre which is also the circumference). The last four chapters might be called something like "Rivers of Eden," & should have the epigraph from the Sepher Yetzirah.[318]

[357] The Hermes chapter comes to a climax in the Mutabilitie Cantoes, but Shakespeare, the court masque, Milton & whatever I can get out of Dante will be involved. The Adonis chapter will be on cycles (Spenglerian & Viconian), & on the various relationships of comparative mythology to Biblical structures. Demonic parody & analogy—Giles Fletcher quote[319] and the white goddess: Milton's P.R. [*Paradise Regained*] passage.[320] Prometheus will be mostly Blake & Shelley, with the analogy of descent & ascent (i.e., the descent which is not to hell & the ascent which is not to heaven). Eros I think is clearer: I think I can use more of the Bible itself.

[358] The metaphor chapter shows me departing from my experience-and-knowledge antithesis and trying to work out a participation thesis. Where this will take me I'm not wholly sure, but I'm going in the direction of that world which is totally symbolic that Jung & Eliade & that lot talk about.

[359] The most pressing question is the strategy of chapters three & four. I've been assuming that I had a third chapter, "Symbol and Spirit," dealing with (a) the decentralizing & interpenetrating process following the apocalyptic vision (b) the whole & part interchange (c) a quite vague notion of a circle (or the infinite centres-of-circles in interpenetration) as distinct from the horizontal line of myth & the axis mundi or vertical line of metaphor (d) a very clear explanation of the contrast of psychikos & pneumatikos, unless that's too Biblical (e) some etymological points in my Royal Society paper.[321] I wanted it to be in particular The Book of the Spirit, following the chapters on the mythical Father & the metaphorical Word.

[360] If such a chapter is forthcoming, then I think of my "intercalary" chapter on the Bible, which may have a Part Two to itself and the Sepher Yetzirah motto.[322] This would summarize the first three chapters in a commentary on the Bible. Parts One & Two seem to want to run in threes, following the Trinity: why Part Three seems to want four I don't know.

[361] Anyway: myth in the Bible. Two creation myths, suggesting the two aspects of nature. Fallacy of "the" historical Jesus at the end: John as the beginning of the N.T., presenting a Christ in whom mythos and logos become the same thing. The demonic & human falls: the former animates at Job & the latter S.S. [Song of Songs] & Ruth. Metaphor climaxes in the apocalyptic identification of all categories of being with Christ in the *other* John, the end of the N.T. (Neither John, of course, either the other one or the beloved disciple.) Then the definition of spirit.

[362] If I'm following the scent, I have a circle (my three theory blocks and the Trinitarian Bible) inside a square (the four confiscated gods).[323] But why is the circle threefold? Or, because the four could be quadrants of a circle too, why is *this* circle threefold?

[363] Or, I might stop this book at Chapter Four, the recapitulation of the Bible, on the principle that a big book is a big evil, and leave the four deconstructions for later.

[364] My hesitation in doing so is that I may not have a Chapter Three. I suppose tactically the best thing to do is to try to finish the Metaphor chapter, and at the same time draw up notes for the Bible chapter. Look, there just *has* to be a third chapter on symbol and spirit: I *can't* get along without it. At this point one has to ask the Spirit to suggest a theme for the chapter on him.

[365] Four: For the writers of the Gospels, the post-Easter (=Pentecostal) Christ is *primary*: "the" historical Jesus *secondary*. Hence they present the latter only in so far as he's consistent with the former. As usual, the Logos ascendancy reverses the priorities. The gospel writers weren't interested in history, but in the power that stops history.

[366] All human souls are symbolically female in relation to a symbolically male God.[324] Surely that's a clue to the third chapter: the spirit speaks a language different from the language of nature.

[367] I'm in the thrashing-around stage again, and this time I wonder if the Bible chapter isn't the *third*, the fourth being the secularizing and democratizing of the Scriptural idea, & forming the transition to Part Two. Possible title:—well, Symbol & Spirit might do. That would leave a

fourth title for a fourth chapter, perhaps going through Boehme to the intransitive poets of praise.[325] Word and Context.

[368] At the beginning of Xy [Christianity] there was a pre-historic Jesus concealed in the O.T. and the post-Easter risen Jesus. That was the Christ that Paul worked with. Only later did it seem essential to insert *a* historical Jesus in between, & that was what the Gospels did. There is no historical Jesus at all in the N.T. outside the Gospels.

[369] There is no continuous literal meaning in the Bible: whatever statement might be taken as literally true or factual is that way by accident. "Levels" (they're not levels: that's a metaphor hung over from the chain of being) of meaning start with the "allegorical." As I said, the allegorical meaning in the Bible is typological,[326] & typology is the reversal of causality that leads to what Michael in Milton calls "spirit" [*Paradise Lost*, bk. 12, ll. 485 ff.]. I note this because I'm still fussing over whether Chapter Three is going to be on the Bible or not. If not, I'm stuck with five chapters.

[370] Anyway, typology has penetrated our own time, especially in all the false analogies from evolution. Man is the antitype of animals, is the assumption; consciousness (or whatever) is what animal or insect behavior is pointing to.

[371] In my symbolism paper I used the somewhat farcical examples of *Axel* & Das Esseintes' trip to England:[327] I should look at Valéry. If I can't after all figure out the Jeune Parque, I should be able to do something with Teste.[328] (That is, the anti-kinetic view of the arts that we find also in Joyce's Portrait.)

[372] What attracts me about Valery is (a) his secularizing of all the religious metaphors of Mallarmé (b) his continuing of the Boehme tradition. Mallarmé really does talk sometimes as though he thought literature was a "substitute" for religion, though of course no "substitute" can have more than an *ersatz* reality. I suppose he would say, if he were using my terms, that literature is the antitype of what religious symbolism hazily points to. This is a defensible view in itself, but criticism has further to go than that.

[373] Well, Valéry: at the end of his Ébauche d'un serpent he says:

> Cette soif qui te fit géant,
> Jusqu'à l'Être exalte l'étrange
> Toute-Puissance du Néant![329]

I suppose this is the same serpent that bites the narrator near the beginning of La Jeune Parque.[330] We start out with things like "nature abhors a vacuum," which is a metaphor. As metaphors are for practical purposes the elements of language, they can't be broken down into more elementary units: they can only be rearranged. One rearrangement is "God made the world from nothing." What was God before he made the world? Boehme says "a nothing longing to be something." At least that seems to me what his Urgrund is a metaphor for.[331] This is one of the metaphors of the *via negativa* that extends from John of the Cross to Taoism with its *wu wei* notion: by doing nothing everything is done.[332] The Abbé Sieyes uses similar formulas for his "Third Estate" epigram.[333]

[374] In Valéry the principle of nothing becoming something is associated with the serpent of self-conscious knowledge. So it's in the direct line of Sartre's Being & Nothingness, which in turn takes up Shakespeare's "nothing" as the total alienation of the ego deprived of its identity (symbolized in Lear or Richard II, by the loss of one's social function).

[375] The allegorical "level," I've said, is really the typological, and is supposed to answer the question *quid credas*?[334] One has to think of *credo* as "what do I assume to be an antitype, the reality to which everything else is related as a type?" Traditionally, the soul or vital principle was the antitype of the physical world, the Platonic intelligible form. With Paul the soma psychikos, the soul-body unit, is a type of which the antitype is spirit, the soma pneumatikos.[335] What is spirit? It's the whole of which each spirit is a part, but with the power of reversal, so that it becomes a part, something the individual *has*. It's also the antitype of birth, as birth is the antitype of embryonic life. Spirit means breath, the most primary of all primary concerns, the great sign of the appearance of birth, the thing we can't live twenty minutes without. Spirit is the antitype then of

air, the invisibility that makes the real world visible.[336] But the real world is not the world that's there: it's the fictional world of *our* creation that's real. So what is real, like literature & mathematics, is an epiphany of spirit. Stuck again. No, not wholly stuck: this is the point where externality is rejected, and hence *quid credas* turns into *quid agas*.[337] Here we leave the metaphor-cluster apocalyptic panorama, and rejoin narrative without being bound to it.

[376] I think I've said somewhere about Bunyan that he believed firmly in the objectivity of the demonic. When Christian is in the valley of the shadow, horrible blasphemies resound in his ears, which distress him the more because "verily he thought they had proceeded from his own mind."[338] A reader today would say that verily they had proceeded from his own mind, and that if Christian is an aspect of the narrator of *Grace Abounding*, verily it was high time they did. Yet Bunyan was right in a way: the blasphemies were not objective to begin with, but once they are audible they start to be objectified, and once they're objectified they're recognized. Start again.

[377] To the extent that they are objectified they lose the power to condition behavior. Spenser makes a similar point about Orgoglio and Duessa: when evil is isolated from its interpenetration with good it becomes nothingness.[339] Note that there's a bad, or moral, interpenetration as well as a good one. The looseness of the terms good and evil doesn't matter: looseness is built in.

[378] I wonder if I'm not still revolving around the Burnt Norton schema of plenitude & vacancy. The reversal of reality & illusion is plenitude, the way of work & creativity. The via negativa, the way of Mallarmé's Igitur & Valery's Teste, is the everything-out-of-nothing aspect. Perhaps "symbol" is the key to plenitude and "spirit" to vacancy. And, of course, perhaps not. Try again. I got some intuitions out of Poe's Domain of Arnheim long ago on the transformation of nature.[340]

[379] All reading begins in the revolt against narcissism: when a book stops reflecting your own prejudices, whether for or against what you think you "see in it," & begins to say something closer to what it does say, the core of the reality in the "objective" aspect of it takes shape & you start wrestling with an angel.[341]

[380] I've been reading Jung's autobiography (dictated mostly to a colleague at the age of eighty, but by a long way his best book). He says that that Kenya tribe he visited had a word meaning, more or less, God, which they applied to the sun, but only to the sun at the instant of rising, and to the moon, but only when the moon was in a certain phase at a certain place in the sky.³⁴² In our object-obsessed language we say "those guys worship the sun, & maybe sometimes the moon." We overlook the fact that for them a "god" is not just an object, or even an object at all: it's an event or epiphany of what may be an object. The event or epiphany is primary, also more primitive: its objective aspect coincides with a subjective moment of self-awareness.

[381] Like other primitive features, this one enters Xy [Christianity]. The real Jesus is not the historical but the epiphanic Jesus, the post-Easter and pre-"Christian" Jesus of the O.T. The Jesus of the Gospel is not presented as a historical figure, but assimilated to the epiphanic one. Incidentally, that makes a lot of my Milton stuff useful.

[382] Spirit is subjectively air because that's the most primary of primary concerns (I mean of course breathing is): it's objectively air because the invisible air makes the rest of the world visible. Spirit, then, is the unity, expressible only by metaphor, of subject and object in which the essential reality of the two are one. The difference between soul & spirit is that soul is *anima*, receptive & creaturely, and above all individual: a group of souls are still aggregates. We use "body" to mean a plurality as a higher individual: that's why it's only "body" that enters the resurrection by becoming spirit. That's where the part-whole paradox begins.³⁴³

[383] Look, I've just *got* to have a third chapter, & can't duck out of it by starting on the Bible. To leave it out would be to leave an antithesis unresolved that would mean total failure. Also a kind of insult to the Spirit, who I hope wants the book written. I've been ducking the question because of the clock ticking and cuckooing, but if the Spirit *is* given greater knowledge among men thereby—never mind how little—the time will be made non-existent, as Blake said.³⁴⁴

[384] Had I world enough & time,³⁴⁵ what would I aim for? Part One:
  1. Myth & concern, as I have it.
  2. Metaphor & identity, as it's going now.

3. Symbol and Spirit, whatever the hell *that* is in theory.
Part Two: 4. The Myth of the Bible.
   5. The Imagery (juxtaposed words) of the Bible.
   6. The Symbolism (Spiritual Meaning) of the Bible.
Part Three: 7. The Bible of Authority (Hermes).
   8. The Bible of Renewal (Adonis)
   9. The Bible of Revolt (Prometheus).
   10. The Bible of Redemption (Eros).
The ideal book, then, would be a tetractys. The myth chapter, which sets out the human condition and its need for help, is the Book of the Father. The Books of Word & Spirit form a pair completing it, then the three Bible books, then the four dealing with the human quaternity following the Bible.

[385] Four I have a good deal of material for. The two accounts of creation, with the demonic & human counter-movements, will give me the outline of the fourfold human Bible. Also the destruction of the historical-Jesus figment & its replacing by the epiphanic Jesus. In John mythos & logos are the same thing. The Law-Creation Bible of authority; the Promethean Job & Isaiah-2 revolt; the Bible of cycles (negative implication) & the Ruth-SS [Song of Songs] Bible of redemption: I think it'll come clear.

[386] Five I haven't much besides repeating the apocalyptic panorama of all categories of being identified with Christ. Perhaps my way & ladder papers[346] belong here as summing up Chapters One & Two. You'll need the *axis mundi* to explain the Hermes Bible, in any case. Six is a complete haze as yet, because three is. But I think it aims at a goal (*telos*) of recapitulatio. Also, of course, "symbol" introduces a completely decentered view of literature and the Bible. Symbol is the *unit* of subject-object identity: metaphor is a verbal phrase unit incorporating the reader. Perhaps Four deals with the Way as far as wisdom; Five with the axis mundi; Six with the epiphanic god who is no longer an object ("Praise {God sous rasure} [rature]").[347]

[387] One: The point about there not being a definitive grail legend before Chrétien is not that there's no evidence for it, but that the illusion that there is one comes from *later* reading, through Malory to Tennyson and Wagner.[348]

[388] I have *logos* supremacy as linked to the work ethic,[349] but there's also a suggestion in another note that work is connected with renewal and play with resurrection.[350] *Mere* work, or drudgery, is simply the squirrel-cage cycle; but at best the cycle is still a cycle: it does come around again. (Schiller's Aesthetic Education of Man is the source here, not Huizinga.)[351]

[389] I think "deconstruction" is something literature does to itself, whether with anxiety or without it. As a critical technique it seems to me popular because facile, a "new criticism" analysis with no holds barred. Of course I may be wrong: this nearly always includes an unspoken "but I damn well don't think so." Not in this case, though: I'm really very uncertain. But my theory of modes seems to me better because it follows a pattern that literature itself creates; in criticism, the medieval four levels theory (the "levels" metaphor is expendable) supplies a rationale for the procedure.

[390] As I've said, there being no literal meaning in the Bible that actually *is* the Bible,[352] GC dealt with the allegorical meaning, which for the Bible is the double-mirror typology. For this book I want to work out some of the implications of the tropological or *quid agas* meaning.[353]

[391] These include, first, the unifying of the two aspects of rhetoric, the ornamental (mythico-poetic) and persuasive (mythos employed in the service of logos) aspects of figurative language. Many problems here: when Jesus ends a parable by saying: "Go thou and do likewise" [Luke 10:37], he doesn't primarily mean, or perhaps even mean at all: "Go invent other parables." So am I not, like the theologians and historians, simply creating one more pseudo-Bible outside the Bible?

[392] Perhaps, but let that go for the moment. One focus here is the possession of literature as an aesthetic object-world, the Nazi-commandant-who-loves-Shakespeare paradox. I've taken to starting everything I write with a personal reminiscence, because I want to involve myself, as the reader I know best, with what I'm reading. I also want to distinguish the subjective possession of an object from a model in the mind around which the lifestyle is shaped. It's linked to K's [Kierkegaard's] either-or dilemma, but the context is very different.

[393] Things seem to be clearing up around my Utopia,[354] one of them being the contrast between software & hardware Utopias. The latter are future-oriented, & dependent as they are on mechanism, they raise the connection with the mechanical that all portrayals of life without self-conflict provide. More's title [Utopia] indicates that the transcendence of time & space can come only from the *nowhereness* of the soul, the "nothing" that Sartre found in consciousness. Sartre's final commitment to Communism was a contemptible betrayal of his own principles, the "inauthentic" lying to oneself under the pretext of being practical & expedient. One doesn't feel that More's defence of the status quo was a self-betrayal of that kind. It wasn't that he died a martyr to the status quo, but that there was nothing to betray his principles *to*, unless one considers H8's [Henry VIII's] self-deification something.

[394] Huizinga's play thesis[355] is deeply involved in this book: one thing is ritual play, as at a convocation, where the pretence that degrees are being conferred at that moment is a *symbol* of a certain process. I suppose this comes under the whole business of sacramental symbolism, the analogy of religion where there is any religion: in Marxist countries demonstrations and the like are symbols within the analogy of solidarity.

[395] Wild guess: I wonder if the point of 3 and 6 isn't an imaginative or literary Thomism where it's not the universal but the spiritual analogue of the symbol that's real? That would equate reality with created "fiction," but would also be a transition to an imaginary literary "Scotism," of a kind that Hopkins was groping for. Hopkins' "inscape" would be a vision in the panoramic apocalypse area, and "instress" the recovery of one's own involvement with it.[356] The spiritual world is the order of being in which what is in this world expressible only by metaphor becomes existential. To reach this we have to go beyond the unities of myth and metaphor to a completely decentered and interpenetrating universe: the stage represented by the decentered Bible.

[396] Perhaps all this last note means is that I haven't yet really understood Hegel's *Phenomenology*. But I don't know: I have no interest or belief in absolute knowledge: I may be climbing the same spiral mountain, but by a different path. The hypostasis of the hoped-for, the elenchos of the unseen [Hebrews 11:1]. If I could articulate that in my own words, I could burn the straw and pass on (I'm thinking of St. Thomas Aquinas

on his deathbed.)[357] Hegel is a Gnostic, of course, and while I have a great respect for Gnostics, I don't altogether trust them. At *their* point of death there's a separation of physical body and spirit, but their spirit is patterned on the soul or mind, & isn't a real spiritual body.

[397] I seem to be moving toward some kind of final statement, but it doesn't have to be a single unified statement. The book these notes are preoccupied with is the main job, but there's a number of other things I want to do that this book can't cannibalize. The education hamper-spanker[358] is on its way, but there are still over twenty unpublished, or rather unreprinted, essays. Most of them will probably get absorbed in Words with Power, but some won't: the Wagner, the Morris, the Vico perhaps, the Vico-Bruno-Joyce, the Castiglione, the More's Utopia paper I'm doing now, the Wiegand lecture, the Royal Society symbols paper, the Smith paper perhaps—that's nine,[359] even if the others (Ontario 1784–1984, the short lyric introduction)[360] get squeezed out, and the various religion papers (Montreal, Chicago, Vision-Belief, Way, Ladder, etc.)[361] get absorbed in here. I think the Ruth paper will still make a tenth.[362]

[398] But now I feel I must do something on Samuel Butler,[363] even if I don't get it done in time for Jerry's Festschrift.[364] I can always dedicate it to him anyway. A book with More & Castiglione weighing down one end and Morris & Butler weighing down the other would be a well unified book. More accurately, they would be four essays on the relation of education to a social model. *Utopia*, *Cortegiano*, *News from Nowhere* and *The Way of All Flesh* (I think, rather than the *Erewhon* books) would be the main foci.

[399] I've also been considering an article on ghost stories & the 19th c. occult (no other century produced ghost stories worth a damn). The main focus of interest, for reasons I've given elsewhere, would be Henry James. Curious that the only one who wrote better ghost stories was also named James.[365]

[400] But as I started thinking about that I got increasingly attracted to an article on "Fairies & Elementals."[366] In studying the "Faerie" theme in Spenser I became aware of the conception of a world occupying the same time & space as England but differing in moral perspective. That's differ-

ent, though. What I'm interested in is mainly:

1. The Paracelsian tradition of the spirits of the elements in Shake-
   spearian comedy & romance (MND [*A Midsummer Night's Dream*]
   and T [*The Tempest*] particularly) and in early Milton, especially
   Comus. I have always had the feeling that there was something to be
   pinned down here that I never did pin down. The parody in the
   Rape of the Lock should be noted too.

2. Romantic developments of this in the Germans (Novalis especially)
   and in George MacDonald. Morris' romances of course, early &
   late. Here we shade off into the occult & ghostly.

3. Lewis Carroll's *Sylvie & Bruno*, one of the most off-putting books
   in the language. But its conception of a "fairy" world close to
   children, dreams, and everything related to what the theosophists
   call the "astral" will bear a good deal of thinking about. I suppose
   Bruno's relentless & nauseating cuteness is his way of coming to
   terms with little boys: Alice is never cute: that's one of the things
   that's so wonderful about her, and neither really is Sylvie.

4. John Crowley's *Little, Big*, a book the author handed to me at Smith,
   seems to know something about this: two of his characters are
   called Sylvie and Bruno, & the name "Bruno" suggests memory
   theatres.[367] Also A.E. Waite's *Quest of the Golden Stairs*, another
   superficially off-putting book.[368]

[401] I've just read Maureen Duffy's *Erotic World of Faerie*: a long, dull,
bad book.[369] But I read it through because it touches on material I want to
deal with. Curious how plodding down the centuries equipped only
with Freudian reductionism produces an exact counterpart of the old
dream books written for servant girls. Hair = pubic hair; cannibal giant =
daddy; bitch-witch = weaning mother; journey, dark man in your life,
good fortune, would produce the same structure. Maybe that *is* all the
fairy world amounts to; if so, the hell with it. But I don't believe it. In
Spenser the Quixote romance apparatus contributes a "Faerie" world
that's a Purgatorio of England itself, i.e., England rearranged into a
moral pattern. More's *Utopia* (and other Utopias) likewise. A narrow
approach, but a genuine one as far as it goes.

[402] It isn't that Freudians are stupid, but that they're so easily satisfied
with what they (think they) know. Similarly with Marxists and Christian
fundamentalists. Discovery, for them, is not interesting.

[403] Faith, the schoolboy said, is believing what you know ain't so. That's why some people, including me and, I gather, Paul Ricoeur, have switched to hope as the real basis.[370] Hope doesn't assert: it says Perhaps A, but then, perhaps B. A sympathy note after Helen's death told me the veil between life & death was very thin. To me it's as thick as the distance to the next star. But if the two possibilities, of nothingness and of something that makes sense, weren't equally present, the mind couldn't grow. If I *knew* that there was nothing, my motivation for going on by myself would drop to zero. If there is something, and I *knew* what that something was, the next life would be essentially the same as this one. So the mystery in death guarantees the liveliness of life.

[404] I've been more or less an unconscious advocate of holism, assuming that everything worked together for the wholeness of the whole, which is Platonic, or that wholeness was what made the work organic & not mechanical, which is Coleridgean. What I now feel is that wholeness is a mimesis of objectivity. It disintegrates when the subject starts merging with it.[371]

[405] I wonder if it's remotely possible to reverse the order of parts One & Two; I'd start then with the Bible & from there go on to the "secular" myth-metaphor-symbol sequence. I don't suppose it would be at this stage. Oh no, how could I make the point that for John mythos & logos are the same thing in Christ?[372]

[406] The part-whole distinction again: the 18th c. sublime-beautiful is an aspect of it. The sublime leads to the "oceanic" feeling of submergence;[373] the beautiful to the sense of possession, which on its lower levels is the elite possession of Fabergé toys. The infinite multiplicity of the "collideorscape"[374] is closer to the reality of beauty than wholeness, which is iconic.

[407] I've said this before: the theologian is doing an essential job up to the point when he unconsciously takes his doctrinal structure to be the real Bible, of which the actual Bible is a parable or example. It's conscious in Newman's remark that the Bible isn't there to teach doctrine but to prove it;[375] but Newman's naive & obsessed mind couldn't take in the Bible. With the rise of descriptive writing we get the Biblical scholar unconsciously assuming that his historical framework *is* the real Bible,

the actual Bible being its parable. He'd deny this in theory, but pursues i
in practice.

[408] The whole-part interchange comes through in the church-work
relationship as well as the church-Bible one. More's *Utopia* depicts a non
Christian state which is bigger and closer to revelation than the Churcl
More adhered to. I don't admire H8 [Henry VIII], of course, but th•
Reformer's claim that revelation comes not through the Church bu
through a dialogue between a teacher-Bible and a pupil-Church wa
dead right. It would have been wrong for More not to resist H8; but hi
Utopia, which tolerates Xy [Christianity] but doesn't enforce it, is mor•
Xn [Christian] than his public life was.[376]

[409] Further on wholeness (128):[377] I still think it's an essential heuristi
principle for criticism concerned with knowledge of the work as object
But there's another stage concerned with multiplicity, identification witl
at a higher level. Note that identification here is of a different kind from
naive identification with a character (a form of controlled lunacy).[378]

[410] If Hegel had written his Phenomenology in *mythos*-language in
stead of in *logos*-language a lot of my work would be done for me. Th•
identification of Substance with Subject-Spirit in the Preface[379] is mythi
cally the central issue of the Reformation, overthrowing the sacramenta•
"spiritual substance" of the Eucharist & replacing it with the growin•
Spirit that takes over the Subject.

[411] I'm beginning to think, perhaps too much, about the word mime•
sis. In Kant's Critique of Judgment the relation between purpose anc
purposiveness without purpose is the difference between work anc
play. Biology excludes or brackets teleology because the work of God is •
notion that undercuts their work. The beauty that might be seen as th•
play (=wisdom) of God is a stimulus to human recreation, which is •
mimesis of the divine creation (if the latter phrase really describes any
thing). Time is the endless Sabbath when God rests and we work.[380]

[412] I think now I have the shape of Chapter Two: it begins witl
resonance, the inter-echoing sounds that suggest magic if external causa
tion were added.[381] From there resonance gradually takes on a visua
quality, and progresses until we reach the metaphor-cluster, the tota

juxtaposition of words. In *mythos*-language this would be what Hegel in *logos*-language calls the concrete universal.[382]

[413] Now: the corresponding movement for One is to start with mythos as narrative, then rise through differentiation from logos to a total narrative that involves both and the participating reader as well. Also the writer as mover, story-teller, whose authority comes from the story, Montaigne's consubstantial form.[383]

[414] If Chapter Three weren't still such a haze, I'd see this more clearly. At the end of Two we're subjects contemplating a metaphor-cluster icon. But we get *our* sense of *identity*, as distinct from the verbal sense, from our experience in time, hence the narrative must be incorporated, & ourselves with it, into the inner & no longer objective structure. So there are two phases to the end of Two, the second of which may belong to the end of Three. I mean the beginning, you horse's ass.

[415] The merging of reader and icon leads to interpenetration, but at that stage the reader is no longer an individual but one with the universal reader. The poet doesn't purify his authority until he's got rid of his ego, and the critic is not a real reader until he's taken his wig off & stopped trying to be a judge.

[416] That takes him into the interpenetrating universe of symbol and spirit. The literary work is now the symbol of literature, in the two senses of symbol: it's a symbolon completed by the whole of literature, and a symbolos that is an augury or epitome of literature. The augury foretells: the symbolos as augury has a temporal dimension too, in absorbing the time-identity of the reader.[384] This I suppose is where typology as conditional prophecy comes in. But Hegel also speaks of the soul becoming Spirit as it proceeds up his spiral: that is, it goes up in a metamorphosis or transfiguration.[385]

[417] Part Two starts with the Bible as narrative, which, like Chapter One, involves the question of its authority. Demonic revolt against this authority contains a positive element (the titanic) that has to be recovered by man, as well as a negative or "evil" one. That's what Boehme (probably) and Nietzsche, along with Blake, were getting at. But what horse shit it was for Nietzsche to identity Dionysus with Prometheus![386]

Dionysus is not life: he's a dying god who won't hang. Prometheus is the natura naturata Christ-figure who destroys Nobodaddy; Christ himself is the natura naturans son of Adam who destroys the Covering Cherub, the watcher of the threshold, and leads back the bride. So the theme of Chapter Four is the purification of the mythical authority of the Bible from history. History really is Antichrist, the devil's scripture, though only in this context.[387]

[418] Chapter Five, the Bible as imagery, similarly purifies the meta-phorical unity of the Bible from its doctrinal unity. Doctrine or dogma is another Antichrist (because irreversible).

[419] Wonder if Hegel has any clear idea of *where* spirit takes over from soul. Eliot at least would locate such a point: the *Ara vos prec* speech in Dante.[388]

[420] The word with power is the metaphor. Metaphors normally have two units, tenor & vehicle, & so are word-phrases, positive & negative magnets. But many metaphors, like "way," are single-multiple words.[389]

[421] "From shadowy types to truth, from flesh to spirit" [*Paradise Lost*, bk. 12, l. 303]. That's Michael instructing Adam, of course: note that you're going up Plato's divided line. Shadows are eikasia; flesh is pistis; truth is dianoia, spirit (in this context) is nous.[390] Or truth could be the trustworthy world of pistis and flesh the individual consciousness or soul-body unit.

[422] Four Bibles in Genesis 1–2, as I've said.[391] Wonder if they're Blake's Four Zoas. First, the Tharmas creation or science naturata world. Second, the Los world of titanic revolt. Third, the Urizenic world of cycles. Fourth, the Orc cyclical revolt. It would be nice to get my next lead from Blake after all. Thus: the participating apocalypse is a *re*creation in which man takes part. Job is shown the demonic world in its titanic aspect, and is told that he can be redeemed from creation because he wasn't a participant in it. But he thereby becomes a participant in the new world of his three beautiful daughters.[392]

[423] Hannah Arendt, quoting Char: our knowledge doesn't come in a testament.[393] The metaphysical systems of the past you don't "believe,"

but you have to swallow, like Milton's God.³⁹⁴ But the Bible is a *testament*, the record of a "will," and the approach to it is different.

[424] The best known of all Oriental stories is the one about Chuang Tse dreaming he was a butterfly, and, waking, not knowing which was dreaming which.³⁹⁵ But this must be badly translated: it can't be an either–or question. The real question was asked by the butterfly in Chuang Tse, and was: "Isn't that big lout of a larva awake yet?"

[425] God must be thought of as the inconceivably transcendent: all thoughts of that psychotic ape homo sapiens being divine have to be dismissed. The sheer bumptiousness of Carl Sagan & others who want to communicate with beings in other worlds amazes me.³⁹⁶ They should be saying: look, there are several billion Yahoos here robbing, murdering, torturing, exploiting, abusing & enslaving each other: they're stupid, malicious, superstitious and obstinate. Would you like to look at the .0001 per cent of them who are roughly presentable?

[426] Three and Six, or symbol and spirit, are likely to be based very largely on Hegel's Phenomenology and Kant's Critique of Judgment. Hebrews defines faith as the hypostasis of the hoped-for, and I've given reasons for thinking that hypostasis here means the traditional "substance," and not Paul's "assurance." Two questions: if we accept the Hegelian thesis that the true substance is subject, where does that take us?³⁹⁷ Two, does this question belong in Three or Six?

[427] I think some of the extra papers now crowding into my mind will get cannibalized. The one on "Fairies & Elementals"³⁹⁸ could go into one of the secular Bibles, probably the Adonis one. And I think a lot of my "lyric" introduction³⁹⁹ should be expanded and placed in Two. First, the mental change from linear improvisation to "verse" is a change in awareness. Also the resonance section could do with some expansion—the aural counterpart of apocalyptic vision—incidentally, that's a factor that can't be absorbed in the visual stage, & is thus probably the entering wedge for the reexamining of the experience. Tolstoy's WP [*War and Peace*] with the Russian complications about *mir*.⁴⁰⁰ Translation and its "sense" cuts off this re-examination to some degree. Hegel & aufgehoben.⁴⁰¹

[428] I gather that Bhaktin's [Bakhtin's] "dialogism"⁴⁰² is gradually re-

placing "deconstruction" as a buzzword. Of course there's dialogue between writer & reader, but much more goes on than that: it's more like an interpenetrating of identities. Montaigne's "consubstantial" remark[403] shows that the writer's ego and the reader's ego *can't* interpenetrate: they're like the old-style atoms, or, more accurately, like the Leibnitzian monads. In this century we have to forget that "atom" means the unsplittable (or did mean it) or that the individual is the "individable." Two egos identifying would be like two billiard balls copulating.

[429] The Blake paper[404] starts with the Ulro Bible: fallen or forbidden knowledge taken as revelation: that "shite it" couplet.[405] The Generation Bible is the MHH [*The Marriage of Heaven and Hell*] Orc-Urizen one; but there are two sides to that. One is the reversed mythical framework I've expanded so often: the other is a proto-Nietzschean Christ-Antichrist, life-asserting & life-denying confrontation. Why Nietzsche identified his life-asserting Antichrist with Dionysus, the most hypochrondiac [hypochondriac] of all dying gods &—even less Nietzschean—the most obsessed with female sexual impulses, I don't know or want to know. Nietzsche is like all the drunken-boat people,[406] except that he's *really* drunken and has a torpedo in his ark. There's no specific revolutionary theme in him: his real vision is of evolution as the exploding force of nature. True, he never has a good word to say for Darwinism—perhaps he's closer to Lamarck—but that's his vision. So he comes back to Nature with its incessant death-rebirth ("recurrence") Adonis pattern, dodging the death-resurrection dialectic.

[430] The Beulah Bible takes in the very tricky business of male-female symbolism versus men-women relationships. The latter for him [Blake] is the fallen form of the other. Pound's fragment[407] will do here and that verse in II Clement[408] & Clement of Alexandria which is pure Blake (Mead I 105).[409]

[431] Why the inhabitants of Easter Island put up all those immense statues is a profound & inscrutable mystery. Almost as profound and inscrutable as why anybody would carve a gigantic head of Theodore Roosevelt on a mountain in South Dakota.

[432] If I were asked if I "really believed" the P.V. [*Pervigilium Veneris*] motto I've given the dedication page of WP (nice that that also stands for

Work in Progress) I'd have to say "not yet." But what else is worth trying to believe?[410]

[433] I am 75 years old, and my wife is dead. There are a lot of what look like winding-up symbols—the Italian conference, the G.G. medal, the Oxford degree, the San Francisco meeting[411]—but I know they're not connected to other symbols or processes. I have what seems like one more major book in me, which I might conceivably finish before too long—perhaps by the time I reach the age at which Helen died.[412] I don't feel suicidal: I just have no more resistance to death, though of course I still have the normal anxieties about it.

[434] I'd like to tidy things up, not leave a mass of irrelevant papers behind. I promised Jay I'd give my literary executor (her) as little trouble as possible.[413] In addition to *Words With Power*, I'd like a volume of 12 essays completed. Four on Utopian & social model writers, two Renaissance and two Victorian: More, Castiglione; William Morris, Samuel Butler. The last isn't completed yet.[414] Four on special topics: at present, the Book of Ruth, Blake, Wagner's Parsifal, Joyce. Four theoretical: the Wiegand, the Smith College, the Royal Society symbolism paper will be three of them.[415] In Italy I was presented with the proposal to do something on the short story. I had previously thought of writing about Henry James' ghost stories, treating *The Sense of the Past* as what his whole work was leading up to, from this point of view. An extension of this to "American Gothic," starting with Poe and including Hawthorne & Melville might touch on some of the things I've always wanted to do—Biblical typology & *Clarel* in Melville, for instance. I don't know about that: *Clarel* seems obsessive, and *Israel Potter* perhaps a shaggy dog irrelevance.[416]

[435] A poem by Gerard de Nerval called "Horus" is a very beautiful white-goddess poem, almost a laboratory specimen of one.[417]

[436] When I was in Japan I visited a Buddhist temple, several buildings all dignified, rather sombre, and in exquisite taste.[418] At the top of the hill it was on was a Shinto shrine, incredibly gaudy, as though it were made of Christmas candy, the bushes around having rolled-up prayers tied to every twig, like women with their hair in curlers. My immediate feeling was that it was good-humored and disarming: I had no hostile or supe-

rior feelings about it at all. So why did hostile and superior words, like "superstitious" and "vulgar" start crowding into my mind? Did *God* tell me he thought it was superstitious and vulgar?

[437] I was reminded of this when I started reading *Steppenwolf*. I started that in the sixties, when every fool in the country was trying to identify with Steppenwolf, and abandoned it after a few pages. I couldn't stand the self-pitying whine of someone totally dependent on middle-class values but trying to develop his self-respect by feeling hostile and superior to them. I was hearing that whine all around me at the time. The next stage, also obvious in Hesse's text, is when you try to raise your opinion of yourself by despising yourself. Like the wrestler: "I got so fuckin' tied up all I could see was a big arse in frunna me, so I takes a bite out of it, and, Christ, it was me own arse."

[438] I'm getting along better with *Steppenwolf* now because my own hostile feelings toward it have minimized. One lives and learns: one doesn't learn very much, but one lives.

[439] Tennyson's Hesperides is still not in Six. The song of the siren in Tennyson's early poems is curiously haunting: it's in the Lotus Eaters too, of course.[419] Also: I seem to be suggesting that the spiritual world outgrows our present genital fixations and goes back to a polymorphous golden age. Also: a passage in *Aurélia* identifies a woman with a garden (I, vi),[420] & cf. Shelley's *Sensitive Plant*. Seems to me a naked female statue in G. Macdonald's *Phantastes* has similar affinities.[421]

[440] Very obvious link I still haven't got: draining off the "Sea of Time and Space"[422] and exposing Atlantis is the same thing as hooking & landing Leviathan, the sea monster who is the sea. Cf. the vision of "land" and the end of Dylan Thomas's Ballad of the Long-Legged Bait.[423]

[441] I regret very much that the gospel reports Christ as saying that the sin against the Holy Spirit is unforgivable [Mark 3:29]. The sin against the Holy Spirit *is* original sin itself. Perhaps it can't be "forgiven," but it must be annihilated, or the whole Christian structure, which depends on a love that forgives *everything*, is a lot of balls. That's what I think now, anyway. An unpardonable sin means a stinker God, and I will never accept such a creature in the Christian set-up.

[442] Footnote on Steppenwolf: what I said about it over the page [par. 437] was utter crap, and I didn't abandon it after a few pages: I read it through, and, as my marginal notes show, with appreciation. Funny how screen memories work: I resented the student hysteria so much in the sixties, and some of them (at Rochdale,[424] e.g.) made a cult of Hesse. So the remark about the wrestler biting his own arse comes home to roost. Not that I think now that Steppenwolf is really a great or profound book, but he's aware of his own irony.

[443] "She died young."[425] The only she in my life died at seventy-six, which in some terms would be a full life. And she wasn't murdered: I refuse to believe that. But everyone who dies loved dies young (to the lover at least).

[444] Protestantism is a wonderful religion: I wish I knew what Tillich meant by his "principle."[426] It has no real cultural substance. One thinks of Hopkins as a Catholic poet: one doesn't think of Byron & Shelley & Keats as Protestant poets, even though two of them were buried in the "Protestant cemetery" in Rome. The hidden genius of the faith of the released Word transmuted them into something rich and strange.[427]

[445] I will try to make this book make sense to me: that's all I can do to make sure it will make sense to readers whose reading is important to me. To say that the others no longer matter doesn't mean I've turned arrogant: it means I've stopped feeling masochistic about them (i.e., "it's my fault for not being clearer; if I just rewrite it once more," etc.)

[446] Confronted by the mysteries of birth and death, one may feel (I may feel) I wish I knew it all. It may be that it's unknown because it's not an objective body of knowledge to be known: perhaps it's a process of being realized out of an illusion. It won't be known until we've finished working at it: the simple way to interpret "finished" is to identify it with physical death, but maybe it's a bigger process than that. I wish John had reversed the syntax he assigns to Jesus: the truth is what makes you free, and then is known.[428] Cf. Jung's notion of sermons addressed to the dead, as though they had something to learn from the living as well as the other way round.[429]

[447] I've finally started to read the beginning of the Mahabharata, which

the editor says he thinks was *designed* as a riddle.[430] A great war starts over a frantically complicated succession story, and that's only a core story later mythologized and ideologized endlessly. In Romeo & Juliet the killer is the feud: we never find out what the feud was about, but we realize that any "knowledge" of it would lead us to something utterly footling, & that in turn, etc. Like Rob Davies and his three novels on a snowball.[431] Once again, Job: don't lose yourself in a labyrinth of pseudo-causes.

[448] I know from experience, and I've read the statement often enough, that if one could turn off the incessant chatter in one's psyche one would be well on the way to freedom. In all my life I've never known an instant of real silence. That, of course, is because I've never gone through the years of discipline and practice in meditation. To come to it cold (as I've said in another notebook) would be like rolling back the waves of the Red Sea and walking across the bottom.[432]

[449] And yet I wonder if there isn't a contrast between chatter and inner dialogue, and that the latter is important to preserve. Chatter is (a) mechanical, triggered by the associative mechanisms that psychology has studied from Hartley to Pavlov. And (b) it's partly repressed, conforming to censorship but full of disguised malice and resentment. The psyche is a Tower of Babel, a structure of pride and dictatorship with a "babble" of voices inside, all unintelligible to each other. Perhaps the ideal is a Quaker meeting, silent until the Spirit speaks from somewhere.

[450] In public school there was an attempt to teach writing by a "fore-arm movement," starting with the whole arm instead of making twiddly voluntary movements with the fingers. I knew I would never learn to write this way, and as far as my observation went nobody else did either, even the teachers. But they worked out better compromises than I did. What I didn't of course realize was that this was really a "Zen" technique, based on the principle of letting the writing emerge from the arm. Perhaps if I had learned to write this way I'd have become a poet or novelist instead of a critic: perhaps some ability to draw would have emerged, instead of the total inhibition of that faculty which has always mystified me.

[451] And perhaps if from early youth I had practised regularizing my

breathing—just regularizing it, not trying any fancy yoga tricks—instead of spending my entire life in short pants, I'd have developed an inner authority despite my physical weakness and outgrown the masochistic self-betrayals that have tripped me up at intervals all my life. God, the things the bull learns the first and only time he is in the ring.

[452] I may be nearing the end, although my powers seem to be as lucid as ever. After finishing Blake I faced the critical Y. Either spread into general theories and make endless mistakes in detail, or dig into one period and do it thoroughly. I chose the former: many of the mistakes I have made have been pure laziness, and could have been avoided. But I think perhaps no one else could have done what I have done, and I think perhaps what I have done has been worth doing. R.I.P. [Rest In Peace].

[453] I'm taking this tone because some of the things I've done recently have been really good: I can still do my job. And I think the first four chapters of WP are good. But that second half haunts me with the feeling that I've tackled too big a job, which probably means that I ought to rewrite it on a different basis—if I can find the basis. I think it's somewhere in the part of Eight that keeps eluding me.

[454] I recently heard of a little boy who drew five horizontal lines on a piece of paper and told his mother it was a picture of a fox hiding behind a fence. The mother said: "I see the fence all right, but where's the fox?" The child protested: "But I *told* you; he's *hiding behind* it." If I knew the answer to that one I'd know more phenomenology than Husserl, and more of the noumenal world than Kant.

[455] Speaking of Kant, it's curious how writers do the opposite of what they're trying to do, often along with what they're trying to do. The question "Is there, or is there not, a God?" is the ultimate in verbal unreality: hell itself cannot contain its utter futility and emptiness. Kant wrote his first two critiques to try to make it less unreal by showing that such a question could never have an answer. Along with doing this, he raised the same question again in the form "Is there, or is there not, a noumenal world?" (Because God, according to practical reason, is to be found only there.) Note that I repudiate the phrase "trying to do" when applied to Shakespeare: it applies only to proposition-writing, conceptual or rhetorical, at least when it concerns great writers.

[456] Similarly, Mallarmé fascinates me because he shows that as soon as poetry becomes pure it's abolished as poetry, and something transcendent (what "would have been the truth," as he said) appears that the pure poem is a symbol of.[433] It's not for nothing that "aboli" is one of his favorite words.[434]

[457] The Joachim of Floris notion, that there's a coming age of purely spiritual Christianity, an everlasting gospel, has always been central to my own thinking. I don't look for it in the future of time, but ideally it's always there. I should quite cheerfully write off Protestantism as a transitional phase to it. But Catholic converts who turn back from the wilderness to Egyptian civilized life will never see the Promised Land. The road to Jesus' spiritual kingdom runs through Luther, perhaps Calvin: it gets pretty dry and narrow there, as Jesus said it would, but the self-sufficient Church just won't do. The same thing is true of Xy [Christianity] itself: it's superstitious compared to Judaism and intolerably inhumane compared to the greatest of the Greeks—but it's higher in human scale. I don't know what I mean by "human" here: certainly not that Christians are more human than Jews or Greeks—I'm following Paul's phrasing.[435]

[458] Lowrie, the translator of Kierkegaard, says that English needs a distinction between a providence that rules and a providence that provides.[436] All metaphors of God as sovereign, ruler, lord, master, king, all relate to the unity of the spiritual "kingdom" which is not of this world, and has a different hierarchy if it has any. As Job found, God doesn't rule this world: Satan does, and what we get is at most a series of angels to wrestle with. The *provision* of providence is different: that's the ministry of angels, or manifestations of God: it comes *from* God, but may come *through* anyone, including departed spirits. I suppose a prophet is a talking angel; there are prophetic figures like S.K. [Søren Kierkegaard], but they often allow conceptual or lower-rhetorical idioms to usurp the function of the kerygmatic.

[459] Adele Wiseman says, referring to her Winnipeg schooling, "many teachers are teachers because they can't bear to have their small certainties disturbed, and want only to imprint them on the unresisting young."[437] That would apply to others besides teachers: she never had to endure the appalling series of parsons I was dragged off to by mother—or perhaps I'm just being romantic about rabbis. (Mother was deaf—a

blissful advantage—but she could see, & what she saw was a symbol of her father.)⁴³⁸

[460] Speaking of rabbis, I heard of a married couple of Polish Jews picked up by the Nazis, the man sent to Dachau & the woman to Auschwitz. Miraculously they both survived & both remarried, assuming the other was dead, & both had children. The woman discovered the existence of the first husband & consulted a rabbi. He said there must be *no* direct connection of any kind with him, otherwise she'd be adulterous & her second-marriage children bastards. Nothing to me what Jews do or think: I simply note how frenziedly anxious humans are to catch themselves in rat-traps, and how eagerly they interpret the will of a God who could *only* be a shit and a stinker.

[461] Note to cheer myself up with: I'm not a great 17th c. poet like Milton, or a great 18th-19th c. visionary like Blake, but I am a great 20th c. reader, and this is the age of the reader.

[462] (I must have said this elsewhere.) The great obstacle to finishing chapter Eight is that I don't know nothing. The grammar is correct, but perhaps "know" should read "understand."

[463] Hamlet tells his mother she can't love Claudius because she's too old for such feelings [3.4.68–9]. Of course it's important for him to believe that; anyway, he's a mother-fixated bachelor, perhaps with slight homosexual leanings, who hasn't a clue about women. (Incidentally, the second time he sees the ghost he completely accepts him as his father & speaks with great reverence to him [1.5], both in contrast to the first time; also, the ghost is evidently promoted to a trusty at least in purgatory.)

[464] Donne, DEO 17: "All mankind is of one author, & is one volume; when one man dies, one chapter is . . . translated into a better language . . . God's hand is in every translation, and his hand shall bind up all our scattered leaves again, for that library *where every book shall lie open to one another*."⁴³⁹ Italics mine: superb phrase.

[465] Calvino, Norton Lectures: "Literature remains alive only if we set ourselves immeasurable goals, far beyond all hope of achievement. Only if poets and writers set themselves tasks that no one else dares imagine

will literature continue to have a function." *Six Memos for the Next Millennium*. The first sentence is for me: the hell with what dunces think they think.[440]

[466] *Jacob's Ladder and the Tree of Life*, ed. by Marion L. Kuntz and Paul G. Kuntz. *Concepts of Hierarchy and the Great Chain of Being*, Peter Lang Publications.[441]

[467] In the old cosmos the order earth, water, air, fire explained[442] many phenomena we ascribe to gravitation. It also had a hierarchical significance.[443] Our cosmos of solid, liquid, gaseous & plasmic states of matter is similar, but has no hierarchy.

[468] Well, I've entered the Elizabethan age.[444] Not one atom of my feeling for Helen has changed: neither is my feeling that we're linked somehow in the spiritual world. But my notions of spiritual union may have clarified: there is no spiritual marriage because marriage has to be ego-centered and a mutual possession. In *that* world all books lie open to one another. (Donne's image, like Dante's in Par. 33 & Montaigne's, makes the book the image of completed man.[445] Perhaps this is a *Three* point: Three is a short chapter.)

[469] Five is also a short chapter at present, because it's unfinished. *Paradiso* and the Mut. Coes. [*Mutabilitie Cantos*] still have to go in. Also an introduction making a transition from Part One. The basis of understanding the Bible being active & creative (imaginative) and not passive or uncritical (historical or doctrinal) we may at first plunge into a free-for-all game where anything goes. Actually, in our time, the anything goes game is linked to all the up-for-grabs guesses about the *historical* Jesus.

[470] But that wasn't true in N.T. times, with all that torrent of Gnostic mythopoeia about Barbelos and Ialdabaoths.[446] The more one looks at this crap (though it contains some profound insights, certainly) the more one admires the crisp clean kerygmatic outlines of the N.T. The problem extends to Classical mythology, where I know slightly more: the kergymatic censorship of myth in the N.T, the gospels particularly, contains some point I haven't got yet.[447]

[471] Morris is only one example of the tale-framework convention of Boccaccio & Chaucer, which has always had a curious fascination for writers, & perhaps for reasons similar to Morris's.[448]

[472] It doesn't matter how often I'm mentioned by other critics: I form part of the subtext of every critic worth reading. Aug. 30/88.

[473] Why are Marxist & Freudian approaches to criticism so sterile and so quickly exhausted when Marx & Freud themselves are so endlessly suggestive and illuminating? I suppose because the centre of gravity remains in Marx or Freud and turns all literature into an allegory of Marxism or Freudianism. (I think something similar is true of feminist criticism, even if it has as yet no comparable third figure.) So I ought to know how silly it would be to turn my book into any sort of Biblical or Christian allegory.

[474] The hope of deliverance from history in the New Testament revived in Lenin-period Marxism. It is no reproach to Marxism to say that it failed to achieve such deliverance: so did historical Christianity.

[475] What we look "forward" to gradually fades out as it is transmitted to posterity and renounced for ourselves, & finally disappears altogether. The essential thing is something to look "up" to, until we begin to realize that there is also a misleading factor in the metaphor "up": i.e., it is not necessarily out of our reach.

[476] The notion that being involved with an infinite personality is an infringement on man's "freedom" seems to me exquisitely idiotic. What has "freedom," at any recorded period in history, ever meant for more than one per cent of the total population? What did it really mean even for them? Certainly freedom is one of my primary concerns, but it always includes deliverance from everything society thinks is freedom.

[477] Areopagitica is still the great turning point: after it, we can no longer contrast the sacred & the secular with the same old confidence.[449]

[478] All irony, whether of content or of form, is relative to a norm, and is unintelligible without that norm. It seems essential to keep on saying

this in an age of "deconstruction," where the illusion grows up that the norms are no longer there.[450] *Tristram Shandy* was "odd" to Johnson and "typical" to some Russian formalist,[451] but it's not typical of anything but a fashion. (When parody becomes very fashionable, the illusion grows up that the norms have disappeared.)

[479] I suppose the Mormon Bible is a parody of the lost histories of the great civilizations that came pouring over the Bering Straits into the New World.

[480] This may sound like nagging, but. What we know personally about a writer we often use against him, making him fall short of some norm. Tolstoy was a noble and orphaned at two, so his work is full of mummy's cuddles and futile attempts to reach the real people. All such limitations are positive contributions to the sum total of human emotion. I have a note on Strindberg to the same effect.[452]

[481] I mustn't overlook the figure of the *widow*, who is an exile figure: I think she comes into Six and partly rationalizes the rejuvenation transition. Penelope analogy. Giles Fletcher calls Eurydice a virgin widow,[453] although from the point of view of the upper world Orpheus was a widower.

[482] Five: relativity of time: transfer the *letargo* passage[454] to here and put Dostoevsky's account of his near-death experience in *The Idiot*[455] beside it as a demonic parody. Mallarmé's St Jean[456] and Valéry's Zeno too.[457]

[483] Six: don't forget that Adonis symbolism relates to the *Two* categories, the oasis one of trees & water, & the agricultural one of harvest & vintage. Well, I haven't really. But "metamorphosis," both in Ovid & elsewhere, ought to be linked to the natural cycle as the return of a *different* life, as well as to the Fall.[458]

[484] Pierre [Bezuhov] in War & Peace asks why the ladder of being should stop with him.[459]

[485] I don't think it's coincidence or accident that feminism and ecology should become central issues at the same time.

[486] Voltaire's Pococurante[460] is something of a wimp, no doubt; but still a relentlessly human standard applied to everything has some point. Is there *nothing* sacred? Not unless it has a bloody good secular record too. This would apply to my trickster-god passage in (I think) Five,[461] which should come back into Eight as part of man's effort to overcome the demon-gods derived from nature & set in the Siege Perilous.

[487] Seven should turn partly on the plenosis-kenosis cycle in Gaster,[462] only in its revolutionary form: whatever is excluded will come back. That's why I'm so attracted to the Genesis 2:3 interpretation of Mallarmé's *Igitur*:[463] whether it's right or not, it makes the Mallarmé story a kenosis followed by an unwritten plenosis. "Igitur" is not the logical "donc," but it does imply a natural following, "wherefore" rather than "therefore." The *full* kenosis-plenosis cycle is for Eight; the nothingness bit.

[488] Re the "virgin widow" across [i.e., par. 481]: that should be repeated in Seven, where the anabasis of Kore[464] is a central theme. The theme of the rescued bride isn't all Six: the bride has to be dug out of the ground, like Kundry, or come to life from a statue or snow-woman.[465] So far this theme, to the extent that it's not neglected altogether, is muddled with Six.

[489] Exchange of identity in Mark Twain: Prince & Pauper, Pudd'nhead Wilson, Huck Finn as Tom Sawyer. Double theme of Seven, I suppose. Yeats' mask theory & his Player Queen.[466] The comic double or twin theme relates to the soul-body duality: the romantic Two Brothers dreamer and dreamee (nice word) theme belongs to Paul's spirit-soul distinction, daimons and such. I have the principle in Four; the detail goes in Seven.

[490] Empire is the demonic control of space; Christ with his spiritual kingdom here and now was born under Augustus. The demonic control of time is the memorial monument: Ozymandias might have been the Pharaoh of the Exodus; Herod had his temple, Nebuchadnezzar the Hanging Gardens, & symbolically Babel: Russia has Lenin's mummy, and so on. The "I am the way" passage [John 14:6] buggers *that* up. Not complete, but I need something in the words-vs-power theme. Power means the Father, who never comes on the scene whenever power is associated with folly and hatred instead of wisdom & love. Re the above on monuments: all monuments are really tombs or cenotaphs, preserv-

ing the illusion of life in the memory-world of the dead. So the tomb of Christ is also the memory of mankind.

[491] This is something not yet clear to me, but I think it's important. I've talked about the interchange of reality and illusion in *The Tempest* and elsewhere: I've talked about the way that technological developments increase introversion. I've also speculated on the connexion between the unrest of the sixties and society's digesting of television.[467] But I was being over-optimistic, I think.

[492] American civilization has to *de-theatricalize* itself, I think, from the prison of television. They can't understand themselves why they admire Reagan and would vote for him again, and yet *know* that he's a silly old man with no understanding even of his own policies. They're really in that Platonic position of staring at the shadows on the wall of a cave. The Pope, again, is another old fool greatly admired because he's an ex-actor who *looks* like a holy old man.

[493] Watching a television panel of journalistic experts discussing the (Bush-Dukakis) election, it seemed to me Plato's cave again and Plato's *eikasia*, or illusion at two removes—show business about show business. All one needs to know about such horseshit is how to circumvent whatever power it has. I'm trying to dredge up something more complex and far-reaching than just the cliché that elections today are decided by images rather than issues—they always were. It's really an aspect of the icon-idol issue: imagination is the faculty of participation in society, but it should remain in charge, not passively responding to what's in front of it. Where does idolatry go in my argument? End of Three?

[494] Irony depends on its deviation from an opposing norm: the sense of losing this norm has been constant throughout literature, though it seems very acute now, and there are even theories (post-structural ones) trying to show that it doesn't exist, or no longer exists.[468] Television has helped to do that, too.

[495] A condensing image is an explicit allusion to something Biblical or conventional in mythology or folktale dropped into a (more) representational context. Melville and Dostoevsky are particularly given to them. The allusion may be casual, parodic, or incongruous (or perhaps really

accidental, though we can very seldom be sure of this), but that does not affect its function.[469]

[496] Five is a study of the ladder of wisdom, and its point is kerygma on a higher level that's gradually emerging in my mind, and may *still* involve some more tinkering with the end of Four. Higher kerygma is a two-way street, the interpenetrating of Word & Spirit, not the "proclamation" of God to Man.

[497] The morals of Five, mainly, are the autonomy of the verbal universe, the expansion of time, and the business about reversing the "merely symbolic" business in that Dante commentary.[470] But there's also that higher kerygma business, which is a reversal of Otto's holiness, the *mysterium tremendum*, which is basically an alienation image.[471] The m. t. is connected with some form of Lacan's *nom du Père*, and with my "trickster" passage indicating that you can't get to God through uniformity alone.[472]

[498] We all wonder, with Pierre Bezuhov (see a previous note [par. 484]) why the level of personal reality should go up to man and stop, even if we can't raise much interest in the nine orders of angels. But the atheistic argument (Sartre) that if we admit the existence of God we're "dependent on" God and thereby lose our "freedom" (whatever that is) is bloody stupid.[473]

[499] Where the hypothetical basis of literature still holds up is the fact that no form of higher kerygma is prescribed as *the* one. That's why, for example, mysticism is so distrusted. But I'm really just reconstructing Buber here: the discovery of "Thou" is, if not *the* experience, pretty close to its centre.[474]

[500] The penetration into holiness is connected with the possibility of understanding, say, the language of King Lear. As I've always maintained, something about such language is recognizable, something that in a sense we've said already in unknown areas of our experience. I'm still revolving around that remark that Oscar Wilde so casually threw out about the music of Chopin[475]—and my own about Rilke in the Masseys.[476]

[501] Moral of Six: love is interpenetration, but it has to extend beyond

the sexual interpenetrating of intercourse. Every act of hostility is penetration with a threat, with a desire to dominate or acquire for oneself. Love means entering into and identifying with other people and things without threats or domination, in fact without retaining an ego-self. That's what the woman-garden expansion means. The rejuvenating of the mother into the bride means (a) the internalizing of the maternal (b) the equalizing of a figure of authority. Shelley after the Coronation of the Virgin.[477]

[502] I need morals for Seven and Eight: one is that in the normal allegorizing pattern of the Trinity the Father represents power, the Son wisdom, the Spirit love. Everyone complains that God seems to exert no power. But divine power can operate only in a context of love and wisdom: it can't work in a context of human folly and hatred. That sounds like Eight: maybe the why-the-Bible? question is the pulling together of Seven. The exasperating thing about this book is that its really seminal ideas, if there are any, come very late, after I'm sick and tired of revising; and the one thing that will really put over the book, the question "so what?" fully and intelligibly answered to a relatively unsympathetic reader, will probably come last of all. I just hope that if or when it comes it won't necessitate a complete rewriting of the book.

[503] The passage about the trickster or stinker God in (I think) Four looks weak where it is, but it does have a development, and I'd like to put it where it is now, though it may belong to some peroration at the end of Eight.[478]

[504] This development concerns the reality of the imaginative cosmos. Matthew Arnold said that many things are not really seen until they are seen as beautiful,[479] and Ruskin and Morris made quite a career out of saying that Victorian England is not really seen until much of it is seen as ugly.[480] You can't stop with the uniform God, because the malicious, the ironic, the tragic, are all realities. To say that a person has no sense of humor amounts to saying that that person is deficient in a sense of reality. Similarly with irony. One has to pass through this, of course: I've noted elsewhere an essay of Kierkegaard where the essential thesis was "God is ironic,"[481] and one can't tie God to any such human construct. But the construct is there: I can see the wise and kindly irony at the end of the Jonah story as divine, though not the malicious irony of S.K.'s God. Kierkegaard was half a nut, after all.

[505] Add to Five the tragic archetype of the fall off the top of fortune's wheel as a repetition of the original fall: you need that to introduce the fall theme in Seven. It's still going in its most primitive form in Ibsen's *Master Builder*; and I must look up the first mountain scene in *When We Dead Awaken*.[482]

[506] Seven themes not really dealt with: hell and purgatory continue the tradition of the world of the dead as some sort of survival (irony of Hamlet's ghost).

Death of female (Lucy, etc.) & anabasis of Kore. Blake's black girl is "not yet."[483]

Ambivalence of lower world in Schopenhauer, etc., linked to selfish-gene. Wordsworthian spiritual nature. Latter = wisdom & fertility.[484]

Return of repressed starts with nature: Horace's tag;[485] Rousseau precedes Marx & Freud.[486]

Parallel of buried seed sprouting in a new air-world is there, I think: Christ as source of food a type of his death & resurrection.[487]

(Eight should deal with the apocalyptic separation of death from life and the cleansing of temple imagery: the latter is only glanced at).

I can't really do without the Resurrection as a type of apocalypse, where "nature" is split & the natural body becomes shit, the spiritual one being food & drink.

Demonic union of nature & reason is in Eight.[488]

[507] Possibilities: transfer the "journey" bit to the end of Three;[489] transfer the food and shit cycle to Eight.[490] We can keep Roethke in Eight; that's part of the nothing-and-everything complex.[491] No: Eight shits, but food and Frazer are Seven; the double is Eight; the prison of Narcissus destroyed by the second Adam is Eight.[492] The technological (mechanical) theme is introduced in Eight because of the unconscious mechanism having to be controlled by a will.[493]

[508] Eight: demonic descent to psychopathic evil: Iago, Cornwall, Swift's nature-reason fusion in *that* context. Demonic ascent to Lucifer tyranny, predators & rulers. Creative descent to nothing (turned to everything by the creative); creative ascent purgatorial practice. Heart of Darkness is in the demonic ascent.[494]

[509] Buber: Thou is the spiritual form of It: it's the Narcissus reflection that destroys the prison of Narcissus. This last links with the Hoffman

Salvatora Rosa story & TS [*The Turn of the Screw*] (Bunyan too in the valley: objectify to fight, otherwise you become an object yourself[)]. I'm sure this is Eight material.[495]

[510] God's power works only with wisdom & love, not with folly & hatred. As 99.9% of human life is folly & hatred, we don't see much of God's power. He must work deviously, a creative trickster, what Buddhists call the working of skilful means.

[511] Mystery of evil: nature is said to abhor a vacuum, but astronomers say there are black holes, & there must be moral black holes too, like the arse of Satan Dante crawls out of.[496]

[512] (Yeats buried in a Christian churchyard.) As for Nietzsche, he may have believed or tried to believe, that the perpetually dying Dionysus affirmed life and that the Christ of the Resurrection denied it, but that hardly makes him an "Antichrist." Hitler is an example of the kind of thing the N.T. means by an Antichrist.[497]

[513] Fix up the remark about socialist realism in Five. That is, cut it.[498]

[514] It is historically impossible that the Bible could have achieved such a unity of structure and imagery, over such a variety of periods and authors. But as the unity is there, so much the worse for history.[499]

[515] 3/12:[500] In Homer what *we* call metaphor is "literal," a reality in its own right.[501] People clung to the metaphors of the Bible for centuries and insisted that they were "literal truth." Calling them metaphors implies an acceptance of the s-o [subject–object] distinction, of course; my diagram really means that there are two bases to start from, one descriptive (natural) and one metaphorical (spiritual).

[516] Plato's spindle in Republic x[502] is a comprehensive axis symbol, and perhaps belongs in Eight, as part of the conclusion.

[517] There are obvious Freudian reasons {except that I've forgotten what they are} for the appeal of detective stories:[503] Freudianism itself owes much of its popularity to the same kind of appeal, Freudian therapy of a neurosis being essentially a search for who done it in childhood. Or what done it.

[518] Eight: pick up the stitch dropped in Seven: the fact that Kingu was killed as a traitor suggests a demonic origin for mankind.[504] (The fact that Christ was executed as a traitor to Jewry & Rome confirms this.) Adam had only one wife: the progeny of Eve (the first one being Cain) and of Lilith are the same.[505]

[519] I've been tinkering with the end of Four endlessly: what may be needed to tie up the argument is a link between the two levels at the top of my diagram (and it should be clearer that there *are* two levels) and my type-antitype argument. See across, bottom [par. 515].

[520] In Carlson's (?) book on Strindberg and myth there's a passage on mythos & logos I should quote in the notes.[506]

[521] I should revise my diagram, cutting the directions (they're reversible), putting two levels of the imaginative in (type-antitype, as above [par. 519]), putting in a "primitive" base where the metaphorical *is* the literal, an identity that gets restated at the top, when we know what a metaphor is but no longer consider it "unreal." Note that regarding the O.T. as a series of "types" makes it (almost) purely literary—literarizes it.

[522] In the Incarnation the Word comes down and the Spirit, having finished his job, goes up. Here the Spirit is the Father of the Word. In Acts 1–2 the Word goes up and the Spirit comes down. Here the Spirit is the successor or Son of the Word.[507] Anyone who calls this a lot of crap can stick it up his ass with the rest of his own crap.

[523] I should recognize that "verbal" has an expanded reference where it includes the six languages of human creation, especially the musical and the pictorial (i.e. the diagrammatic). I don't know if I can get into the business of painting as an "unborn" art beginning in caves, or sculpture as the hypothesis of biology, but there are certainly architectural expressions of the creation and cosmos, from Stonehenge and the Pyramids to the cathedrals of the west and the stupas of the east. Incidentally, the reality of beauty (Arnold's principle)[508] is implied in the word "cosmos" itself. There's a mathematical language too; of course, though I don't know it.

[524] Of the six arts, mathematics is out of the picture in the Bible, although kabbalism tries to bring it in; the visual arts are played down, though Solomon's temple was not just architecture, but had a freedom of

sculptural decor, & probably pictorial as well, discouraged later. The narrator confused the wise builder (Hiram, the Masons call him) with the idolatrous follies of the historical Solomon [1 Kings 5–7].

[525] Re Iago & unmotivated evil: anyone can construct his own hell and trap himself in it for the rest of his life. Once he dies he's no longer in that context: I don't believe he's caught "forever" with the consequences of his actions in life, but as there's nothing in him to get to any "heaven" I should think he probably just vanishes, as many believe everyone does. Ibsen's button-moulder.[509]

[526] Critics may ignore the language of myth and metaphor; but no poet can possibly be a poet of any significance who does not learn to speak it constantly & consistently.

[527] I want to keep away from theological language, not because I don't recognize its validity but because it would be a rat-trap for me and would over-complicate an already cumbersome book. Two things, though: (a) Paul's analogy of faith belongs with my spiritual dialectic (b) Eight, probably, should conclude with some consideration of catastasis and apocatastasis.[510] The latter is, I think, Irenaeus' recapitulatio & Kierkegaard's repetition;[511] the former is more particularly (as in Ben Jonson) a false though plausible conclusion: the one arrived at by the police in detective stories just before the great detective explains it all (I must have a reference to Hoffman's Mme. Scudéry story).[512] In Revelation it's the triumph of Antichrist, Blake's consolidation of error.

[528] Nothing I know of in literature comes anywhere near expressing this ultimate fusion of Word and Spirit, this final push past the mysterium tremendum. It would be Stevens' great poem of earth,[513] which isn't here yet, and Mallarmé's.[514]

[529] Add to doubles in Seven: the mystery of iniquity is Antichrist, and the Iagos of the world are tragic parasites, who can't exist except in a destructive relation to someone else. There are also science-fiction doubles, anticipated by Henry James in his time-travel double (The Sense of the Past) and parallel-worlds double (The Jolly Corner).[515] The Ivan-Smerdyakov relation in Dostoevsky is closer to the Iago-Othello one (someone existing destructively in relation to someone he would other-

wise be forced to admire) in the regular "double" form. I haven't mentioned the male-female double in *Twelfth Night*, either: cf. Balzac's Séraphita.[516] Borges and I.[517]

[530] At present my diagram has kerygmatic meaning three bloody things (a) ordinary rhetoric (b) the epiphanic-antitypical outgrowth on top of the imaginative-poetic, which is what at first I wanted it to mean (c) "spiritual" rhetoric, which may be a lot of shit. I don't really think it is, given that the 19th c. Natur-Geist distinction has now entered criticism & shifted attention from text to the reading of text. If I put kerygma firmly on top of my diagram, I can straighten out a rather kinky argument.

[531] . . . what the funeral service calls, etc. We shall have occasion later to notice that the reasonable is the opposite of the rational, and spiritual dialectic may give us what the funeral service calls the comfort of a reasonable religion, in contrast to the arid and fatuous discomforts of a rational one. In terms of this book, it gives us the counter-logic of a reasonable and metaphorical Bible. I think my Dante-annotation point could come in here.

[532] A more polite way of putting the point on top of p. 160 [par. 522] would be: anyone who regards this as a lot of rubbish is a soul in ignorant bliss.

[533] There are only two branches of the human race: those who belong to the bourgeoisie and those who wish they did. There is no such thing as a proletarian consciousness.

[534] Verlaine said take rhetoric & wring its neck *not* Valéry.[518]

[535] The end of Eight, thanks to a merciful God, is coming into sight. It's a stretto taking off from my purgatorial section, on the various relations of the creative-demonic to the—well—ouranic. Yeats' two Byzantium poems go near the end; Eliot's Little Gidding has to do with terrifying but benevolent descents; Verlaine's Crimen Amoris with a masochistic fascination with Rimbaud's demonism (titanism) and the ultimate supremacy of God. Cf. the fascination of Byronism in, say, Shelley's Julian & Maddalo, Verlaine's poète maudit and the descent of the fourth level from the old demonic. Ch. 119 of *Moby Dick*.[519]

[536] Victor Hugo's Fin de Satan and Dieu;[520] Goethe's Faust dragged off to heaven as arbitrarily as his prototype was to hell; the condensing images at the end of Purg. & Par. [*Purgatorio* and *Paradiso*], Nietzsche's Superman. Arrogance has to be directed against someone or something: Ahab talks of a personified impersonality, i.e., Nature.[521] In Job God descends. I haven't got educational repetition to fit yet, but it must belong. It's suggested in "Byzantium" in the progression of spirits.[522]

[537] It's wrong, or at least unresolved and immature, to be arrogant toward & dominating [of] either Nature or women—everything Nietzsche says about women indicates that his Superman is as male as a gent's piss house. The mature position (this concerns critics, not poets; poets do what their imagination tells them) is my Genesis-Exodus one. What begins as objective becomes a mysterium-tremendum; philosophically, the holy is the God of the gaps;[523] then it's stripped of authority (which is really counter-arrogance) and becomes simply order, the supporting, supplementing, inexhaustible counterpart of human creative energy. The spindle of Plato[524] disappears at the impersonal stage.

[538] Stevens' "great poem of earth" probably can't be written, because the narrative has to end with a vertical vision looking up & down. Even War & Peace ends with the contrast between those two states (Mir in Russian means a lot of things besides peace). Mallarmé's "great work" certainly wasn't written, but maybe a comparative study of the Bible and the literature we have may give critics, *in critical terms* only, some notion of what it would be like in outline.[525]

[539] Fn. [footnote] (probably) on "Parnassian" (Hopkins' term) as a third kind of rhetoric, the habitual language within his poetry that a poet gets accustomed to using. I thought I had this somewhere.[526] (Maybe it's Eight, too; part of the habitual bit.)

[540] I think I have everything now that would obviously belong in such a stretto, except Shakespeare, more particularly the romances.

[541] Reality of beauty & ugliness (156, top [i.e., par. 504] goes with the up-down perspective I take off from.

[542] Eleanor's Stevens book, commenting on the "Snowman," has a

footnote referring to Rosalie Colie on 17th c. paradoxes of nothing-ness.[527] Check along with Adams' Nil book.[528]

[543] It is a terrible thing to reject love, even a very dangerous form of it like the vampire love of neurotics—I, of course, think of Norma.[529] But sometimes one can express genuine love only through rejection: after all, the neurotic can't *unite*, or go out of (in this case) herself.

[544] I think I understand what Jung means by animus & anima, but I don't believe that only a man has an anima and only a woman an animus. I think everybody has both.

[545] I'd like to get rid of the blocking metaphors about the burden of the past, maintaining standards, keeping up traditions, & other euphe-misms for staggering under guilt feelings. This again connects with my use of the Bible. In its historical & ideological context the Bible is male-centered, white-centered, Christian-centered, theist-centered. In its mythi-cal & metaphorical contexts these limitations become metaphors for something that includes what they exclude. Perhaps these centres carry the predominant emphasis in the culture of the past: as Newman said of English literature, the bulk of it will always have been Protestant.[530] One has to recreate. That's why, of course, there's so much yapping about deconstruction and, more especially, "supplements." The real supple-ments are implied in the text, not in the psychology of the writer.[531]

[546] Narrative is a horizontal journey; it can't express, for example, love: it can only keep pursuing an object of desire that retreats to the last page. That's why there has to be a thematic stasis: love would involve the reader's participation. Those who can think only in either-or categories, & can't see that an antithesis is part of a thesis, naturally assume that if something isn't diachronic it must be synchronic, & therefore static, unchangeable, immutable, & all the other unfashionable things ("my name is Ozymandias"). But it's objective & static only as long as it's not understood: it has to enter into an identity with the reader. We think of the "sub"ject as being under the objective, including an objective text, but the subject is metaphorically on top.

[547] The interchange of whole and part I've mentioned is an extension of what is called in criticism the hermeneutic circle. How do we under-

stand the wholeness of a work of art? By studying the parts. But how do
we understand the significance of the parts? By studying the whole.
There is a vogue now for deprecating holism, but it is an indispensable
metaphor: if we want education we also want a "university," despite the
miscellany of activities; if we look at the stars, we want to feel that we
live in a "universe," despite the discouraging number of galaxies. Apart
from that, "we are all members of one body" is the extension of holism
from literature into life. There can be no sense of exhilaration, no expansion of the spirit, without wholeness.

[548] "It is expedient that one man die for the people," said Caiaphas,[532]
and every human being agrees with him. So I used to say. What I'd
emphasize now is that according to the Christian doctrine of atonement
God's plan of salvation justifies the faith of Caiaphas (he was the first
person to be so justified).

[549] When I started criticism I knew that there was a difference between "creation" and criticism because I myself was neither a poet nor a
novelist. I knew that I was just as "creative" as though I were, but I
worried then, as was appropriate for the time, that criticism was regarded as parasitic. Now the perspective has reversed, like one of those
trick drawings, and now, in the phrasing above, the poet must die that
the critic may live. Criticism's paradoxical task is to indicate the bounda-
ries of literature by obliterating them, just as one may indicate the existence of Russian literature to English readers by translating Tolstoy into
English.[533]

[550] Translation is a key word now: the Bible attracted me because,
poetic as it was, it seemed the essence of translatability. The critic translates literature into another linguistic structure (basically descriptive, but
adapted to its figurative subject) that joins literature to other aspects of
culture.

[551] I wish my notes weren't so damn elliptical: re Jung, top of 165 [par.
544]: the metaphor or fantasy of a being of complementary sex doubtless
throws the conception into higher relief, though the conception is only
incidentally sexual. And the burden of the past is echoed in Bloom's
anxiety of influence.[534] Incidentally, the burden of the past makes pastoral myths inevitable. (This way of writing is trendy now, but it's a most
irritating form of rib-nudging.)

[552] Marxist & feminist criticism belong in Seven, with the return of the excluded. As one can't alter a ruling-class or patriarchal past, one has to talk about a future, talk up the few bits of proletarian or feminist imagination in the past, or put the heroic stature on the consciousness-raising critic. All these are crap, more or less. But I mustn't get too psychological or Tibetan-monkish, at the end of Four or anywhere else. Kerygma is also—perhaps primarily—a *social* vision, an attempt to see a society freed from ideology. Gibbon was, from a naive point of view, chasing a ghost, at best a metaphor inscribed within his sources, there being nothing "out there" that actually declined and fell.[535] (My classing history with description of external events is impossibly naive, history being a discourse; but the descriptive is an element in history.) The present vogue for "historicity" extends the conception of horizontal narrative into everything: the great importance of the axial perspective is that it shows the relativity of the historical.

[553] Patch up parabola in Mut. Coes [*Mutabilitie Cantos*], & link with arrow parabola in MND [*A Midsummer Night's Dream*]. You said that before, but the hell with that. I mean the parabola of Diana's cunt.[536]

[554] The great intuition I got from Spengler, and later from Vico, was the sense of every historical phenomenon being symbolic of every other phenomenon contemporary with it. That's more or less what neo-historicism has got into now, the Marxist element in it having forgotten that it once had a transcendent perspective on history.

[555] Seven turns partly on the purloined-letter archetype, the thing that sits there staring you in the face while you're knocking yourself out hunting for it and not finding it. Some say it's a clitoris and others that it's a phallus. I think it's the kerygma of God, the verbal message everybody wants to kidnap but can't get hold of.

[556] Marxism shows an odd resemblance to Aristotelianism in earlier centuries. In the sixteenth century & later Aristotle became an influence on literary criticism precisely when he began to lose his dictatorship in logic, metaphysics, and psychology (De Anima). Marxism is a literary influence in non-Marxist countries just when it's on the skids as an economic theory in Marxist countries.

[557] The Bible says that God created man and that the Word became

flesh. This on Hegelian principles contains the fact that man makes (himself) God (which he can do demonically or apocalyptically) and that his flesh (soul-body) becomes Word, or intelligibility. The two are complementary, not contradictory.

[558] Freud was a conservative pessimist transformed by disciples into a revolutionary optimist; Marx was a Utopian transcender of history transformed into a determinist of "historicity."

[559] Derrida says structuralism is wrong because you can't get outside a structure to examine it. That's a misleading metaphor: you enter a structure from the "inside" & it becomes a part of you. Only it doesn't stop at the individual, but creates a spiritual substance: it's one's infinite extension.

[560] Transfer the sentence about why keep jumping from the Bible to literature to the Introduction. The Bible of myth & metaphor expands literary experience into some very unexpected quarters. That Bible is also the spiritual Bible, something infinitely greater than the guide to conduct that legalism & doctrine try to make it out to be.

[561] We're possessed by the quiet of the "silent night" incarnation vision, with its peace & good will, & forget the verse in the Book of Wisdom it's linked to.[537] The arrogant, boastful, jealous, trickster God can descend in some very unexpected ways.[538] The God descending in the whirlwind to Job is in a way more malicious than Satan, but he completes Job's protest for all that.

[562] The possible documentation available in the whole of literature is so huge that any examples give an effect of thinness.[539]

[563] Kerygma of course transcends all value-judgments on literature: quel effroyable toc.[540]

[564] (Recap.) There has been a good deal of discussion over Poe's story The Purloined Letter: does the letter, for example[,] represent a clitoris or a phallus? I am not much excited by such critical allegories;[541] but if we must have allegories, a story of a verbal message that everybody wants to kidnap, but can't because they can't find it, & can't find it because they

can't see it, & can't see it, not in spite of the fact that it's staring them straight in the face, but because it is, is much closer to the kind of thing I've been talking about. After all, a letter *is* a verbal message.542

[565] A certain amount of Platonism is inevitable with social institutions: every student, every churchgoer, every voter, has some *idea* of the university or church or government which is not destroyed by the pedantry or stupidity or dishonesty that he finds in the operating institutions.543

[566] Intro: much criticism today is in the tradition of the worst ages of Biblical commentary, except that its allegorical basis is feminist psychology or Marxist sociology rather than theology.

[567] Graham Greene's Ministry of Fear combines amnesia & twin themes: a man has his memory destroyed in a bombing raid and becomes a nuthouse inhabitant under a different name. Allegory of totalitarian brainwashing: he's the victim of a spy ring.544

[568] One has to resist the temptation to see in metaphor nothing but an easy out for any kind of logical argument. There are "logical" or fitting metaphors, there are mixed metaphors, & there are what Stevens calls metaphors that murder metaphor.545

[569] Goethe's Prometheus poem could be mentioned with the "right worship defiance" group.546

[570] I'd like to scrap a lot of the stuff at the end of Two: it's a dreary rehashing of what I've written before. Poets invent their own history: poets & other people use pastoral myths. The point is not that myth falsifies history, but that history falsifies primary concern. The "overthought" is the ideological content, or what is, more or less, being "said." The "underthought" is the progression of metaphors that express the primary concerns. Don't rehash Henry V: quote the Edward III passage and point to the two levels of meaning.547

[571] I think I should cut what I have on the Crucifixion, or the latter part of it, & substitute perhaps my Caiaphas point.548 If I keep what I have, I should alter it to something about a negative primary concern: we

do this to God, so *the* (mythical) Xfn [Crucifixion] is the dead end of ideology.[549]

[572] In Three, on the other hand, I should add what I'm now trying to stuff into Eight about the irony of narrative as such & the necessity of the "sub"ject's being in a superior position.

[573] The Orientals say you should get outside the rush of thought through the mind, & realize that it isn't you thinking—in other words all such gabble is at best ideologically conditioned, at worst just ego-shit. Stream-of-consciousness means something that's never really conscious. The verbal sewer is an infiltration of "historicity" into the individual: it's nonsense to say we can never get clear of it.

[574] I don't know what to do with this: dramatic forms, including music, have a positive temporal factor in their structure. By that I mean only that a play has to be staged in two hours or whatever. The time factor in reading a novel is there all right, but it's a relaxed personal-time factor: you can take up War & Peace and put it down again, taking six months to read it if you like. Poe's short stories & poems to be read at a "sitting" stresses the positive time factor, and heralds the approach of the electronic media.

[575] Transfer the irony-against-norm point to 3/31.[550] I'm wondering how much of this chapter is inorganic repetition: I can't remember how much is in GC & how much is in the paper I wrote afterwards.[551]

[576] Seven: revolutionary criticism, whether Marxist, Freudian or feminist, seems to have to go through a stage of second-rate pedantry where it is intelligible only to fellow-believers, before it outgrows a quixotic phase of trying to remake history (that's wrong: Quixote wanted to continue what was there). As Newman said of English literature, "it will always have been Protestant,"[552] and the real critical enterprise can hardly be concerned only, or primarily, with what we do from now on. Incidentally, doubles can be expanded: I don't know if I mentioned the secret sharer in Conrad, but I ought to expand the TN [*Twelfth Night*]-Séraphita[553] point to include a reference to feminist criticism and my difficulties with Jung's anima.

[577] Swedenborg, with his hypnagogic visions of a hell world below & a heaven world above the middle world of waking consciousness, is an immense influence in the 1750–1850 period: Balzac's *Seraphita*, de Nerval's *Aurelia*, etc.[554]

[578] Four: add to kerygma: social consensus primary & literary v-j's [value judgments] about, e.g. the Koran irrelevant. I think it's in Five that I have the passage about the mystics & how they became what they beheld: this was the one grain of genuine insight behind the frenzy of notes I wrote on the sun Cantoes in the Paradiso, the fact that Dante had included Joachim of Floris.[555] For Eight, look up Lucian's dialogue on Prometheus (Prometheus es in verbis).[556] Speaking of Eight, did I squeeze out the externality of the demons in *The Pilgrim's Progress* when I transferred the journey part to Three? If so I should put it back.[557]

[579] Six should say that the traditional patriarchal emphasis, along with the dying-god (usually male) myth with the female nature in the background, is ideological manipulation, not an inherent principle of myth.[558] The Cinderella archetype is an example of the opposite development: Cinderella is quite as important an image of human purgation as Prometheus. The ewig-weibliche[559] theme is of course male-centered too.

[580] I can't say what I really think here: I'd kill the book if I did. I think social feminism, genuine social & intellectual equality between men & women, a centrally important issue. Feminist *literary* criticism is mostly heifer-shit. Women frustrated by the lack of outlet for their abilities turn to pedantic nagging, and the nagging pedantry of most feminist writing is a reflection of frustration unaccompanied by any vision of transcending it. As Newman resignedly said of English literature, it will always have been Protestant.[560] Perhaps female (not feminist) writing has a great future, but that doesn't make its effort to rewrite the past any less futile.

[581] In the previous note I had to stop & think before writing the commonplace "bullshit." I must look up the passage in D.H. Lawrence where a white peacock is associated with women: I remember the phrase "all vanity and screech and defilement." I think it's in *Lady Chatterley*: it's

not in *The White Peacock* itself. But if I remember correctly it's still a peacock, not a peahen.[561]

[582] Six: (after *Seraphita* probably): although I think every human being has both an animus & an anima, still there is one Jungian theme I can adopt, though I got it from Blake. A stabilized male-female relationship within the psyche is the basis for imaginative progress: without an "anima" or animus a male or female becomes left with what Jung calls a shadow and Blake a spectre, "a ravening devouring lust continually" [*The Four Zoas*, Erdman, 360, l. 37].

[583] Eight needs both Bunyan and Goethe's *Faust*. Faust doesn't really descend to hell: he pushes that off on Gretchen. At the end of the second part he's dragged off to heaven as arbitrarily as his prototype was to hell.[562] Christian (one has to assume an identity with the narrator of GA [*Grace Abounding*]) goes off to the wicked gate staggering under a burden of "sins" that are almost all merely anxieties, and, as above [par. 578], externalizes his demons. The titan with the vultures is a larger view of what is more frequently somebody scratching fleas: Beelzebub is only the lord of flies, after all. Demons behave very like insects: one can always shoo them away but they always return, and their strength is their persistence in returning. But a virus invisible to anything short of an electronic microscope can destroy a human soul.

[584] Nothing, in Eight, leads to the negating of negation, where nothing becomes everything, or at any rate something, & potentially everything. From there I somehow (nohow-contrariwise) get to four interconnected themes that sum up the book: the purgatorial, the technological, the educational, and the Utopian.[563] These represent respectively the tortured Prometheus, the fire-bringer, the Prometheus of forethought (*in verbis*) and the creator of man. Except that the model society leads to the fifth concluding vision, the paradise on top, the eternity which is an "artifice" rather than an authority. How these themes connect I'm not altogether sure, but I have some clues.

[585] I think I should get my catastasis stuff out of Eight, where it's blocking me, and put it wherever I've got my other detective-story point (I think Seven).[564] In my four final patterns, the technological leads to Marx's instruments of production, & from there to the fact that the

ultimate i's of pr [instruments of production] are words and numbers. Besides, what I'm really looking for at the end is not apocatastasis, but recapitulatio, whether that's in Irenaeus or not: a *new* creation.[565] Also all the upward patterns are summed up in the Resurrection, which recapitulates the progress of human life itself from nothing upward, but makes a second up-thrust after its death.[566]

[586] In Job the descent of God with his revelation of the "old" (really the unspoiled, or, in Christian terms, unfallen) creation is followed by the restoring of Job to a new creation.[567] For Blake the beautiful new daughters would be poetry, painting and music, which are also prominently featured in the later cantoes of the *Purgatorio*.

[587] The world across death is the invisible world that enables the new creation, that of human art, to become visible. I said that the question whether Yeats in Byzantium is talking about life after death or about the poet's transforming of reality is one of those either-or questions that have to have a both-and answer.[568] I don't think Dante is predicting his own salvation at the end of the Paradiso: I think he's predicting the salvation, that is, the guarantee of the reality, of his poetic vision.[569]

[588] The klimax of the ladder is not a life "following" this life in an extension of ordinary time, but a transcending of time (and space too, I suppose). Hence the "letargo" passage in Dante. Incidentally, the Argonaut allusion is repeated from the beginning of the Paradiso:[570] I must find out why.

[589] The technological-purgatorial modulates into the educational process of *habitus* or *hexis* in which the poet, painter or musician perfects his skill.[571] It's here that questions of beauty & ugliness become relevant, and, perhaps after all, of catastasis (shit) and apocatastasis (unified apocalypse vision of body-as-food[)]. Maybe I need to do a lot of transferring from, especially, Seven.

[590] That leaves just one stage more, the forming of society into one "body," the Utopian theme that may form the subject of my next book. In the *Purgatorio* the increasing emphasis on poets & painters in the later cantoes, climaxed by the appearance of Statius, introduces the theme of art in the context of an improving condition.[572]

[591] I keep notebooks because all my writing is a translation into a narrative sequence of things that come to me aphoristically. The aphorisms in turn are preceded by "inspirations" or potentially verbal *Gestalten*. So "inspiration" is essentially a snarled sequence. Many of the nuts and cranks who write me letters are inspired, but can't get to the verbalizing stage. Some of them are nuts because they accept the pernicious Shelleyan fading-coal fallacy,[573] and think they're descending to commonplace when they attempt sequence.

[592] I've said in Eight that the real instruments of production are the verbal, mathematical, and pictorial creative powers of man. The sculptural & perhaps architectural are included with the pictorial (architecture *is* science, Blake says [*Milton*, pl. 27, l. 56]), and it seems clear that the musical is included with the verbal. I know about my circle at the end of the AC footnotes,[574] but there are implications here that should be looked into.

[593] Some of the people Dante meets in hell, such as Vanni Fucci, hate to give their names:[575] there's a close parallel in such dialogues to the ghosts in No plays. If the setting of the Inferno were Bardo it would be a less barbaric poem, if not necessarily a better one.[576]

[594] Beauty & ugliness go *out* of Eight, and should go wherever I talk about the autonomy of the metaphorical cosmos, if that isn't the Introduction. If it is, I'll have to do something else.[577]

[595] Look up Sergis Hackel's book on Blok (Oxford, 1975).[578]

[596] Regarding the beauty & ugliness bit [pars. 504, 541, 589, and 594]: the Platonic tradition in particular did what it could to bugger up science by introducing aesthetic categories into the objective world. It looks prettier this way; therefore that's the way God must have made it. This is the "cosmetic" fallacy, as we might call it, remembering the etymology of the word.[579] The cosmetic fallacy recurs in philosophers (Kepler & Hegel provide examples) where some simplistic mathematical formula tries to save scientists the trouble of being inductive. The author of Job is infinitely shrewder: he talks about the power and mystery of the creation, not about its aesthetically satisfying qualities.

[597] Amassing themes for the Epilogue: the simplest metaphor is good-

up, bad-down. The axis one is more complex, because there's a split between creative & demonic, but both can be up or down. Demonic descent from above means a trickster god or a Satanic sky-god. Nobody believes "in" a demonic god up there: a lot do believe in a benevolent one, and they include me. That modulates in the direction of my Exodus-Genesis vision, human effort striving "upward" against a descending vision of order that complements it. That simply recapitulates Job. My original notion of the Bible as a kerygmatic vision coming down from up and secular literature as a response coming up from down, and actualizing something like the Chinese (Taoist) heaven-and-earth imagery, haunts me, but I doubt if it will work.[580]

[598] Unless, perhaps, "earth" is the existential and "heaven" the essential world. That's a by-form of an earth-act and heaven-word setup. Babel is action with confused words.[581]

[599] So Nietzsche's remark that it's hard to get rid of God as long as we believe in grammar[582] does contain a genuine intuition, silly as it sounds. There's no reason I can see to want to "get rid of" God, and grammar isn't a thing one believes in; but I have always made an order of words part of my thinking, and have always suspected that my "verbal universe" *was* the creation. The metaphors surrounding music: harmony, correspondence (i.e. counterpoint), scale, concord (cf. the Russian *mir*) belong here too.

[600] This sounds as though I were heading for a Platonic conclusion, with a duality of form above and whatever it is below. But Platonism, like Judaism, is full of the legal fallacy, that right action is informed by words. It doesn't go through the two Beulah gates of ivory and horn.[583] I think Platonism's context is the continuity of institutions, as in a previous note [par. 565]. The authoritarian fallacy always assumes this kind of descent: it thinks of man as responding, whereas it's really God who responds, Blake's eternity in love with the productions of time [*The Marriage of Heaven and Hell*, pl. 7, l. 10].

[601] A sense of humor, like a sense of beauty, is a part of reality, and belongs to the cosmetic cosmos: its context is neither subjective nor objective, because it's communicable.[584]

[602] With all constipated bureaucracies, even expressions of orthodox

ideas are suspect if their expression is original. Once an ideology goes downhill, it becomes too stupid even to understand itself.

[603] All human creativity drifts upward through the ivory gates from libido to ego, bringing a mixture of vision and violence, love and cruelty. A sense of articulate order comes down through the gate of horn.[585] Creativity is a purgatory fuelled by the "blood-begotten spirits,"[586] refined into love & wisdom through words. Without words it's only the Babel of power with its confusion of tongues.

[604] Look at the end of Strindberg's Keys of Heaven.[587] I wonder if Joyce knew this play under that title: the last words of Finnegans Wake, before the sentence completed in the first page, are "the keys to. Given!"

[605] My sequence leaves out the drama and the symposium: the Platonic dialogue, in particular, moves toward some kind of epiphany. Plato does not speak in his own name, so he's beyond the logocentric and in the imaginative area.[588] The epiphanic climax even links him to the kerygmatic. Links also with polytheism & discussion of gods among themselves in Homer; links with Kierkegaard's "aesthetic" writings under pseudonyms;[589] links with the Book of Job and with the conclusion to my book, which so far is a fucked-and-far-from-home mess.

[606] I suppose there are once again two points of epiphany, an upper one of the symposium; the group drinking wine & becoming one body, and a lower one of the dialogues of the dead—Lucian & the black-comic people from Strindberg to Beckett—my Parsifal point too. The upper one may qualify Buber's insistence that he & she are ultimately part of the It-world. The angel, the messenger speaking for someone else, is what's involved.

[607] Wordsworth's nature as an inner vision of Paradise: it has a sublime and a beautiful aspect. The beautiful is the conventional Eve-garden, but there's a sublime Lilith-weeds and wilderness side too, which has a slightly alienating but also a complementing side.[590] This has a parallel in the Romantic Esauism,[591] and it's not impossibly connected with my doubled female convention.

[608] Cut the demonic-letargo point[592]—in fact you should go carefully through the book taking out over-clever complications. Also hee-haws.

[609] This Chaos book I've been reading quotes von Neumann as saying that science doesn't explain or interpret: it makes (basically mathematical) models.[593] I think a model-book (on Utopias) lies ahead of me: its main elements I have, but the fact that *every* work of fiction is a Utopia, i.e. a nowhere, a description without place, hasn't really sunk in yet.

[610] I may have overdone the schematism, as usual, in my Natur-Geist diagram at the end of Four. But it's only in the *Geist* context that we can have a "polysemous" structure. When the "literal" is not descriptive but narrative-mythical; when the conceptual (not in Dante, really) is the metaphor-mosaic; when the rhetorical is the spiritually rhetorical, addressed to the *inner* life—then we can have a polysemous structure. Not always the inner life, but rhetoric with no element of the homiletic, the appeal to an inner vision, whether of society or one's self, is Natur-rhetoric that can't ultimately avoid its own debasing.[594]

[611] I John 3:9: no one begotten of God commits sin. Put this in place of your stupid paragraph on the puer aeternus in (I think) Four. The late-parents business comes in here too.[595]

[612] The first three forms of discourse in chapter one become, in their spiritual form, three elements of a "polysemous" verbal structure which can only be poetic. Descriptive becomes description without place, the fiction or revelation. Conceptual become[s] the underthought, the underlying progression of metaphors that won't quite do. Ideological-rhetorical becomes the parliament of the spirit, the voice inside (Sermon on the Mount), the symposium leading to epiphany (Plato), the vision of social order (also Plato and Jesus' kingdom).[596]

[613] Leopardi, in one of his notes, says what I say about the uniqueness of Jesus[597] (I say it about Buddhism, though): that Jesus was the first to define the enemy of mankind as the world—in short, man is his own devil. (I don't need to unscramble that silly parenthesis: I'm not publishing this.)

[614] I wonder if I could push Leopardi's remark another step: man's enemy is the world: that is, man himself as aggregate instead of body. And he can't be anything except either an aggregate or a spiritual body.

[615] Job is a symposium ending in an epiphany of the creation pre-

sented by God. The Gospels are a symposium of Jesus and disciples ending in a God-man risen from death and hell. In poetry there is no direct address: in rhetoric there is nothing else.[598]

[616] Re my remark about Caiaphas justified by faith [par. 548]: cf. Dante's *De Monarchia*, where he says Pilate acted justly in his own context.[599] I should add Dante to Milton & Victor Hugo as a political poet who couldn't find his own political ass.[600]

[617] Two things in Plato that keep haunting me: why the tragedy-comedy business at the end of the Symposium,[601] and why the Thoth-writing business at the end of the Phaedrus?[602] The first attracted Fred Sternfeld, who said only Shakespeare and Mozart had done it.[603] I wonder if it has something to do with the chronicler of Socrates, who put him into dialogues resembling comedies and also spoke of his tragic death. I've long realized that the second was in part an ironic comment on the rhetorical speech that Socrates' friend brings along with him to "refresh his memory."[604] But there's something more I haven't got.

[618] "Words with power." Words without power don't matter: power without words inevitably turns to genocide, and then to self-genocide. Where there is no vision, the people perish [Proverbs 29:18] (Joel):[605] that's a descriptive statement, not a metaphorical one. What I call in One the "impersonal" turns out to be the person Thou.[606]

[619] Does it matter whether Jesus' feeding multitudes with practically no food happened or not? Answer: the story is profoundly and suggestively true if it did not happen, and quite unbearably cheap and vulgar and silly if it did happen.

[620] Eight: the Revelation "defiled with women" crap[607] links with the puer aeternus mythology of I John 3:9.[608]

[621] In an age of primary concern the hewers of doctrine and the drawers of boundary lines seem deficient in charity.[609]

[622] When feminists are told that their criticism is infantile they always reply that of course new ideas are deeply disturbing. Their ideas are not new: *they're* new.

[623] I think I am at the point now (subject to the revision of Eight) when I can put what I've left out into footnotes. Dylan Thomas' Winter's Tale seems to have been left out:[610] another point, that only secondary concerns are distinctively human, can be squeezed into the present Eight. So can the two memories, which relate to the two aspects of Job. But I did leave baptism out of the shit in Seven,[611] and I guess it's one for the corn plasters.

[624] "Literature is the total modality of mythology."

[625] Fn. [footnote] to Four: Jesus' mustard seed of faith [Luke 17:6] illustrates how kerygma normally comes as a shower of seeds.

[626] Look at the Chapman Tears of Peace quote again (for a footnote)[612] and find out where Soul becomes Spirit in Hegel.

[627] Word about going *up* to Jerusalem in Ezra [1:3] that's something like ma'alah.[613]

[628] Turning away from quest (Faust's Erdgeist, Dante's three beasts) recurs in the Job climax. (Turning away from past & Satan but seeing leviathan after all.) Wagner & Shelley, Tolkien & the renounced cycle I perhaps don't need, as I've got them elsewhere.

[629] Chief Seattle's magnificent speech in 1851 when the whites proposed to "buy the land" of his people.[614] I thought I had it, & maybe I do; otherwise a footnote.

[630] Only animals have entirely primary concerns: secondary ones are the distinctively human ones. For primary concerns to become primary again we need a reintegration with nature.[615]

[631] God: the transcendental signified of the old model is actually the universal signifier, the giver of names through Adam. Created beings (Seiendes in Heidegger) are the signifieds of ordinary languages, but the signifiers of their own creation. Creation is the awakening into a world of meanings, as Keats' famous statement about Adam's dream[616] in fact implies.

[632] Re above [par. 630]: secondary concerns are linked (a) with laws

postponing instant gratification (b) basing the major arts on *distance* senses.[617] Censoring of smell & deprecation of taste (Plato's cookery) [*Gorgias*, 462d–465d].

[633] Words with power: Luke 4:32. Jesus says some mysterious things about power ("all power is given unto me") [Matthew 28:18] yet is helpless in a human context.[618]

[634] Job can't look back but up & down to the end of the narrative which is his present situation. Brooding memory that breeds superstition & vain repetition, & practice memory that sets free. Lost paradise & future hell-distortions of anxieties of time.[619] Put together. Especially Job.

[635] Woman born of man (Eve) type of male-center & female-circumference. Man born of woman the wanderer revolving around the hortus conclusus at the centre.[620]

[636] I used to say that hypocrisy was really a virtue, meaning it as half a joke. But when our worst impulses start clamoring that they're our "real" feelings, we realize how debased reality can be even when it's real.

[637] I've been rereading my Utopia article—I mean the one I did for Holy Cross.[621] Like all my good articles, it contains an entire book in itself, and I'm wondering if I should write out the book.

[638] Most of it is familiar stuff to me: the prestige in the 16th c. of Plato's Republic & the Cyropaedia. The ideal state as the allegory of the wise man's mind: the role-model figure of Cyrus & the 16th c. tradition of the Institute of the Christian Prince. The deadlock between the Castiglione tradition (Elyot's Governour; Faerie Queene, Sidney's Arcadia as (according to Fulke Greville) a model state) and the Machiavellian view of Cyrus & the Prince generally.

[639] The greatest-form for prose point is not in the paper. The educational-encyclopaedic ideal (medieval) and the social-model one. Contrast between static, monastic, withdrawn-from-history Utopias like

More's & Campanella's and hardware technology science-fiction ones like Bacon's Atlantis, which brushes aside the natural-virtues point of Utopia.

[640] The Utopia as nowhere (cf. Faerie) and the eutopia; the purgatorial form; influence of Lucian & the katabasis form; Rabelais' send-up of Utopia, which he admired: Erasmus, who also admired it, has a send-up in Encomium Moriae & said Utopia *was* actual & model England. The humanist in-joke & the crap nervous Catholics draw from it.

[641] Burke & Rousseau; *natura naturans* natural society vs. Burke's art-as-nature and Swift's gifted animal. Erewhon's Book of Machines argument & the luck-or-cunning thesis. That's verging toward the question of what I want to do with all this. So far, the point seems my humanity-as-world versus spiritual interpenetrating kingdom.

[642] Mandala symbolism (I could call the book, or a chapter in it, *The Squared Circle*, or *The Earth's Imagined Corners*). The stuff about Solomon's temple in the first volume of Purchas;[622] the city in Revelation; the theocracy of the Torah.

[643] Plato gets his priorities right: the philosopher-king orders the guards; the Machiavellian reversal of this is the road to hell, like Calvin's theology of unconditioned will. Note that Utopians are anti-Thomist; they're post-nominalist humanists, like More himself.

[644] The liberal who won't join the revolutionaries gets forced into a reactionary position. More's life; Rafferty's story.[623] The sentimentalist who wants to believe in the conservative facade—of course the facade itself is also a model. Hythloday is *culbute* and More's own "informing" (educational) view.

[645] Why am I writing all this out? Because the ideas have excited me for fifty years (e.g. Dumézil's red-white-blue men and Plato's classes, though I don't believe that set-up is just Aryan). Montaigne on the Cannibals and the beginning of the natural-society debate, with its Tempest overtones. But while all the elements are rooted deeply in my mind, where am I *going* with it all? Is it really the third book in the Bible series,

incorporating both my Utopia article and the educational-contract one the New Statesman reprinted?[624] Is the educational contract in the Bible? (Yes, it's part of wisdom).

[646] Then there's all the Utopia : city :: Arcadia : garden stuff I got from Morris' NN [*News from Nowhere*], which spills over into pastoral in one direction and Thoreau in the other. Thoreau's experiment in economy raises the question: is expecting good value for money a primary concern? Yes, surely: Ruskin & Morris, in different ways, realized that shoddy, tasteless, overpriced goods always means that somebody is sweating somebody else's labor. Which means, of course, that the economy of waste violates a primary concern. That's one of the things Buckminster Fuller's *Critical Path* is about.

[647] My article on Spiritual Authority in the 19th c., which I've nearly forgotten, bears straight on this subject.[625] So far I'm just collecting references to what I've already written, which is hardly good enough.

[648] A student recently said to me: "I don't see how you can keep on believing all that stuff for so long." That is, she assumed the axiom "faith is believing what you know ain't so," & further assumed that belief on such terms was an intolerable strain.

[649] *My* approach to faith turns it into *gaya scienza*, a joyful wisdom: most of the conventional approaches turn it into a burden of guilt feelings. Critics who distrust me because I don't seem too worried about inconsistencies (Murray Krieger, Bill Wimsatt)[626] can't tune into this notion of faith as a dancing ballet of intuitions, affirmations, counter-affirmations, "doubts" or retreats from dogma, & a pervading sense of "anything may be 'true' or 'false,' but whatever it is, the whole pattern has a design and a movement."

[650] Of course all my Spengler-Toynbee stuff,[627] my "butterslide" writings,[628] and my studies of Yeats' pseudo-history,[629] would be relevant to the squared circle. But perhaps the third book is not about Utopias but simply about the intermediate verbal cosmos. Perhaps the two things are one thing.

[651] I have never understood why that blithering nonsense "the me-

dium is the message" caught on so. Apparently the terms "medium" and "message" are being aligned with "form" and "content" respectively. And while it would make sense to say that form and content are inseparable, a medium is just that, a medium. It's a vehicle, a transmitter, a means of communicating words and sounds and pictures. It is not and never can be a form. The form of a verbal message is as verbal as its content. The content of a musical message, say a Mozart quartet, is a musical form. It may be heard in a concert hall or over the radio or read as a score in a book, but such varieties of media touch neither form nor content. On Magritte's pipe principle, the content of a picture is not the objects it represents, but its form or pictorial organization.[630] But painting itself is not a medium: painting cannot be a means of transmitting painting.

[652] The same data that demonstrate the non-existence of God to Ivan Karamazov demonstrate his existence to Alexei, and there is no third criterion to appeal to, even if Dostoevsky himself agrees with Alexei.

[653] Reading a "Leavisite" attack on me: Canada is full of critics who are like those bright blue recycling boxes: they diversify the scene even though there is never anything in them but junk.

[654] I suppose a central question, in One, which I ducked, is: what mode does criticism itself belong to? It's the activity, I think, that interrelates the modes and demonstrates their mutual interdependence. *Literary* criticism, in my approach to it anyway, has the specific task of inter-relating the imaginative to the other three. Distinguishing without dividing, the critic separates mythology from ideology, concrete metaphor from abstract argument, self-contained language from servomechanistic description.

[655] Patrick White's *Solid Mandala* is a double story, as I should have known.

[656] Utopia book: start with metaphor as model, looking at Max Black's book, and then myth as model (pattern repeated, figure in carpet). Harrington's Oceana. Becker's (I think) Heavenly City of 18th c. Philosophers and Manuel's book on (I think) 18th c. confronts the gods. Sacvan Whoozit on New England again. The body metaphor would be

as important to this book as the royal metaphor was for GC and the *axis mundi* for WP. Start with Purchas on Solomon's Temple: the whirligig of time for me.[631]

[657] By that I mean that my standards reverse those I was brought up on. Everybody said in the 40s that Hakluyt was a wonderful editor and Purchas loaded up his stuff with rubbish.[632] Spingarn speaks of Henry Reynolds, the greatest critic before Johnson, as though he were an idiot crackpot.[633] The fact that there's so much resistance means that the myth people are supremely important, of course: but I still don't have the why of the resistance.

[658] Why can't I learn languages? Because I can't bear to read anything unless it contains potentially something I can base a critical judgement (no) aphorism on. You can't find such material in the opening pages of a Russian grammar. In other words, pure vanity.

[659] The yogis claim that the most childish thing you can say is "I wish." If you want something, either go after it or get past the stage where you think you want it. Bullshit. The minute you say "I wish" you're starting to construct a model. It may be only a Land-of-Cockaigne model, but it's the beginning of imaginative life. The thing is that when it leaves the imaginative and enters the practical sphere (which is what the yogis are talking about) it becomes the "I want it all and I want it now" motto of yuppie-puppies. And that *is* childish.

[660] I've been resisting playing the piano for so long that I will perhaps never get any skill back. I don't know why, but instead of relaxation it's become a mechanism for churning up the gibbering monkey's recital of embarrassing memories. My adolescent interest in Classical music (I could never hear anything in popular music but an unpleasant noise) was obsessive, a reaction against Monctonian, parental, & school environments. I was never very good: my sense of rhythm was poor and I have always been too lazy (and weak) to play up to speed and volume. I had dreams of being a great composer but never worked at them as I worked at my writing. Why this furtive scurrying approach? Far worse, I can't play in public because the same gibbering monkey sits at my ear and says at intervals "all right now, it's time for you to make a mistake."

I always really wanted it this way: I wanted to read everything and scurry over the top of the keys. This caused conflicts when I finally did take lessons. I've been wondering recently if my relation to my brother[634] had anything to do with it. He left some music—I remember Mendelssohn's Rondo Capriccioso and Raff's Am Loreley-Fels—which convinced me that he was a very able pianist. But perhaps he wasn't: perhaps he just bought them and didn't play them. Anyway, my mother's feeling that she had only one son and that I was a second-rate substitute for him (God provided the substitute, but God can be a pretty blundering fool in evangelical minds) may have affected me in some ways. Fortunately I was always too indolent & selfish to make silly efforts about it, trying to "prove" myself and the like.

[661] The Bible *is* a colossal literary tour de force, whatever "more" it is, and the canonical instinct is so sure, in the large view, as to suggest a direct intervention by God. I don't see this in the Koran, & I don't see how anybody could see it in the Koran. But what does this lead to? Apparently to the reflection that God is exactly like me: in a world howling with tyranny and misery all he cares about is getting his damn book finished.

[662] Qoheleth's nothing new under the sun is about knowledge; his time for all things is about experience [Ecclesiastes 1:9 and 3:1]. The former is the cycle of the revolving mother from whose womb we never get born; as soon as you say the latter you've invoked the creating father and his appearance in time as the (separating) Son.

[663] I shouldn't overlook my own remarks, like the one on p. 3 [par. 6]: "food expands into a concern with bodily identity."

[664] That footnote I so admire in Robert Cohn's book on Rimbaud[635] has to do with the cycle of the old *man* giving birth to a son: Santa Claus & the New Year, full fathom five, a veillard [*vieillard*] in Mallarmé, etc. One should add Dylan Thomas' Winter's Tale and also a paragraph on the Father-Son relationship in (I think) Seven.[636] See if you can find that amazing patristic passage where the Father shits the Son.[637] Pound, Canto 13.

[665] Perhaps I should add *The Beast in the Jungle* to the Nothing section.[638]

[666] The network cluster: Chaucer's House of Fame, of course; Jonson's Staple of News; De Quincey's Mail Coach essay; the fascination of various people (Bennett, S. Lewis) with hotels; McLuhan: I don't know that I've got hold of anything here, only the network of rumor is a parody of the spiritual body. Henry James: In the Cage.

[667] It would be nice if God willed that I should write a Century of Meditations.[639] But I wouldn't want to plan such a book as a dumping ground for things I can't work in elsewhere or as a set of echoes of what I've said elsewhere.

[668] Such a book would feature (a) completely uninhibited writing, like my notes on the romance book[640] (b) completely uninhibited metaphor-building, as in some of my undisplaced plot-reconstructions. Ideally it's a book to be put away in a drawer and have published after my death.

[669] Levy's Gate of Horn: the Malekula chapter: souls of dead meet a spirit-figure who draws (I think) a half-pattern in the sand they have to complete.[641] Overtones of Oedipus & the Sphinx (her riddle was the other half of the Oedipus-Laius-Jocasta threefold pattern). Ishmael Reed, Mumbo-Jumbo.[642] The overtones go as far as Browning's notion of the next world completing the pattern of this one. And Yeats' Purgatory— well, his double-gyre Heraclitus movement.

[670] The Critique of Judgment purposiveness-without-purpose and the intuitions I got from Poe's Domain of Arnheim don't really seem to have got in. Sometime I must read that *Chaos* book.[643]

[671] God, it would be wonderful to write a whole book in the discontinuous aphoristic form in which things actually come to me: I'd still have the sequence problem, but not the crippling angel of continuity to wrestle with. The hell with it, at least for now.

[672] Well: the Utopia essay is unpublished, I think; I'm working at Henry James & the Comedy of the Occult;[644] perhaps a "network" essay featuring De Quincey will work out. Minneapolis suggests an 18th c. topic:[645] wonder if I could get anything out of Berkeley's *Siris*. Law— Boehme, Byron, etc. too, and Lowth.

[673] Some of my readers say that my approach lacks rigor; I hope it also lacks rigor mortis. (If this goes in the reaction to Kermode goes out:[646] I'm sunk if I start slapping all the mosquitoes. One has to sacrifice one's blood to insects who need it to fertilize their own wretched little lives; but in this area I should have some control over the itch.)

[674] Perhaps the main theme of the next book is the supplementary relation of the Utopia, the human construct that by itself is worried & exclusive, & the Arcadia, the divine provision of a habitable Nature that by itself is full of—well—mosquitoes. The latter is what brings in the Arnheim-CJ [*Critique of Judgment*] stuff across [par. 670].

[675] We went to Simcoe[647] "for Easter," and Elizabeth wanted to go to Arizona "for Christmas." Curious how much holidaying consists of running away from holy days.

[676] Another dream book of mine is a novel where the hero dies, or eventually discovers he's dead, and is about the world of the dead and the appearance this world makes from that perspective. I dislike Charles Williams, but I have to admit he had the guts to try this.[648] The point would be to make it like Alice's Wonderland, so good-humored the reader wouldn't think "morbid," & yet so convincing he'd shiver.

[677] The hell with that. Prometheus is emphatically a trickster figure, though he tricks gods rather than man. So my last chapter is really the defining of the trickster element in God himself that I mentioned earlier.[649] Nietzsche & others are tricked into being Christian missionaries.

[678] I think the primary concerns are food, sex, property & free movement, besides breathing. Property, in the Aristotelian sense of the material extension of the personality, includes money (*very* primary in 19th c. fiction), shelter or housing (house as body in dreams), possessions of all kinds, including clothing.[650]

[679] This vast book on model societies:[651] at any rate I'll have to find out what the hell natural law is, and read people like Halévy.[652] Wonder if my network metaphors really belong: there seem to be two things involved: Utopias and communication. I'm going to have to put in a request for a long pre-senile life.

[680] Two big books, on social models and on communication, would give me a L ⏋ ∧ ⋏ sequence, unless FS & AC plus two volumes, one of collected essays and one of collected public lectures, form that sequence,[653] and the four starting with GC are the second sequence (V Γ ⅃ ⊥ I think they are.)[654] Otherwise the second sequence is the shadow of the GC sequence in the spiritual world. In either case the die is cast, or the cast has died, whichever comes first. I've had more time and better health than most people, so less excuse. AMDG:[655] yet how can God really be glorified by me?

[681] Well, there's this book. I've put a note on criticism as the theory of words into One,[656] and a clarifying alteration of the four concerns into Two.[657] Three seems hardly to need much addition, though the kairos theme, Eliot's still point in reverse (and Yeats' SB [*Sailing to Byzantium*], where the movement is from cycle to chain of being instead of from horizontal line[)].[658] Four needs a lot of fixing up still: it's always been a bugger of a chapter. The sequence persuasion > hypothesis > myth to live by, plus the top 189 note [par. 649], still is more confused than I want it. Also I'm not sure about spiritual & physical bodies as two halves of the same thing (incorporating the Malekula-Oedipus half-riddle theme on p. 194 [par. 669]) belongs in Four or Eight.

[682] In the second part there should be a paragraph added to each chapter dealing far more explicitly with the concern involved. The most elaborate would be the free-movement theme of Five:[659] the Psalm 23 wanderer vs. the exile who can't go home;[660] the opening of the prisons to those who are bound; the ideological hierarchical ordering of rank and social status (in Henry James most of the characters never really think about anything but sex & money, but as they can't say so they have to pirouette around all these social-status ritual dances).

[683] Probably I should say at the beginning of Five that there are three things to be considered: the myth, the concern the myth expresses, and the ideological adaptation of the myth. Besides the demonic parody, of course.[661]

[684] Anyway, it seems to be also Five that contains the reversal pattern that I first got out of Milton's psychology:[662]

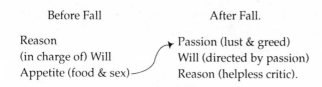

Before Fall	After Fall.
Reason	Passion (lust & greed)
(in charge of) Will	Will (directed by passion)
Appetite (food & sex)	Reason (helpless critic).

[685] This modulates after the Romantic movement, in a way perhaps most clearly indicated by that nut Nietzsche.

[686] That is, the traditional pattern is that the primary gift of God to man is reason, and the reason should be in charge of the will. The from-Rousseau-on pattern is that man owes his being to Nature, not God, who supplies him with an amoral will as his primary driving force. Reason or consciousness now assumes a *critical* function.

[687] Some of this should be spread evenly: if so much is piled into Five, the other three will look like perfunctory fillings-out of an empty schematic design. The concern of Eight is property, and property eventually modulates into the extension of individual & social power, which eventually turns [out] to be machinery. The rebel angels, like man, have to be redeemed, purgatorial & not hellish figures. Perhaps the Malekula half-riddle split comes into focus here.[663]

[688] Perhaps Seven has an insertion or two: it certainly has baptism, which I unaccountably left out. Also the point that nothing gets shat but shit. God has no positive enemies: nothing is his enemy after the apocalypse except nothing (I mustn't forget to add Henry James' *Beast in the Jungle* to Eight). Neither can he be touched by blasphemy.[664]

[689] Words with power should come into focus probably in Eight: man is born using his consciousness in the service of the selfish gene;[665] that develops in the direction of Nietzsche's will to power. The purgatorial process transfers power to the instrument of consciousness: the word. The relevance of machinery is that our behavior is mechanical now: purgatory reverses this to the control of mechanism.

[690] Machinery, once evolved from the dinosaur stage where control of it is a prize in the class struggle, becomes an extension of consciousness very closely related to the arts. The sons of Cain invented both, and they

must be redeemed, once the goal of their behavior becomes forgiveness instead of Lamech's vengeance.[666] My reference to Lamech should cite the "seventy times seven" antitype in John.[667]

[691] I can see why crazy Nietzsche thought his Dionysus gene-born principle was a life force:[668] wisdom, says Yeats, is the property of the dead [*Blood and the Moon*, l. 49], meaning, as something in Yeats knew if he didn't, that it's the ambience of the spiritual world, starting with the moon.[669] The spirit & the soul-body below the moon are an antithesis.

[692] Don't forget the benevolent trickster who makes Freud & Marx & Heidegger Christian missionaries (obvious at a glance at any theological journal).

[693] *Four* things to get clear in all four variations:[670]
1. The aspect of kerygma or myth to live by.
2. The myth itself & the concern it grows out of.
3. The ideological adaptation of the myth.
4. The demonic parody.

[694] I think I'm about ready to absorb Dante into the book now: reality is heaven, hell, & the purgatorial process. Hell doesn't "exist," but it's the world we *have been* making and ought to stop making. It's the pure past, the bottom of God's revelation to Job. Blake's doctrine of Los's halls, where no hair or particle of dust can pass away [*Jerusalem*, pl. 14, l. 1], overlooks or does something else with hell: a hell of the past that never passes away is as irresponsible a nightmare as Dante's in the ordinary reading (including mine). The phrase in *Jerusalem* is "the outward shadows of possibility."[671] I still think the *Inferno* was a monstrous concession to stupidity and malice, but I hardly see what else he could have done.

[695] Eight on machinery as final possession: the dynamo, in Henry Adams' phrase, regenerated along with the Virgin.[672]

[696] The Spirit is essential man, man as *responsive*: what he responds to is the verbal world, not the objective one. This means that he is no longer a subject, but a writer of the dividing Word.

[697] It is true that I attempt overviews, and my style in consequence

features what are called, in the sweeping cliché of tunnel vision, "sweeping generalizations."[673]

[698] Near the end of 1989: the text of WP is roughly off my hands. I have a dozen or so essays worth reprinting. Emmanuel has made a request which is an unreasonable imposition, but in view of, etc., has to be taken seriously.[674] I gave a lecture on More's Utopia at Boston College which I later altered to an inaugural Newman lecture at McGill.[675] I have very little use for Newman, but I can use him for a partial integration of my views on Utopias or model communities and the university, along with a religious dimension totally different from his.

[699] Then I talked about "Literature as Therapy" at Mt. Sinai Hospital,[676] and out of it came the suggestion that poetical language is the language of a counter-environment, directly opposed to the ideological rhetoric that aims at kinetic influence. Myth & metaphor confront the environment instead of trying to adapt to it or speak for it. So I have two lectures there: the first on the university as Utopian and religious community, the second on the confrontation of poet & public (cf. Yeats' *King's Threshold*, which has two sides, one illustrating Yeats' importance as a poet, the other his silliness as a carpet-knight). For the third I'd like to go off into very deep waters.

[700] The second one takes off from a point emerging in the Henry James lecture:[677] realism is poetry compromising with the objective world; for a poet reality is verbal, and truth is what tentatively emerges from a consensus. I can make this the theme of my NEMLA address,[678] and adapt it to the Emmanuel sequence. I must read Maritain's Mellon lectures:[679] when I acquired the book at Princeton I couldn't read it because that Thomist illusion was even then going over the hill. But separated from that it makes some sense. So the first two lectures will put their roots down in Catholic ideology, & the third will try to show that roots aren't the whole plant.[680]

[701] I told the doctors about mother & Scott's novels, suggesting that romance creates a counter-delirium.[681] We don't buy Galen's sympathies and antipathies any more: they don't exist in nature (amethysts for drunks, saffron for jaundice, etc.). But they may exist in the reality-realism metaphorical-objective context. The confrontation technique in

the casting out of a humor. Jonson, Shakespeare's *TS* [*The Taming of the Shrew*], the Fool-Edgar in *Lear*. My point in the *Lear* lecture about words fighting evil (my 1940 experience with Churchill) at the centre of the words-and-power conflict.[682]

[702] I suppose what my bourgeois liberalism really amounts to is the sense of the ultimately demonic nature of all ideological constructs. In the 30s & 40s the Thomist one had Gilson & Maritain in the front line: they were gentlemen, of course, but a mean-minded fascism lurked in the background.[683] I knew that the Thomist setup was an illusion, and that Marxism (which didn't have any gentlemen) would eventually be exposed as another illusion.

[703] The R.C.'s [Roman Catholics] have moved closer to Protestantism in the last two or three decades that [than] I would earlier have believed possible, and I suspect that even my central belief that a church mired in history has to be constantly "reformed" by dialogue with a Word of superior authority is one a good many Catholics would accept. Newman was a pint-sized Marxist who thought he believed in a historical process: he actually believed (as in *The Arians of the 4th c.*) in a mythical repetition of events. His "Via Media," too, was a dim vision of an autonomous Word.[684]

[704] So the lectures[685] may go in a roughly Hegelian pattern: first the historical process and the informing principle; second the confronting poetic Word; third the redemption of history through (but not by) the Word. Note that the subjective and objective worlds are the same, the individual ego being a historical product: it's just that they seem opposed because of a cloven fiction that really unites them. I want to get this out of Kant (CJ [*Critique of Judgment*]) rather than Hegel.

[705] At Princeton I bought four books to keep me up to date with the mid-50s: Maritain's, Malraux's *Voices of Silence*, Auerbach's *Mimesis*, and Curtius on medieval literature and Latin. At that time Curtius was the only one I could read with any real profit: *Mimesis* was all very well but I was working out an anti-mimetic theory of literature; Malraux said a few excellent things but was full of bullshit; Maritain, as I said, kept busting his skull against this preposterous "Art and Scholasticism" thesis, insisting that critical theory just had to come out of St. Thomas, who cared as much about the arts as I do about basketball league playoffs.[686]

[706] In the myth-metaphor world all truth is paradox: a Hegelian thesis where thesis contains and implies antithesis, but lives with it and doesn't transcend it. A is/isn't B. This did/didn't happen. Maritain derives the person or individual from the Incarnation, which releases the Self from the idolatry of things; but the individual doesn't come from there: he comes from society. In insisting on this Marxism had the real principle. But it's only in the individual that paradox can exist, as only Self can enter the interpenetrating world. I was always shocked by the Marxist use of "the masses."

[707] The 30s of this century were frightened by the power of the masses led by a mass-man, and religious people turned to the Incarnation, the Word made flesh, as the source of verbal as opposed to brutal power. But the Incarnation is only the Apollonian or order side of the Word; the Resurrection, the Dionysian expression of the power, completes it. Well, who denies that? I'm trying to get at the tension of opposites.

[708] The final lecture[687] is concerned with the Utopia as the symbol of what oversees the historical process and continuously informs it. A Utopia in a future at the end of history is an illusion. Newman doesn't seem to have thought of a Word in dialogue with the Spirit, only of a Spirit immanent in the historical process.

[709] Malraux says Spengler's book started out as a meditation on the destiny of art-forms, then expanded.[688] What it expanded into, I think, was a vision of history as interpenetration, every historical phenomenon being a symbol of the totality of historical phenomena contemporary with it. That's what fascinated me, though of course I didn't know it for many years.

[710] Escape literature is confrontation literature: whatever evades this world faces, or sets up, another one. A Galenic sympathy exists between plot and the "insane" world (the world of dreams, fantasy, improbabilities) and a Galenic antipathy between the metaphorical world and the "sane" world, the verbal reality versus objective realism. Of course realism (as in Goya's Disasters of War) will impress us as reality if we're under the sedatives of idealism—I dealt with this in the Whiddens under the rubric of "stupid realism."[689]

[711] Scott was a source for the 19th c. opera—Donizetti's *Lucia* & Bel-

lini's *Puritani*, the latter very loosely adapted from *Old Mortality*. I think not Verdi, though Verdi drew from a Romantic tradition that Scott did a lot to solidify: Hugo, Dumas, Schiller, etc. Nobody could imagine an opera of that period based on Jane Austen. If I try to rehabilitate Scott as a romancer, I should also try to rehabilitate melodrama. That term is usually used with contempt, & I've used it so myself, because of the way it approximates lynching-mob mentality in its hiss-the-villain setup. But there's a legitimate type of melodrama where characters and plot outrage "probability," yet seem to live in a logical world. I find Scott very hard to read now, but there are a lot of important critical principles extractable from him.

[712] The Waverley Novels form a gigantic epic stretching from the First Crusade (*Count Robert of Paris*, a most discouraging introduction) to Scott's own time (*St. Ronan's Well*, an even more discouraging conclusion.) (The effective sequence runs: T [*The Talisman*], I [*Ivanhoe*], FMP [*The Fair Maid of Perth*], QD [*Quentin Durward*], K [*Kenilworth*], FN [*The Fortunes of Nigel*], LM [*The Legend of Montrose*], OM [*Old Mortality*], perhaps PP [*Peveril of the Peak*], RR [*Rob Roy*], LL [*The Lady of the Lake*], HM [*The Heart of Midlothian*], W [*Waverley*], R [*Redgauntlet*], GM [*Guy Mannering*], A [*The Antiquary*].) In such a sequence there is bound to be anachronism: sometimes identifiable mistakes, sometimes large-scale reconstruction (e.g. the Fleming in *The Betrothed*). The former is noted by contemporary reviewers (Balzac on QD [*Quentin Durward*]), and some of them make silly moral issues out of them. The point is that anachronism is never creative, as it is in *Cymbeline*, for instance: there are rules to the game, as there are in detective and science-fiction stories, and Scott's historical-novel genre is formulaic popular fiction of exactly the same kind.

[713] Why write a historical novel when the pattern of history is fixed? That question perhaps indicates why that particular genre went out of style—until it suddenly revived with Umberto Eco's *Name of the Rose*. The idea is to set up a romantic myth in the middle of a historical situation.

[714] I don't want to read the whole shelf: a group of three, K [*Kenilworth*], FN [*The Fortunes of Nigel*], QD [*Quentin Durward*], would be enough. Notice the strong emphasis on the character of the ruler. Elizabeth I,

James I, Louis XI. It's not exactly a great man theory, but as history it contaminates history with romance. (No, that won't do either. The ruler is a focus of primary concern, the sub-ideological substratum of history, and he's the real centre of the action, not Nigel or Quentin). Against the ruler is polarized the chieftain: Fergus in W [*Waverley*], Rob Roy, the too-late Jacobite in R [*Redgauntlet*], Charles the Bald in QD [*Quentin Durward*] and AG [*Anne of Geierstein*]. The trampling down of the tribal Highland culture by middle-class Hanoverians is the central inspiration for them all.

[715] For mother's generation Scott was the pinnacle of serious secular reading: no one realized that he inverted [invented?] a popular formula, and isn't "serious" in the way Jane Austen or Balzac are. This point has been confusing me: it's involved me in one of those "revaluation" antics I detest so much, and which invariably appear when there's a confusion of genres. If Scott had been allowed in his day to be, if not "obscene," at least as sexually explicit as Fielding, he'd have been more centrally in the Milesian tales tradition.[690]

[716] I should make more of the point that revaluation results from a confusion of genres.

[717] The "subject" swallows everything objective to it: hence the pan-historical critics of today, the Hegelian pan-philosophical absolute knowledge, the pan-literary universe which only three people understand: Blake, Mallarmé, and myself. The *final* answer, naturally, is interpenetration.

[718] Back to this silly creative-critical dichotomy: what's "creative" in me is the professional rhetorician, the saviour of occasions, the person in constant demand for convocation addresses, after-dinner speeches (which I almost never give) and church services. This stuff being mainly oral, the bulk of it has disappeared. (Into Los's Halls,[691] I trust.) But it's what I really do best: I'm one of Jung's feeling types, a senser of occasions. My summing up of the "Options" U of T conference and the "Violence" CRTC [Canadian Radio-Television and Telecommunications Commission] one showed me at my best:[692] similarly with my Chancellor's greeting to the lyric conference,[693] my Ben Jonson dinner speech,[694] my "benedictions,"[695] etc. etc.: I'm usually first-rate at impromptu. I forget what point I was going to make of this.

[719] I've already said, in prefaces & the like, that I'd greatly prefer to see the occasion preserved:[696] the lyric conference introduction is a good example. As a paper contributed to the conference, it looks rather silly, to me anyway. Naturally, I've had some resounding flops. I'm also particularly good, or used to be, at answering questions: my ability to translate a dumb question into a searching one has often been commented on. This should be leading to something useful, but it hasn't yet. The central thing is that my "creative" faculty is the power of *personalizing* occasions. My written texts are, whatever Derrida says, incarnational or prophetic, and reading them ought to lead to reincarnating them.

[720] The Virgin Mary is mother: Mary Magdalene is the forgiven harlot, often linked maritally to Jesus by apocryphal writers (D.H. Lawrence[697] and that holy blood squad).[698] Typologically this is correct. Mary of Bethany is the Sophia-daughter, the kernel of the church. It is she who persuades a sorrowful head-shaking Jesus to dig up the corpse of Lazarus and set it going again [John 11:1–46].

[721] I didn't need to travel as far afield as the Hindu hermit in search of the territorial imperative: every fucking couple wants privacy and darkness. That's "shame" only in a neurotic or Satan-inspired context. Incidentally, agape is sexless in the N.T. because spiritual intercourse simply interpenetrates: physical intercourse is impossible without penetration, invasion, or, if the woman is unwilling, violation. God screwed chaos for six days and separated on the seventh, panting. Chaos thereby split into cosmos, the child, and Schekinah, the surviving companion. The light and the dark, plenitude and vacancy. The prototypes of all the light and dark doubles—no, not quite.

[722] "In the beginning" is really, as there's no article, "in beginning" or "to begin with." "God created the heavens and the earth" sounds like a very easy statement, whether taken as factual or as mythical. That's because everybody assumes that "God created the world" means "God made the world." But if created means simply made, then divine creation is a metaphor projected from the fact that man makes things. And the Hebrew word *bara* [created] is never used for what man makes.[699]

[723] Interpreting "creator" as "maker" is vulgar: it reduces God to at best a demiurge or more often the watchmaker. God of Paley[700] and the

rest. On the human level we use "make" for the useful arts & "create" for the fine ones. Bach didn't make the B minor Mass: he brought it to birth in his mind, like a virgin mother: well: it had a father, the whole tradition of music up to his time.

[724] I used to say that creation was the revelation of the objective order to a conscious subject, and didn't exist, as creation, before human consciousness. Not intended as a history of how nature came into being. To say God made the world *ex nihilo* is the Critique of Pure Reason answer: the world is pure phenomenon, epiphany or manifestation with nothing for its inner substance, a conception more Buddhist than Biblical—that doesn't make it wrong, but I'm looking for the Genesis meaning. "Out of matter" isn't even grammatical, if I'm right in thinking that matter is energy brought down to the point at which we can live with it. (Perhaps at death the spirit enters a world of higher energy, a tachyonic world where $e = mc^2$ would no longer hold.)

[725] Here comes Schopenhauer with his Wille-Vorstellung view, and his fantasy that we inherit will from the father and representation from the mother.[701] So God the Father is the eternal will, and human consciousness the power of objectifying that will as a representation. All humanity is female, then, to Schopenhauer's disgust and orthodox delight.

[726] Were the world now as it was the sixth day, there were yet a chaos, Browne says.[702] The sabbatical vision was not only creation becoming objective to God. It meant *unveiling* the creation, which had been chaos, and putting the veil on himself as the Schekinah. This seems close to Luria's withdrawal theory.[703]

[727] Traditional Xy [Christianity] says there's to be a final judgment of man by God, which will of course be just. Theodicy is a dishonest judgment of God by man that says he's innocent though the evidence is definitive that he's guilty. Guilty of what? Of not arranging the world in accordance with human desires. Such a judgment is about as relevant as a dog's judgment on a picture: "inedible."

[728] If "make" (see across [pars. 722–4]) is a lower-level metaphor for "create," then create, while it may include making something, doesn't

stop with that, but produces what Blake calls an emanation. I don't see that I'm getting anywhere with this yet. God creates specifically *life*, or at least living things, though the B Minor Mass is potentially alive. In some respects it's a ghost: it can be invoked in séance or performance. In Genesis God speaks but never appears.

[729] I'd like to get a good book on Scotus Erigena, or a translation of his book on the Division of Nature. He seems to be a commentator (Martianus Capella, Boethius, Dionysius)[704] and there's said to be a lot of the usual shit in his book. But some of his ideas make St. Augustine look like a nut in a sandwich board. He seems to be a transplanted Greek, closer to Clement & Origen & all the sanest & most cultivated Christian writers. (The story that Origen castrated himself is probably pure Western charity.) He got 19 theses condemned by a synod, which proves his eminence as a thinker.

[730] The first & last epiphanies of God, creation and apocalypse, correspond to the first & last appearances of the human being, birth & death. I'd like to know how far words can go in exploring the silences and mysteries surrounding these events. It's partly the old Mallarmé problem: black words on white space: what does the white space say? the nothingness from which the words emerge? What is said *around* the words? Mallarmé himself said that when you reverse black and white the white turns into the definitive book, the (rewritten) Torah.[705] But.

[731] Three Maries. Mary the mother, paradoxically a virgin, which makes mythical sense. Mary the forgiven harlot, often associated maritally with Jesus, which again makes typological sense. Mary of Bethany, the Sophia daughter (which would make Lazarus Jesus' son). Hell: I've got this [par. 720].

[732] I may have this too: re the Paul de Man scandal:[706] why should we expect public figures to be role models, exuding all the approved sentiments? His record could hardly be worse than Heidegger's, but who denies Heidegger's importance? Heidegger, Frege, Spengler, George, even Wagner: all people of great importance: every one a kraut clunkhead as dumb as the beer barrels in Munich. Jung too, for all his dodging. Sartre: the incarnation of the *Trahison des clercs*,[707] the juvenile delinquent of the intellect. Camus used to complain of being taken as a moral oracle,

but that was just the public saying: "Sartre and Camus—well, at least Camus is a grown man."

[733] I think Kierkegaard understood the conception of imaginative literalism very well, but his "either-or" dialectic contrasts the aesthetic and the ethical. Well, in many contexts they are a contrast. But he never got through to the final insight: the ethical *is* the aesthetic transformed. Ethical is kerygmatic in my context.

[734] Ignatius (Ephesians 19) speaks of the virginal conception, the birth and the death of Christ, as three things (a) hidden from the prince of this world (b) as mysteries of a "cry" (krauge) in the stillness of God.[708] In Magnesians 8 he speaks of the Word that proceeded from the silence.[709] Scholars argue about whether he meant to identify God and silence, as apparently the Gnostics did: some early editorial meddler inserted a "not" into the passage.[710] But the language is still living and metaphorical. There's an analogy to the Schekinah in Jewish thought. Also, I think, Ignatius would have taken Byron's remark about history as the devil's scripture [*The Vision of Judgment*, 1. 689] very seriously. I'm brooding over two forms of pseudo-history: the legendary poetic history (Trojan war, Grail romance, etc.) and Heilsgeschichte, the sacred narrative plotted by God in the silence and taking the plan-of-salvation form. Ignatius also, in exhorting friends not to make him avoid martyrdom, says if they love him in spirit (let him go) he will be a word, but if they love him according to the flesh (try to save his body) he will be a mere voice (phone).[711]

[735] Schopenhauer on the will: he speaks of the absurdity of fearing only *future* non-existence and of saying: I was born in 1912 and will live forever. Hence reincarnation (which he says should be called palingenesis)[712] is reasonable enough. Nature cares only about the species in the world of will, not its individual manifestation (Vorstellung); but (a sharper insight) below the phenomenal world the individual-species dichotomy may not exist. But his vision doesn't include any spiritual order: will and phenomena are both aspects of nature and that's all there is. Wonder how true that is also of Oriental visions he was so close to. According to him we derive our participation in the will-world from the father & the idea-world from the mother.[713] Beyond that father and that mother there's no ancestry.

[736] Blake was Xn [Christian] because for him only Xy [Christianity] identified the divine and the human. His was probably a monophysite view, but the two-natures one may be just rationalized hierarchy again. He also clearly thought that only Xy [Christianity] had a real conception of spiritual substance (or reality). That's what I'm trying to get some notion of now: I'm rereading the *Paradiso* for the somewhat unusual purpose of getting information about the spiritual world.

[737] Siger of Brabant, William of Ockham, Nicholas of Autrecourt, Peter Abelard, Meister Eckhart, Roger Bacon, Scotus Erigena: in all repressive societies most of the really first rate people are either accused or suspected of heresy.[714]

[738] For Heilsgeschichte, practically all the events in Weltgeschichte are really non-events. That is, what should or could have happened merely fails to happen. That's another way of saying that W [*Weltgeschichte*] is a demonic parody of H [*Heilsgeschichte*]. The great man in W meets with his councillors and decides to go to war. That's decision; that's making history; that's positive action. If he decided for peace, that would have been a non-event in W, but a genuine event in H.

[739] Well, I finished The Double Vision: I don't want to add another syllable to it, but I may get some flak of the "too difficult and too short" type. What I might consider is a fourth lecture on "The Double Vision of God." Here I'd pick up a theme from WP about the Jehovah of the Old Testament being not God but an intensely humanized being as violent and unpredictable as King Lear.[715] This came back to me when a publisher sent me *The Book of J*, a new translation of the Yahwist narrative, with a commentary by Harold Bloom.[716] Jehovah is not a very likeable character, because, like Lear before his abdication, he has no vulnerability, but just keeps on doing damn fool things. He is not a man, that he should repent, says one of his more nauseating flunkeys.[717]

[740] According to that liturgical piece Charles Heller showed me, the Jews were always clear about the metaphorical nature of the "revealed" Jehovah.[718] The Christians weren't, though they were partly protected by the New Testament, where Jesus' Father is better behaved and far more reticent. The Moslems, on the other hand, got stuck with a God who's a nut and a crank, and they're led by unscrupulous people who

want to make this obscene creature a political fetish. In the sign of a stinker-God shalt thou conquer. I've got all the material for the Gods constructed on the analogy of nature or social aristocracies, but can I say anything really new with it?

[741] It's beginning to feel as though "The Double Vision of God" were next on my schedule: if so I'll get help with it; if not it'll end on the cutting room floor with no hard feelings. I should look at things like *Fear and Trembling*,[719] which make a certain sense out of the old bugger's capers.

[742] Milton: man can do nothing except destroy his own idols: all creative power is from God, or the Spirit (Blake's imagination, of course). Such an essay would emphasize my pro-Hebraic bias, despite the Jehovah-riddle. Bultmann and Harnack are Marcionites: they want to attach Logos to the *Greek* logos. The reasonable is the opposite of the rational.

[743] I have to strike out the passage about the fourfold vision being beyond my scope.[720] The double vision separates the metaphorical from the natural vision: the former is the grammar or linguistic expression of the spiritual vision. In the vision of God the metaphorical becomes in its turn a new form of natural vision.

[744] So I have to go back to anagogy. I think I see a connection between the anagogic vision and Milton's rule of charity in reading the Bible.[721] The real revelation in the Bible is that of the divine plan for redeeming man, so everything that seems to indicate the enslavement of man, or rather God's approval of enslavement, indicates a wrong reading.

[745] Of course the spiritual vision *of* God *is* God: Narcissus is transcended, but the metaphor (Paradiso 10) is still there.[722]

[746] Dante and the monstrous moral perversions the priestcraft of his day compelled him to accept. Hell is human life as "mere nature," as Blake says:[723] purgatory is the effort of the spirit to emerge from this. I have now a skin cancer and a hiatus hernia, besides other ailments—very petty compared to what other people have. If I say "thank God," it's only because that seems ordinary politeness; my thanks are really for the gift of life and consciousness, and I'm not fool enough to think my

ailments are punishments or trials or that the fact that they're relatively minor has anything to do with my virtues or merits. Diseases are the revenge of nature for getting born: a lifetime of the nervous irritability of my lifestyle was bound to produce these particular diseases. If I recover, my spirit is throwing them off in an effort to continue life on this plane; sooner or later something will separate them for good. Even Lazarus, on the narrative level anyway, would have had to die again. So would all those healed of palsy and the like in the Gospels. *All* healing is casting out the devils of nature. *And* the psyche we acquire from nature.

[747] One very widespread myth (ancient Egypt, the Orient) is that the psyche consists of several elements, which break apart at death. Let's follow out the Oriental version for a bit. Everybody has, I've said, a lost soul, and should make sure it gets good & lost. When you bust up, the crucial question, as with multiple personality cases, is: which one is the real you? When Helen died, the real Helen became an angel in heaven. There was also a sulking and egocentric Helen, who would become a preta or unhappy ghost, and wander around Cairns[724] for a few hours and then disintegrate. Lycidas was a Christian angel, a pagan genius, an absence, and a drowned corpse. Helen was a pile of ashes, an absence to me, and an angel: perhaps she's a genius to me (or anyone else who loved her and is still living or not living and still confused).

Notebook 50

This notebook was discovered in the bedside table of Elizabeth Eedy Frye after her death in May 1997. Internal evidence indicates that it was written during 1987–90, though most of the entries come from 1988–89. Frye mentions, for example, the 1987 tour of the United States by the Pope, and he wrote some entries during his trip to Russia during the fall of 1988 (see par. 731). Two entries are dated: paragraph 756 ("June 1989": the reference here is to the Tiananmen Square massacre) and paragraph 761 ("July 14/89"), Frye's birthday. The later entries were written after the publication of Words with Power *and only a few months before Frye's death: there is a reference to a trip to Yugoslavia Frye took in September 1990 (par. 808) and to a review of that book that appeared in November 1990 (par. 809). The notebook is in the NFF, 1993, box 1.*

[1] If I can bring it off, what I'm trying to work out is the way the four major or primary concerns expand into literature. That sentence is illogical: I mean I'll publish the complete scheme if I work it out, bits and pieces of it if I don't, and stop with this diary if it doesn't exist.

[2] I think the four primary concerns are food, sex, shelter and play. My first indication of their immense expansiveness came when I was studying the ramifications of "lust" and "greed" in *Paradise Lost*. (Food and sex in their demonic forms.)[1] Freud has shown something of how the Eros theme straddles over the whole of literature. Marx ought to have been our guide to Prometheus, but Marxism froze into a dogma about dialectical materialism that knocked it out of the real centre of literary criticism. The same thing happened to the Freudians, but the revisionists got in earlier, and so the critics got more leeway.

[3] The Prometheus theme starts with the kernel of shelter, which expands in two directions: toward construction, the centrifugal direction, and towards home, the centripetal one. Such books as G.R. Levy's *Gate of Horn* and its successor[2] deal with ramifications of building imagery for the gods and the dead. Most ladder imagery goes here too: spirals, towers, the winding stairs deconstructed by Eliot (*Ash-Wednesday*), Yeats (*The Tower, The Winding Stair*), Joyce (Finnegan's ladder) & Pound (tower of Dioce).[3] In the Gospels, note the phrases of Jesus about "ascending & descending," and the climax in the first two chapters of Acts, with the Word ascending and the Spirit descending.[4]

[4] I think the discussion of Prometheus has to come first, partly because he's the more specifically "creative" Zoa and partly because I think the Eros ladder is secondary.[5] But I've written a good deal on Eros in literature and on how the sexual act becomes allied to the literary one.[6]

[5] Frazer collects lots of data on the food anxiety, but of course he can't think, so I have to work out all the Eucharist and other ramifications. It's closely linked to the psychology of sacrifice, and an extraordinary amount of positive law consists of inhibitions about eating and drinking. It's as though the inhibition that stops or postpones eating has a lot to do with the growth of consciousness and its detachment from the natural environment. In the Bible it ends with the restoring of the tree and water of life, and the invitation to drink (the climax parodied in Rabelais).[7]

[6] The conception of play I got originally from Huizinga, from whom I deduced the principle that work was energy directed toward an end, and that play was the end, energy for its own sake.[8] In society work is a penal effort imposed by society and accepted for the very little amount of play it allows. I imagine Nietzsche has a lot to say about this emancipated energy ("gaya scienza"), though its "will to power" connections are a product of frustration, at least so far as they're aggressive.

[7] Buckminster Fuller thinks science originated in South Pacific navigation, where the stars had a practical use. Also that the Bronze Age began in Thailand and spread to China, where copper & tin are both found. When it finally got to the Mediterranean, they had copper in Cyprus and had to go all the way to Britain for tin. They couldn't have discovered that two soft metals would make a hard alloy except by accident.[9]

[8] The navigator, then, was the first scientist, and an astronomer. Pyramids & other buildings were aligned to the sun & stars, & had no room for anyone alive except for an astronomer. Germ of Il Penseroso, of course.[10]

[9] I think the business about those not defiled with women in Rev 14.4, which sounds so damn silly, is a deliberate contrast to the Watchers of Enoch who were, allegedly, so defiled.[11] Actually it still is silly, but the typological symmetry redeems the silliness. Why it should and how it can I don't know, but it just does.

[10] That very pathetic passage in Gilgamesh where they set a whore to trap Enkidu, and he loses his link with nature.[12] The fall in Genesis is similar, of course; but *what* is the link between virginity and the paradisal link with animals? And with magic (compulsion over nature)? In Blake Urizen loses the link without benefit of whores, but that's because for Blake it's the fall into the cloven fiction of intellect & morality that's primary, not the fall into sexes. Song of Songs: garden & spirit of garden. The chaste in Revelation, above [par. 9]. Orpheus with his lute. What I'm approaching is: why did Jesus have (a) to be born of a virgin, with Nativity ox and ass (b) to *be* a virgin? I have the Morris passage,[13] of course, & Alice couldn't have held Wonderland if she'd got even as far as the menarche, to say nothing of intercourse.[14]

[11] Schiller's essay on the Aesthetic Education of Man is the source of the Huizinga play thesis. Also Becker's *Denial of Death* speaks of "Eros, the urge to the unification of experience." He must have got that from [Norman O.] Brown: I'll look.[15]

[12] Brown also quotes from the Tao Te Ching, though unfortunately his reference is only to Needham, & the Tao Te Ching is such a bloody amorphous book one can't find anything in its chaos of translations (I wonder if a sort of translators' variorum would work with such a book?):

> He who knows the male, yet cleaves to what is female
> Becomes like a ravine, receiving all things under heaven
> (Thence) the eternal virtue never leaks away.
> This is returning to the state of infancy. (28).[16]

This ties up two things. The time I consulted the I Ching for general advice & got, without any moving lines, the second K'un hexagram,[17] and Jung's notion of the soul as the embryonic female (*anima*) a man carries around with him.[18] Jung's "animus" is something quite different, a disease of consciousness perhaps. Whenever Jung speaks of the animus in his women patients he starts to lose his temper—a sure sign he's missed his point. I suppose the notion of carrying around an embryonic male is so natural to a woman that it's at a depth he can't reach.

[13] What was the point in creating Eve? I suppose it was to give the anima a local habitation and a name.[19] I heard of a man in the CBC or NFB [National Film Board] who died of a cancer caused by an undeveloped Siamese twin he'd been stuck with, or to. I suppose every death has something of that in it.

[14] I think feminism is being very silly when it objects to words like "mankind" instead of just letting them fossilize. A kind of niggling pedantry is so deep in women that it seems almost a built-in characteristic. It isn't, of course, but it's a very deep social conditioning, and that's what I think the "animus" is. The real animus, the male soul of a woman, is what makes her a real woman, to use a phrase stolen by crackpots.

[15] *Cocteau's World*, ed. Margaret Owen (1972) has the scientist Poincaré telling Cocteau that "the chance of a rhyme sometimes makes a system emerge from darkness."[20]

[16] There are four main bodies of verbal expression. Two are mythical and rhetorical: one of them is literature, the other the area I've been calling ideology. The other two use logos language, one constructively, the other descriptively. In descriptive language centripetal features like figured speech and ambiguity are minimized: they can't be abolished, but they are subordinated. The constructive sphere of logos is metaphysical: descriptive writing is words in front of physika, constructive writing is works behind or after ta physika.[21] Constructive writing is generated out of ambiguity and metaphor. Literature represents the maximum concentration of figuration, and the ideological area uses rhetoric kinetically. I've always suspected, too, a Hegelian form of polysemy. Descriptive writing, corresponding to immediate sensation, is *aufgehoben*[22] into constructive writing: that in turn is caught up into the metaphorical & rhetorical structure of ideology. Then that's caught up in

the poetic, where the centripetal is at its most concentrated. That may bring me back to conventional meanings of "literal."

[17] Descriptive writing tries to make words a mirror of externality: its convention is to persuade us that its words reflect things: a Lockean setup of a tabula rasa on which *diverse* impressions are recorded. Then the mind collects them and puts them into a construct. In this process the metaphorical roots of thinking become visible (aufgeheben, pharmakos, etc.). This is an allegorical phase (never mind just why for the moment), where doctrine, belief, & truth apply as fact applies in the preceding phase. Diversity gives place to unification. Then we move into a third quid agas[23] phase of ideology proper, where rhetoric takes over from logic & is used kinetically (the diverse reappears). Then we move into the poetic, where metaphor is at its most concentrated. Blake stops there: I can't, quite, because the Biblical kerygma is at a level that's not that of either quid agas or the poetic. (It's not absolute knowledge either). I suppose what I'm writing is a draft of Chapter Three.[24]

[18] The "unhappy consciousness"[25] or "sick soul" I suppose turns up at the end of the ideological stage: I don't know. The Utopia or social model is on the two > three boundary.[26] Maybe there's a distinction between the level itself and the level as swallowing all the lesser levels. Thus the top level is poetic; the top level absorbing the others is Biblical apocalyptic. Works of art are holistic in the iconic stage; then they decentre as they unite with the perceiver.

[19] One thing I seem to have left out of the GC was the jubilee year or sabbatical age: the type, I suppose, of which the antitype is the millennium or Messianic kingdom. Ascendant classes squeeze this out to preserve the continuity of their privileges: hence moments of deliverance are irregular.

[20] The symbol is the minute particular, the spiritual atom, the monad full of mirrors (perhaps after all *not* windows), the grain of sand reflecting the (spiritual) world, the primitive like an orb.[27] Its context can be present or absent. In the former case it's the centre of the world: in the latter the world is decentred. Or the metaphors could be liquid instead of solid: when present (the context, I mean) we have "oceanic" submergence; when absent, the whole is the part of the part.

[21] Try again. First we have verbal structures designed to convey information from the outside world. This means (a) a rigorously consistent
and constant sense of the separation of subject and object (b) a criterion
of "truth" in the sense of the factual (c) a sense of words as reflecting
phenomena or replicating events.[28]

[22] Here verbal figuration is minimized: ambiguities are avoided, and
so is every aspect of structure except the linear. The first thing this
reflective use of language reflects is the memory, hence the first use of
writing is to record commercial transactions, laws, etc. The link with
memory persists in the myth of the Muses & Mnemosyne & in the Thoth
episode of *Phaedrus* [274e–275b].

[23] Eventually the sense of the simultaneity in the structure separates
out as the antithesis of recording. The antithesis, then, in Hegelian fashion, swallows its opposite and we have dialectic, where A "follows"
from B. The highest development of this is the metaphysical system,
which is generated out of the metaphors and ambiguities still lurking in
the language. Also, of course, out of the syntax. This is what is best called
logos language, which I should drop for what I've now got it for.

[24] The motive for dialectic is seldom disinterested, though some, like
Spinoza, are close to it.[29] See the passage in Robert Musil about verbal
imperialism.[30] So dialectic turns into rhetoric or ideology proper. Aristotle said that rhetoric was the *antistrophos* of dialectic, and that dialectic
should always take the lead, the essence of rhetoric being fact & logic,
appeals to emotion being suspect.[31] That starts off the polite fiction that
the impersonal facts show A to be true, the fact that I desperately want A
to be true being suppressed or treated as coincidence.

[25] Rhetoric is figured language like poetry, and shades off impercepti-
bly into the mythical and poetic. Because it makes assertions, it "answers" to dialectic. It's Bultmann's kerygma also, but that illustrates
another principle: kerygma in Bultmann is still answering to dialectic &
excludes mythos, whereas it ought to be *totally dominated* by mythos and
should be *its* antistrophos.[32] Only I imagine that real kerygma is on the
other side of mythos or the poetic, which again brings us the "code or
art" phrase again [sic]. The metaphors of poetic grow out of apocalyptic
vision just as metaphysics grows out of those metaphors.

[26] I think each verbal area goes through the two stages of time-hearing and space-understanding (criticism).[33] Criticism of this kind reveals the "ground" of what is understood to belong to the next phase.

[27] Thus: we read a book about history or gardening or aeronautics. When we try to understand it as a whole we see that it is an assertive verbal structure related to, etc. Assertive verbal structures, that is, dialectical arguments culminating in metaphysical systems, come next. We try to understand St. Thomas Aquinas or Leibnitz or Hegel & find that they are historically & culturally conditioned products, i.e., works of ideology. We look at ideological structures and find them products of poetic myths and metaphors. We look at literary structures and find them products of a totality of imaginative vision (Tao, apocalypse, various Buddhist, Hindu, Moslem terms) where the subject-object and time-space distinctions no longer exist.[34] Behind the "code of art" I don't think we can go.

[28] In the ideological area we see that some (Spinoza, St. Thomas) lean toward the metaphysical & others (Kierkegaard, Nietzsche) toward the poetic. Note the determinist partial code: Marx, Freud, the religions, etc.

[29] The first chapter—and I think it has to stay the first chapter—is "Myth and Concern," and it defines the writer's authority.[35] But it could be called "The Illusion of Myth." Mythos is the verbal encapsulating of will, movement, power. Whether power is the supreme good (Nietzsche, Marx) or the supreme evil (Schopenhauer, and I think Blake) is a major issue of our time. I think directed power is evil—it aims first at revolutionary action, always with a kernel of dictatorship—and then at Star Wars games—but is good if its end is in understanding.

[30] Chasing the siddhis, the will o' the wisps of magical powers, is what a lot of technology does. The real drive & energy of myth is clearer in music, with its allegro fugues & their imitative entries. In literature there's the cyclical quest where we either come home again (Sam in Tolkien)[36] or attain Kierkegaard's repetition, recreating the original form. In history cyclical movement is a by-product (Babylon in Augustine, life under a "providence" in Vico). Here's where my "way" article goes.[37] In really great will-to-power music (Beethoven's 59:3 finale)[38] there's a sense of another power, internal & external at once, the fuel of the engine.

[31] Anyway, the way in the Bible (Chapter Four) meets its axis mundi full stop in "I am the way."[39] This is the midpoint of an axis mundi symbolism that starts with Jacob's ladder and ends with the metaphor-cluster identified with Christ in Revelation. From there it goes on to the tree of life in kabbalism and the various hierarchical constructs in Neoplatonic, Gnostic & Mithraic followers, & of course the four levels with its Ptolemaic & chain of being derivatives. Lurking analogy of the human body, & a hierarchic analogy there too. One book I read suggests that the mandala is a squashed or non-hierarchical tree of life.[40] I've given musical examples of the will to power in fugal & imitative-entry patterns.[41] Axis mundi ones start with the Scarlatti binary mirror-form (tonic-dominant, dominant-tonic), which becomes an actual mirror in stunts like the rovescio. Variation forms are something else again: they belong to an exfoliating evolutionary structure I haven't got clear yet. The dance or tactus rhythm in music brings in my work-play antithesis. The will to power is evil if it's work, because, unless it's practice work, the end in view is bound to be destructive.

[32] We all belong to something before we are anything, so we're all born from a symbolically female social body. To the extent that we're individual we're symbolically male.[42] Fitting actives to passives was the original job of Eros, according to Donne, but he must have got confused.

[33] Practical criticism derived from my AC is based very largely on modal transparency: i.e. seeing such things as myth & romance patterns in Joseph Conrad. Conrad is a particularly good example of an over-determined writer. Note the counter-historical direction of such criticism. It seems the opposite of deconstruction, which is based on that mysterious variation form I haven't got yet: Derrida's "construal" meaning is the theme. I've written a paper on Stevens as a variation-writer:[43] most great variation structures in music hover around the 30–33 mark: boxing the compass or filling out the phases (I have just 24) seems involved. Gozzi I think comes up with 36.[44]

[34] Buddhism is superior to Xy [Christianity] in the way it gets past the aural-visual time-space antithesis: Revelation gets to the panoramic apocalypse, invites us, like Rabelais, to have a drink, and that's it.[45] Buddhism understands that the next step, or participating apocalypse, is interpenetration, which destroys the antithesis of the inclusive and exclusive.

Hence being a Xn [Christian] is one way of being a Buddhist. Xy [Christianity] has the spiritual crusade, the effort to consolidate the death-principle & hell-principle, and get rid of them by clarifying their nature.

[35] It looks now as though there has to be a first chapter on the four levels of meaning. I'd like to get rid of the metaphor of levels, with its hierarchic overtones, but I don't see how to avoid it, considering the way they're related. A spatial metaphor like "quadrants" won't work.

[36] Start then where you always start, with the centripetal-centrifugal dichotomy. The progression that follows is not historical: it's almost the reverse of historical. First come the two phases of the Aristotelian mimetic. I no longer think Aristotle is talking about art & nature: I think he's talking about two kinds of logos-writing. Naive mimesis is descriptive writing, corresponding to Hegel's certainty of immediacy.[46] Here the verbal reproduces something objective at secondhand: in other words we read to gain information about something outside the words. Here language has to minimize ambiguity and figuration: the one-to-one relationship of signifier to signified is emphasized as far as possible. It's not completely possible, of course: its great strength, however, is in its capacity to create the categories of "truth" and "fact." Even the arts appeal to this level: "I just paint what I see"; "a camera dawdling down a lane," & other metaphors appropriating truth & fact for their vision.[47]

[37] Aristotle realized that this form of mimesis was reversible, and that the "true" relation of art to nature was an internal relation of form (art) to content (nature). This threw the main emphasis on the interconnection of words. Here we're in the area of logic & dialectic, where the *following* of one proposition by another, inner coherence, & the like, are what is primary. This form of logos-writing inherits from its predecessor the sense that the objective alone is real & the subjective & emotional unreal. This discovery accompanies the growth of writing, which emancipates verbal communication from the human body (the repository of memory). Abstract language, which eliminates the individual sense-perception, is the essential vocabulary here: note that while abstractions descend from concrete metaphors, they break their connection with them (Anatole France) in favor of their connections with each other. So logos writing is eikon-writing turned inside out. The most elaborate form of it is the metaphysical system or cosmological skeleton.[48]

Late Notebooks, 1982–1990

[38] Eventually it becomes clear that metaphysical thought is generated out of diagrammatic metaphors (they're not invariably diagrammatic, I suppose). So just as logos-writing is eikon-writing turned inside out, so logos-writing also is turned inside-out by its metaphorical growing kernel (I'll find the right words eventually) and turns into kinetic writing or rhetoric. Eikon writing attempts to come to terms with the physical environment; logos writing tries to solidify the human community in the middle of it.

[39] The next two areas of writing are the kinetic & the poetic. Here the verbal basis is rhetoric, and training in rhetoric, which covers both oratory & poetry, is the study of the figurative, ambiguous, centripetal aspects of language. The next chapter, on myth & concern, deals entirely with the relation between these two aspects of rhetoric, so cut out every reference to logos you've made in it.[49] All kinetic writing is ideological, and aims at rationalizing power or authority (or challenging it, which is the same thing).

[40] Plato's *Republic* begins with Socrates destroying the thesis of Thrasymachus that justice is what is to the advantage of the stronger. The regular Socratic eiron-alazon role is clearly central, but there are bigger ironies involved, two in particular. Plato is aware of one, but I think not the other. Socrates demonstrates nothing about justice: he demonstrates only that the *word* justice is a "good" word, and belongs in a context of "good" things. Thr. speaks for the wordless world of power: he's the prototype of Machiavelli and Hobbes and Marx and late Nietzsche and all the power followers: Mao with his "power comes out of the barrel of a gun," Stalin's "how many divisions has the Pope?" But he is telling us about the real world, whether he's defining justice or not, & Socrates isn't.[50]

[41] For Socrates the word justice can exist only in a world where such words mean what they ought to mean. *To mean is to acquire power*. So he accepts the challenge of his disciples, and proceeds to set up a counter-world, a society illustrating the meaning of justice. Such a world can exist within the individual, whether it exists within society (or as a society) or not. Modern synonyms for original sin, like "fascism[,]" refer to the isolating of power, holding power without the need of rationalizing it. Socrates, like Hegel, is trying to build a verbal structure that will contain power. That's the bigger irony Plato *is* aware of.

264

[42] Well: Thr. [Thrasymachus] is a sophist who teaches rhetoric and (ugh) charges money for doing so [*Republic*, 337d]. Plato has a great contempt for rhetoric and its sense of the relativity of good & evil. For him dialectic is the *cure* for rhetoric.

[43] But dialectic is or attempts to be beyond history. To the extent that a dialectical structure becomes, in time, historical, it is revealed to be a work of historically conditioned ideology: in short, of rhetoric. That's the larger irony I don't think Plato was aware of: that his philosophy, in its historical dimension, was a super-sophistic rhetorical ideology.

[44] So we get what might be called lower kerygma: proclamation derived from, or allegedly derived from, dialectic. Aristotle says that rhetoric is the *antistrophos* of dialectic [*Rhetoric*, 1354a]: that its reality is "objective" argument (or syllogisms adapted to enthymemes). Lower kerygma is the stage of law, full of prohibitions & penalties, & increasingly given to censorship in the arts—Plato is almost insane about this in the *Republic*. Bultmann's kerygma excluding myth is in the same tradition, as in fact is all theology.

[45] But the inexorable turning-inside-out process goes to work again, and reveals the *mythical* core of ideology. Ideologies are always post-revolutionary and social: poets emerge as individuals to recreate a pre-revolutionary state of play and innocence. This takes me into the second chapter, where I deal entirely with isolating the genuinely poetic & mythological core of ideology. In the third chapter I reach down to the dialectical level and extract its metaphorical core. Dialectic, with its imagery of following & pursuit, belongs to the way or quest archetype; ideology to the axis mundi or confronting one.[51] The fourth chapter, a complete haze as yet, recaptures the symbolic core of the descriptive.

[46] That's Part One. Part Two is specifically about the Bible. The first chapter (Five of the whole book) deals with how the higher kerygma crystallizes out of myth: God out of the gods. Higher kerygma cannot be analyzed for a sixth phase,[52] so far as I can see: it's the ultimate power that words carry, the primordial light of consciousness antecedent to the dawn. Then follow chapters on Biblical myth, Biblical metaphor, & Biblical symbolism. These have to do with way-narrative (with the quest-cycle subordinate), the axis-mundi dianoia, & the decentred interpenetrating structure succeeding the apocalypse. (It's not a struc-

ture, of course). Now if I had a coherent notion of Part Three I'd be all set.[53]

[47] Of the two forms of *logoi*, the descriptive is reflective of the external and the dialectical is circumferential and internal. The two forms of *mythoi* are similarly related, except that their milieu is society rather than nature (social science, including modern historiography, adopt[s] descriptive techniques, but they reduce {if that's the word} society to a natural object when they do so).

[48] Naturally I want to show that the higher kerygma redeems the poetic, and that the Word has to go through the valley of shadows, the whispered or shouted *lies* of literature, to get to its real home. Even Barth can't see that, much less the people who want kerygma to exclude myth. In Milton's PR [*Paradise Regained*] Christ is tempted to go to school to Athenian culture: he refuses, & by refusing he redeems Athenian culture & makes it profitable for us to go to school to it.[54] As ED [Emily Dickinson] says, he refunds us our confiscated gods.[55] But this must go along with the transcending of what is usually meant by faith.

[49] On the dialectic level, because of the subordinating of the subjective, it's impossible to distinguish what one believes from what one believes one believes. As I've said, it's only on the quid agas level of ideology that belief acquires any reality. We have to go through the poetic, where no one can believe anything, before we get anywhere near the hypostasis-elenchos level, where belief has passed beyond the stage of the *dependent*.[56]

[50] Chapter Four may have something to do with my symbolism essay,[57] as I've assumed, especially if it's reclaiming the descriptive. But more, I think, with the lyric sketch,[58] with the reference to word-*magic*: not kinetic magic anymore, but the unlocking of a word-hoard that's not a cupboard. Fantasy, dream, hallucination, condensation, displacement, are all possible ways along with consciousness. Also, that reality is the process of creating the here and abolishing the there. Such phrases as "Brightness falls from the air" are keys or talismans.[59]

[51] Utopian literature, like Plato's *Republic*, marks the transition from the second to the third level. Perhaps legendary history (Arthur, Aeneas)

is the corresponding third-to-fourth transition. Note that in the attack on idolatry as a worship of human artefacts we have a passing through the *arts* to the higher kerygma, or would except that it almost invariably collapses back to the doctrinal level. And of course when I speak of the poet as an individual emerging from an ideological community I am speaking of a very gradual process. At first it's all pure convention, and individual variants attract critical attention.

[52] Why do I set up such a deafening clatter of inner talk in my mind? Probably for the same reason that villagers gossip and urban people intrigue: to keep myself reassured about the reality of the ordinary world. If I'd shut up and listen I might be able to hear other things. It corresponds to the senses' filtering out and giving us the reality we can take. My whole life is words: nothing is of value in life except finding verbal formulations that make sense. Yet the great secret in reserve is something you can't reach unless you shut up. That's what Zen has to communicate. And how does it communicate? By flooding the world with books about silence. Words are to us what water is to a fish: dwelling-house of being, says Heidegger.[60] Yuh. The real temple is the tent.

[53] Anyway, I seem to be stuck now with twelve chapters, not ten. Three parts: Theory, Bible, Literature. Four themes. First, overview; second, myth-narrative-concern-movement-immersion in Time. Third, metaphor-imagery-dianoia-space-axis mundi. Fourth, symbol-decen-teredness-fragmentation-comminution-interpenetration. This last has only hunches for theory & Bible; it has however a closer literary link than the others, namely French symbolisme. (Unless Goethe's *Faust* takes over, & I don't think it will.)

[54] How to distinguish the clatter & chatter from my central work with words? No real boundary; but I know well enough when it's nothing *but* chatter. I can't turn it all off, but I could, perhaps, get more control of it. And perhaps after a couple of years of trying to shut off babble I might get a second or two when I'd realize what genuine quiet would be. Even before that, a quieter mind might increase the intensity of experience. The aim would be the receptivity of the infant Samuel [1 Samuel 3], but I don't expect that (though I'm not excluding the possibility of learning things in other ways).[61]

[55] Barth, as I've noted, says the three ways to preaching are dogmatism, mysticism (which he calls self-criticism) and dialectic.[62] It simply doesn't occur to him that one *must* go through the shadowy valley of lies, illusions, and demonic epiphanies to get closer to the Bible. I have to be emphatic on this point, because *all* the opposition I get is to the suggestion of trying to sell a dialectically-dominated faith (not the Hebrews faith,[63] of course, as I'll explain in the right place).

[56] Without the superstition of dialectic control, faith becomes vision. Dante "believed" and Goethe didn't, but Goethe's last scene in *Faust* has all the traditional faith-trappings. Only Faust is "saved by works": he gets an E for Effort. Wonder how far the will to power dominates the modern world. Most power goes in the cyclical rhythm of recurrence, as in Poe's Ligeia—there's that woman again.

[57] The verbal factor that turns descriptive into dialectic writing is essentially syntax, the centripetal emphasis consistent with the other emphases on the objective and assertive. Syntax is an emphasis on the *ordering* of words, and goes with the sense of consciousness as having a verbal monopoly. Verbal statements must *follow* others in a certain ordered direction.

[58] Once we've got logical & dialectical ordering, we discover a less objective juxtaposition among words, & hence *metaphor*, in the largest sense, crystallizes out of syntax. Metaphor usually comes into dialectic structures in a diagrammatic form, then develops more figuration and emotional appeal, as quid credas modulates into quid agas.[64] "Belief," as we usually use the word, has to do with the domination of dialectic over rhetoric, and persists from at least Plato to Barth & Bultmann.

[59] The metaphorical basis out of which ideology emerges, and brings us thereby into the concerns of time, usually takes some form of hierarchy. Out of ideology, in any case, there crystallizes the myth, or story. In proportion as myths grow out of their ideological matrix and become individualized, they become playful. An example would be Shelley's Witch of Atlas, which has so little ideological content it bothered Mary.[65] From here we go through magic, as in my lyric paper,[66] to the conception of consciousness as one of many sources of verbal communication. Dream is not something beginning with Rcsm [Romanticism], as a glance at

Chaucer would show; and the association of manic and mantic is Hebrew & early Greek, not to speak of shamanism.[67]

[60] I've got things mixed up here. Individualized myth is play, but it's
primary concern too. That's the theme of Chapter Two: Chapter Three is
concerned with literature as confronting the critic, recapturing ideology,
and showing its continuous tradition in the transparency of modes. Then
that mysterious chapter on symbols and the spirit: that's the one that
features magic and play and fantasy and madness and parody.

[61] Now: it's either in this chapter or the next one where I get from
poetics and mythology to kerygma. If it's this one, the book will have
eight and not ten or twelve chapters. It probably will anyway. This is
probably the book, if I contain such a thing. Bible and literature get
mixed together in myth, metaphor, symbol and kerygma.

[62] The next four chapters (I mean the second four) deal respectively
with way (horizontal line), ladder-tree-mountain-axis (vertical line; hierarchy); circumference (cycle of time; universe or one-turning) and centre
(i.e. the omni-centred world). Hermes; Prometheus; Adonis; Eros.[68]

[63] Well, anyway: how do I get from poetics to kerygma? Note that
Bultmann doesn't know there is a lower & a higher kerygma. The lower
includes the sermon (as the *word* sermon shows), and should be totally
under the domination of myth. The higher is an outgrowth of myth, not
an exclusion of it.

[64] In descriptive writing the *verbal* content (not what we usually think
of as content in that connection) is syntactic prose. When this content
turns into form, a content of metaphor reveals itself within. When *that*
becomes form, myth (order, narrative, time, quid agas) becomes the
content. When myth becomes form, kerygma becomes the content.

[65] Kerygma can never, except in the sacred book, become form, and
even there its form is provisional. That's because its habitat is the
decentered, or rather omni-centered, universe. When myth starts to take
form (I have some hesitation in working this out on a form-content basis,
but it'll do for the moment) the first thing that crystallizes is gods. Here
(too) are gods, says Heraclitus lighting a fire.[69] The movement completes

itself when gods become God, and spirits Spirit. This corresponds to the individuality on the human plane that marks the emerging of literature. The total individual, who permits us equally to be absorbed in him and to separate from him, is the universe, the one-turning reality. That isn't pantheism, except that when we're talking about an unfallen world we're all pantheists. What proclamation proclaims is *presence*, and the presence of presence busts the universe.

[66] I talk very well; it would be nice to know what I was talking about, but if I did I might stop writing, as St. Thomas Aquinas did when he died.[70] If it's necessary for me to know I'll be given the knowledge.

[67] Horizontal line; vertical line; circumference; centre. These are metaphors from plane geometry, but that's not a difficulty. The first will be a short chapter, because every linear narrative (even the pre-Homeric formulaic poems) has what Frank K. calls the sense of an ending built into it.[71] That ending is either an axis mundi symbol or a return to the beginning of the cycle. Biblical narrative is longer in Judaism than in Xy [Christianity], naturally.

[68] Figuring out the second four chapters will be hard work, but I mustn't think in terms of, say, stuffing Dante into 2. Dante will spread over 1, 2 & 3 anyway, and Goethe, or at least Faust, over 2, 3 & 4. The 3rd or circle chapter will likely be the one for this: Dante faces the three beasts, can't take them, and his running away takes him through the whole cosmos. Faust wants magic rather than theology, summons the Erdgeist, can't take him, settles for a deal with Mephistopheles, but goes through hell to heaven—note that his quest is in time rather than space metaphors. And the Bardo Thodol, with its flash of light that practically everyone misses, & has to go through the cycle again.[72] My FW [*Finnegans Wake*] point about the cycle being the only "symbol" for what's beyond a cycle, is in AC [323–4]. Ist nur ein Gleichnis:[73] everything's an analogy or mirror. In spite of all the "die That" crap, Faust is *not* saved by works.[74] He's dragged off to heaven by Christianized Valkyries in spite of himself. Keats' *Endymion*, another road with a detour sign.

[69] Jesus speaks of hypocrisy, which may be a vice in the gospel context but is the one absolutely essential cementing force that holds society together. Morally, it is the greatest of all virtues. I'm overstating, I know:

I'm just trying to get clear the complete "otherness" of higher kerygma from the lower or social kind. As Milton says, in society we are contiguous, like bricks in a wall, not continuous as in the spiritual world.[75]

[70] I've suggested that a social function of Judaism may be to break up the monolithic agreements of ideology. According to Joyce (FW [*Finnegans Wake*]) the poet is a Jew:[76] he backs up ideologies by conforming to his own tradition.

[71] Myths tell us about the actions of gods. There are no gods, so myths are verbal narratives only. But the stories of gods recapture (a) the concrete (b) the disinterested (c) the bodily.

[72] I've said that if man can alternate between absorption in the universal and the individual carrying the universal,[77] then obviously God can too. Jesus is the particular or individualizing aspect of God, and as such he individualizes the supra-personal essence, the ground of being, the super-duper whatzit, as the Father. Jesus' own Father was the Spirit. Individual & personal terms like "Father" are always metaphors: terms like super-personal essence and the like come from the analogy of being.

[73] What's the initiative excluded from the higher kerygma?[78] Something that goes outside the verbal, which is why it can't have much of a role in my book. It starts after we've finished the Bible and accepted its invitation to drink [Revelation 22:17]. But Zen & others say that it's a renewal of vision, the same world but seen in enlightenment. If so, the five modes go round in a circle. But that won't work: it just brings back the old cloven fiction. No: the conception of interpenetration can't be avoided. Although, once again, there could be a cyclical movement that represents ultimate failure, just as reincarnation is a cycle representing the failure to achieve the Chih-kai Bardo flash.[79] Somewhere there has to be the notion that return to this world doesn't mean being hitched to a death-journey.

[74] Metaphorical unity of Babylon & Egypt: in N.T. times there was a town, or garrison, in Egypt called Babylon.

[75] Try this for Part Two:
    Dialogues of Word and Spirit (i.e. the infiltrating of Biblical myth, or

whatever, into literature—or vice versa for pre-Biblical myth and literature).

The Dialogue of the Ladder (Eros, air).   Urizen.

The Dialogue of the Garden (Adonis, earth).   Orc.

The Dialogue of the Ark (Hermes, water).   Tharmas.

The Dialogue of the Furnace (Prometheus, fire).   Los

Only maybe the right order is 3, 2, 4, 1.[80] Whatever the order, it won't work unless I can show convincingly that these are the quadrants of the total vision of the Spirit when it animates the Word, and that this Spirit is the initiative excluded from literature.

[76] No, the order as I have it looks more promising. The most systematic one, the axis mundi, starts off; then follows the cycle of time, then the dive into the depths of nothingness, then the rising out of it in a totally decentred form. The last is the ultimate recovery of myth: fire may be the leading symbol, but it's a Hiranyagarbha fire in the waters,[81] where you drink what's been drowning you. One thing is that the proposed order is damn close to Eliot, especially the sequence of elements.[82] What I want is an outline of the spiritual world, found equally in the Bible and literature, to which the most unsympathetic reader can't just say "so what?"

[77] Identity and Difference. Identity is love; difference beauty. On the seventh day of creation God looked at what he had done, it became objective to him and therefore beautiful. Love goes with absorption into the whole, or into the loved one's body; beauty goes with the individual, carrying the whole inside him, getting all the fun out of an objective world & none of the uneasiness or oppressiveness.

[78] In OUR beginning is the Word, and our end too. We never get out of the rainbow arch that stretches from Alpha to Omega. The wordless, like the discarnate, is one of those "substraction" sums, and means nothing.[83]

[79] Prometheus: carrying fire in a fennel stalk: revolutionary symbol (cf. the Russian Communist paper Iskra[84] or spark[)]. Invention of gunpowder gave it a demonic force; atom bomb still more. Hiranyagarbha again: organic heat bursting the seed open. I wish Dante had put furnaces in the planet Saturn. He got enough of them in hell, God knows.

[80] If there are numerous individual myths but only a few species,

maybe the same thing is true of symbols. Which is (so far) the postulate of Part Two. But I'd like to see a hologram structure in Part Two: each one the whole of God, both as genuine in itself and as ideological distortion. Like the Four Zoas in Blake.

[81] 3 and 4, above [par. 76], form a double spiral: 3 is a systole going down a maelstrom and contracting to nothing, 4 a diastole rising up through the waters like the sunrise and exploding or expanding to the circumference. That's a little closer to my building-blocks of metaphor dream.

[82] There are, of course, genuine and false gods. The god of progress, who demands that we sacrifice everything for a posterity we know nothing about is a Moloch demanding adult sacrifice for (unborn) children.

[83] I've been wondering if my four "dialogues" couldn't be about the Father, the Son, the Spirit, and the Bride. But I don't quite think that will work in that form. What must work somehow is the expansion of "myth" in Chapter One. So far I've dealt only with myths that link the social world with the non-human world. These are Spirit myths: there are spirits of nature and spirits of human nature. But there are also myths that express the primary concern of the ego to become an individual and stop being blinded by Galatea.[85] Those are the psychological or Father-Son myths, with the Oedipus theme at the centre.

[84] Everything goes in cycles, especially fallacies, which go in simple circles, with no trace of spiral development.

[85] Why do Americans continue to cherish Reagan, including millions of Americans who know he's an ass? I think they're bored by their own indifference to the world, but can only focus their minds on a boob-tube leader.

[86] The etymology of "universe" suggests that everything turns around a centre, that centre being the personal centre that calls it a universe.[86]

[87] Chapter Three: total dianoia, or apocalyptic panorama of juxtaposition, has to be recovered in (spiritual) time.

[88] I am about to write the world's profoundest poem, with apologies to William James, the only one who has touched my level of genius:

> Hogamus, higamus,
> God is polygynous.
> Higamus, hogamus,
> Christ was androgynous.[87]

[89] If faith is the substance or hypostasis of hope, does that mean that literature as a whole is an expression of hope? Or that polytheism is?

[90] Eugene Vance: From Topic to Tale (1987) for the influence of logic in tightening up medieval narrative. The set piece is Chrétien's *Yvain*.

[91] Here's something that opened out at the end of One, but may belong in the Garden dialogue. This is the magical link between virginity and the natural world. The virgin is customarily but not necessarily female. Very early, in the Gilgamesh epic, we have the pathetic story of Enkidu, a wild bull of a man, so strong he terrifies everyone. So they send a prostitute to seduce him, and after she's done her job the beasts reject him.[88] Then Adam & Eve fall: they develop a self-consciousness about sex that loses them the control of the garden and the animals Adam had named. As soon as Miranda's ready to marry[,] Ariel gets his freedom: the Lady in Comus is linked to benevolent nature spirits as long as her virginity holds out. Alice could hardly have held her Wonderland together when she reached menarchy, much less marriage.[89] Cf. Isaiah's "a little child shall lead them" [11:6]. So Virgin & Spirit seem designed for each other. I wonder why: Diana is of course associated with animals. The Virgin Mary has the ox & ass & the manger, & early Mesopotamian seals feature a virgin (or mother) surrounded by animals. It seems as though there's something about the *conscious* sex act (sex in the head)[90] that commits one to the human and ideological (knowledge of good & evil) world. This is something different from the white goddess, who's an inveterate fucker even if she does renew her virginity, and from the black bride, even though Blake's Little Girl Lost, protected by a lion, seems to be black.[91] Perhaps the virgin-nature link means that nature has yet to be united to man, and all fucks before that are premature. A garden enclosed; a fountain sealed [Song of Songs 4:12]. But what is the

Spirit doing knocking the apostles over and starting the church? Assembling the bride, apparently, but what a whorish bride!

[92] What opened up One was a set of three kinds of myth. One was horizontal, identity-with myths, human links with a lost nature. Two are the Oedipus-Narcissus myths that Freud discovered to be linked with infantile efforts to differentiate one's individuality from others, starting with parents. These are identity-as myths, and they bother the hell out of ideologues. Then there are circumferential, or perhaps temporal, myths: Where was I before I was born? Where do I go after I'm dead? What the hell, generally? I'd like to call these, respectively, myths of the Spirit, the Son and the Father. What makes me hesitate is that I might get stuck with this scheme for Part Two, and I'm by no means sure it's the right one. The fourth, in that case, would have to summarize all the female figures. Part Two, at least, has to be worked out in some other way.

[93] The ogdoad of trigrams in the I Ching are father, mother, three sons & three daughters. At present I seem to have Father-Mother, Son-Daughter (Sophia), Bridegroom-Bride, Spirit-Virgin (as above [par. 91]). I'm not sure there is a mother—there isn't one in Blake—but the Faustian descent to the Mothers may be part of the Igitur nothingness descent (choice of you as embryo, chance that she may go on to her next period).[92] Ark dialogue is what I have. The Virgin-Spirit one could work out to the Garden dialogue, which leaves the Bridegroom-Bride for the Furnace and the Son-Daughter for the ladder (that can't be right).

[94] At present the most likely sequence & pairings seems [seem] to be: Father-Mother-Ladder-One; Spirit-Virgin-Garden-Two; Son-Daughter-Ark-Three; Bridegroom-Bride-Furnace-Four. There must be a lot of shit in that. One thing is clear: if Part Two is really "Dialogues of Word & Spirit," the word part is an analysis of the Bible and the Spirit part a survey of secular literature. (The above would look better if Father-Mother and Son-Daughter were interchanged.) One thing; the cyclical Mental Traveller-Odyssey pattern of mother-son, bridegroom-bride, father-daughter, spectre-emanation definitely won't work in this context.

[95] The electromagnetic sequence runs in what is most easily visualized as a straight line, from infra-red through the colors, red to purple, then

the ultraviolet, X and gamma rays. But in our sense experience of color purple is a mixture of blue and red, and takes us around a circle. A parable of the way in which the cycle is sometimes the only symbol of whatever is beyond the cycle.

[96] Four: philosophers, mystics, Gnostics, all set out by describing God as a something so super-duper, that no words can possibly describe him. He's above Deity (Gnostic John), above Being (or its ground, as in Tillich), above anything you can possibly put into words. O.K. But how could so stratospheric a conception be a character in a human story, which is what he consistently is in the Bible? I think one has to universalize the conception of epiphany, manifestation (Vorstellung, Schein). That led a lot of people to think of Jesus Docetically: that won't work; he was a physical reality *and therefore* an illusion. So are we.

[97] There's a "Hymn of Glory" in the Jewish morning service, composed by a medieval poet who died in 1217, that says:

> In images they {the prophets} told of thee, but not according to thine essence; they but likened thee in accordance with thy works.
>   They figured thee in a multitude of visions; behold thou art one under all images.[93]

[98] The furnace cluster includes the alchemical uniting of red king & white queen (or the opposite, as in Shakespeare's PT [*The Phoenix and the Turtle*]); the "need-fire" ritual with a naked boy & girl going into the dark to start a fire (by twirling a stick in a hole, I suppose); the Hindu Hiranyagarbha, the seed of fire in the waters; Prometheus' fire in a fennel-stalk; Isaiah's smith [54:16]; the glowing Jerusalem of the Apocalypse; Blake's Los symbolism; the tradition of hell as imprisoned fire; the candle of the Lord that gives light to the world [Proverbs 20:27]; Abraham's furnace {a bit out of line} [Genesis 15:17], and, of course, Nebuchadnezzar's crucible-furnace [Daniel 3:19–30], where three become four.[94]

[99] Part One is a little clearer: my AC modes go into Two; so does Gibbon.[95] Three I think goes as far as interpenetration and the whole-part interchange. Four takes in the point across [par. 96], and leads to some tentative grouping of myths like the Father-Son-Spirit one I've

been brooding about, which won't quite do in that form. I still want Spirit to be the excluded initiative of *all* myth.

[100] Jesus is a Son, but the Son & the Bridegroom are different: that's why the gospel Jesus is presented as a homosexual (actually androgynous). The difference comes out in the wedding at Cana [John 2:1–11], which I have no doubt means a wedding where Christ himself was the bridegroom. But *that* wedding was not a biographical event in Jesus' life: it's a parable of the Second Coming. Whenever there's a son there's a mother, and Jesus declares his independence of his mother here. The Bridegroom is the sexual Jesus: the Bride is the people, of course, but Jerusalem is the Second Coming of the Virgin individual carrying the Word.[96]

[101] Similarly Ruth is the Bride from the Strange Land who becomes a mother: the fact that she's a great-grandmother of David doesn't alter that. And it's *her* mother—her Jewish mother—who has the son.[97]

[102] Towards the end of Three should come some emphasis on magical realism: the *Watt* & *Les Gommes* and Williams thing I mentioned before.[98] To which should be added Joyce's Epiphanies, i.e. "real" events heard with illuminated hearing, or whatever the adjective for hearing should be.[99] It'd be nice if this could be a Part Two snatch.

[103] Maybe the way or quest is a garden theme: as soon as it hits the Word it stops being a way and becomes a wandering of the 23rd Psalm type (though there's a way there too:[100] I was thinking of the temple as tabernacle development[)].

[104] Interesting in the Mental Traveller that it's only the *Female Babe* that springs out of the fire and is the fire [ll. 44–5].

[105] How much should go in Four and come out of Part Two? The Two creation myths, perhaps; some of the building blocks like the way (horizontal line), the ladder (axis mundi), the everywhere centre, the nowhere (*or* everywhere) circumference. A possible cycle of upper descent (incarnation, son & daughter, brother & sister, Adonis), lower descent to hell & the parents, lower ascent through fire, upper ascent to the garden. Oh, hell.

[106] The soul is the old Father, Adam, Joseph; the body the old mother, the *adamah*. The Spirit recreates the body-soul unit (soma psychikos) which withers away, and the soma pneumatikos, bridegroom & bride, takes its place.[101]

[107] I think your upper & lower descent & ascent is all right fundamentally, and they are certainly featured in the quest of Christ. But I think I'm confusing myself by thinking of each as a halfway. They're parallel & complete, the parallel being formed by the two creation myths. Still, they have a centre of gravity in each of the elements: Adonis, descent to earth; Hermes, descent to water; Prometheus, ascent in fire; Eros, ascent in air. Look up the *logoi spermatikoi* [generative reason] of the Stoics, which are obviously relevant. I just wish there was more in the Bible.
                            (Of *that*, I mean!)

[108] Valéry, writing of Mallarmé: "Language thus becomes an instrument of "spirituality," that is to say, of the direct transmutation of desires and emotions into presences and powers that become "realities" in themselves, without the intervention of physically adequate means of action."[102] The whole paragraph is very important: Valéry can certainly write when Mallarmé is telling him what to say.[103]

[109] Levirate marriage: perhaps a Hebrew incorporation of the old white goddess sequence.[104]

[110] Why does the Word have to be born from a virgin? Because if it weren't the Father would be just one more Zeus-fucker, prolonging the agony of nature.

[111] Why does the tradition of prophecy end with a severed head? Perhaps because the blood of the martyrs is the seed of the church, & there's an ancient belief that the head is the repository of seed.[105] So JB [John the Baptist] is an Adonis figure of renewal, not the resurrection-figure that ends renewal.

[112] I think my hazy notion of Part Two will take shape if I work on it without panic. "Dialogues of Word and Spirit."[106] The Word is, more or less, what's in the Bible and the Spirit is the response of extra-Biblical literature. The first is "Dialogue of the Mountain," dealing with Spenser's Mut Coes [*Mutabilitie Cantos*], the Paradiso, the spiral-ladder and kin-

dred imagery[107]—but I'm beginning to think more in terms of straight mountain-tops: Zion, Moriah, Sinai-Horeb, Carmel, and their counterparts on Olympus (perhaps Etna) & elsewhere. This is the Bible of authority, chain of being, etc. Eventually the mountain, after passing the metamorphosis of the Word (Transfiguration) moves into the stars and the great cosmic dance begins. {Adonis; upper descent; incarnation, air}.

[113] Dialogue Two (the order may vary) is the sexual or Eros Bible. Song of Songs, Beulah, white goddess & black bride, Eve, virginity & the animal world, Shirley, the survival of Eros, gardens in the 17th century— it's all a bit miscellaneous as I have it now. {Eros; upper ascent; ascension; earth} {No: reverse earth and air}. Dialogue of the Garden; symbolic sexual relations.[108]

[114] Dialogue Three: the seed. Saving remnants of Ur, Sodom, Noah's ark; JB's [John the Baptist's] severed head; descent to lower world of nothingness; Igitur and the chance-choice darkness. {Hermes, water, lower descent}.[109]

[115] Dialogue Four, the furnace. The golden city; the escape from the Egyptian furnace of iron and the Babylonian Nebuchadnezzar one; logoi spermatikoi [generative reason]; candle of the Lord [Proverbs 20:27]; alchemical union; need-fire; {Prometheus, fire, lower ascent} Oh, hell, I've got all this, and without confirmatory texts it *does* sound the most awful crap.[110]

[116] Every word demands a reply, Lacan says:[111] epigraph for the dialogues. Everything in literature is a reply to something in the Bible. By the way, the seed dialogue is Adonis, I think: the severed head is normally buried, like Bran.[112] (Gods, elements, are all Christmas-tree baubles: they'll take shape when the tree does). Get after the fucking tree.

[117] Verum factum doesn't just mean what's real is what we make. It means that the real is what we participate in making. You have this in 3, but don't fail to connect it with what GC says about Job delivered from a creation he didn't participate in, a wholly-other universe of accident.[113]

[118] The unity of God results from the internalizing of gods in man. The gods are now human moods, and the moods are emanations of God.[114]

[119] Once more, it isn't *that* the 1920s poets were all fascinated by staircases and ladders and towers and spiralling mountains: it's *why* they were. It isn't *that* the French symbolistes were fascinated by John B's [the Baptist's] severed head and descents to nothingness: it's *why* they were.

[120] Why is there so emphatic a prohibition against lighting fires on the Sabbath? Cf. the Xn [Christian] emphasis on the Mithraic birthday of the sun.[115] There's a lot about God as fire in the Bible I still have to work out. Cf. the Parsee fire-worshipping element in *Moby Dick*, with its Promethean "right worship is defiance."[116] Exodus 35:3.[117]

[121] Chapter 4, I think, ends with John's identifying of *mythos* and *logos*,[118] *mythos* being there (a) to incorporate the literary (b) make doubt possible & so build up belief as an internalized authority (c) *present*, e.g. the Xfn [Crucifixion] instead of putting it against the ghosts of the past (d) giving us a "historical Jesus" who isn't that at all, but the same kind of discontinuous epiphany he is in the O.T. & the rest of the New. When we get to "Spirit" as the answer to "Word," the series of excluded initiatives stops: the next step takes us into the wordless.

[122] Re the severed head of JB [John the Baptist] & the buried head of Bran;[119] it's an Adonis fertility symbol, JB's decreasing being a "must" for Christ's increasing. The notion of the head as a gigantic testicle is less absurd than it sounds: according to Onians, it was believed for centuries that the heart was the seat of intelligence (or "belly" in Proverbs 22:18)[120] and that the function of the brain was to supply sperm for the genitals (what a woman's brain was for I don't know).[121] Perhaps the shift to the brain as the seat of intelligence has some parallel with the Genesis 1 firmament in contrast to the sexual fall (sex in the head).[122]

[123] I must find out more about why Joyce was so interested not merely in the word "epiphany" but also in the word "epiclesis."[123] He didn't know much Greek, and I doubt that he was an expert on liturgies—the word "epiclesis" is outside the R.C. [Roman Catholic] liturgy anyway.[124] Cf. Dylan Thomas' Winter's Tale. Incidentally, the book that eventually became PAYM [*A Portrait of the Artist as a Young Man*] was built up from epiphanies (which were often "actual" images, experiences, & reheard fragments of conversation, etc.[).] What I "incidentally" started out to

remark on was the fondness of Canadian writers (not just Alice Munro).*
Dubliners is also an epiphanic sequence of Dublin. Could the notion that
the Gospels were a discontinuous sequence of epiphanies have filtered
through to Joyce somehow? (At the time of his schooling Irish Catholics
were brutally ignorant of Biblical scholarship.)

[124] Three: There's just enough reference to the history of *logos* in John
1 to make it mean: up to now we have thought in terms of wisdom
(sophia): now we have to add the literary or mythos category to logos.
Logos & sophia are son and daughter, complementary but not (sexually)
united. I think when logos grows to include mythos, sophia becomes
defined as something by itself, or herself.

[125] Two accounts of Creation: one all distinction & separation; the
other all union and reconciliation. Are they the accounts of Word and
Spirit respectively?

[126] (I may have this): Faith is the *substance* of hope: is the literary vision
the fictional or analogical vision of hope? Of course some people don't
hope.

[127] Why is it the *Spirit* who speaks by the prophets? Why not the
Word? And why that mysterious mutter about the unpardonable sin
[Matthew 12:31]?

[128] The distinction between God and gods, Spirit and spirits, Word
and words, is of course essential (I think also between Father & "fathers,"
meaning the way of the fathers, the tradition of wisdom). But the capital-
ized unities are not Platonic Forms. Are they, as I've been thinking, concrete universals? Or metaphorical class-individual identities, as I've also
thought? Or, as I'd like them to be, something that excludes "or"?

[129] We are always in the place of beginning; there is no advance in
infinity.

[130] . . . The infantilism that is so exasperating a feature of popular
religion.[125]

---

*for novels made up of short stories.

[131] Part Two may be about, not how the Bible has influenced or even infiltrated literature, but about how literature has brought the Bible to life. If all four modes are present in every mode, the fifth one must be too: i.e., there must be a kerygmatic mode in literature, and it's the primary job of the critic to explain what it is. Perhaps this confers an immense responsibility on the critic, but I can't help that. The critic, after all, is neither the phoenix nor the turtle, and he should avoid the temptation of believing that he is the eagle. He is simply the bird of loudest lay [Shakespeare, *The Phoenix and the Turtle*, l. 1].

[132] I wonder if the soma-psychikos is the father-mother residue who are the giants at the bottom of the soul. They don't have to be stupid (Dante) or greedy (Rabelais), or even creative senses (Blake MHH [*The Marriage of Heaven and Hell*]). Big people & little people (GT [*Gulliver's Travels*]): I had something about that I've mislaid.[126]

[133] The oldest idea I had for this book, the two levels of nature, now seem to be hooking onto the two somas of Paul.[127]

[134] Part Two:[128]
   I've consolidated a certain amount here: what I want are four "dialogues of Word and Spirit." First, called "dialogue of the mountain," is about the axis mundi. There isn't such a thing in nature, but there sure as hell is one in the human consciousness,[129] derived perhaps from the backbone-tree analogy. The whole notion of the need for authority comes out of it. Why do people put up with tyrants & privileged classes? Because they've got an axis mundi stuck in their fool noodles. Still, if there's a demonic one there must be a genuine one—perhaps, though, its genuineness emerges more clearly in the cave one, although I don't much like the idea of one scheme finished by another. Besides, you ascend as well as descend.

[135] The second dialogue is on the garden, which also doesn't exist in nature, but is created out of nature by a sense of love and beauty. This is the sexual Bible: its end is not so much Yeats' perfect fuck as the total mergence indicated in the Bridegroom-Human and Bride-City union in the Apocalypse. I don't mean human, of course. Interpenetration is on the other side of sex: that's the why of the what. The what is mostly

spirit-wind and virgin in garden—enclosed garden and sealed fountain. The fuckless Christ of the first coming (no "coming" at all, of course: the fish-Christ, not the sperm-pourer[)].

[136] The third dialogue on the seed deals with unexplored possibilities of being in parallel worlds & the like. Dream-life and life-past death analogy will have to come in. A lot of the imagery here is submarine, and ends with drinking (internalizing) the *water* of life: getting soaked in it is something else.

[137] Fourth on the furnace I think takes in the problem of suffering and martyrdom: Egypt as furnace of iron; the martyrs of Nebuchadnezzar. Blood, fire, treading the winepress of the grapes of wrath. Abraham's "furnace": cf. Smart as well as Blake's Los, Little Gidding, Byzantium, fire of life image.[130]

[138] I have to alter the self-delusion bit: what I say is true enough, but I shouldn't suggest junking it all. I may yet find myself stealing from the Seth books,[131] and of course there's James Merrill, who extracted an epic from a ouija board.[132]

[139] I think I left out the business of the spirit of life being the spirit of death as well (Siva and Shelley OWW [*Ode to the West Wind*]), from the point of view of the seeds who don't grow.

[140] The furnace includes suffering humanity: the genuine "holocaust." Christ's tomb is a cave of the natural body and the crucible (a descent to hell) of the spiritual one. The fire-seed that pushes through the fennel-stalk, the fuse of the flower, the phoenix red bird of fire, Hiranyagarbha, the glowing flame-city Atlantis-Byzantium. Jerusalem rising from the sea—there's enough to work on.

[141] What about the "way" business? I suppose as space is curved you don't go from here to there at all, but always go round in a circle unless you hit the way that's Christ. The only real quest is ascending the ladder, which is reactionary authority only when you *don't* ascend it. I suppose that means there's no horizontal line, apart from the life-death one.

[142] P creation:	J creation
Cities, construction; the Word; discrimination	Gardens; living space; spirit; union
World of particulars	Interpenetrating world
Assumption of Dante	Assumption of Faust

[143] Reincarnation is not a doctrine, whether true or false: it's experience, a kind of self-guided fantasy. The conception of interpenetration makes it easy to see how one can enter various personalities.

[144] What's at the top of the ladder? Babel was a confusion of tongues, so one of the things on the journey from Spirit to Word is Zephaniah's "pure speech" [3:9]. Note the images I used in Chapter Three. Pure speech would be metaphorical. The separation of word and thing would no longer exist.[133]

[145] Holocaust as crucible: Blake's blacksmith Los comes out of 2nd Isaiah, whose chief theme is the suffering servant.[134] Little Gidding & the bombs of London.[135]

[146] The concluding scene of *Faust* always bothered me: he's dragged off to heaven just as his prototype in the Faustbook was dragged off to hell. I shouldn't have said he was saved by works [par. 56]—he isn't; he's just completed one of the meanest acts of his ignoble career. But he isn't "saved." Dante isn't "saved": he just goes to heaven.[136]

[147] Pure speech is not fusion of word & thing, but of word with spirit, coming the other way from "logocentric" incarnation, where the Word is made flesh. Cf. Mallarmé, *un sens plus pur* [*Le Tombeau d'Edgar Poe*, l. 6].

[148] The virgin is the garden; the bride is the city. The spirit-virgin cluster goes with the homosexual or asexual Christ. One could take the state of innocence as pre-sexual, the way the fuckless fathers take it, but when God created Eve as a mate for Adam she was clearly a sexual mate, and God took the opportunity to institute the state of matrimony. But the second Eve, like the second Adam, had to be celibate because she's already identified with the sealed-off garden of Paradise. Hence, as I've said [pars. 10, 91], the association of virginity with a magical control of animal & plant worlds (they're herbalists too).[137]

[149] Cave dialogue begins in the womb of the mother and the intense will to identify with animal forms. Painting as "unborn" and sculpture as "born" arts. The emergence of the (threatened) son in the "ark" (Noah-Moses-Exodus sequence). Preservation of original darkness & mystery in the Holy of Holies. Labyrinths & false directions; world of seeds, most of whom are "lost"—the potential other worlds or paths. Roads not taken of course consolidate in the fall story. Manger & ox & ass—I've got all that in GC, for God's sake. Look up Borges' story The Garden of Forking Paths—I suspect it may go back to Shelley's Zoroaster meeting himself in a garden [Prometheus Unbound, 1.1.192–4]. This links in turn with the cluster in my Harvard lectures: dream as split in body of dreamer; forest as sinister female body, hunting imagery with interchange of hunter & victim (Actaeon), and, of course, Narcissus.[138] Not much of this very clearly in the Bible, but a lot of it is what the Bible is trying to escape from.

[150] In connection with pure speech at the top of the ladder, the tree would have a (usually singing) bird with HS [Holy Spirit] associations: Yeats' SB [Sailing to Byzantium], Marvell's Garden, etc.[139]

[151] Levy, G.H.[R.], 50–1, 159, says Australians identify journey of its animal ancestor with its body. "I am the Way" (her quote too). "That Rock was Christ." A lot of my stuff is pretty second-hand. On p. 286 she says Macrobius calls Dionysus the underground sun. He leads the choral dance of the stars in Antigone 1146–7: link with Comus.[140]

[152] John 1:51. The descending angels presumably bring the Word of God, said more than once to be delivered by angels. The ascending ones bring the prayers of man, which according to Paul are really prayers of the Spirit [1 Corinthians 14:14–15], up to God.

[153] Furnace: world as Purgatory (Kung):[141] Blake's Orc, concealed in MHH [The Marriage of Heaven and Hell]; last judgment by fire. I've said Yeats's Byzantium & the "holy fire" of SB [Sailing to Byzantium, l. 17]. Why the hell is the Virgin the burning bush (Chaucer)? [The Prioress's Prologue, l. 16]. I suppose she's the carrier of the Word in the enclosed garden, which is a burning tree.

[154] It's common knowledge that Kekule's discovery of the circular

atomic structure of the benzine molecule is linked to a dream of the ouroboros, and that the DNA molecule is linked to the double helix. Nothing is discovered out there that isn't in some sense already here.[142]

[155] The subjectivity of the symboliste poets, including Rilke, still bothers me. Perhaps literature is all typical, a world where things-events have become symbols but are still signifiers of something else that's signified. It expresses the fiction of hope but not the hypostasis of hope. The final utterance is prophecy. The two stock phrases associated with prophecy are "the Word of the Lord came to" and "I will pour out my spirit . . . and they shall prophesy." In prophecy Word and Spirit are no longer proclaimer and listener, but the same thing, Jesus metamorphosed with Moses and Elijah. (Note the *return* of Elijah theme, something not really taken care of by John the Baptist.) Here the distinction of signifier and signified has disappeared, a totally verbal (communicating) world where words *are* the things they mean—except of course that there are only spiritual realities, not "things."

[156] Jesus isn't really homosexual, of course, but he certainly is withdrawn from sex. Androgynous, as I said before [pars. 88, 100], recovering the original Adam before sex in the head started.[143] Not that that really works either.

[157] A metaphor can't be reduced to a "literal" statement: it can only be exchanged for another metaphor. Obvious, but worth saying somewhere.

[158] Leviticus 16:19, on the Sabbath, can't really mean "afflict your souls":[144] it must mean "hold your souls together"—in other words, turn off the chatter.

[159] Song of Songs: Bernard of Clairvaux, a thoroughly nasty (I would even say evil, because he preached crusades) man, preached 86 sermons on the SS with the avowed aim of erasing every sexual image in it. Poets have consistently shown a better sense of proportion about it: Spenser's Epithalamion.[145]

[160] Folly of either-or views of the book [Song of Songs]: there's the country (rural) wedding songs, but the sexual connections of "vineyard" connect with the fertility of the land, hence a king-land wedding, with

the bride as earth, is a concentric reading. So is the Jewish one, where the bride is the Shekinah, and the Xn [Christian] one of Christ & the Church, with the Virgin the garden & fountain. But the St. John of the Cross S.S. isn't superior to the image of a man fucking a woman: that's central, & St. John & the rest are peripheral. What I don't find in the book is any clear trace of Danae imagery: the bride laid on top of a tower for the god to drop on her. The land imagery is there, certainly, & the seasonal imagery.[146] If the garden & fountain are the Virgin, who is a mother, the progression to stage Four is a movement from mother to bride, a rejuvenating movement in the opposite direction from ordinary life—the mourning mother modulates to the anabasis of Kore. Look up that Greek folk play cited by Cornford.[147]

[161] Of course the final "consummation" (quote Blake on the pompous priest)[148] is an embrace beyond the wildest polymorphous dreams (why are they perverse, by the way? isn't that word just as obscene as what the geldings have done to the sex act, as in Blake's Chapel of Gold poem?).[149]

[162] I don't think my four gods will really work: what I seem to have is: Descent from the Mountain (Incarnation); Walking in the Garden (Teaching ministry); the Conquest of Hell (Passion); the Conquest of Death (Resurrection).

[163] Yeats, Letters (728 in my ed.): to Joseph Hone, says the confusion of the modern world comes from renouncing the hierarchy of being from man up to the One.[150] That comes from what he's heard about Plotinus, I suppose: one wouldn't expect Yeats's weathercock mind to hold such a view consistently, but it fits his carpet-knight & similar obsessions, as any hierarchy would have its political counterpart.

[164] Wyatt has a poem about "I am what I am," which I could use if I'm forced into a personally defensive position by the Canadian clucks. In this book I should expand "thematic criticism" a bit. The theme is not something in the poem (I said that in the MLA piece,[151] now junked) but the totality of the poem as a simultaneous presentation to the reader. The two levels of underthought and overthought may have any relation to each other from near-identity to contradictory clash. Keats said, very truly, that we suspect poetry that has a palpable design on us,[152] but often an audience will not accept a poem unless it has or professes to

have such a design. I may also add to my Zen flower remark the Tibetan tankas (I think), the mandalas & yantras used as objects of contemplation. *Distinguish from* the Zen golden flower or titles like *The Golden Bowl*, which are expanding symbols.[153]

[165] Four: I'm still in search of a genuinely "charitable" vision of spirit that can unite everybody. My "arrest of the mind," the intensifying of consciousness that grows out of the imaginative response, is, I recognize, a bourgeois-liberal conception: a Marxist could say: your poets may talk about primary concerns, but what do they do about forming a social order that actually does something about them? I know the standard answers, the first being that the moment you start doing so you get involved in ideological postponements & excuses, & the end disappears in a labyrinth of means. However, that's a negative and, worse, a merely counter-ideological answer. There's still the gap between belief & rejection of the entity of God, identified with everything "spiritual" by Xy [Christianity]. To me, God means the unlimited nature of the human heritage.

[166] The seventh chapter should be, or start with, the journey below hell. The coded inscriptions buried under the sea or underground belong here. A creation myth recorded by Berossus (Levy & others have it: I'll look it up) has to do with burying the tablets of destiny under the sea. The Rcs. [Romantics] have Wordsworth's Arab dream in The Prelude [bk. 5, ll. 68–165]; Blake's Prophecies on the Atlantic Mountains;[154] the instruction given to Keats' Endymion at the bottom of the sea [bk. 3, ll. 234 ff.]; Poe's cryptogram at the South Pole (=bottom of the world);[155] earlier, the pillars of Seth saved from the flood.[156] Jung would have no trouble explaining these: I want more. I want Mallarmé's Igitur & Coup de Dés, for one thing; the descent to the Mothers in *Faust* (but connected with the paleolithic cave as the maternal womb[)].[157] Somebody gets dunked in that exasperating H v [Heinrich von] Ofterdingen story.[158]

[167] Back to thematic stasis for a moment: there's a myth that one's life appears as a total vision at the moment of death or near-death: I have yet to confirm this in my own experience. But I've always been fascinated by the Chih-kai Bardo business in the Tibetan Book of the Dead,[159] and it fits

here. The complete picture comes to us in a jigsaw puzzle box, and criticism is the art of putting it together.

[168] The way or journey is a series of cycles (journey of course is from journée) where we get "up" in the morning and "fall" asleep at night. At a certain point the cycle stops for us—there's finally a winter-night-old age-sea point with no spring-dawn-birth-rain following. We all take that road; the question is whether (or when) an upward spiral moves against it. It does, of course, but there must be a point at which rebirth must give place to resurrection. Anyway, back to seven: the journey below hell is the "descend lower" of the Quartets, where we pass beyond demonic parody.[160] The point of death is also, in cosmology, the descent of energy into the chaos-inertia heat death of entropy (all four of those words I just used are trdnl. [traditional] attributes of hell). Virgil, of course, doesn't go below hell: he slides over the top of it.

[169] So Chapter Eight, God save the mark, is, or may be, the journey above heaven, the journey to the primordial light above the sun, moon, firmament, and waters (chaos) "above" the firmament. Apart from the Paradiso, I haven't many clues here.

[170] Most of the submarine-coded information images listed above [par. 166] are metaphors of internalization. I think Patanjali's word for this is samayama, getting the strength of the elephant by meditating on the elephant.[161] Rilke goes back to the caves of Altamira.

[171] Myth & history, & Tennyson's last lines on the last battle of Arthur, I must insert, perhaps in One.[162] In Five, my emphasis seems to be heavily on the individual side, perhaps because the contemplated object presents itself to one person at a time: the consensus is a group formed by individuals. Hence the emphasis on the "arrest of the mind," negatively, the mysterium tremendum before God's holiness (Barth-Otto), as in Jacob's original dream. Positively, the kerygmatic burst through the mythos (the Quakers speak of "openings" in Scripture through which the Spirit pours).

[172] The way up & the way down are bloody well not the same,[163] or at least they don't become so until Seven and Eight. In Five & Six there's the

creative double spiral, which is ascent & descent all right, but its parody is the closed cycle or ouroboros. DNA molecule & Kekule's dream.[164] The white goddess is this in Six.

[173] Eight includes Thou art That[165] and the flight of the dove to the dome, the dialogue of Monos & Una. That's still at least metaphorically individualized, and I have to work out the assumption (in the theological sense) of the interpenetrating world. Perhaps the last word could be Tom o' Bedlam's "Methinks it is no journey."[166] Tom o' Bedlam is a shaman, & I start off Part Two with the shaman's ladder. It passes through the prophet, with his "the Word came to" and "I will pour out my spirit upon." (I've got this elsewhere [par. 155], so I can be elliptical.)

[174] The sublime & the beautiful is an aspect of the oscillation between the oceanic submergence & the particular emergence. The furnace is, as I've said, the crucible of revolution, bringing up from the depths the écriture, the writing on the wall, that puzzles the tyrant. Iskra, the "spark," was Lenin's magazine or whatever.[167] There's a burning operation that vitrifies forts & makes them look metallic—reference in Graves to Welsh Triades,[168] & one of Paul Fort's pseudo-mysteries.[169]

[175] Anyway, I think the kerygmatic breakthrough always contains some sense of "time has stopped." The sequential movement has become a focus, or fireplace. In intensified consciousness the minute particular shines by its own light (or burns in its own life-fire).

[176] "And having heard of the city, they went there." Popol Vuh, III.4.[170] Graves has a phrase about "the ancient lawsuits of the goddess against the god": no doubt he'd read the Mut. Coes [Mutabilitie Cantos].[171] (I think Graves may have something about the trees coming earlier than the sun because they formed an alphabet.)[172]

[177] ". . . the infinite varieties of human self-deception."[173]

[178] A remote analogy to the P creation story, where the Word, later the Son, creates a separating "firmament" after turning on the light, is a primal-scene myth in which an indignant Son separates his naughty fucking parents, pushing one, generally the Father, into the sky & leaving the mother on, and as, the earth. First cousin once removed: the Xn

[Christian] myth as reversing the Oedipus one comes I think into Seven (or perhaps Eight). Note that the Spirit and Garden are magically pre-sexual, and modulate to a Virgin Son with a Virgin Mother. What follows next is the apocalyptic version of Blake's Mental Traveller cycle: the male grows from the virginal Jesus to the matured Bridegroom of the Second Coming, while the female principle rejuvenates from a mother to a Bride.[174] I wish I could keep this out of Six: I'd have nothing for Eight that I see now—but I may not.

[179] Schrödinger's "consciousness is a singular of which the plural is unknown" reverses what is axiomatic to any hearer or reader that c. is a plural of which the singular is unknown.[175] The remark repeats Heraclitus' aphorism (one of the two mottoes for FQ [*Four Quartets*]) that although there is a common Logos, each man acts as though he had his own.[176] This suggests a way out of my bourgeois individualist impasse. First we have the erotic alternation (Six), where, as in Donne's Extasie, the lovers die each other's lives in union, and live each other's lives when separated into two bodies. Alchemy and the red and white union. Alice is a white Queen, taking over from a sheep-mother, & the Red King dreams about *her*, not the Red Queen.[177]

[180] Speaking of unexpected reversals, there's WS [Wallace Stevens] saying that beauty is momentary in the mind but immortal in the flesh [*Peter Quince at the Clavier*, ll. 51–3]. This poem is therefore more about the Song of Songs than about Susanna (or just as much).

[181] Hopkins' Heraclitean fire: the Resurrection is the fire of life that turns the burnt-match carbon of the natural body into the diamond-carbon of the spiritual one. Here the Hr. [Heraclitean] fire is the fire which consumes, not the fire of life.[178] "It is death to souls to become water" [Heraclitus, fragment 49], but there's also the water of life. Rabelais, of course: I don't yet know what to do about him.

[182] *Where* do I put the pure cycle? I'd like it in Seven, to start off with. Or rather, I'd start with the horizontal line or way, then show that a "journey" is an up-and-down movement, then that death is the rejoining of the pure ouroboros circle. The theme then modulates to the journey below hell, as above (!)[179] and, perhaps, the whole drunken boat bit goes here. A revolutionary polarizing construct, reducing the whole show to

black oppression & white supremacy, might even make sense of that insane Sibyl's leaves poem in Hopkins [*Spelt from Sibyl's Leaves*]. Ouroboros serpent and the repressive sexual neurosis is acquired at the fall. Note that the pyramid-ziggurat mountain is also the *tomb* of the king.

[183] My four gods are coming back, I think, in the order Adonis-Eros-Hermes-Prometheus. If I can get enough Eight material to make an effective conclusion I'm through. The chariot of fire in Blake[180] is both Elijah's chariot and the chariot of the Triumph of Love.[181] One of the last epigraphs should be Tom o' Bedlam's "Methinks it is no journey."[182]

[184] Three: epopt*ae*, not epoptes: plural is wanted.[183] Seven, if I'm right, could start with the tree of repressive morality and go on to the Noachic flood. Its illustrative material should move from the recovery of Atlantis in Blake, Shelley & De Quincey (the recovery of land at the end of Faust II belongs also) to the Symboliste movement from Igitur to the Jeune Parque. The Mental Traveller and FW [*Finnegans Wake*] should go here as cyclical parodies (also Yeats' Vision) of what in English are apocalyptic visions—that is, if I can explain them without the other. Also, though it may repeat AC, the cycle below in Dante's 26–33 Purg. & above in Virgil's Aen. 6, indicate[s] just what status reincarnation has as part of the illusion of rebirth. (What I was really after was that identical recurrence nonsense that drove Nietzsche even crazier than he was, along with parallel nonsense in Yeats's Vision & Dialogue of Self & Soul. I can't even formulate this stuff without starting to lose my temper: it's the modern version of a literal hell.)[184]

[185] For Eight, apart from Byzantium, Little Gidding and Hopkins' Heraclitean Fire, all very limited in different ways, I don't know what to draw on, and will be largely on my own. Curious how little Job there is so far in the book: no new light on it at all.[185]

[186] Fire is perhaps the archetypal expanding symbol, growing from spark to a world consummation. Smart on Abraham's furnace.[186] First judgment by water and last by fire, Cancer & Capricorn respectively holding all the planets. Cyclical fire scheme in the Stoics, ekpyrosis.[187] By the way, my order is now the Eliot Quartet one, HEAP [Hermes, Eros, Adonis, Prometheus].

[187] Berkeley, *Siris,* says all language about the soul is more or less metaphorical, 171.[188] Heraclitus says that the Lord of the Delphic oracle neither speaks nor hides, but "signifies" (semanei) [fragment 18]. This brings me to the conception of the expanding symbol, the seed becoming a tree, which I think is a central theme of Seven, and would get me over the "subjective" aspect of symbolisme. Notice that Rilke uses the image of the springing-up tree at the beginning of the Orpheus sequence.[189] (Orpheus may well be the key myth for this chapter:[190] note the severed head again.)

[188] In the great "love is as strong as death" passage in the SS [Song of Songs 8:6], the LXX [Septuagint] renders love as *agape.* (Another point I've forgotten: God, I wish I wouldn't do that.)

[189] The first Adam was beyond sex; consequently the second Adam had to be presented as the virgin son of a virgin mother. The second Adam had a bride, like the second Christ.[191]

[190] Where does the analogy of myth go? Logically in Part One, in Four. The expanding symbol should be introduced in Three (I have it there but not enough of it).[192]

[191] Five: the descending spiral cannot be represented architecturally, but *only* in words.

[192] In Through the Looking Glass the alchemical marriage is celebrated between the Red King and Alice the White Queen, where it's symbolized by a mutual dream.[193] As Alice is the second white queen, in something like a filial relationship to the bumbling and scatterbrained earlier queen who turns into a sheep, her reaching the Eighth Square is also an anabasis of Kore. The Alice books are inexhaustibly suggestive, one with cards & one with chess, one ending with a trial and the other with a banquet, and the riddle in the second: Why are all the poems about fish? They're a source of the kind of mad and unprintable intuitions that supply most of the real power in this myth game: too bad people are so stupid I have to keep them secret.

[193] Heraclitus (last page [par. 187]) should be brought into Three, I think, with the expanding symbol. Or maybe: end of Six & the interpen-

etrating screw: those who have arrived at "belief" in a spiritual reality through experience will estimate those variously: those who haven't will remain in the imgve. [imaginative] perspective. I should think this would belong more logically in Four.

[194] Isms, feminism & Marxism most obviously, are plate armor for the second-rate: people with nothing to say can always spout their line. But the established religions aren't much different, except that a cooling of pressure in an ideology gives the more flexible individual more of a chance to emerge. The whole business of the individual emerging from a solid mass [of] social conditioning needs to be handled very carefully. The whole principle of ideology is that everybody spouts some kind of line: it's the personal examination of it that matters.

[195] Revision of Two: I am speaking of the writer's function: in practice, writers being simply the human race, there is a great deal of mindless following of convention. When the convention happens to be deliberately violent or shocking, the devotion of the less original writers to it may begin to seem irresponsible. It doesn't follow that social authority is justified in interfering with the process by censorship.

[196] Three or wherever: underthought and overthought may be in any kind of relationship to one another, from near identity to wholly ironic contrasts. Among the latter is Eliot's paradox.[194] Autonomy of underthought is a feature of poetics.[195]

[197] The whole section on the Spirit and the transition to kerygma needs more careful expression. Of the chaos of myths waiting for the Spirit to brood on them, ranging from the profound to the frivolous, the reverent to the obscene, which can be "believed"? Belief here means the creative use of a recognized fiction. Myths that cannot be "believed" remain in the imaginative corpus, as possibilities only.[196]

[198] Six is now relatively plain sailing, I think: Seven can begin with the Romantic revolt in the name of Eros, the reversal of the traditional four levels, and then go on to descent-exploration myths, where Word & Spirit, perhaps, meet at the bottom, where in the middle of nothingness they would still be different aspects ("persons") of the same thing ("sub-

stance").[197] I suppose some revision of Jung's collective unconscious would turn up here: anyway, if Job gets in at all it would be here.

[199] I think the Mut. Cantoes [*Mutabilitie Cantos*] finale would most logically go in Eight, simply because that's the metamorphosis chapter. This chapter starts, or may start, with lightning and Viconian thunderclaps coming down and volcanoes going up. Titans, including Shelley's Prometheus, are under volcanoes. Find out what the Neptune & Pluto people in Faust II were talking about, and why Goethe listened to them.[198] Revolution is the social form of metamorphosis.

[200] Seven, then, is the Adonis chapter, and moves upward cyclically, as in evolutionary theories & their mythical analogy of progress. Its approach to the nothingness problem is negative. Eight is the chapter that deals with titanic revolt & the eventual human conquest of the titanic.[199] I think this is a feature of Job: also the end of *Moby Dick*: the right worship is defiance.[200] In Seven Frazer's original sacrifice is the demonic parody of the divine symposium;[201] in Eight the Oedipus pattern has the same relation to its apocalyptic contrast.[202]

[201] Two things in the Introduction revision: the English language, whether rightly or not, has decided that "man" and "he" shall include, not exclude, "woman" and "she." In language, usage fossilizes, as in Quaker & mongolism, & the notion that "man" necessarily & always excludes or subordinates "woman" is[203] the kind of literalism that is under attack all through this book. Second, the reader should be warned that symbols are not things, solid & stable objects: they are more like themes in music: they keep modulating into other things: yet they don't really lose all identity. FW [*Finnegans Wake*] examples, maybe.[204]

[202] The only disadvantage from my point of view is that readers unacquainted with the earlier book may find startling omissions (Revision of P).[205]

[203] P rev.: Robert Graves called his WG [*The White Goddess*] a "grammar of mythology,"[206] and while my view of it is very different from his, I still believe that there is such a thing as a grammar of mythology, & I think my work gives a few paradigms of it. {Fluidity of concepts here}. In

my younger days a senior colleague, disconcerted by my leaps in metaphorical identifications, said, "Well, you can just do anything, then."
You cannot, if you are speaking with some fluency, "do anything," but
you can express anything.

[204] (Also: transfer, I think, the anti-historical business to the preface.[207]
And add, perhaps: there is a lot of superstition about history, fostered
partly by Marxist reverence for the historical process. History is mainly a
record of psychosis & paranoia: the notion that it will turn into something sane and intelligible is an illusion unless other factors are brought
to bear on it. One of these is typology, dealt with in GC: others are
mentioned here.)

[205] A book of creation myths, *Alpha*, suggests that some societies are
not very interested in creation myths: why, an anthropologist studying
that society would have to tell us.[208] (I think I have the indignant son
pulling apart his naughty fucking parents, pushing the father (usually)
into the sky and leaving the mother on, and as, the earth [par. 178]. This
creates a "firmament" that gives gods and men a chance to breathe. This
myth is Maori, or at least Polynesian.[)] The author of Alpha says
Neumann says that the word ouroboros occurs in the *Timeaus*:[209] I don't
think Neumann would know, but I'll check.[210]

[206] Revision of 5: there are many by-products of the chain of being:
some of them are listed in the second chapter of Foucault's *Les mots et les
choses*.[211]

[207] To create from nothing makes reality an epiphany or manifestation, a phenomenon, *Schein*. But an epiphany of what? According to
Eckhart, of God's desire that there should be something rather than
nothing.[212]

[208] Why the hell can't I say, in tracing the outline of Seven, that I go
from nothingness to the reversed chain of being, and from there to the
drunken boat? I don't think the titanic fall (perhaps not even *Shirley*,
though we'll see if it emerges in Six) goes in Seven: rather in Eight[213]—
anyway, the recovery of myth begins with the human conquest of the
titanic. (If I were writing another Finnegans Wake I'd be interested in the
fact that the ship called the Titanic sank in April, 1912, when I was an

embryo, and that "the recovery of the Titanic" is in the news right now.)²¹⁴ I'm interested in the Titanic sinking because it was the first tangible sign that European civilization had lost its grip on reality and was about to throw away its cultural leadership of the world.

[209] Left out of the above: the only explicit Biblical statement that God made the world from nothing is in II Maccabees 7:28, which is pretty damn late.

[210] All my dialogues seem to start with creation myths: I wonder if the kind of awareness symbolized by "creation" isn't the real beginning of human consciousness.²¹⁵ Seven seems to be starting with the egg-myth, the painted cave as the embryo of metaphorical identification. Painting is the art of the unborn, I've said [par. 149], and maybe the iconic, the presenting of the objective as a flat picture (the *Bildung* of Wittgenstein's *Tractatus*)²¹⁶ isn't the starting point of consciousness. It certainly seems to be the starting point of this book, where the recovery and incorporating of the excluded initiative of experiencing literature marked the first step from the *Anatomy* that I've taken.

[211] The thematic development of myth, though it moves within history, is not really historical: that's why people interested in mythology, like me, get called anti-historical. Of course the "that's why" is really a detritus of superstitions about history. Catholics & Marxists both lay claim to historical infallibility, & regard themselves as containing the essential meaning of history (never mind the grammar right now). As long as they preserve these infallible illusions, they remain simply antitheses of Protestantism and capitalism respectively. History needs to be counterbalanced by other things (mainly myth) before it ceases to be Byron's demonic scripture [*The Vision of Judgment*, l. 689] (also Blake's "garment of war" [*Milton*, pl. 42, l. 15]) and Joyce's nightmare,²¹⁷ a record of man's paranoia and psychosis. The "fall" was man finding himself in a world of time and law. Time meant that half his life was a journey "down" to death; law provided the illusion or dream of Babel & Jacob's ladder, that one could climb by steps & degrees. (This suggests an as yet unwritten conclusion to Five.)

[212] Once in Pakistan it began to rain: a man from Belfast walking with me had an umbrella & spread it over me, saying he was glad to help

preserve "a better brain than my own."[218] There are many obvious reasons why I should find such a remark irritating: the most important, perhaps, is that I feel that within the very wide area of normal intelligence I think all brains are pretty well alike. I have always loved music better than words, but I think I'd have been a second-rate musician, a commonplace church organist. In other areas, like business, I'd be a dunce. We all start from scratch: the immense differences in where we arrive are largely a matter of luck, plus conditioning of various kinds. That's one reason why one *has* to believe in a God who knows what people are and pays little attention to what they do. (Why do I leave out the crucial word?)[219]

[213] Well, Six. The first section revolves around the rejuvenation or emancipating of the female. Mother modulates to wife: the Virgin (a mother is naturally virginal in relation to a son) becomes the bride. Hence the very ambiguous remark Jesus makes to his mother at the Cana wedding.[220] Also Demeter and the anabasis of Kore. Also, Ruth whose son is really Naomi's. Naomi is thus one of the late bride stories (Sara [Sarah], Hannah, Elizabeth), where again there's a kind of rejuvenation, not mother-to-bride but crone-to-mother.[221]

[214] A modulation of this is the foreign-harlot theme dealt with in GC [155], which *must* be attached to even very virtuous women, though with them it may be only a false accusation. Susanna is a type of the "jealous of Joseph" element in the story of Mary. Then there's Ruth, who's a Moabite descended from the incest of Lot & his daughter. This last is a parody of the theme of the levirate marriage. Tamar is also accused of being a harlot, and of course Jerusalem is a harlot turned bride, as I said in GC [156–8]. Ruth also has what Keats calls a "deep one" aspect[222] and it's possible that some phrases in SS ("my own vineyard have I not kept" [Song of Songs 1:6]) carry some of the same overtones. Then there are folk tale themes, like the one in The Wife of Bath's Tale.[223] Documentation for poet's knowledge of the identity of paradisal garden and bride's body include Campion's Cherry-Ripe, Vaughan's Regeneration, and Marvell's Garden.[224]

[215] Section Two is the demonic or white-goddess cycle,[225] the reason for breaking from the Mother-Goddess (you're an embryo until you do, as in GC [107]): the cycle represented by the serpent (skin-shedding and

ouroboros) as a death-reversal process that ain't *it*. Here we have the hero's rejection of the goddess: Gilgamesh of Inanna [Ishtar], Adonis of Venus, Odysseus of Calypso (politer, but essentially the same, especially when we realize that the Circe theme is a part of it, as the Gilgamesh poem shows).[226] Mental Traveller in Blake; Tobit in Bible.

[216] The son of a late birth is always a victim: Isaac goes through the Akedah, Samuel is "devoted" to the temple, John the Baptist and Jesus are martyred.[227] I don't know what happened to Obed: maybe the proxy saved him.

[217] Creation and fall are positive and negative aspects of the same vision. One is of the brave new world, ordered (spiral mt. [mountain]) and beautiful (Eros ladder). The other is of "thrownness," of alienation from this world, where all creation is recreation, the recovery of something lost. These two visions recur in Jacob's dream of the ladder & his fight with the river-god that crippled him [Genesis 28 and 32].

[218] Mountain & garden are very close together: it's been quite a job separating angelic and erotic ladders. Cave & furnace are going to be damn close too. The mountain is, I think, the vision of the primary concern of construction; the garden, of sex; the cave (the place of seed) of food; the furnace of the imprisonment ending in freedom of action and thought. Food ends in the Eucharist vision of eating God & being eaten by him; play ends in the dance or Marvell's longer flight [*The Garden*, l. 55]. Methinks it is no journey.[228] Both Seven & Eight are alchemical, Eight especially. And purgatorial. A Mother Church with a Papa, which reverences a chaste Son and a virgin mother but subordinates women within itself, is a purgatorial Church, waiting further deliverance.

[219] Incidentally, internalizing or subjectivizing, as with the symbolistes, is part of the crucible-purgatory pattern. Such internalizing begins as a renunciation of cyclical experience (i.e. the white goddess cycle). Hence the femme fatale figure of Salome and the severed head (or, equally, the severed balls, whichever part you're looking at).[229]

[220] The femme fatale seems logically a part of Six, which she is because the white goddess is. But she also has a role in Seven & Eight as the siren false emanation who decoys her pursuer like a mother-partridge,

the alastor illusion. The pursuer has to realize she's inside & start there (Keats' Psyche, not impossibly Valéry's).[230] Find out what the "receptacle" is in the *Timaeus*.

[221] Dance as a mimesis of fucking: I've never believed that the "navel" in SS [*Song of Songs*, 7:2] was a euphemism for cunt, because her feet are in sandals and she's dancing. Dancing begins in imitation of the mating dances of animals. Orchestra, of course, & Penelope's web in that poem, recurring in "Burnt Norton" [ll. 56–71].[231]

[222] Internalizing is voluntarily plunging into the prison of hell and demonic parody, and then the deeper prison below that & which produces it really: the prison of Narcissus, the stade du miroir.[232] Mallarmé, of course, tried in Igitur to hit the real bottom, & says in a letter that he had to go through all that just to get a vision of the universe, the only alternative being left shut up in one's self.[233] Evidence that interiorizing is by no means an end in itself. I think (only a vague guess yet) that Seven ends with gradual release and Eight with metamorphosis and discontinuous breaks. I must look at Pelikan's book on continuity[234]—that's another purgatorial element in the Mother Church.

[223] Theocritus' poem on the festival of Adonis [*Adoniazusae*], & the babble it records, has precisely the relation to Adonis that two Christmas shoppers have with the birth of Christ. Obvious but interesting; cf. the roll call of strange names in Gerontion of the people who've eaten and drank God.[235]

[224] Speaking of Gerontion, Ronald Bush's book on Eliot says that Eliot originally added a second epigraph to the MM [*Measure for Measure*] one: Inferno 33, where Alberigo says he doesn't know what his body is doing in the world above [ll. 122–3]: i.e. he may still be "alive" even though he's in hell.[236] Gerontion is likewise a compulsively reflecting mind cut off from a body, a sterile seed like the ones at the opening of WL [*The Waste Land*], blown around by winds. In short, a severed head.

[225] The Tudor mystique of royalty of course goes back to ancient & in fact Biblical times, with its focus on the royal Psalms, especially 2 and 110. But the chain of being, while it continued the same symbolism, rationalized it much more completely. Add note to Five.[237]

[226] Cave & furnace both start underground, and at least the furnace looks as though it included alchemy. Eliade's book on alchemy suggests that trying to hurry up nature's *time* was the point about the actual process.[238]

[227] The fall brought death (the inevitability of downward movement: if there's anything else to the psyche it can only go up); time or sequential movement (reverse the order) and law, the illusion of advancing by degrees toward a final trial and judgment. This should go at the end of Five, the sex part being left for Six.

[228] The point about the note at the top of this page [par. 225] is SS [*Song of Songs*]: the ease of transition from the king to the god.[239]

[229] The theme of martyrdom, the souls under the altar yelling how long, is part of Eight. The martyr practically proves resurrection, as the word itself ("witness") shows. Like other apocalyptic symbols, the martyr has a demonic parody, the terrorist, who kills or tries to kill first. His mendacity is identical with that of the inquisitor who kills the martyr. But all genuine martyrs, I think, die in an equally good cause, and will probably be promoted from the witness-box to the jury, if God really bothers with a trial.

[230] Returning to the alternating sense of "oceanic" unity and heightened individuality, I wonder if the unifying sense comes particularly from the Spirit of love and community, and the individualizing one from the Word, the two-edged sword that divides and discriminates, in the mental, spiritual and physical life. I may have something here if it's not unconscious self-glorification (i.e. the critic makes a unity out of his poem).

[231] Eight (peroration material): the concern for free play, unimpeded movement, and freedom is concern for life itself, separated from death.

[232] Myths are seeds: the kerygmatic ones are the ones that grow out of imgve. [imaginative] possibilities and become part of one's post-genetic code. This is what Jesus meant by his faith & grain of mustard seed [Matthew 17:20]. I think even Paul's dying seed [1 Corinthians 15:36] sprouts into kerygma, or in response to it.

[233] Hiranyagarbha: the golden egg laid by Prajapati,[240] the Spirit brooding on the waters, not a dove this time but a goose laying a golden egg. Evidently H. [Hiranyagarbha] becomes eventually the Logos—Radhakrishnan on the Upanishads.[241] Maybe the Son myth separating heaven & earth is a Seven starting point, the egg-seed an Eight one.

[234] I don't know if I have much to say about sacrifice I haven't said in GC [180–6]. The Ymir myth of archetypal sparagmos; a horse in the Upanishads, a bull in Mithraism, a lamb in Revelation (slain at creation). Maybe I should add a note in Five that the dragon-Kingu myth wasn't so obliterated after all.[242]

[235] Then there's the human > animal sacrifice progression (Akedah and Passover). Reverse of this is Abel lamb-offering, accepted because it was bloody, followed by Abel's own death [Genesis 4:4–8]. I think the Genesis narrator is genuinely puzzled by the stinker-god in his sources sometimes, but maybe it'll come clear.

[236] The Pope is touring U.S. now [September 1987], trying to tell American Catholics that they can't pick & choose what they will believe out of a dialectically conceived doctrine. The point is that everyone, Catholic and non-Catholic, picks & chooses how he will believe, & that's really what my book is about. In revising the book there should be quite a lot about the difference in charity between a dialectically conceived doctrine and a mythologically-conceived one. The latter will never be adopted by my church, but it will be by an increasing body of the public.

[237] Six: Esther (and the more vulgar but pictorially more interesting Judith) is a third female rule type, the savior of Israel who reverses the usual temporal structure of power. Esther is really a concubine, not a queen, scrubbed like the kitchen sink before she goes in to the Top Fucker. That links her with the *New* Testament Rahab (note Dante),[243] the justified harlot (perhaps thought to be Boaz' mother by Matthew [1:5]). Also with the culbute theme in Hannah's song [1 Samuel 2:1–10] and the Magnificat [Luke 1:46–55], which in turn links with redemption *by* woman.[244] And *don't* forget Shirley in Six.[245]

[238] When Berdyaev says in an essay on Boehme that Boehme's whole thought comes out of an intuition about fire, and that this links him with

Heraclitus,[246] I start running around in circles barking wildly, even if I don't know quite what he means, and am inclined to wonder if he does. However, I've always known that Boehme linked the Father with fire and the Son with light.

[239] Rousseau became the first modern revolutionary thinker because he was the first thinker to emphasize the primacy of primary concern.

[240] God help us, maybe it's in *Six* that I need the Polynesian myth of the Son separating the fucking parents and giving gods and men a chance to breathe. Vestige of this, as I've said, in the Genesis beginning of turning on the light and creating the firmament [par. 178]. So the *descent* of the bride in Revelation is the end of that. She doesn't have to descend: she could be hidden in a cave with a lion guarding her, as in Blake's Little Girl Lost.

[241] Mallarmé is very heroic in the way he tries to sink himself in myth & metaphor so completely that the kerygmatic will speak through. "The pure work implies the disappearance of the poet as speaker, yielding his initiative to words."[247] That's the regular rhetoric-poetic distinction: don't let the ego quack: let the words come. But it also echoes Jesus' advice to the 70 not to rehearse what they're going to say [Luke 10:4], which means that kerygma is *on the other side* of the poetic from rhetoric. "Since the immortal word is tacit, the diversity of tongues . . keeps everyone from uttering the word which would be . . truth itself in its substance." He goes on to say that then poetry wouldn't exist:[248] it's what I call an analogical structure. So you can't have a sixth initiative, once you've gone from the Tower of Babel to Zephaniah's pure speech [Zephaniah 3:9]. Note the kernel of Derrida in the first quotation.

[242] The male virgins in Revelation [14:4] (I probably have this) are the antitype of the fucking sons of God in Genesis 6. The combination of great visionary and silly bugger in John the Divine is very clear here: the silly bugger said "not defiled with women," the great visionary saw the antitype. Page bloody 4.[249]

[243] The mountain dialogue is based on the concern of construction (*not* of shelter, which is psychologically quite different). The garden is of course based on sex; the cave on food (which expands into the physical

absorption with the environment; the oceanic direction opposite to construction), and the furnace on freedom, moving from the prison to its opposite. The intransitive praise spoke of by Erich Heller is the song of freedom.[250]

[244] The newspaper story, with its headline breaking through in large type, is a parody of the kerygmatic breaking through the mythical. I suppose there is no such thing as a continuous kerygmatic; even if there were, our reading of it would be discontinuous. Watch a student underlining what strikes him in his reading. One hopes that he owns the book.

[245] Part Two again. The mountain dialogue is, I think, realized except that it looks to me as though the Romantic reversal of the four worlds ought to go into it. It's not exactly a demonic parody, but it *is* a contrasting vision, and in a sense the descending hierarchical vision is a demonic parody, i.e. of the real descent of the gift of tongues.[251] The garden dialogue has the white goddess cycle as its parody. I should do more about the redemption *by* woman I mentioned [par. 237]. One reason for the virgin birth is the need for sublimating Eros. The disdainful mistress of Elizabethan lyric is a parody (she's descended from the white goddess) of the Ewig-Weibliche muse who keeps hauling us up: she's the only authentic mother-figure I've discovered. The desire to *possess* this mother is another parody. I don't see how I can keep the Oedipus parody out of this dialogue: it's the real demonic form, and the w-g [white goddess] cycle is again a reminder that the true mother, though she may be violated, is never possessed.[252]

[246] Anyway, Two of the four major concerns, construction and sex, are incorporated in these dialogues. Now, Three and Four. Three revolves around the concern of food, but of food only as a central symbol of absorbing the environment. Its demonic parody is the divine cannibal feast in the background of Frazer (this is not "historical": in the Eros dialogue, what four-year-old actually screwed his mother and killed his father?). Freud buggered up his own thesis when he invented a historical father-killing: the old man always ducks: he never gets sacrificed.[253]

[247] Well: the usefulness of food & drink accounts for the symbol of eating tree-fruits in Eden. Then comes Abel with his blood-offering,

which God prefers to Cain's vegetable harvest-offerings.[254] Passover takes precedence over Pentecost-harvest and Seventh-vintage. Here's an interesting contrast: God just loves blood and murdered animals, but man is strictly forbidden blood in his diet, though if he eats meat he's bound to absorb some.[255] The fact that animal blood is a not wholly satisfactory substitute for human blood I don't need to elaborate on. Les dieux ont soif:[256] the gods must be fed or they'll die. The crudity of this image conceals the meaning the prophets keep hammering at: the sacrificial *life* keeps the gods going: the gods live by the myths we live by. Woden and Mithra died of disbelief, not starvation.

[248] The communal meal is the image of an interchange between the individual and the group: the ocean and brook interchange. The God-Man's body is revealed among, and as, the group—I have all that.[257] It develops among other things the symposium form, where a Platonic form is ideally created. What literary elements I can use, beyond Burns's John Barleycorn, is not yet clear. Well, the Convivio form itself, of course: VW's [Virginia Woolf's] *The Waves*.

[249] Banquet of wrath: the harvest and vintage of man in Revelation [14:10–20], developed out of the treading of the winepress in Isaiah [63:2–6]. Martyrdom goes here: the blood of the martyrs is the *seed* of the church: the blood of Christ saves: in martyrdom the apocalyptic and demonic images are superimposed. Cannibal giants & so forth: I have a lot of this.[258] What *devours* is death, and ultimately time.

[250] Food modulates into metamorphosis. Start a section with your point about metaphorical identification in the Paleolithic caves. That leads to the figure of the shaman in the beast skin, acquiring the power of the beast[259]—is it samyama in Patanjali?[260] From there we go into drama as the central form of metamorphosis. Careful to keep it separate from sexual metamorphosis, where *two* are involved: the Christ of the first coming was the Eucharist Christ, with no bride. So the Mut. Coes. [*Mutabilitie Cantos*] must go here after all. *Ritual* and drama.

[251] Dream is the digestion of individual experience. Amnesia, the break in continuity, and twins, projection-metamorphosis, start it off.[261] Then the enveloping female wood, where you get et by Diana's hounds, and of course metamorphosis downward.

[252] Metamorphosis upward is, in its antitype, the transfiguration of Christ into a Lacanian full word.[262]

[253] Each dialogue has a kerygmatic and a demonic form. The Freud (Oedipus) and Frazer demonic forms are clear for Six and Seven. In Five, the apocalyptic form is the ascent of wisdom (mental freedom, Blake's mental fight) and the descent of order. The demonic form is the Babel ascent of pride and the descent of tyranny. They're always mixed, of course. In the Quartets, where it's all kerygma, the way up and the way down can be the same: Yeats' Blood and the Moon has both upward ascents, though both in an ironic context. Maybe Nietzsche and his absurd notion of recurrence is the presiding genius of the mountain, only the genuine form of his recurrence fantasy is the wheel of fortune.[263] Note the falling rope-dancer in Z [*Thus Spake Zarathustra*].[264] Germans, even Goethe, are always trying to rationalize the Homeric hero,[265] who really *hasn't* any vision: there's no Krishna on any Homeric battlefield.[266]

[254] Kerygma is *spiritual* rhetoric, rhetoric delivered from ideology by being on the other side of myth. The gospels contain the teachings and parables of Jesus: they're "logocentric," but they come to us in continuous (to some extent) written form. The kerygma is—and I use the term advisedly—the *resurrection* of the living speaker from the written myth.[267] Or rather, the living word. The Sermon on the Mount isn't a harangue. To choose a text for a sermon makes a myth into kerygma. Kerygma is the completion of the personal possession of the written word: it's linked with mantra, but without the "vain repetition" [Matthew 6:7] that often goes with that. It's the actualized form of the "myth to live by," assuming that the real life is a spiritual one, delivered once for all from all ideologies or rationalizations of power.[268]

[255] I have often wondered why I'm so hooked on detective stories: I read a Freudian explanation of them once that seemed utterly convincing, at least of my addiction, and then, in true Freudian fashion, forgot and mislaid it.[269] One thing that occurs to me is double meaning: a casual remark or incidental episode suddenly becomes *relevant* in that second world where the murderer is identified. Miniature apocalypse with Satan cast out and all the other details moving together in identity.

[256] I wonder if Valéry's *jeune parque* is mother Eve rejuvenated as a bride. The serpent that bites her (or the narrator) is certainly the Edenic serpent.[270]

[257] Well, Eight. Start with Boehme and his fire: God is nothing and wanting to be something is a fire. When he gets to be something the fire acquires light. I don't know whether he actually says that God without light is Satan, but Satan is the darkness that doesn't comprehend the light.[271] Then *Igitur* and its reduction to phoenix ash or whatever. If igitur means therefore it means the death-end of causality. Mallarmé speaks of the alchemists as *nos ancetres* (*nos* meaning poets, of course) and this chapter-dialogue is an alchemical one.[272] Maybe Jung is its presiding genius. Marx isn't: he talks about a transfer of power from employers to workers, which is important in the conception of the recovery of myth but isn't based on the primary concern of freedom, though it's certainly related to it. Edmund Wilson claims he's [Marx is] full of Promethean imagery and that he read Aeschylus' play every year,[273] but even if this is true (and it sounds awfully phony) he's not a mythical focus. Blake's Los, the blacksmith at his forge, is the essential Prometheus-Bible link;[274] I wish I knew the background to Smart's remark about Abraham's furnace "coming up at last."[275]

[258] I wonder if there shouldn't be a second preface, to Part Two only. It could include the theory of displacement, which I so badly need, the analogical use of myths of the Classical origins, a defence of my procedure of taking the Bible and not just going all out for comparative mythology. I need to explain clearly what I'm doing, so I'll know too.[276]

[259] Where does the drunken boat go? I'd hoped to keep it in Seven, and to keep, by the same token, Seven as the water chapter. But the seed of fire *in* the water won't go away. Hiranya goddamn garbha: even the Indians don't know him, or it.[277]

[260] The spiral mountain-temple contains the dead body of the king, or the sleeping Albion. Fire brings him to life, as Los explores him with his planetary lamp. Job is dead when he's prosperous, and starts life when disaster strikes.

[261] Republic X is fantasy-myth, of course: people don't choose the

tragic, miserable, humiliating lives that so many of them live. They don't choose either to be born in the world of nature, where such lives are inevitable for the great majority, where the decision to take a chance does not abolish chance.[278] In short, the world is a fiery purgatory to the extent that it makes sense. Or, in water, the belly of Leviathan. Leviathan's belly or the brick kilns of Egypt: whatever, God himself must be purgatory, as Kung says.[279] Not a vale of soul-making but of spirit-making.[280]

[262] Re across [par. 257]: the Industrial Revolution has its demonic side—the dark Satanic mills[281]—but positively it's Prometheus taking the fire out of the fennel-stalk.

[263] Mother, bride, daughter (Sophia): no Council ever declared that they were different persons of the same substance, or that anyone who confounded the persons or divided the substance would go to hell. After all, the entities involved, whether real or "only" symbolic, were "only" female. Perhaps for that reason they have become major conceptions in literature.[282]

[264] The Preface to Part Two would say something about a grammar of mythology and the Frazer-Freud origins of it: Graves, who uses the phrase, Eliade, Campbell, and Jung's Psychology and Alchemy. The illustrations to that book, which are the essential part of it, cover my whole territory. (I think the text is largely crap, though there are striking remarks in it that emerge through the preaching.) The tradition is Vico and Schelling. I suppose the chief principle I want to get across is that of displacement (the other half of that, the condensation of pure metaphor, is close to Freud's conception of condensation; my displacement is almost the opposite of his.) The tedious straw-thrashing of criticism, circling around issues there should have been a consensus on years ago, might be just mentioned.[283]

[265] But demonic parody needs to be at least referred to, so as to save obscurity and perhaps explanation for those who haven't read or grasped the point of GC. Also, of course, the difference between demonic and analogical myths outside the Bible.[284] And—especially important—the fact that symbols behave like liquids, not solids: they tend to keep their volume but not their form. That's also true of the myths containing them,

especially the ones with expanding symbols. The expanding symbol needs very careful explanation: it's a place where readers grow dim.

[266] Seven is based on the Frazer stuff I've already written about, so I can summarize most of it and go on with what I've talked about less: the original sense of sacrifice as (a) an effort to reach the spiritual in communion[285] (b) the willingness to lose the physical. This last modulates into the acceptance of *death*.[286]

[267] For someone like Mallarmé "believe," like "praise" in Rilke, is an intransitive verb.[287] *What* they believe, or rather say they don't believe, isn't important: it's the language they use that's important. I must learn to distinguish subjectivity from internalization: perhaps the latter is the climax of Seven. Stevens' supreme fiction[288] and Emily Dickinson's "Circumference."[289] When Mallarmé speaks of "glorieux mensonges"[290] (of belief) he doesn't, with respect, know whether they are mensonges or not: he means only that when *he* talks about "resurrection" he doesn't want it pinned down to the gospel one. But he means resurrection, not just getting up in the morning. I think this is increasingly what *we* have to mean by the Hebrews belief definition [Hebrews 11:1], whatever the author meant.

[268] God is a spirit: man is a mixture of spirit and shit. Whatever isn't spirit gets shat, including I think his soul—I still feel that soul is something to get lost, not saved.

[269] If Eight is going to be the end, it ought to be a climax, and if it's a climax it can't scrape together a rubble of miscellaneous ideas. It has to be based on something very central, like the belly of Leviathan, and focus on the Father. And in the Bible, Job, the poetic and Christian Genesis-Exodus. The redemption-purgatorial theme, the go'el.[291] I had a context for the restored daughters I've mislaid—I think in Blake.[292] The restored daughters in Blake are internal but not subjective—that goes back a long way.

[270] Rousseau may wonder why man is born free & yet is everywhere in chains,[293] but it was Blake who realized that as long as man lives within a hierarchical or tyrannical mythology, all his social institutions will be of the same shape.

[271] I'm not too worried about my compulsive reading of detective stories: until the shape of the whole book is utterly clear in my mind, serious reading would only distract me. Two very central ideas I've left out are (1) the progress from mythical to kerygmatic is identical with the progress from type to antitype (2) exploiting imitative harmony & the like is verbal *play*, magic released from the futile work of trying to affect the world out there.

[272] In allegro music you're not aware of the vibrations of the individual notes; in driving a car you're not aware of the individual revolutions of the engine. All narrative maintains a certain *speed*: the speed conceals our awareness of the individual metaphors. *That's* why we need criticism, rather than the analogy of the definitive response (except that that's another aspect of the same thing). Three.

[273] Add to Crucifixion: you say it's a historical event, but doesn't its essential power depend on its historicity? Would it be anything at all if it were simply a story like *King Lear*? (Anything at all in kerygma, that is, not myth.) The answer I think is that that side of its reality is not so much historical as personal. That isn't just a quibble: the historical is only historical, and can only be recorded by historians, whereas the personal can be metamorphosed into myth. But not pure myth: the pure myth repeats; the personal happens once & for all (Hebrews 9:26), and thereby pulls history around into a shape. The recurring historical event, the repeated church ritual, are part of history's dream of revelation; myth reveals the personal; it doesn't just repeat, & so leads us to the kerygmatic.[294]

[274] Food in chapter seven: it symbolizes the illusion of acquiring and the reality of assimilating. See Gabriel Marcel's *Being and Having*. The Strephon of Swift's poem is distressed that "Celia shits," but if she didn't she'd *be* shit, like a miser.[295]

[275] Four: hope for a "future" life, whether resurrection or reincarnation, is a common and frequently articulated form of hope. I imagine that everyone has some hope that his life exists in some other dimension than ordinary time, but this is an area where self-censorship is very active, and most such hopes never get anywhere near verbal formulation.[296]

[276] Part Two is getting clearer: creation of wisdom and love: redemption or reconciliation of (human) love and wisdom. All my educational philosophy goes into Eight. HEAP [Hermes, Eros, Adonis, Prometheus] is right; also the Blakean sequence Urizen, Tharmas, Orc, Urthona. Blake changed the emphasis from Orc to Luvah when he realized that Orc was not really his Eros but his Adonis, though I doubt that he really got all of Tharmas clear. I wonder if I'm getting it clear for him. Don't think in those terms. The initial letters of the Zoas in their right order make up the word Urthour.

[277] Also: the formulas of popular fiction reflect the primary concerns. Five is based on the amnesia-twins formula of romance I looked into in the Norton lectures.[297] The central document is FW [*Finnegans Wake*]: the sleeping Finnegan and the cyclical HCE. Also De Quincey's view of the dream, the reverse of Freud's.[298] I must reread The Ministry of Fear.[299] It's the concern of construction, metaphorically of creation. Hence it's the concern of concern, the anxiety of anxieties, the poet wondering how much of what he "says" is the reality of illusion, the analogy of kerygma, and how much is reflection of the ideological Babel-babble around him, the illusion of reality.

[278] In Six the concern of sex-based love and union takes the form of the Harlequin romance or Cinderella archetype, the recognition of the bride. Some positive talisman is the clue to her identity, like the slipper, or the ring in Sakuntala. The removal of a "stain" or handicap is a negative talisman. In the Nortons I spoke of the descent of Ishtar,[300] but perhaps that belongs in Seven: the quest of the Sophia figure of the Gnostics of which the gospel of John is a counter-Gnostic reversal.

[279] Can I really go on with the AC principle "the poet says nothing" in this context? Shouldn't I say that the poet "says" whatever is ideologically compulsory, and sets forth only the total vision where what he "says" doesn't count? But I can't keep quoting tags from Emily Dickinson & such and refuse the phrase "as ED says" to her.

[280] I've said my educational ideas go in Eight [par. 276], & some of them do, but surely my central one goes in Seven: the symposium is a *banquet*. The Book of Job, by the way, is a parody symposium, one in

which Job is increasingly isolated from his friends, a Lazarus under the table, a Timon—part two figure (naturally there's more than that).

[281] I think the popular archetype of Seven is the detective story, which in turn is based on the primitive feeling that no one dies: one is always, so to speak, murdered by death. It takes a long time even to admit that it's death: before that you look for a tangible murderer. When at last it's recognized to be death, you get the ritual of "carrying out Death." The expulsion of the scapegoat or death figure is an essential part of the Frazerian feast: that's what *really* draws the survivors together in a new unity (p. 74, top [par. 255]). I've not seen that clearly before.[301]

[282] For Eight, it's the thriller where hero or heroine fell into the clutches of the villain, who explains the plot up to then to them in the context of the vision of the whole-of-life-before-death convention. They're nearly always threatened with death, escape by some wriggle or gimmick, & may acquire their knowledge of the conspiracy at the price of some wound or injury. Odin loses an eye: Christ rises with the five wounds.

[283] The Frazerian banquet, above [par. 281], splits into the real king, who's eaten & drunk and vanishes, and the mock king who's driven out. Reality & illusion paradox again.[302]

[284] I don't have a central model in modern literature except FW [*Finnegans Wake*] for the first. It would be funny if it turned out to be La Jeune Parque after all. Eight could be Igitur, except that that's so sketchy. (The J.P. would be Six.) But I'm sure I've got an argument with a shape: being & doing; being & loving; being & having; being & becoming. The difficulty, as always, is in distributing the material: I now think sacrifice goes in Eight, as part of a theme of renunciation. Identification of victim with the god of sacrifice.

[285] Things that seem silly or arbitrary fit as antitypes: the celibate in Revelation (I have that [par. 242]) as an antitype of Genesis 6; the cursing of the fig-tree by Jesus [Mark 11:14], which looks merely peevish, like the silly stories told of his childhood in the apocryphal gospels, is an antitype of the cursing of the serpent [Genesis 3:15]; striking Zechariah dumb [Luke 1:20] for expressing the same incredulity that Mary does ("How shall this be?" [Luke 1:34]) is the antitype of the laughter linked with Isaac [Genesis 18:12], etc.

[286] The apocalyptic ladder is the spine of universal man (*Thespis*, 396);[303] the Tower of Babel is the rising and falling prick. The cursed serpent ("on thy belly shalt thou go") is a collapsed spine *and* a limp prick. Kundalini banished to the perineum.[304]

[287] I'm thinking of a prefatory note to Part Two that will warn readers about displacement,[305] demonic parody, and the *liquid* quality of mythical thinking (i.e. the way lust & greed spill all over history in P.L. [*Paradise Lost*] xi–xii as war & exploitation).

[288] Also, though this may have to come out later: all four dialogues use places as metaphors for verbal structures. Jacob's ladder has the analogue of the "tower of words" (see if the phrase is in D.T. [Dylan Thomas]);[306] the garden the "anthology" or verbal intercourse (Donne's "sonnets" & body-book);[307] the banquet the Platonic dialogue; the crucible or whatever the one volume of Dante's last canto.[308]

[289] The demonic parody of Danae is Iphigeneia or Jephthah's daughter on top of the altar,[309] though that could be kerygmatic in the context of Eight (or Seven). Don't leave out things like the sleeping beauty theme,[310] or the link between *adamah* and the "material-maternal" association.[311]

[290] Whatever one thinks of the Tertullian paradox ("I believe *because* it is impossible"),[312] the opposite of it is that trying to reduce belief to the credible is a waste of time and desolation of spirit. One doesn't bother to believe the credible: the credible is believed already, by definition. There's no adventure of the mind there. (Didn't Coleridge say that Donne was a Christian because it would have been so much easier to be an atheist?)[313] Belief is the Wright brothers getting a heavier-than-air-machine off the ground after the most distinguished scientists had "proved" that it was impossible. In short, belief is the creation that turns the illusory into the real. Being kerygmatic, it emerges on the further side of the imaginative.[314]

[291] The phrase "God is dead" may have made some sense in the Nietzschean context, but as a slogan it's sheer idiocy.[315] It is far more likely that in the twenty-first century the birds in the trees will be singing "Man is dead, thank God." What really is dead is the antithesis between a subjective man and an objective God. Nietzsche, by the way, was a

power and will worshipper, and because everything man *does* goes in a circle, he *had* to wind up with his identical-recurrence horseshit.

[292] The Word of God is brought by angels (cf. "evangelist"): note the point made about an angel being a manifestation as well as a messenger. (I've got this now in Five.)[316] The Xn [Christian] identifying of angel & evangelist ties this up & makes clear that as what a messenger brings is a word or message, the real Jacob's ladder is a tower of words. I can't find the last phrase in Dylan Thomas, though he keeps coming close to it. October.[317]

[293] The Exodus 31 law about devoting every firstborn son to God makes every Jew an Isaac.[318] In Isaac shall his seed be called [Genesis 21:12].

[294] Eight, the counterpart of Five, is the descent of wisdom, as Five is its ascent, and starts with Blake's reversal of the four-level hierarchy, going on to Shelley and the drunken boat complex.[319] Seven, the descent of love, probably incorporates my Two-Brothers amnesia-twins complex as well as Frazer.[320]

[295] Red & white are the colors of erotic love (Shakespeare's PT [*The Phoenix and the Turtle*], Valentine's Day,[321] the flower in MND [*A Midsummer Night's Dream*, 3.2.102–9], the episode in Parzival); the colors of its demonic white-goddess parody are red, white and black. Red & white are also the colors of Jesus' bodily resurrection, the animal body and blood where the red principle is the life.

[296] Five: Browne's remark about the seventh day means that human art imitates nature which (or who) is the art of God.[322] That won't do. But the "sabbath" implies the need of a conscious being to objectify his environment, rely on his distancing senses, and postpone the instant gratifications of food & sexual mating. This last links with the dietary laws of the O.T. & the maudlin cult of celibacy that starts with the New. It's why secondary concerns must exist, though it's a perversion to make them dominant on the plea that they're what distinguishes us from mere animals. Unless we go back to the proper reverence for the animal in us that evidently the Magdalenian painters had, we're sunk—sunk in the deluge. That doesn't mean we should imitate the shrew, eating three times its own weight every day just to stay alive, or, like contemporary

Americans, assume that we have a right to fuck everything with a hole in it. There's a middle course in such matters. The implications in this entry are quite important: the function of law in sublimating impulse I already have, but not the "human" aspect of secondary concern.[323]

[297] Linked to this is: creation is a vision of the environment as ordered, something to be explored by science. Hierarchy, authority, command & obedience, are all perversions of order. They're rationalized by saying the ultimate source of authority is God, but he isn't: he's totally blacked out by human authority. Similarly in education: the authority comes from the subject taught, not the teacher or the teaching institution, whether church, university or monastic order. The "transcendental signified" is actually the universal signified. The created beings (*Seiendes* in Heidegger) are the signifieds of ordinary language, but also the signifiers of their own creation (i.e. they're part of the natural Bible, the second Word of God). Adam, the giver of names, is the first incarnation of God.

[298] Angels ascend & descend on Jacob's ladder: angels are messengers carrying *verbal* messages: I've got this.[324] It's the growing sense of *verbum factum*, of truth as *facta* rather than *data*, that has given language its tremendous contemporary importance. The fallacy of doing produces the tower of Babel, which becomes half the wheel of fortune, and the "rise and fall" of empires, a ritualized ouroboros, just as ascent & descent are a verticalized journey. The change from horizontal to vertical metaphors keeps nagging me: I don't know where to put it: perhaps in the interchapter (prefatory note to Part Two expanding into an introduction).[325]

[299] Ascent (beyond "heaven") is the concentrating and transcending of consciousness; descent (beyond "hell["] and death) is the reinforcing of consciousness by fantasy & dream.[326] There's also the Eliot plenitude-vacancy movement: it still isn't clear.

[300] So ascent from the surface of the earth into the sky is a metaphor for the concentrating of consciousness into the spiritually creative, Blake's mental fight, and descent from the sky to the earth is a metaphor of revelation, or the presenting of data to consciousness. The angels bring down the Word in Paul, and the Spirit's prayers, informing God what we *really* want, go up.

[301] And descent from the earth into the world under earth or water is an exploring of the resources and—so to speak—food supplies of consciousness. Ascent to the surface of the earth is an escape from prison. D.H. Lawrence, Rimbaud's Saison en Enfer, and, essentially, Heart of Darkness take us to various levels of depth. Hell is one level, death is below it, and annihilation below that.

[302] Keep in mind the social as well as the individual metaphors. Hell is a tyranny, dictatorship, rule of the elect—Milton's hell—or a concentration camp with jailers—Dante. The movement of escape begins with assembling the saving remnant and declaring solidarity with the "wretched of the earth," as in Rimbaud's identification of himself with "niggers."[327] In the upper semicircle community concentrates into communion, represented by the ambiguous term "body," which may be an intercourse of bodies (Six). The societies below hell are ghosts & shades like those of Homer with knowledge of the future & mysterious code messages to communicate from the bottom of the sea, the south pole, or the centre of the earth.

[303] Maybe the reversed quest (Dante's beasts, Goethe's Erdgeist, Keats' Endymion, etc.) is linked to my theme of halting the quest of the "way." Yoga (yoking), arrest, shipwreck, halting the momentum of time, are all examples of the way mythical thinking, cosmology & the like try to shore up the endless flux of time. History is diachronic but history-*writing* is synchronic: it selects, rejects, censors, condenses & displaces just as the dream does. Derrida's insistence on writing is an insistence on simultaneity as well. After that, depth perception, realizing that the presented surface of things is only the first look.[328]

[304] The giants & midgets at the bottom of the world are, in part, shifting perspectives on "reality." They descend perhaps from the animals of the paleolithic caves.

[305] I've noted Samuel Butler's claim that the reasonable is the opposite of the rational[329] ("claim" is a silly word): the explanation is in the half-truth setup of dialectic. In the Euclidean world the shortest distance between two points is always a straight line, but we do not live in that world.

[306] Note at top of page [par. 303]: the *study* of the arrested-flux is a process in which the movement of time is resumed. Here the flat surface becomes, in Borges' phrase, a garden of forking paths.[330]

[307] Look: Seven is the one that starts with the Blakean reversal of the four-levels and goes on to the ark & the drunken boat. I don't know how it gets from there to sacrifice and dying seeds and saving remnants, but it does. Eight starts with Poe, the world of clocks and mirrors & its deliverance, ending with a deste fabula conclusion: the analogy of literary characters & ourselves: *ye* are gods.[331] So Eight should deal with the annexation of the demonic by the human. Long before the "God is dead" crap we had "the devil is dead," in Skelton and elsewhere, which was crap too, but at least accepted the Beddoes principle that there's no external or non-human devil. Bunyan's projecting nonsense goes here.[332]

[308] Note that the Tom o' Bedlam song[333] really suggests a heart-of-darkness type of journey, as Browning divined when he used another theme from *King Lear* for his "Child Rowland" poem.[334] The heart-of-darkness journey is an Eight theme. Corresponding to it is the Mut. [*Mutabilitie*] Cantoes theme in Five, related to the transfiguration or metamorphosis where Jesus as the total Word (with Moses & Elijah) stands over against the Ovidian met. [metamorphosis].[335] The latter is a metaphor for the separation of subject and object that ends in the subject's becoming an object, in short, being annihilated, made *nothing*.

[309] The four levels of time and space (Davies quote) should go at the end of Six, not Five, as part of a general summary of superterranean symbolism.[336] Seven includes sacrifice, & also includes my hunch, going back fifty years, that sacrificial symbolism implies a stinker-god.[337] Even the atonement theory has the smell of farts from the back parts of God about. It's a central point I've never really worked out, but all the stinker God aspects of the Bible (*and* Milton), of course, are bound up with it.

[310] Of course the sulphur-smell is from the demonic fall, if I can ever figure out from that yammering ass Boehme the extent to which that fall involved the divine nature. The important theme is that just as the superterranean imagery absorbs the angelic into the human (and eventually the divine through kenosis, the one kernel of truth in the God-is-

dead crap[)], so the descent theme absorbs the demonic into the human. Man has to sift through the demonic to find his enemy, & identifies the enemy finally as death. Carrying out death consolidates the community (end of Seven).[338] Or Eight.

[311] Another theme I've never got clear is the role of elemental spirits, who are so often sulky, unwilling & dangerous—demonic, in short, & quite often devils. But, as in *Comus*, they can include guardian angels. Goethe's *Faust*, in spite of my growing disillusionment with Goethe, has a lot to do with this: Erdgeist, Homunculus, the lot.

[312] Descent is the wonderful servant archetype, the collecting of forces, Satan rousing the devils, men raising Cain, or the city of Cain. The quest for Siddhis—one shouldn't chase after them, but one certainly should collect them.

[313] Chess in Bardo? Is it a modulation of dice in Bardo? A chess move is a decisive choice that may not abolish chance, but sets up a train of consequences that forces it to retreat into the shadows.

[314] Perhaps sacrifice is the carrying out of death *in reverse*, identification through death to union with God—well, obviously it's that. This identity with death turns into an identity across death.

[315] Seven: descent themes. At first blocked off: there's nothing there but hell, and stay out of that. That's a product of the moral repressiveness starting with the fall, and creates the Freudian *repressed* underconsciousness. Among the things that got stuffed into this collar are the parental (or ancestral) figures. They link with the dead generally: note the Anticlea theme in Odyssey XI and the redemption of Adam and Eve in the Harrowing of Hell. (Actually the first one out is John the Baptist, who's the dreamed-of brother, the Pirithous or Theseus rescued by Heracles.[)] Jesus' remark about hating one's parents [Luke 14:26]. I think I'm dimly glimpsing the road to Oedipus here, and the sacrifice of the son to the father. Black rams turn up in Odyssey XI [ll. 36 ff.].

[316] See if you got the "one flesh" metaphor producing the one flesh child: it should be in 3/19. Genesis 2:24.[339] See too if you have what you

planned for the PN2 [Prefatory Note to Part Two]: everything man *does* goes in a circle. Check Tao & grace.

[317] The Penguin Hölderlin says he says, in a letter of 1801: "the free use of what is proper to one is the most difficult thing of all."[340] No German, no precise reference; just a statement that it's one of the few written after his return from Bordeaux.

[318] PN [Prefatory Note]: re Giles Fletcher: the "positive analogy" is also the "Gentile type."[341]

[319] I've often wondered why Blake makes those silly remarks about imagination having nothing to do with memory,[342] when he must know damn well that it does. I think the fourth level is that of pure duration, continuity, the superstitious fear of breaking a link, the traditional clanking chains of the ghost, the neurotic's archaic heritage, the ghosts of parents and ancestors, even the genetic code. It's the hampering aspects of *that* memory he's worried about; he knows about the habitus-memory too.[343]

[320] Wonder if Eight is a synopsis of modes of freedom: freedom through freedom itself is forgiveness, release from the law of the accuser; freedom through assimilation is education; freedom through love is that; freedom through work is habitus. The first, which is the fourth, is the story of Job, & gets him into the right place.

[321] Most history is the cycle of empires (∩); Biblical "history" is not history at all, but looks at what we call history as an interval between a paradisal prehistory and a recreation of that paradise in post-history (∪).[344]

[322] The real curse imposed on Adam & Eve was the family: not just a patriarchal family, even though that may be the worst form of it, but simply the family, in which children are brought up in a hierarchical structure with the design of losing their childhood when they become adults. The genetic child (the child*like*, not the child*ish*) is prehistoric: post-historic man is the creator or recreated (not the adulterated) child. Hence Jesus on preserving the child in us; hence the way that fundamentalist devil-worshippers go in for periodic orgies of child-spanking, pref-

erably, of course, girls. (At least the fundamentalist journals I get sent occasionally seem to have regular cycles of such articles.) The family is a cyclical principle.

[323] The verbal angels of Enoch & elsewhere become (demonic) *teachers*, like Blake's prophetic blacksmith. Compare the children of Cain in Genesis: also the role of Prometheus and Thoth in Plato: also the demonic reputation of the smith and the taboos on altars built with iron. Usually (and especially in Enoch) these demonic teachings are wrapped up in a reactionary and obscurantist what's-the-world-coming-to package. Precisely the same reactions accompany technological developments in our day: there is always some truth in them, of course: there are no unequivocal signs of progress. Also, technological development is often stimulated by war. What's stupid is the attack on genuinely civilized arts, like the invention of music by Jubal Cain[345] or of writing by Thoth. Writing, by the way, is the emancipating of the memory, and belongs to the redemption of duration.[346]

[324] There's a link here too with stories like Arachne and Marsyas: the human artist gets it in the neck (or wherever) for competing with the gods who claim that *they're* the artists.[347] Projecting devil-worship again.

[325] Stages in descent: hell is near the top, and underneath it is the world of potential reinforcements of consciousness: dreams, giants, fairies, elemental spirits, ancestors, preverbal residues—everything repressed. Note that here too there's a merging of subject and object: the objective is projected and usually dangerous, the subjective important. In Schopenhauer the lower of the two levels of nature is practically hell. So the real journey down is one that starts below the sea. There's identification with the proletariat ("je suis un nègre," says Rimbaud, after saying he's blond and Gaulish [*A Season in Hell*, sec. 2]—never mind the genuineness of the identification, only the fact that he makes it) and the identification with the powers of nature in the paleolithic caves.[348] Identity & assimilation are different things: the latter is my theme here, I think: it's closer to the food archetype. Themes of isolation & desertion as one approaches death: Beowulf at moor, Jesus & Buddha forsaken by their disciples.

[326] *Below* death is self-annihilation or kenosis: the creating of a vacuum. This links with the end of Job & the institution of the Eucharist: nature

abhors a vacuum, and a new society rushes in to fill it up. Percival in Virginia Woolf's *The Waves*. It's the uncanniness of murder and the reintegration of society with new meanings. Death, in short, is followed by the death of death. In Burnt Norton the bottom of the descent (section 4) is followed by a conspectus of art in section 5.

[327] This seventh chapter is getting rather uncomfortably close to Blake, especially the MHH [*The Marriage of Heaven and Hell*] diagram. People in Blake's day couldn't understand why man was born free & was everywhere in chains, or why the oppressed put up with oppression when "Ye are many, they are few" [Shelley, *The Mask of Anarchy*, l. 155]. Blake saw that if your myth-created ideology was hierarchical, you couldn't function outside that hierarchy. As for his lack of influence in his time, the only commentary needed on that is the line:

> Wisdom is sold in the desolate market where none come to buy
> [*The Four Zoas*, Erdman, 325, l. 14]

And, of course, it was Blake who saw that the real Bible was a revolutionary structure, founded on the Exodus type and the resurrection antitype.[349]

[328] There are many dangers in following out the roots of consciousness as they take one into fantasy & "spirits" and the like. The main danger in the upward journey is idealistic discarnation, the escape of the pure soul, Marvell's drop of dew.[350] One of the central—probably *the* central—*axis mundi* image[s] is that of the erect human body, and when the soul is exhaled back into the skies, it becomes a ghostly body that's bumless, gutless, and shitless, to say nothing of prickless & cuntless. A lot of obvious things go here, including the Celia shits point & Strephon's wimpy idealism; the sexual-excretory association.[351] "Bumless & gutless purity"—I like that phrase.[352]

[329] I think the 19th c. fascination with St. John the Baptist's severed head (cf. Valéry's M. Teste) belongs here: Lawrence, of course. Also Valéry's Zeno: the paradox of the zenith.[353]

[330] Freud's pleasure-principle is supposed to collide with a reality-principle: what it practically always collides with is an ideology-principle, something already headed for the slag-heap of eternal verities.

[331] The first book of *Paradise Lost* shows the devils discovering the two infallible formulas of children's fiction (boys['] anyway: I don't know about girls[']): the golden treasure hidden underneath the world and the conspiratorial society about to overthrow the world. I suppose even such genuinely evil things as the Nazi myth of a conspiracy of Jews sitting on a treasure of the world's gold belong to it. Gold and shit, of course.[354]

[332] God, I wish D.H. Lawrence had some sense of real satire: if he had he'd have been by long odds the greatest fiction writer of the century.

[333] I must be coming into my Finland station: a great swarm of things, such as Wallace Stevens' "Description without Place" are finding their right places.[355] Still, I think I should continue my policy of reading nothing but thrillers until a draft of the 8th chapter is completed.

[334] {In the Introduction}. I suppose it is true what I think Roland Barthes says somewhere: that only rereading counts, because all first reading faces not a text but a mirror.[356] But I now feel that there is a very large class of readers for whom a text can never be anything but a mirror, & who will never discover in any page of print anything beyond a reflection of what they already think they think. I used to feel that if people persistently talked nonsense about me it was my own failure to be sufficiently lucid, but now I realize that that is only teacher's masochism. The notion that every "reader" is a potential reader of texts is something I no longer assume.

[335] I feel that I want a narrative for Eight like the others, and not a series of climactic examples. I may be wrong in thinking the Frazer cluster belongs in the second part of Seven—we'll see. But Eight—I've done this before, I know, but I have to keep on doing it until it comes clear—seems to me to deal more with family, Blake's Storgous appetite [*The Four Zoas*, Erdman, 341, l. 10], perhaps with the redemption of continuous time, the vacuum of kenosis & the community that forms around it, the swallowing of the old shit-sack and his resplendent resurgence as the Father (note that this reverses Comus' swallowing of his sons, the normal sacrificial pattern), the pattern absorbed in the ∪ one, the Xn [Christian] turning inside out of the Oedipus story (no, dear; mummy doesn't get fucked after all), the sleeping-father Arthur-Albion figure.[357]

[336] Without the descent theme, the ascent can never be anything except an authoritarian ideology. That's one of my "self-justifying" formulas—perhaps the central one.

[337] Difference between parody and demonic parody: Rabelais' oracle of the bottle is the former; the demonic outrages primary concern. But they come close together in, e.g., Jarry's *Roi Ubu*. (Only it's Ubu Roi, an ape's way of saying Oedipus Rex).[358] Here the reader's sense of concern has to take over: this is my old point that the evil can always be redeemed by being *seen as* evil.

[338] Add to Six: in Five we distinguished the kerygmatic myth of order and knowledge from the ideological cycle of authority & obedience. In the context of Six the kerygmatic myth of love & beauty has to be distinguished from the ideological sado-masochistic cycle.[359] The Virgin symbolizes a love that can never be possessed or perverted into jealousy, as well as the inexhaustible nature of love.

[339] Start Eight with the fall of the rebel angels; then go on to Prometheus the Titan, then to the Titans as Gods before the gods, then to the reigning God as, not the Father, but the usurping Son, the archetype of all Antichrists.[360] Thence to the Oedipus cluster.

[340] Now two transitions I'm less clear about: one to Poe & the technological imagination (also, eventually, Moby Dick) the other to Narcissus.[361] When Blake opened FZ [*The Four Zoas*] with the fall of Tharmas he came at once to the Spectre of Tharmas and his "self-admiring raptures."[362] Something to do with the Deluge myth & the whole theme of demonic parody as holding up a perverting mirror to the apocalypse. I don't know what to do with science fiction.

[341] The shitsack Nobodaddy God is, then, really an Antichrist or Narcissus or Two-Brothers reflection of both the real Son & the latter's still living Father. And does it really matter whether the Son kills the Father or the Father the Son to prolong his own life? But surely this is *Seven* material. I have an instinct to shoot the works on Seven, & let God supply the ideas for Eight (as he did of course for Seven) but that's checked by the already emerging outline for Eight.

[342] I don't have the Oedipus complex clear yet because it's a two-way

street. The son dethrones his father & reigns in his stead, pretending to be a father, but as father he keeps murdering his sons to prolong his own life. Thus Cronus is both a Golden Age legend & a hideous ogre devouring his children, too stupid even to distinguish them from stones. Also the O.T. Jehovah isn't the son of anybody, in contrast to Zeus, who got born, and Jupiter despite the "piter" side of his name.[363] But (first born) sons belong to him, & they get redeemed.

[343] Explicitly, the part is "in" the whole; implicitly, the whole is "in" the part. But the way that the chicken is in the egg is different: a world of interlocked energies. I suppose this is what the hologram-paradigm people[364] are getting at, not that I want it.

[344] The myth of ascent is a quest for liberty or self-realization; the myth of descent is first of all a quest for equality. Shit and death are democrats. The opening pages of *Moby Dick* are crammed with images of descending into a Charybdis whirlpool, but the first positive discovery Ishmael makes is his human equality with Queequeg.[365] The descent here is the descent of love (including a perspective in which tolerance is love at a distance), where we realize the iniquity of proletarians or excluded groups. Doubtless this could extend, as it does in some Oriental religions, to forms of life other than human, but the extension would take us beyond the range of the normal Western cultural imagination. But that's why religion is the worst possible basis for society, because all communions sooner or later turn their backs on each other. *Eight* is the descent for wisdom, the reinforcements of the dead (something different from the *kataplous* form,[366] which is Seven[)].

[345] Blake's inversion of the mythical structure of authority is important (for me) because it's just as Biblical as its predecessor. The authoritarians forgot that the central event of the O.T. was the Exodus, the refusal of Israel to live under the tyranny of Egypt, & that its N.T. counterpart was the resurrection, the refusal of God in man to live under the tyranny of death and hell. Also that the final (eschatological) events are repetitions of *those*, not of the giving of the law or the forming of the church.[367]

[346] Milton, as Blake realized, was quite able to distinguish the revolutionary from other upheaval movements: the devils in Book Two [of

Paradise Lost] are not plotting revolution; they are plotting the imperialistic conquest of a foreign outpost.[368]

[347] Steppenwolf is told that his werewolf myth about himself is a "mythological simplification," because everybody is hundreds of personalities.[369] But he goes on with his werewolf myth all the same. It seems that there is something numinous about all simplifications, even the early speculations that oversimplify. One would not attempt a NASA program on a basis of Heraclitus, but his oracles can be seminal just the same. Similarly of course with the gospel.

[348] Seven: the Romantic cosmos, discovered by Blake although Rousseau got the credit for it (I know he was earlier, but he kept to the discursive languages), was of course not a discovery of the new but a rediscovery of what had been buried. The seeds of an archaeological imagination were sown in the time of Byron's sojourn in Italy & Greece and Napoleon's in Egypt. The motto of Shelley's PU [*Prometheus Unbound*], the "Amphiaras" passage from Cicero, contains the phrase "sub terram."[370] Except that what's buried underneath and dug up may be submarine as well as subterranean, hence the reappearance of Atlantis in PU from under what Blake calls the sea of time and space.[371] No explanation for its appearance: it's just there. I must look at the two themes in PU that concern me in this context: the rejuvenation of Mother Earth and the anabasis of Kore.

[349] This Atlantis theme is the most solid link with the Bible I see at present: it corresponds to the hooking & landing of Leviathan, not as a monster in the sea but as the sea. Ballad of the Long-Legged Bait & "nothing but land" I must have somewhere.[372]

[350] Otherwise, this area seems non-Biblical, which is why I call it a secular scripture. It's concerned with man and the occult powers he's acquired or could acquire from Nature. So far as Nature is female, she has a redeeming role the Bible rather grudges her. In the metamorphosis downward recounted by Apuleius, Isis has this redeeming role, and A's [Apuleius'] Isis is explicitly linked by G. de Nerval to his Aurélia.[373] Aurélia (the name) comes from Hoffmann's Devils' Elixirs, of which more later.[374]

[351] Speaking of archaeological imagination, what is earliest "sub terram" material is paleolithic cave-drawings, with the intensity of their metaphorical identification with animals. Some of them are human figures in beast skins, a fertility symbolism that goes on for centuries.[375] Where I go from here is, first, to folk tale themes, then to Romantic systematizings of them, and then—this is still boggy ground—to the Orc-Luvah transition, the Eros figure of the divine child becoming the Adonis figure of divine sacrifice.[376] Xy [Christianity] seems to have dug this up from Judaism, but maybe not: Israel could be a Persephone figure.

[352] Folk tale themes and motifs: the animal helpers, the elemental spirits, the grateful dead, the animals who carry out impossible tasks, all belong to the theme of lost but recoverable powers of nature, the identity with "animal forms of wisdom," as Blake calls them [The Four Zoas, Erdman, 406, l. 31], that we've given up or never realized we had.[377]

[353] Magic objects are lost and recovered: when not lost they may turn into just ordinary objects. Dream-waking relations in the Sakuntala themes of forgetting (amnesia as the key to the dream) and remembering through some talisman of recognition[378] (note the link in Proust between this and "temps retrouvée["]; also the Winter's Tale "gap of time" [5.3.154]). Objects cast into the sea (of the unconscious) and recovered through a fish or simply, like Pericles' armor, fished directly out of the sea [Pericles, 2.1].

[354] Perpetual food: leviathan given Israel to eat in the wilderness [Psalm 74:14]; Jesus as the saving fish ("how can this man give us his flesh to eat?" [John 6:52]).[379] Fertility rites are charms for rebirth in another form, and rebirth is the type (not a demonic parody really, though it could be one) of resurrection.

[355] Surefire romance themes are the buried treasure and the secret society that finds it. One would expect such themes in Tom Sawyer & Treasure Island, but they are also in the first book of Paradise Lost.[380] Unfortunately such a theme can readily turn pathological, as in the Nazi myth of a conspiracy of Jews sitting on the world's gold. Incidentally, the mythical kernel of such folk tale themes as the hero with golden hair (Grimm) is the sun passing under the world at night from west to east.[381]

[356] Eventually the dreamer & the hero he dreams of consolidate in the figure of the double or doppelganger. This figure may be hostile (Poe's William Wilson, the double in Aurélia, & some in Hoffman) or helpful (two brothers theme).[382] The hostile develops toward the polarized brother-struggle theme so prominent in the Bible. All identical-twin themes are linked to Narcissus, of course: the self and its reflection as an object. Look up Lacan and perhaps Otto Rank on this.[383]

[357] According to Jung, the hostile double is a "shadow," and eventually turns into a soul of the opposite sex (anima for man; animus for woman. As I've said elsewhere, I don't believe in the animus except as something sick: the woman is sufficient to herself).[384] This means a mystic marriage in the psyche below the level of consciousness—quite different from the Song of Songs one.

[358] The Resurrection, then, is the marriage of a soul & body which forms the spiritual body. The body part of this marriage is female: the empty tomb is recognized solely by women, except for that fool who stuck Peter into John's account [20:1–10]. (Perhaps the "and Peter" of Mark [16:7] was stuck in too.)[385] The fact that Jesus took on flesh in the Virgin's womb has certainly been dinned into Christian ears often enough; but the fact that he took on flesh in the womb of the tomb at the Resurrection, and that there's a female principle incorporated in the spiritual body, seems to have got strangled. The real tomb of Christ was the male-guarded church. Maybe here I should deal with the essay in *Shirley* or Genesis 6:1–4, where the story is not the standard curse-the-woman crap, but splits in two, half of it becoming the wedding of what she calls Humanity and Genius.[386]

[359] At what point does the struggle of brothers turn into a father-son struggle? The Christian story as one of which the Oedipus story is a demonic parody is one of my main themes. What look like father-figures (I'm *sure* I've got this elsewhere [par. 342]) are often usurping sons, like Zeus: Jehovah is unusual in having no father. Stinker-father & stinker-son do their best to sacrifice each other, to get *their* knife in first. I suppose Boehme was trying to separate the real Father brought to recognition by the Son from the Nobodaddy creature who's really Satan, but has the same ancestry.

[360] I think I can work out an argument for Seven: it's what to detach from it and put in *Eight* that's really the bugger. Seven, though it's in the Bible sporadically in the form of tales that have folk tale analogies, like the Samson stories, Jepthah's [Jephthah's] daughter, the birth of Moses, etc., doesn't seem Biblical. But it's really the *under side* of the Bible, the story of the first Adam rescued by the second Adam, the dream of history that wakes in kerygma, the amnesia of Israel that eventually recognizes its God, in Xy [Christianity] through the talisman of the Resurrection of the body with its five wounds.

[361] Miscellany: "don't touch me" is better [than] "don't cling to me" [John 20:17] (me apton: some scholars think the original was me pton, don't be afraid). Rabboni, in the same passage [vs. 17], is a word normally addressed to God. Too bad for Isaiah 7:14 the word "maiden" didn't occur to the LXX translators: would the word "kore" [girl] have been available? Above, the beloved disciple got to the tomb along with Peter: that plus the curious Epilogue (chap. 21) does look like something stuck on or in by a cult. Surely I've got my "vulgar fraction" crack somewhere about 14½ zodiacal signs: numinous simplifying.[387]

[362] "Supposing him to be the gardener" [John 20:15]: well, that's what he was, and Mary M. [Magdalene] was identical with the garden at that point.[388] Oh, God, I wish I could WRITE. That apocryphal remark of Jesus about when you put the inside & outside, male & female, etc. also belongs here.[389]

[363] Also, there are subterranean themes in the Bible: I think Job is one; I've never figured out Joseph, but he's clearly another; there's Jonah & Tobit of course, and the Dives-Lazarus reversal.

[364] I think my distinction between the historical & the personal aspects of Jesus could expand in the direction of showing how only the personal has the power to be recreated. The most primitive societies think of their significant acts as repetitions of myth: repetition in the present is what ritual is all about: the "truth" of the Virgin Birth is not whether the accounts in Matthew & Luke are historical facts, however factual, but in, say, Meister Eckhardt's [Eckhart's] sermon telling us that every Christian has an obligation to become a virgin and bring the Word to birth in his own soul.[390]

[365] That's one of the places where I want to WRITE: another is wherever I explain the illiterate vulgarity of the question: "Do we have to believe in God in addition to all this?" If the word "spiritual" has any function for you—and even Marx uses it—your God is alive, & you don't have to think in such stupid terms as "*a* God."

[366] I must cover my ass about Blake's horror of natural religion & later of Rousseau;[391] he's all Prometheus, & gives up Adonis to the female will.

[367] The secret society, Robin Hood's band in the forest, the Grail knights (I have Melville & Ishmael's discovery of Queequeg), seem to have an egalitarianism, though this theme lends itself all too readily to paranoia or perversion (i.e. emergence with a new authority).

[368] I wish I could get more *eating* into Seven—after all, it *is* the Adonis chapter, and along with eating, sacrifice. I've said that this Seven stuff is not explicitly Biblical but the under side of the Bible [par. 360]; yet there was a time when I felt that sacrifice was *the* central theme of the Bible. Trouble is (or one trouble) that there's so much of it already in GC.

[369] Oh, God, I do want Eight to be terrific: a big recognition scene where the Resurrection redeems a female Nature, where Word & Spirit evoke the original Father, the god before the gods, where apocalypse renews & transforms the creation, where the U-shaped comic ending reverses the cycles of history, where resurrection abolishes rebirth and revolution-culbute abolishes revolution-turning wheel.

[370] Regarding the personal as amenable to myth & repetition: whether the Virgin Birth "really happened" is inorganic: even a historian who believes it couldn't work it into a historical narrative. Eckhardt's [Eckhart's] statement that every Christian can be a virgin and give birth to the Word[392] is personal. Historical facts are in the cloven fiction of yes and no.

[371] Mallarmé's "Cantique de Saint-Jean" deals (among other things) with the paradox of time out of time, absorbing into human experience what Davies assigns to God. "Burnt Norton" deals with the Christian kairos, the descending movement of the Incarnation (though perhaps

one shouldn't call that kairos). The reverse movement is in Shelley's "car of the hour arrives":[393] a passage in P's [Prometheus'] opening speech mentions this. The passage of homogeneous hours rolls along until there is a mutation.[394] This, applied to the apocalypse, is the real kairos. Los is the Spirit of time, repeating the prophetic message of "in that day."

[372] The Resurrection peroration & the gardener belong, I'm pretty sure, to the end of Six. *Eight* has (a) a concentration on metaphors of *time* (hither to space, as images are objects in space). Evolution the model—applies to nature. Progress is the authoritarian perversion of this, along with social Darwinism. (b) a concentration on the ∪-shaped myth of comedy, in Rousseau, the Communist Manifesto, & the Bible (also McLuhan & perhaps the rise of existential metaphor in the sixties). (c) why did God "choose" not a national, much less an imperial, community, but an aggregate of *tribes*? Tribalism, in short, is a theme.

[373] Philip Gosse's rationalizing of creationism[395] sounds stupendously silly, but from the point of view of this book it is not really without sense. Creation is not God doing something at the beginning of time; it is the revelation of the order of nature spread out as a revelation before a conscious being, at the end of an immensely long process during which man was not conscious. Note that the argument of Job follows precisely this argument—oh, God, look where you're going. Anyway, Eight has to recapture some of the narrative interest of the opening chapters.

[374] I don't know if I'm gonna get anything to eat in Seven or not; but I think the Frazer bit belongs in Eight after all. I've said that Eight revolves around time: the conception of evolution dominates it. Evolution gets perverted into "a man is the lord of creation" hierarchy, which even if it's true is a very dangerous state of mind, because of the way it leads to exploiting nature. That in turn gets corrupted into progress, where "civilized" means "better weapon technology" and "primitive" means those who get enslaved or exterminated. The moral horror of progress, however, is less in imperialism than in sacrificing the present to the future, which is precisely what the killing of the divine king is all about. *Do ut des* means: I give now; you repay me later (or you're a cheat, suppressed). The prophets say that God never signed any such damn contract.

[375] Then there's the kairos moment which is in but not of time (I think

that may be a clearer formulation than Eliot's). That is, it isn't linked to sequence. The moment of opportunity, the *right* time, often turns up in a tragic or ironic context in Shakespeare. The mysterious "hour" of Shelley's *Prometheus* is kairos in another context: it sounds phony, but so does the kairos estin engus [the time is near] of Apocalypse. Its metaphorical kernel is the unknown but inevitable moment of death.

[376] The *missed* moment, the peripeteia, which starts the cycle turning again, has fascinated me ever since I met it in the Chih-kai Bardo. It's in de Quincey, of course, and in FW [*Finnegans Wake*], where I've dealt with it.[396] I don't know if the renounced quest belongs, though it's central in PU [*Prometheus Unbound*]: in Macbeth the completing of a revenge quest sets time free, & I suppose Pr's [Prometheus'] renouncing of the curse on Jupiter that keeps Jupiter in business does the same.

[377] I should leave the *social* (tribal) descent for Eight.

[378] I'm again at the point in the book where I wonder if I know what the hell I'm talking about. What's ahead of me in Seven is the double, and the argument should trace him from shadow (Narcissus, shade in Hades, pure illusion void of substance) to hostile anti-self (Steppenwolf and its "mythological simplification," Poe's William Wilson, Hoffmann's Devil's Elixirs, Salvator Rosa, etc., de Nerval's anti-self in Aurélia, the struggle of brothers theme radiating out from it) to Lacan's alienated ego, to the final point where the real body is Los & *not* his Spectre, the spiritual body in fact, the Second Adam who takes over from the first.[397]

[379] I think that's straightforward enough: it's the interchange of my reality and illusion argument. But in Jung the shadow turns into the anima; in Shelley Mother Earth is rejuvenated into a bride-sister, and I wonder if a lot of what I now have in Six shouldn't go in Seven. Is there a lower-world marriage where Mother-Earth rejuvenates? Alchemy hints at it in its ritual marriage of red king & white queen (Alice again).[398] Donne's Canonization & Shakespeare's PT [*The Phoenix and the Turtle*] may belong here after all, because of the close association with death. Death of course is the ultimate screwing of the Mother. Certainly Dylan Thomas' Winter's Tale sounds like that.[399] The NT, apart from the Easter women, gives us no help on this: perhaps that apocryphal remark does,[400] but it's pretty oblique. I've never said explicitly that the Xn [Christian]

Nativity & the Xn [Christian] Pieta correspond to the Venus-Eros & the Venus-Adonis relation, but perhaps they should. (Hell, I mean they *do*: perhaps *I* should say so.). That means saying explicitly that Christ is an Eros figure as well as an Agape one. The O.T. isn't much help either, except for the beauty of Job's daughters.

[380] The basis of the female-garden identity is that the alienated subject, the Moi, can only confront an alienated object. In proportion as the ego-feeling switches over to the spiritual body, the object becomes an emanation.

[381] I hope I don't have to try to crack that infernal Jung book again (Mysterium Conjunctionis), though its existence shows how important he thought the theme was. But, as I've said [par. 357], I don't believe Jung's animus really corresponds to the anima: all humans are symbolically male, and they all have animas. The animus is part of something still residually alienated, like the female in Nietzsche or Paul.

[382] The attendant or guardian spirit who guides the descent—Virgil in Dante, Raphael in Tobit—seems to be just that:[401] he doesn't take over the personality. If female, such a spirit would be an Ariadne figure.

[383] I may be in for a lot of transferring: if the tribal *society* is what the Promethean descent is all about, my medieval conspiracy theories go in Eight. Tribalism ought to be opposite of racism—Queequeg & Jim. It also ought to be the opposite of a sexist or sectarian group. I wonder if it's a classroom or symposium. It's like the society that forms around Job at the end, the regenerate form of the false society of the "comforting" accusers.[402] The trial (AW) [*Alice in Wonderland*] is the parody of the banquet symposium (TLG) [*Through the Looking Glass*].

[384] The Word ascends in two stages: the Transfiguration and the Ascension proper. Blake says: "Know that after Christ's death, he became Jehovah" [*The Marriage of Heaven and Hell*, pl. 5]. When he ascended to his Father, he was assimilated to the inexhaustible source who is the real Father, the antitype of Satan-Nobodaddy the sky-scarecrow. The counterpart was the former of the apostles with the gift of tongues.[403] That's in two stages too, I suppose, the first being the Last Supper. I'm blithering, and I'm lost.

[385] Perhaps the four levels of time and space go all the way back to Five. And I think I should say that making male & female sexes the symbols of human subject and natural object was confusing & perhaps wrong, but we're stuck with it.

[386] Emerson, American Scholar, speaks of Swedenborg, as a visionary of the lower world, making analogies between the repulsive and the evil that are typical of what I say about nausea in Swift.[404]

[387] Eight, the Prometheus chapter, doesn't say much about Prometheus: the Titan Albion-Finnegan figure who's all men.[405] This is the total man whom the small esoteric society will eventually waken. I must get Five & Six from Jane[406] and start rearranging. The Mut. Coes. [*Mutabilitie Cantos*] go in *Six*: Mutability herself is the Triple Will, hell & earth thrusting into heaven, and her lawsuit (trial) winds up Six. Now I have to work in the Transfiguration or true metamorphosis.[407]

[388] Judaism is wrong: the tribal society has to expand into a gospel to the whole world. And Judaism is right, because if it didn't stay out the unified would be (as it was) perverted into an attempt at the uniform.[408]

[389] Where does *nothing* go? Seven, if I'm right, & *Igitur*. Despair, the desire not to be. And where does deliverance from *duration* go? The pressure of ancestors and the genetic code? Surely in Eight. Ancestors turn up in Igitur. Find out more about Foucault's idea that "mankind" didn't appear as a concept before the 17th c.[409] Certainly the Albion-Finnegan all-men-as-one-man image is Romantic, as are most of the developments of the Titanic Arthur myth (Barbarrosa),[410] though that's more like Tolkien's Return of the King. But the metaphorical possibility was always there, even when, as in Egypt, all men *were* the Pharaoh. Also the Kingu myth of the dismembered God.[411]

[390] Re the androgynous Adam: the anxieties of a patriarchal church denied this (Augustine, natch). I should explain at greater length that an originally male Adam makes no sense in the *sequence* of the myth: also that the undeveloped doctrine of mother-virgin-bride indicates a heavy censorship in this area.[412]

[391] Let's see, now: Eight should have the *social* or secret society de-

scent, the esoteric analogue. This small group wakes up the universal man, or all men, explicitly in Xy [Christianity] and Marxism. I want kerygma to get beyond the antithesis of esoteric and exoteric, and not be simply the "proclaimed" exoteric.

[392] Start again: the Frazer & Oedipus clusters seem to be the peroration themes. Deliverance from duration (history) too. Time certainly, evolution & progress themes as above [pars. 372, 374], progress leading to the Frazer cluster & the psychology of sacrifice. Maybe buried here is the "do this in remembrance of me" [Luke 22:19] that's always confused & puzzled me: continuity plus sparagmos, the invisible or spiritual single body being substantially present. Where's literature in all this?

[393] A secret doctrine is a seed-doctrine: a condensed intuition that grows and unfolds into first myth & then kerygma. Secrecy appears in the gospels at the last supper, the betrayal, the undercover arrangements for the Last Supper. In the Frazer myth, the divine king is first there; then he's dismembered, eaten & drunk by the tribe, & vanishes into the lower world: their guts.[413] Some of him reintegrates the tribe into a single body—his—the rest gets shat. That's the bodily part, which reintegrates as a spiritual body: the soul part, which is also spiritual, ascends. I dunno. The reality of this seed-kerygma progress is education, as I've said. Literature is seed: criticism is the kerygma of what's in literature.

[394] Surely your passage on shit & corruption is pretty sketchy: you've left out the whole *baptism* bit: the descent into the water to wash off the dirt. A descent that's also a death, separating the drowned Egyptian (or Phoenician, for Eliot [*The Waste Land*, pt. 1, l. 47]) from the redeemed Israelite. The return from the lower (submarine) world has to be balanced by the return from the subterranean: one is new life from "birth" ("water and the spirit" to Nicodemus [John 3:5]), the other new life from death.[414]

[395] Secrecy: the narrative or sequential kind, where you're teaching chapter one, and conceal chapter two, which depends on it, until tomorrow. The ironic kind, where the *teacher* asks the questions to create a space for the student's mind to grow. The esoteric kind which is academic freedom, protection against the malice of fools. The apocalyptic kind, where you explain something with complete lucidity to someone

who says: "I don't find this convincing." *Nothing* can be done about such people: that's one of my auguries of experience. They're self-censored, and while all censors are irrational bigots, the self-censored are the worst.

[396] Another of my auguries of experience is that there are two kinds of theory. There are the dialectically organized theories, which lead to interminable argument & create innumerable schools, schisms, sects & cliques. Then there are theories that lead to theories, to a synoptic view of the subject. Those who complain about being imprisoned in my "system" are looking at it as an argument. But if I go to the top of the Empire State building for a view of Manhattan and see the Chrysler building, what I say is "there's the Chrysler building." I do not say "that's where the Chrysler building fits in."[415]

[397] End of 4: this is where literature & the Bible really meet, so it's the climax of the narrative. Myth is the content of literature, and literary criticism is the kerygma of literature. Myth is the content of the Bible, and Biblical criticism is kerygma. The transition is both one of contraction and of expansion. Contraction is map-making, putting the whole area into a portable and intelligible form. Expansion is recollection in tranquillity. Here's Morton Smith's book proving that Jesus was precisely what Blake said he was not, an ambitious miracle-monger.[416] Maybe that's what his contemporaries saw: it can no longer be what we see.

[398] One: a metaphysical "system" is a spatial metaphor; since Hegel at least all our modes of thinking have been put on a temporal basis, so that we now think in terms of arguments or narrative movements. Dialectic has come to mean increasingly a sequential or narrative use of conceptual language, with the traditional procedure of consolidating the false opposite & throwing it away.[417] The phrase in *Steppenwolf*, "mythological simplification" [pars. 347, 378], is immensely useful: it's Occam's razor in mythology, and my whole spiritual > natural mythical dialectic is based on it. Ordinarily, the opposition of reality & illusion is based on the fact that there's one reality and innumerable illusions: I'm trying to follow Prospero & reduce the rabble of spirits of illusion to one illusion— which is the work of art (drama).[418]

[399] The journey into chaos, Satan's Miltonic journey in reverse.

Nietzsche's will-chaos, more concrete than Schopenhauer's, was nihilism. There may have been a positive "transvaluation" goal at the end, but he never saw it; he settled for a Dionysian mock-heaven praising the affirmation of life eternally recurrently. He wasn't a proto-Nazi, but he deserved the reputation of one: if we compare him with Yeats, who stuck his nose much further into the Nazi mess: with his prophetic ability *that's* what he should have been obsessed with, not Xy [Christianity].[419]

[400] Robert Graves told Jay[420] that everyone was either a murderer or a suicide, meaning, I suppose, that the sado-masochist cycle hits everyone somewhere. He added that all the nice people were suicides. That's Nietzsche again: he couldn't get clear of antithesis & cycle, so he keeps saying down with the suicides, up with the murderers. The ass brayed yea.[421] If I put the Antichrist into my double dialectic, I should quote "And is old Double dead?" [*Henry IV, Part II*, 3.2.58]

[401] The double is a huge and daunting subject: there's the shadow-double (Hercules in Hades in the Odyssey), the twin-double (Amis & Amiloun),[422] the mirror or portrait double (Dorian Gray), the mechanical double (Frankenstein, though not strictly a double)[,] the *Erbfeind* [old enemy] double (William Wilson), the anima double (Twelfth Night, PU [*Prometheus Unbound*]), the animal double (Steppenwolf), the spiritual double (Blake's Los & S of U [Spectre of Urthona]) and a double dozen more. My clues are Lacan's alienated moi, Jung's shadow > anima, the Biblical first & second Adam, possibly Otto Rank.[423]

[402] I must have written—in fact I know I have—about Don Juan and Faust as tragedies of love and wisdom respectively.[424] True, Goethe's Part One is really a Don Juan story. Hoffmann's fantasy on Don Juan, which I think profounder than Kierkegaard's, takes Juan as a Lucifer defying a God he despises—a very Nietzschean Juan.[425] There's a strong suggestion that "hell" is a vulgar anticlimax for what really happens; and the Oedipal suggestion of Donna Anna as the tragedy of a redeeming mother-figure is there too. Heathcliff is someone very close to his [Hoffmann's] Juan (as Edgar is to Ottavio).[426]

[403] It's the second part of Faust that, as I've said [pars. 68, 146], drags him off to heaven as the original Faust was dragged off to hell (cf. the "done for" & "redeemed" aspects of Gretchen (the wimp brother is there too, even if he isn't really a wimp) at the end of Part One) [*Faust*, pt. 1,

ll. 4580–4612]. Faust Two *is* a tragedy of wisdom, though one that relates very oddly to Goethe himself. Too much science (all that Vulcanist-Neptunist crap) and not a tight enough grip on mythology. Dangerous as it may be to say so, Goethe simply didn't know enough about the Biblical tradition.

[404] Joseph, in Genesis, has always totally baffled me: he bulks so large and so crucially in the Bible's greatest book, but what to make of that I don't see. I've encountered several times the assertion that he's a type of Christ; but what's really Christlike about him? I've investigated Mann,[427] but without result. The one thing that interests me is that he descends to Egypt and becomes, not the Pharaoh or temporal ruler, but his adviser, a Castiglione courtier. Castiglione's book has always fascinated me, although it would be easy to call it a futile and silly book, because it grasps what for me are the central myths of education: the guardian angel teacher, the attendant spirit who doesn't interfere with the ruler's will but whose advice directs and shapes that will. That would make him a type of the Spirit rather than the Word.[428]

[405] There's a link here with something that always has gnawed at me: that Genesis is a book of descent, moving from Eden into Egypt, & Exodus, of course, is the re-ascent. I've been groping too for some link in Seven or Eight with my educational ideals; but maybe I should save them for the core of my next book (which of course I could make a whole book of public lectures) on More's *Utopia*, Castiglione's *Courtier*, Morris's *News from Nowhere*, & Butler's (nominally) *Erewhon* and (actually) *Life and Habit*.[429] Rounded out by some rereading of Plato, Rousseau (*Émile*), Engels (*Anti-Dühring*). That'll keep.

[406] I've just reread the first four chapters, and I think they'll do, even though I'm a bit disappointed with the tone of Four. Two or three sentences in the Introduction to take care of the polemic part of it, a sentence clarifying the spatial "system" and temporal "argument" (I might even incorporate, perhaps in a footnote, my Musil quotation).[430] But I'd like to expand the Prefatory Note into an "interchapter," making a real transition from Part One to Part Two. That would stick the two parts irremediably together.

[407] Two things, one limited & the other big. First, in the *Anatomy* I passed beyond "new" or rhetorical criticism (without knowing much

about it) because I was dissatisfied with its lack of any sense of context as a part of literary meaning. Right now I'm passing beyond post-structural criticism (without knowing much about that either) as a mode with no context either, but simply a reinforcing of an "anything goes" in literature itself with an "anything goes" in the critical approach to it. I don't think I want an explicit reference to this (there wasn't one in the Anatomy) much less any hostile comment (if I did that I'd have to read more than I want to of the stuff). But in my view of the Bible as a model of kerygmatic criticism, which I think of as getting past the imaginative creation for its own sake without going back to the old ideological dialectics, I think I'm passing beyond "deconstruction" into a reconstruction no longer structural. (Actually that was all in GC for those who could read it there.)

[408] Now, the big thing. I have to insert my four levels of time & space into Five, and expand my four-level cosmos, however repetitive. Also I've been ducking Dante & Hegel, who belong *here*. I'll reread it, but I've devoted the first ten or twelve pages to my "journey" metaphor and I don't think they fit. I think a journey paper might well go into Twelve Essays,[431] as one of the group including the Wiegand lecture,[432] and I'll go back to that paper, modulating into something else when I hit Jacob's ladder. But I rather doubt that it belongs here—I've left out some good things, like Roethke's poem.[433] My original reason for including it was that it picked up the narrative themes of the opening chapters.

[409] No, I'm wrong: I've been more ingenious than I thought. The journey stuff does belong, but perhaps I should expand the "Prefatory Note" into an interchapter that will both summarize Part One and introduce Part Two. In it I should put, in a very oblique way, the myth-kerygma point across [par. 407]; also the demonic parody and displacement points I've got; also the counterpoint of Biblical & extra-Biblical myths. Then, perhaps, the journey as the central narrative (*mythos*) > kerygma transition.[434] Then in Five I can put the levels of time and space at the end, and bring it level with the other chapters.

[410] I still don't have anything to eat in Seven, although I promised it in the present version of the Prefatory Note. Perhaps the descending self gets eaten by the double, or vice versa: what the member of the tribe eats is what he's one with. Well, it could easily come out of the PN [Prefatory Note], and I still lean to the idea of combining the Oedipus & Frazer for a smash ending.

[411] Re the Xfn [Crucifixion] bit at the end of Three: the "historical" view is once again "in the beginning was the act (event)," and the words are servomechanisms. The presentation through myth tells us that our longing to crucify *somebody* is a state (cf. that Dickens idiot, "far better hang wrong f'ler than no f'ler" [*Great Expectations*, chap. 52]) in which the victim (not enemy, as I have it) is God. That's what brings all other crucified victims into focus. But crucifixion itself (if not of Jesus, certainly of other people) *is* historical: it's different with the Incarnation (including the Virgin Birth) and the Resurrection, which are not historical but irruptions into and out of history from another dimension. As "this really happened" events, they split the response into the yes-people and the no-people, but even the yes-people can't fit it into history, which accommodates only the historical. These belong to the up-and-down thematic stasis, and their reality is not "this happened" but "this can happen." Meister Eckhardt [Eckhart] makes sense on the Virgin birth.

[412] The second-level sense of place as home or kindly stead explains why the chosen group is tribal, not national or imperial.435 Creativity decentralizes & breaks down: even technological progress is toward simplification.

[413] I wonder if Seven can be built around Frazer & the Eucharist, and Eight around baptism (seed of fire in waters: the dialectic of cleanliness & filth[)]. Certainly no, I'm wrong—baptism *at present* belongs at the end of my shit & corruption passage, death being the ultimate shit.436 The only thing that disturbs is the Adonis-Prometheus aspect of it, & that's not important.

[414] But: Eucharist means descending to earth & rising in air; baptism, descending to water & rising in fire. And maybe shit & corruption does [do] go in Eight, with the demonic fall & the human body image. It seems tacked on where it is. If death is shit, the Eucharist is a type of resurrection—well, of course it is. No, I think both sacraments belong in Seven, whatever goes in Eight.437

[415] I'm re-reading Hoffmann, and working on Seven certainly makes it easier to see what his pattern is. In "The Golden Pot" the hero is in love with two women, one a pleasant commonplace girl who dreams of being the wife of a Hofrat [privy councillor], & thinks he'll be one, the other appearing as a snake on a tree who's a daughter of an "Archivist,"

actually a salamander who lived centuries ago in Atlantis. The hero settles for the snake girl & her home in Atlantis; the other girl marries another man who does become a Hofrat. So the hero renounces the ordinary world for an imaginative one "below." But Hoffmann's conception of the double is so flexible that it's quite possible that the action takes place on two levels, that the two men & the two women are actually one.[438]

[416] [E.T.A. Hoffmann's] Fräulein von Scudéry (I thought using actual people in stories was a modern device, like Freud in [D.M. Thomas's] *White Hotel*) must be about the world's earliest detective story, and it's a perfect example of the genre, complete with catastasis. That is, the police have worked out a plausible but false solution, & then the great detective reverses it into the true one.[439] The catastasis story is a more complex version of the type in which a series of episodes is rearranged to provide a meaning, as in Melville's story *Benito Cereno*.

[417] Then there's the Salvator Rosa story,[440] an extraordinary treatment of the double theme, as the painter is also an actor in a commedia dell'arte, & is also sponsoring a runaway marriage of a younger painter & a delectable young woman who's imprisoned by her miserly & senile uncle who wants to marry her (dispensation needed). Figaro situation, of course. Hoffmann is obsessed not only with doubles but with daughters with mysterious magician-fathers—I think that may be a central lower-world archetype. Here's the one farcical treatment of it I've found: the old boy is cured of his miserly & lecherous humor by seeing his double (S.R. [Salvator Rosa]) on the stage. Except for the faint Sophia traces, there doesn't seem to be much of this father-daughter archetype that belongs in Five or Six. I suppose what Chamisso's Schlemihl loses in his shadow is his lower-world context:[441] Hoffmann's reversal of this makes the "reflection," evidently, the persona: that's why it's so silly to lose it. Vampire theme along with it.

[418] Insight is kerygma with a subjective focus: it's what Nietzsche or Kierkegaard or other prophetic writers have. What's missing is the sense of canon: many writers making an individual writing community. The context of a writer is, first, his other writings; second, his *Zeitgeist* historical and cultural context; third, his generic context. But none of this makes a *canon*.

[419] Rousseau says in his first work that as he has nothing left to hope or fear for, he's "in peace at the bottom of the abyss," a poor unfortunate mortal, but as unmoved as God himself.[442] Except for "mortal," that makes him Lucifer (disregarding the paranoid whine).

[420] I've been worrying about the absence of Seven material in the Bible; but there's of course a series of dream visions from Abraham to Joseph. After Moses, though a lot of it gets banned (Witch of Endor) [1 Samuel 28], it revives in the prophets. And, of course, even Jacob's ladder is itself a dream. I think I see here the larger pattern of Eight beginning to form. From shit to schekina in six easy jumps. From nothingness to somethingness; from somethingness to horror; from horror to wrath; from wrath to judgment; from judgment to charity; from charity to beauty; from beauty to glory; from glory to presence. Sounds vaguely kabbalistic.

[421] Rhetoric has always meant both the moral or persuasive and the tropological or figured. That's because it's intermediate between the dialectical and the poetic, deriving its kinetic aspect from one neighbor and its ornamental aspect from the other. Nothing new here, of course, but it's better to get these things as clear and explicit as possible.[443]

[422] So the poetic has an ideological aspect that merges into rhetoric, and an oracular aspect that merges into kerygma. I've been ducking this point, but if it all doesn't get into Four it has to emerge in Eight. I can hardly say explicitly that it's the function of criticism to see a super-kerygma forming out of literature; but what else do I mean? And what else does the book mean?[444]

[423] I've fastened onto the *axis mundi* because that's the central *dianoia* symbol, the type of everything in myth that's counter-historical. Also it's the only possible imaginative basis for the new creation that kerygma proclaims. Coincides with my point about the objectivity of the meridian of longitude.

[424] Quote the Brobdingnag king on humanity having instead of reason a quality fitted to increase its evil qualities, instead of what you have.[445] Don't preach: don't allow a syllable of preaching.

[425] In reading Goethe, or reading about him, I have often been discon-

certed by a certain vulgarity and tawdriness in his mind, his ideas, even his personal life. I can't help wondering whether this isn't simply because he was a "great man." The same thing is much more obviously true of Victor Hugo. Some renunciation of "greatness" seems essential to the highest intensity, that intensity being the revelation or kerygma which is what literature points to. "Greatness" is linked to the heroic, of course: these two fit Carlyle's "Hero as Poet" category, but Shakespeare doesn't, nor does Nietzsche, whose real "greatness" is in his renunciation of greatness. Another Eight point, I think.

[426] What's new in the previous note is that "their vulgarity does not detract from their greatness" should read "they were vulgar (fell into vulgarity occasionally, of course, is what I mean) *because* they were great." Nietzsche's Superman, on the other hand, is kerygmatic man, and he's appeared at least once in Jesus.

[427] I suppose there must be books on "the dream in the Bible," but I won't have time to read them. I said in GC that the OT was primarily law to Jews and primarily prophecy to Christians [*GC*, 84]. Prophecy comes through hallucination, trance and dream: it's a volcanic explosion from below, and it sets the law on fire and burns it up. Only I doubt if I can say that. The reason is (I say) not that I'm afraid of antagonizing readers who are Jewish or liberal Christian, but that I have so genuine a love & respect for Judaism (as Christ did). I'm back to my metaphor of the fire of life that reveals and the fire of death that annihilates.

[428] I didn't finish my hero note: the hero as poet, like all other heroes, is a tragic figure working out the dialectic of the divine and the human. The tragic unites the heroic with the ironic: the ironic residue, so to speak, is the *poète maudit*. The ability to write very well very easily may lead to Kierkegaard's disease: the esthetic barrier against the kerygmatic. Shakespeare was saved (perhaps) by the fact that he couldn't be a great man or public figure, yet even he wrote the Merry Wives of Windsor, which, no matter how much can be found in it (I found most of it) is basically crap. Dante & Milton are closer to being genuine (whatever that means) hero-poets, but of course they stuck to the kerygmatic source.

[429] Re spirit: the overtones of "spirited" and "sprightly," like many of the overtones of *esprit* and *Geist*, suggest the exalting of conscious-

ness. It's true that phrases like "in good spirits" have their origin in proto-medical theory, but even *those* spirits climb ladders. Nietzsche's *gaya scienza*.[446]

[430] What's on the other side of kerygma? I think that in a way it's a return to the descriptive, but not the "literal" descriptive that postulates the non-verbal. It's rather Stevens' "description without place," which Stevens says is "revelation," referring to the Biblical book [*Description without Place*, pt. 6, l. 1]. Revelation itself *is* kerygma: beyond it is the world of words as seen by the Word. Most mystics say that this stage is beyond words: Paul still hears language, though a language that can't be repeated "here" except in incarnational form. The descriptive-literal is the old creation, man looking at what God hath wrought; the post-kerygmatic descriptive is the new creation that follows the apocalyptic or winding-up of kerygma.[447]

[431] Longinus, you idiot. Why did you leave him out of chapter four? Most of him is the fragmentary, oracular, individualized, that's-for-me kerygma.[448] In proportion as kerygma becomes continuous and holistic, it becomes social as well. The new narrative however is the reader's life, not the old narrative in the text.[449]

[432] The Bhagavadgita XV speaks of the axis mundi as a tree, but speaks of eventually cutting it down [vv. 1, 4]. Getting rid of the here-to-there ladder image is implied all through my Part Two, and should be a theme of Eight. No way, as they still say. This of course nullifies the opening "journey as metaphor"—Heraclitus' up & down motto.[450]

[433] I think Four is reasonably clear now except for the absolutely crucial question: what *really* is the difference between low & high rhetoric, ideology & kerygma? Perhaps I can't really answer it until the end of Five, but some obvious things are there now: ideology tries to control the imagination and direct it: kerygma as *I* conceive it doesn't. One believes that in the beginning was the act; the other believes that in the beginning was the word. One works within the categories of society as it has them: the other invokes categories like eternal & infinite.

[434] Five should incorporate a cut-down prefatory note at the beginning, and end with the categories of time & space. It should also make

clearer the fact that every vision of order gets debased by being turned into a (purely ideological) vision of authority. There are always three versions of an archetype: the purified kerygmatic version, the authoritative ideological version, or vision of authority metonymically though positively related to it (best you can do for now), and the demonic parody. In Five the kerygma is a vision of order in creation, where authority is internalized; the ideological analogy is authority, the descent of power & ascent of obedience; the parody is the descent of tyranny and the response of anarchy. Lear starts with the analogy of authority, descends to the tyranny of Cornwall answered by the anarchy of the storm. Out of this Lear gets an insane glimpse of genuine order, consolidating on his love for Cordelia.

[435] Although Five & Six are the Parnassus peaks of wisdom & love, the main emphasis is on descent in Five & ascent in Six. The presiding genius of Five is Hermes, the psychopomp who brings the dead to their natural place, the thrice-great teacher of wisdom, the trickster and thief that snatches our lives away when they start to get interesting and fills our senses with illusion. Seven and Eight are in emphasis (*both* movements are *always* there) the descent of love and the ascent of wisdom (Freudian slip, maybe: I'm very ambivalent about all this).[451]

[436] Six needs clearing up: the two orders of nature are still there, but there are at least two aspects of them. In one, lower nature is red in tooth & claw,[452] the anarchic nature of ruthless competition where the predator rules. The upper level is that of the equally ruthless exploitation of nature by man. Then there's the "real" imagination-based nature, beautiful & tamed on the upper level and sublime otherness on the lower level (dramatized in the light & dark heroines).[453] Shirley here.[454]

[437] Eros is primarily a reversal in time, a movement toward reversal of youth (*Faust*) or childhood (*Purgatorio*). Hence the first movement is toward the mother, or more accurately the virgin or inaccessible mother. It goes back through earlier stages of history & culture, often idealizing them (both the Bible & Renaissance-Classic & Romantic-medieval idealizings show this; also Virgil, even Homer's bronze age), its ultimate goal a lost Paradise. Here possession & being possessed are the same thing ("know as I am known" [cf. 1 Corinthians 13:12]). So primarily there's the ascent to the virgin mother, the hortus conclusus who's also Paradise, sometimes represented by the moon at which a phallic moun-

tain points. Beatrice first appears as a scolding mamma: Matilda is the image of pre-sexual innocence.[455] Fern Hill.[456]

[438] The demonic parody of this vision is, of course, the vision of the siren's cunt ("ventre") in the Purgatorio[457] and Faunus glimpse of Diana's cunt in the Mut. Coes.[458] Beatrice appears to expose nothing but her yacking mouth. Beatrice is above: everything regressive about Xy [Christianity] is in her. The actual Eros goal however is something for which the polymorphous perverse is a better image than the genital.[459]

[439] The Eros theme is connected with the progressive loss of the shadow: in the Adonis descent-of-love world, where the shadow falls between action and consciousness,[460] the shadow or double becomes a primary feature (not prominent in the Bible, but cf. the Witch of Endor's summoning the shadow of Samuel [1 Samuel 28], and, of course, the Hebrews conception of the Torah as shadow [10:1]). Hence the cult of the synchronized orgasm as an Eros symbol today: spontaneous merging of action and consciousness.

[440] Buber says (I must check) there's something maternal about his Thou.[461]

[441] Prometheus is forethought or ascending wisdom, leaving his shadow-bound brother behind along with Pandora. Pandora is a baggage: that is, she's identical with her box.

[442] There seem to be three stages: the virgin mother, who represents the analogy of authority; the forgiven harlot, and the bride. In the Bible the archetypal harlot is the Rahab who allowed the Israelites to penetrate into the moon-city of Jericho, and so destroy the moon. In Dante the "moon" extends over Mercury & Venus as well: the earth's shadow, & Rahab comes at the end of that.[462] The bride can't appear in an orthodox Xn. [Christian] poem. All this takes more shape for me as in my old age I enter Yeats's "dreaming back" phase.[463] Once Helen was gone she became Ariadne: my love for her intensified and entered a new life, and that's my road to the stars now. I only wish the "unforgetting" process would be more extensive.

[443] Considering what I've learned from Shakespeare, there isn't much from him so far. Leontes kills the anima inside him, but she revives at the

words "our Perdita is found" [*The Winter's Tale*, 5.3.121] although Perdita, like the second female in MT [*The Mental Traveller*], has to come to the man she loves [l. 49]. Each man kills the woman he loves, but finds her alive again after she's been hidden. The Tempest world is submarine & temporal: the renewal of the previous world, symbolized by Milan, doesn't amount to much, except for the seed of something genuinely renewed in the F-M [Ferdinand-Miranda] marriage, the vision of the world saved from the flood, and the chess game, whatever that is.[464] Perhaps chess, like the sword-mirror-purple flower complex in Yeats's dialogue, is "emblematical of love & war" [*A Dialogue of Self and Soul*, l. 19], the Adonis world caught up & sublimated.

[444] God knows I know how much of this is blither: it makes unrewarding reading for the most part. But I have to do it: it doesn't clarify my mind so much as lead to some point of clarification that (I hope) gets into the book. Hansel & Gretel's trail of crumbs.

[445] Postponed "consummation": Miranda doesn't get her cunt popped until after the play's over, though Perdita I think does. *Does* she really marry Florizel? Shakespeare's audience obviously fussed over such points.

[446] I should cut the passage about all texts being incarnational: it's probably bullshit. It may even arise from an impatience with the anxiety of Jewish scholars to get rid of them. In Christ there's a progression from incarnation (natural body or flesh) to epiphany (spiritual body): all his post-Easter appearances are epiphanic. I've said in another notebook that epiphany is to pneuma what logos is to incarnation [11e, par. 17]. Christ as flesh was the end of the physical creation: the world spread out for understanding as object. The incarnation is also the end of all "in" metaphors: the soul in the body, God in man, man in the world. Note how "in" begets hierarchy: the Ptolemaic onion begot the chain of being. But "in" also suggests the ascendancy of sound or hearing over the vision that's "out there." Epiphany is not really out-thereness, but helps to overcome the domination of in-ness. The demonic parody of incarnation is life in death, the ghost of Hamlet's father who refuses to stay in Hamlet. Or find it's Mother Nature in whom we live and move and have our being as embryos. The person *in* the substance is another aspect of the same thing.

[447] I think this "in" business should go at the beginning of Seven, in view of the way that down and in are connected. Doesn't that apocryphal remark of Jesus begin "when you make the in outside"?[2465]

[448] I've just reread *To the Lighthouse* and am now rereading *A Passage to India*. The first has three sections: an exposition, an analytical or sparagmos development, and a recapitulation. Two themes: getting to the Lighthouse and the painter Lily Briscoe's vision. Neither comes off in Part One: in Part Three they come off simultaneously: Mrs. Ramsay holds a society of 15 people, including a husband and eight children, together in Part One: she has nothing to do with the failure to get to the lighthouse, but does seem to have something to do with frustrating Lily's vision. In the middle section she and two of her children die. I'm not sure I've got it, but the theme of descent in the middle is essential. In PI [*Passage to India*] there are three parts, the middle one again a descent. Xn [Christian]-Moslem axis in One; Xn [Christian]-Hindu in Three: in between the descent to caves (which contain mirrors) disintegrates the society and takes them down to the bedrock of pure ego (I compared it once to the voice in Dostoievsky's Notes from Underground) that turns Mrs. Moore from a Hindu goddess into a tired & crabby old woman (my narrative sequence doesn't fit the book, but it doesn't matter).

[449] I think Eight should be a "recovery of myth" chapter, summing up the kerygmatic points of the book, & hence should include something about education as internalized authority, & how internalizing it doesn't affect its objective aspect, merely purifies it. Also, if I'm right about the in as down [par. 447], Seven is a highly individualized and psychological chapter that Eight should counterbalance.

[450] Five: going up the ladder is normally an individualized mysticism, as in Plotinus. Plotinus has no sense of community, hence no sense either of what Jesus meant by a spiritual kingdom. But (I need to add this to the Preface to Five) on the P.R. [*Paradise Regained*] principle that Jesus redeems as means what he renounces as ends, I think Xy [Christianity] also redeems the Plotinian flight of the dove. It puts up a signpost indicating the correct path in the Transfiguration (metamorphosis): Jesus as the total Word. That's why the Mut. Coes. [*Mutabilitie Cantos*] has to go into Five (the Diana-Faunus theme, the descending metamorphosis, is for Six).

[451] The statement in GC [112] that there were pagan & Jewish gnostics as well as Xn [Christian] ones is misleading, & should be so characterized in a footnote. I intended a distinction between Gnostics & gnostics, but it's still misleading.

[452] The climb up the ladder from the surface of this earth is a climb out of history. The climb up from the subterranean world to the surface of this one is a climb *into* history: its type is the Exodus, the beginning of the history of Israel, and its antitype the Resurrection.

[453] It's bloody confusing to read in Revelation that the redeemed are all male virgins, never "defiled" with women [14:4].[466] Not that anyone ever took it—well—literally: cf. the 14th c. *Pearl*.[467] Its demonic parody, as I've said [par. 242], is Genesis 6:1–4: the Rev. [Revelation] bunch are sons of God who stay where they are, & don't go "whoring" after lower states of being. Gen. 6 is in Eight, along with *Shirley*: I think, incidentally, that "giants" [Genesis 6:4] really means "heroes," & that God is really saying he won't have the divine-human alloy or mongrel that's the Greek hero. Cf. the age of heroes in Hesiod.[468] Incidentally, I've got just about nothing on the *tragic* quest: some of it goes in Six under the white goddess, some of it may be in Eight, as in that giant-heroes verse.

[454] Cyrus says that the descent-to-the-Mothers passage in Faust II, which is so endlessly suggestive but nothing more than that because Goethe himself didn't know what he was talking about, may turn on the fact that in German mütter & mythe make a pun.[469] That links the passage with what I've always thought (and often said, unfortunately) about the myths in Morris's *Earthly Paradise*.[470]

[455] One thing that seems to have got squeezed out of the old Six is the crack about the people who understand everything but don't know anything because they lack the energy to know.

[456] The Bhaktin [Bakhtin] "dialogism" seems to be the turning of ideological autonomous discourse into a broken-up autonomy of imaginative writing.[471] Maybe what Bhaktin [Bakhtin] says is infinitely subtler & more complex than that, but I'm losing my superstitions about the infinite mysteries concealed in whatever I don't know. Whatever's in him, the academic rabble is capable only of picking up one idea packed in bullshit.

[457] I used to say that Rev. 12 is a third version of the birth of the Messiah,[472] and I still think I'm right. But I might compare it to the Matthew-Luke infancy narratives at the beginning of Five as an example of what I mean by undisplaced myth.

[458] Six is pretty complete now, except for Diana's cunt in the Mut. Coes. [*Mutabilitie Cantos*] as a white-goddess metamorphosis,[473] & for the Wordsworth-Traherne child as close to Eden (part of the Eros climb as a journey toward youth).[474]

[459] I think my Bhaktin [Bakhtin] hunch can be considerably expanded for the beginning of Seven, where "dialogism" involves drawing on the resources of one's inner community. God speaking to Job, for example. It's the beginning of what I'm starting to think of as the tremendous vision that takes control of Eight, what Blake would call the building of Jerusalem, the spiritualizing conquest of reality by positive illusion, *nearly all of which is unknown and unconscious*. The creative artists are important because their works are the only visible and audible models of what is going on. The rest of it is a mysterious process in which the activity of God takes place through human beings, both the living and the dead. This last brings back Jung's sermons to the dead, one of the few things in Jung that have really held me: the notion of the dead as not knowing "it" all, but continuing to learn through the living.[475]

[460] The elemental spirit is the spark in nature touched by human consciousness: things like Annie Dollard's [Dillard's] (I forget her name) teaching a stone to talk and some book on my shelves about how a spirit in a stone can be evoked.[476] Such a spirit is to a natural object as a dog is to a fox or wolf. There are two such spirits in this room: the Chinese lady, who's a guardian spirit, and the African reliquary. Helen loved them both, so they're not just objects, but have something of what they were designed to be. There are undoubtedly evil spirits too, but not here. I didn't mean to get off on this tack.

[461] Hölderlin's *Brot und Wein* ends with a communion image where after a period of absence & exile the gods will return, earth & its fruits supplying the bread and the thundergods of the sky the wine.[477] This would go nicely in Six, but I wanted communion images for Seven. Hölderlin also has a late and unfinished poem to the Virgin Mary in which he treats her as transitional, a figure of the present exile & absence,

just (or much) as I do.[478] He'd make a footnote: I'm not sure that I want him in the text. His remark that every pure source is a riddle (Der Rhein)[479] is a Job point again.

[462] Also, keep in mind Hölderlin's last poem, on "Spring," especially the last two lines about everything coming to unity and identity in Spirit, mostly out of Nature. Also Keats's letter about a vale of soul-making.[480] Blake's Jerusalem, of course, is the new Jerusalem of the Everlasting Gospel, not a Jewish, Christian, or eclectic city. A city where you can't tell God from man except by the absence of evil.

[463] Six: don't forget the male-female things ascribed to Jesus in the Gospel of Thomas. The Gnostics didn't know much, but they did have that hunch, and they may have had proto-Boehme Urgrund hunches I should look into.

[464] Five: I've been waffling around this, but Five deals with kerygma as the presentation of the world as an order to which the appropriate response is understanding. That makes it still to some degree objective, even though understanding is a latent or potential creation. That's why Six is needed to complete the vision of creation through illusion. Beauty is always something of an illusion, but it implies a more intense creativity. That's why Five is really a descent theme *from* an upper world (see the 124–25 note [par. 435]), although both movements are there, as descent of beauty is also in Six, though the emphasis falls on ascent.

[465] Seven: the "descent" to a "lower world" has the added complexity of moving from the "out" to the "in" world (128 [pars. 446–7]): thus Milton's Satan "falls" to a down world, but the fall is an image of being imprisoned inside himself—S.K.'s [Søren Kierkegaard's] shut-upness.[481] Similarly with positive descents: Anodos in *Phantastes* is making a journey into himself that's really a cathodos.[482]

[466] The release of repression in *Emile* leads to the Savoyard vicar and his natural religion, and natural religion is a red herring, a new form of literalism or constructing verbal replicas of the non-verbal.[483] The traditional fear of idolatry does have a genuine kernel: the word comes from the lower, out of *nothing*. Faust's mother, Mallarmé's Igitur, Boehme's Urgrund, Heidegger's Das Nicht, are some of the efforts to grasp this. Also, I suppose, the St. John of the Cross ascesis Eliot talks about.[484]

[467] The reason why natural religion is a red herring is that one can learn from nature only what is natural, just as one can learn from history only what is historical. (This last is why I call it "illiterate" to believe "in" (accept as historical) what breaks the pattern of history, like the Virgin Birth or the Resurrection.)[485]

[468] What "natural religion" obfuscates is the emerging descriptive power of language (which couldn't really develop until the sense of its limitations had also developed). Humanity was being differentiated from animals *and* God, not simply placed on a chain between them. I wonder if this is connected with Foucault's idea that "man" is a post-17th c. conception.[486] After all, it's part of the same chain-break as the Copernican revolution.

[469] Re above: language reconstitutes itself in the Void: it first seems to be refunding our confiscated gods,[487] but these are only by-products of a realization of literature as the nucleus of language. This is Seven: one needs to go deeper, into the gods before the gods, for Eight.

[470] Josephus compares the Titans to the rebel angels [*Antiquities of the Jews*, 1.3.1], and while titanic and gigantic are different, these "huge and mighty forms" are also the "giants who formed this world" of Blake's MHH [*The Marriage of Heaven and Hell*, pl. 16, l. 1], the "giant forms" of J.[488] On the upper level Genesis 6:1–4 is about a Hesiodic age of heroes; on a deeper level it's about the entrance of the demonic into human life.[489] Similarly with the superficial & the occult meanings of "dukes of Edom" [1 Chronicles 1:54].

[471] I wonder if Chapter Five is really final: seems to me there's a point about "mere words" still to be clarified. This is coming to a head in Seven, where the sense of a reality transcending or completing the verbal seems insistent (e.g. in John), & yet the sacramental mummery (as I see it now) is as footling as any other "literalizing." Or conceptualizing: we can't say that spirit is form and word—well—"matter" (i.e. energy).

[472] In Blake the "Spectre" sums up the shadow world: the "spectre" insists that he's the "real self," but he ain't. I've always been puzzled by Blake's denigration of the "memory," which he certainly knew was essential.[490] Perhaps his "memory" is the past but persisting subject, corresponding to the past but persisting object of "female will."

[473] The one unanswerable question is, what is the relation of death to life? Everyone agrees that death is the end of life; everyone feels impelled to add the word "but." What follows "but" is where the yacking starts. Not exactly hot news, but I want to get around the form of the question that starts with something assuming an unchanged category of time, like "is death the end of life?" In the N.T. death is a necessary stage to be passed through, symbolized by baptism. All sacraments are metonymic, *put for* the spiritual experience.

[474] "Who hath seen me hath seen the Father" [John 14:9]. That is, every Father is the Son of another Father, as Zeus, the Father of gods and men, was the "usurping" (Milton's word) Son of Cronus.[491] The usurping Son blocks out the Father: that's the Oedipus setup. The incarnate Son is the manifestation or epiphany of the Father.

[475] One dream I've had: the second part of Eight might be a more detailed account of four levels of vision. The Mutability Cantoes are second-level: the Transfiguration metamorphosis, the Ovidian metamorphosis or Diana's-cunt level, & the final Sabbath vision, all belong there. The top level would almost have to be Paradiso 33, the lowest level perhaps "Byzantium," which I feel I understand better than *Igitur*. The Adonis level is up for grabs, so far: maybe something like Keats's *Endymion*. No Shakespeare: I wish I could get rid of my Catholic incubus about *Cymbeline*. *House of Fame*?[492]

[476] The two elements in Cain, the farmer and the smith, relate to Seven & Eight respectively. What separates them is the murder, the human-sacrifice act. After this Cain goes into a wanderer or exile stage that's a parody of the Abel or Psalm-23 wandering, a descent from the "kindly stead"[493] into the alienating space-world. This last joins Cain with Israel, even with Christ, who had nowhere to lay his head. The benevolent wanderer returns in Rcsm. [Romanticism]. (Wordsworth's *Excursion*.)[494]

[477] I am not (directly) concerned with the familiar complaint that the elaboration of critical theory makes literature less accessible to the student instead of more so, but I am concerned with a direct & inductive response to literary experience.

[478] The Witch of Endor [1 Samuel 28] is the Biblical counterpart to the

summoning of Thersites in the Odyssey.[495] Presumably (I don't know) she's accustomed to the vague entities that drift through seances willing to claim any identity suggested, and she's utterly dismayed and terrified to find that she's tapped a genuine world of spirits, & that she's invoked the "real" ghost of Samuel. As I have always thought Samuel the shittiest prophet on record, I don't wonder he turned up: if not technically an evil spirit, he'd be full of spite and malice.

[479] I'm reading a book that impressed me, Gopi Krishna's *Kundalini*. The introduction writer says we in the West need a new vocabulary for spiritual reality,[496] a thing I strongly felt in writing Chapter Four (and might perhaps add: see p. 135 [par. 471]). Even the commentary is rewarding, though it's by a Jungian.[497] (Note: during the war I had racist prejudices against Germans, feeling that there was nothing so dumb as a dumb Kraut. When Jung started talking about Jewish consciousness and the dangers of entering into Oriental attitudes, the farts of a dumb Kraut polluted the air: I think he outgrew that, at least in that autobiography,[498] but (as with Spengler) I distrusted the dumb Kraut for a long time.)

[480] Anyway, Kundalini woke up in him accidentally and almost literally buggered him: I wonder whether prayer, the sacraments and the like aren't really forms of *sedation*. Masturbation too, considering where she is.[499]

[481] One thing the Jungian said was that there's in each of us a collective mind (this sounds like something quite different from the collective unconscious).[500] I suppose it's originally the hallucinating voice of wisdom, urging caution & prudence and obeying social conditioning. It chatters and jibbers incessantly inside me whenever I'm writing, and is a bigger hazard than the steaks frying in my ears. That's why I can't read hostile critiques of me: most of them come from people who have nothing but a collective mind, so all they do is externalize all the monkey chatter I keep hearing anyway. Whether this collective mind is in Jung or not, it's certainly in Samuel Butler as well as in me.

[482] The narrative of Seven is fairly clear now, though it'll take a lot of work before it's a convincing narrative. Now everything depends on Eight: the narrative of that will make or break the book. This is one of those totally unhelpful notes I can only stare at.

[483] The people with collective minds, above, have only *idées reçues* for its (their) content. They're the people I referred to who understand but don't know. Knowledge is based on recognition, a sense of fitting together: the mere understanding I speak of is this in the purely objective, or rather objectified world; real knowledge is based on conviction, the subjective complement of the same thing.

[484] Tree of planets (arbore): Paradiso 18:29. Maybe cut the saetta sentence, but put in the Marsyas-Glaucus point (i). Identity of I & me in 19 (Giove, sphere of justice). Contrast of approach to the Hebrews definition of faith in 24.[501] Dante's journey through earth, air & fire: his journey *metaphors* are mostly sea voyages.

[485] Again, I keep thinking of improvements to Four that may belong in Eight. One is the goal of spiritual authority, the authority of experience established in science, & which I try to establish an analogue for in literature. Another is that the reinforcing of consciousness "below" gathers material for language: the intensifying of consciousness "above" is often said to go beyond words into the wordless.[502] It doesn't really: it's still linguistically structured, but the intensified speed & efficiency gives that effect, just as every highly competent skill contains details not consciously attended to.

[486] It's easy to accept the proposition that there was a historical teacher and martyr known as Jesus of Nazareth. It's easy to accept the Christ or Messiah myth of a Virgin Birth, Resurrection and Ascension of an Eternal Word who is Son of God as, in a mythical context, a coherent and intelligible myth. Even though it is a concoction of Old Testament prophecies, and involves some very screwball interpretations of the Old Testament. But the centre of Christian faith is the identity of these two things. What kind of identity? If we say historical identity, we're involved either in fundamentalist irrationalism or in Bultmann's "demythologizing" crap. If we say, as I do, metaphorical identity, aren't we going in some aesthetic or Docetic direction? I have to come to terms with this in some both-and way.

[487] At the top of the ladder words & thoughts attain such high speed that we're unaware of them (SB's [Samuel Butler's] unconscious knowledge). With this higher unawareness the sense of succession-time disap-

pears, or perhaps moves into a new dimension. The demonic time are uniform moments waiting for a mutation.

[488] I started AC with a hunch about centripetal & centrifugal directions of verbal meaning [AC, 73–4]. This has expanded into a tendency toward individual & a tendency toward "oceanic" consciousness. Now, an individual is a community in a state of cooperation. I've spoken of the different linguistically structured aspects of our personalities:[503] they're members of the individual Parliament representing the cells & bacteria which are the population at large. (If they really did represent them, our health would be superb.) Well, I suppose God also is (a) one and (b) maker of all things. As one he's nothing, as there's *no* individual; as all things he's epiphany or manifestation or Word that proceeds out of nothing.

[489] If the last note on 139 [par. 487] has anything, St. Augustine was right in saying that time was a product of the fall. So, perhaps, was continuity by reproduction (although "be fruitful and multiply" [Genesis 1:28] belongs to the P account). So is tradition. So is evolution and its historical by-fiction progress. There's no progress, but there is an accumulated consciousness, preserved through memory, which eventually makes for a qualitative change. The Dante of the 13th c. is "below" but grew "above" it into further centuries.

[490] I have no idea what I'm talking about, but I'm struggling with reflections derived from Butler's *Life & Habit*, trying to get both the Priestley lecture clear and Chapter Eight.[504] I think Eight is potentially a tremendous vision, covered up with the caked dirt of my own ignorance, confusion, prejudice, and sense of loss, so I approach it cautiously like a picture restorer: every silly and blithering note may uncover some original color from another quarter-inch. But it'll take a long time at this rate.

[491] After saying that a hen is an egg's way of making another egg, he [Butler] goes on to say why we find the statement bizarre. We can trace the silent processes by which the egg becomes a hen, but when a hen lays an egg she cackles (and we're very impressed by noise) and we see an egg where previously there was no egg. So a hen laying an egg connects in our minds with (a) revolution and (b) special creation out of nothing by the word. An egg becoming a hen connects only with evolution and

repetition. (In the P account cackle and bird are separated into different persons, but they're both there: the egg ought to be there too, as it is in Orphic and Hindu (Phanes, Hiranya-garbha) myths.)[505] I've always been fascinated by the Hiranya-garbha myth, the seed of fire in the midst of the waters (Radhakrishna[n] says its the Logos),[506] the prototype of Prometheus' fire in the fennel-stalk. In the P account there's the waters, the brooding bird, and the light. I suppose an egg would have stuck another "literal" object in front of the idolators.[507]

[492] Butler is superb, not on the cosmos of existence, but on the cosmos of persistence, the continuity and the persistence of memory and identity in time. He doesn't consider reincarnation except in its hereditary form. One of the books I thought had some clues was Itzhak Bentov's *Stalking the Wild Pendulum*. He says meditation can discover reincarnation as a fact (I've always doubted this) and that we survive death as a "body" of information.[508] I find that word irrelevant: most of it's misinformation, and does misinformation go to hell? Better to say we survive as the Word-body we have made, & then integrate with the Word. I hope all my twitches mean I'm cutting off pieces of my Word that offend me so I can enter the kingdom without them. I don't really want to *know*: all knowledge is a limitation of hope, and my hope is both irrational and infinite (as my dedication page suggests).[509] If the ultimate reality in the world is love, there can be no love without recognition. I suppose "love" is the conscious tip of an iceberg that goes down to automatic (if it is that) "attraction," or cohesion, as in (I think) Empedocles. The flight of the alone to the alone is a lot of crap: there's no such thing as an individual: that's one of the hierarchic illusions. Every individual turns out to be a functioning community. And if everything is community, and love is reality, love must include recognition, which is also discovery, anagnorisis. Recognition is the "moment of truth" in a real and not a slang sense; also it's what holds a work of art together (at least in moving arts, like literature and music).

[493] Don't forget the emphasis on spiritual authority as the only kind that enhances the dignity of those who accept it. All personal authority comes from teachers who want to stop being teachers. After his Ascension Jesus stopped being a teacher, and his authority then became simply the authority of the Word. The Spirit, we are expressly told, has no authority of his own: he's the subject entering into the authority.[510]

[494] On p. 140, top [par. 488], I think I was expounding Boehme's doctrine of the Ungrund. God is one; there is no individual; therefore God is nothing.[511] Or one and nothing are, as in modern computers, the two aspects of everything. God made all that is: hence all that is is an epiphany or manifestation. Of what? Of nothing. What did God make the world from? From nothing, that is, his own nature. This is, I suppose, the real Sunyata or void, not the *hebel*-void of "vanity."[512] An epiphanic creation is a model for our recreation.

[495] Perhaps add to 4: I don't "believe in" the Virgin Birth as a historical fact, but I "believe in" it as a poetic myth. That could mean (though it doesn't) that I don't take historical facts seriously. It certainly does mean that I take myth (and literature) very seriously indeed. That doesn't mean (once again) that I take seriously what they *say*: what I take seriously is the structure of what they present.

[496] But if I'm asked about the "Jesus of history," even about the Resurrection, things get more complicated. The revolutionary element in Western myth makes a point in history essential.

[497] Kundalini is the ouroboros, the serpent coiled up chewing her tail. She's also the coiled-up seed, the seed of the spiritual body. According to Gopi Krishna[513] & others, if she wakes up without warning she'll kill you or drive you nuts, because she's going about the city & seeking her beloved, who's in that mysterious cranium chamber. She may wake up in a near-death experience; she may be locking up gently without one's knowing it.

[498] I distrust all the evolutionary hypotheses connected with meditative techniques, partly because they restore the pyramid-hierarchy of aristocratic levels leading to God the monarch. And they're all *above*, at least in Itzhak Bentov's book, which is very good.[514] Why do I have some above & some below? Because the poets put them there. And why do the poets put them there? Because of the revolutionary culbute, which they tend to leave out. As man has decided to transform his environment instead of adapting to it, it's probable that the word evolution, in its traditional sense, no longer applies to our future. The rules of the game have changed.

[499] This last remark turned out to be the keynote to the Butler-plus-ne

paper I did for Felp at Lethbridge.[515] Along with it went the contrast between habitus-hexis practice memory and conscious memory, recalling the past into the present. I said the former was a control of time, the latter merely an awareness of it.[516] The argument should become a central part of Eight.[517] But *what* is Butler's unconscious? It's not Freud's repressed unconscious, or Jung's archetypal unconscious. It's the Promethean unconscious that will eventually become a superconscious (after all, it's Butler I quote on this).

[500] The up and down metaphors are spatial projections of psychological in and out metaphors based on the cloven fiction. After they go, the ladder, like Homer's chain [*Iliad*, bk. 15, l. 19], is pulled up.

[501] Some archaeological bugger has just "discovered" that the Exodus is a myth. Well, it's central to the Bible, and everything in the Bible that isn't a myth is an excrescence. *When* will people learn that the Bible approaches history *from above*, that it's subsumed in myth? The purely historical belongs to experience: every event is unique. The purely mythical is simply repetitive, & belongs to knowledge and conscious memory. Practice or habit memory, in its social aspect, develops the repetition of myth into the crisis or kairos of history. It was this perception of "historical process" that has made Marxism so powerful a movement in this century. But the belief in historical process has spawned some horrible superstitions in our time: it can't seem to manage the vertical lift that would take it out of the future and put an end to history.[518]

[502] I can't get rid of the recurrent feeling that the basis of organization of Part Two is all wrong and leads to an intolerable thinness of texture. Some of it I was seduced into by the desire to use papers I'd done earlier, e.g., the "journey" bit in Five.[519] And yet that does belong, only I left out the Biblical archetype, the journey *from* Egypt *through* the wilderness *to* the Promised Land *by* the guidance of God (Christ in Paul [1 Corinthians 10:4]). The "by" and the "through" tend to coalesce, making the Egypt-desert-P.L. sequence the model for the Inferno-Purgatorio-Paradiso one. In the middle section is ordinary human life: that life is either a journey to death or a purgatorial journey (vale of soul-making), and that the presence of God is what makes purgatorial sense of life. Similarly with F.Q. I [*The Faerie Queene*, bk. 1], only I don't want to repeat GC.

[503] The Introduction gives Rev. 12 as undisplaced birth-of-Messiah myth,[520] but should anticipate the demonic-parody theme with Jacob-ladder vs. Babel, Tamar vs. Lot's daughters (Tamar was Judah's daughter {in law}, incidentally).

[504] People have always known that metaphor was deeply rooted in the Bible: St. Thomas Aq. explains this of such phrases as "the hand of the Lord" [*Summa Theologica*, pt. 1, quest. 2, art. 1]. But they don't seem to have drawn the inference that metaphor is *functional*, or the inference that its presence *excludes* descriptive accuracy.

[505] Wonder if I should rescue Michael's critique of some recent fool & incorporate it into the introduction, however briefly & reluctantly.[521] Theories of polysemous criticism seem to me to rationalize the inability to read what is there. I'm so lucid I seem to nag people into "construal" readings, and they don't like it.

[506] We can only exchange metaphors, as they're the bedrock of language. Five starts with the journey which is horizontal, from here to there, as typified by the Exodus. That turns out to be a metaphor for the vertical journey up (purgatorial) and down (natural, towards death). This comes to a symbolic climax in Moses, the only one to see the Promised Land, the only one except Elijah (and Enoch) who didn't die. (The Michael-Satan dispute indicates the double nature of his end.)

[507] The up-and-down metaphors, which establish the *axis mundi*, turn out to be metaphors for an in-and-out journey. But those are misleading too, because it re-establishes the subject-object duality we're trying to get rid of. So we realize that that too is "only" a metaphor for the spiritual-natural contrast in Paul, which again is hard to talk about without the metaphor of "levels," which suggests the up-and-down projection again.

[508] What Stevens calls the "metaphor that murders metaphor" [*Someone Puts a Pineapple Together*, l. 27] is a metaphor not realized to be a metaphor, & so "taken literally." Note that such an unrealized metaphor becomes metonymic, i.e., the "best available" metaphor, & so starts us on the downward path of authority & hierarchy. The Biblical archetype of

this is the dream of Joseph of ascendancy over his brethren, which pushes them all into Egypt [Genesis 37:5–11].

[509] My distinction between *habitus* or practice memory and awareness memory is probably close to Bergson's "matter & memory" thesis.[522] The ultimate that all the journey metaphors point to is the contrast between free creative action and imprisoned brooding inactivity: Blake's memory of the Selfhood, the Spectre of Urthona's despair, is linked to the role of awareness-memory as an *accuser*, fighting the power of deliverance.

[510] Among the ambiguities of "nothing" ("there is nothing to be afraid of" and Heidegger's "dread reveals nothing"[)] there is the supremely terrifying "there is nothing to stop you." Hitler & his like hear only the first half of this, until it's too late.

[511] One: I don't say it's possible for a philosopher to be totally disinterested: I say it's possible for him to adopt the literary convention of the impersonal. Adopting a convention is a momentous choice: being somebody is only a condition. There are disadvantages: when the in-here-and-out-there metaphor is adopted by conceptual writers, it suggests, as it does everywhere, the subject-object cloven fiction; but in conceptual idiom it gets stuck there.

[512] I wish I could express this business of concept as *frozen* or *stuck* metaphor more clearly: in particular I wish I could convey the sense of utter unreality the phrase "Is there, or is there not, a God[?]" has for me. The disagreement between theist & atheist is a dispute over the verbal formulas that have no meaning. That's been said as far back as logical positivism, except that they thought that only the theistic view was meaningless, which means they got nowhere.

[513] My original hunch, that because Job is not a participant in the creation he can be delivered from it, was sound, I think. But he's a participant in the new creation that's established in ch. 42. The old creation was only God: it climaxed and ended with the creation of a conscious being who could repeat the Sabbath vision. The new creation must have man, because God wants it that way.[523]

[514] Does the fact that descriptive techniques of writing don't start to

mature until the 17th c. have anything to do with Foucault's thesis that the conception "mankind" came into existence then?[524]

[515] People get the end of *Huckleberry Finn* wrong: they think it's a Katzenjammer Kids comic strip with a dishonestly happy ending. Tom Sawyer is portrayed all through this book as a Quixote figure driven out of his mind by silly books. But if he were only that he'd be a pathetic figure, and he's not: he's a calculating person, intercepting his aunt's letters with a psychotic's casualness and knowing all the time that Jim was legally free. He wanted the adventure of it, he says, but Jim takes all the risks; he doesn't really, even if he does get shot in the leg. In short, he's exploiting Jim like any other slave owner, but on a level of cruelty so refined that Jim (and Huck, who's also being exploited) can't understand what's going on. I read somewhere that Mark Twain planned a story in which Tom sells Huck into slavery, which shows, if true, that he quite realized what an utter creep Tom Sawyer was.

[516] Critics, or people adopting that position, are curious people: because I'm fascinated by the spiral-staircase shape of Hegel's *Phenomenology*, I'm immediately described as a Hegelian. Partisanship is even more automatically assumed in philosophy than in literature.

[517] I'm trying to reread Kierkegaard now: I don't find him an attractive personality, because he seems to play the same cat-and-mouse game with his reader that he did with poor Regina—and that God played with Abraham and Job. He's a trickster writer, in short, and interests me because a literary critic sees him as doing the opposite of what he thought he was doing, obliterating the barriers between the aesthetic, the ethical, and the religious. That is, he's clearly a "metaliterary" writer, like Dostoievsky, Kafka and perhaps Nietzsche (well, Mallarmé too).

[518] I probably don't understand his conception of repetition, & perhaps I'm not intended to. I wish I could be as confident as Karl Barth that I'm "forbidden" to deal with things that don't interest me anyway. (Cheap sneer, of course.) But perhaps, if repetition is eternity, as he says, maybe it's that apocalyptic contrast to Nietzsche's identical recurrence, which is the same thing as the orthodox Christian doctrine of hell. Dante's hell after death is not part of divine revelation: it's exactly what it seems to be, an invention of the devil, as long as the devil is in "his own

place," the traitor at the bottom of the human mind. When properly externalized, hell becomes an aspect of human life, and that's where divine revelation comes in. The ferret doesn't know it's ferocious and "cruel," man does, and the quotation marks around cruel fall off when the ferocity is conscious.

[519] (Directly across [par. 516]). Hegel thought that Xy [Christianity] was a mythological anticipation of the real truth of his own philosophy;[525] that makes him at least an honest philosopher, or rather theologian: all theologians attach belief only to their idioms.

[520] One question here is that of the symbol and what it's a symbol of. Conceptual writers from Plato on always think a myth is a symbol *of* their damn dialectic. But the myth is the self-contained symbol; that's *it*. So what's the "plus"? Partly recollection, in the sense of incorporating and accumulating the other modes. Partly too the waver between the panoramic and the participating apocalypse: you have to be sometimes an individual *observing* revelation, pointing it out, which you can only do in language that's symbolic *of* it. You have to sail to Byzantium as well as be there.

[521] Another thing that interests me about Hegel is the eating or cannibal image that ought to be my chapter Seven basis. The Absolute eats everything up to itself, like Pantagruel in Rabelais II: the *Begriff* starts at the hidden centre & ends *as* the circumference. In that sense the Phenomenology is an Odyssey, because that's what Odysseus does in the last twelve books. But after you've eaten everything you have to divide again to love or to reproduce. That's why Xy [Christianity] is so uneasy with any identification with God that goes beyond loving God. But you do go beyond, that God may be all in all [1 Corinthians 1:28].

[522] I haven't finished Four, though maybe it's in Five that I have the conception of an *angelos* as meaning that messenger and epiphany are the same thing on the spiritual level.[526] But what of the angel to be wrestled with, the God of Job & the Akedah? I suppose one clue here is the *reversal* of the action: Isaac is not sacrificed; Job is restored. Considered as stories, these reversals merely confirm the absurdity of the original situation; considered as myths of revelation—well, that's S.K.'s [Søren Kierkegaard's] "repetition."

[523] So there are two levels of myth: the story level and the revelation level. Hardly surprising, except that I don't want to be brought back to the "levels" metaphor. The absurd story reflects (still a revelation!) the irrational human situation, and so can't be replaced by some other verbal construct. Abraham is "justified" by his faith when his test turns into a trick or illusion: in Job we see the trick at the beginning. Of course poor old Agag doesn't get put together again [1 Samuel 15]: I have no algebra for him. (Algebra, in Arabic, means the reuniting of broken parts.) Tribalism, good & bad, is involved here.

[524] *Fear & Trembling*, we're told, is all about Regina, who seems to be, in the terms of Burnt Norton, the Muse of vacancy as Beatrice was of plenitude. No one can "condemn" S.K. for his behavior about her: if you do you start lying to yourself on some "I'd have done better" basis. But it is permissible to say that *Stages on Life's Way* is a tedious book—not that there isn't such a thing as creative tedium, as Beckett so well shows. *Repetition* is all about her too, but an important conception gets smuggled in in a very furtive way.

[525] Repetition develops, in a Hegelian way, spirally & through *aufhebung*,[527] in three stages. In the first stage freedom, existing in pure experience, dreads repetition as the thing that would spoil it; in the second it comes to terms with it, and as it were harnesses its energy (this is the *habitus*-repetition I got from Butler, though S.K. doubtless wouldn't think so); in the third freedom & repetition are identified, where repetition is eternity and a new creation. It's heaven, in short, just as Nietzsche's recurrence is hell (p. 149 [par. 518]), the place Antichrist goes to prepare for his disciples.

[526] Re my note on Hegel (bottom of 149 [par. 519]): what he did in theory S.K. does in practice, closing off his "literary" works with their pseudonyms and starting his "edifying" works with prayers. As I say, he achieves the opposite of this [par. 517]: his great books are literary, with metaliterary features: there are no "levels." He invariably says his most valuable things in the "literary" works, where he can pop on a mask and disclaim responsibility.[528]

[527] He also distinguishes memory & recollection, saying that children have excellent memories but no recollection (because no past) while old

people may retain recollection even if their memories are impaired or lost. It sounds as though "recollection" is the word that translates as *anamnesis*, and refers to an accumulation or structuring of the past.[529]

[528] *The Sickness unto Death* is a work of casuistry, an existential rhetorical form which is not kerygmatic, except in so far as it uses the Lazarus myth. It's another example of pre-mythical rhetoric usurping the post-mythical kerygmatic.[530] *Fear & Trembling* is also casuistry, though in a less concentrated form. Casuistry means that the ethical area is not one of freedom: it's a labyrinth. S.K. realized this, or came to realize it, in theory; but he never found a genuinely kerygmatic style: his "aesthetic" style is much the closest to it, but one in which a Socratic irony enters.

[529] To start with my own situation: I think in cores or aphorisms, as these notebooks indicate, and all the *labor* in my writing comes from trying to find verbal formulas to connect them. I have to wait for the cores to emerge: they seem to be born and not made. Because of this, continuity is associated with moral duty, as in Coleridge. This is old stuff. But *is* there a kerygmatic style? What's confusing me just here is the Kantian "the critical path is alone open," which historically means that the conceptual idiom is now permanently aware of a fully matured descriptive idiom contemporary with it. This quality of awareness recurs in the distinction between the genuine rhetoric that respects conceptual and descriptive integrity and the mob rhetoric that howls them down. It doesn't have to be conscious awareness: usually it's better if it isn't.

[530] The rhetorical idiom speaks out of an awareness of conceptual idiom (and descriptive, at least now), but uses figurative language as it were "unconsciously." Kerygmatic utterance has to show some awareness of the mythical & metaphorical (though again it doesn't have to be conscious awareness). I sound very muddled: I'm trying to get past the blocking metaphor of "levels" and superiority of one idiom to another. Knowledge *of* God is not more "important" or "higher" than knowledge *of* a flea: all knowledge conveyed by words comes from the Word.

[531] Six: the J creation myth tells us that we acquired a state of mind after the Fall that sets up two premises: "sex is shameful" and "God made it," with the conclusion, "God ought to be ashamed of himself" avoided.[531]

[532] Perhaps I can't get this book really clear until I've faced the complexities in the question: what is the *critical* idiom; what am I writing?

[533] Whenever I introduce kerygma I should speak about Kierkegaard & Tolstoy (perhaps Dostoievsky too). All these were great literary artists who wanted to "go beyond" the literary, but were confused about what idiom was appropriate. S.K. particularly didn't "go beyond" the aesthetic; he merely betrayed it, & the further he got from it the more obsessional he got. He simply went "back to" the dialectical. Such a metaphor as "back to" suggests levels again. Two things stand out: (1) the kerygmatic has to appear in a mythical setting or context (2) metaliterary writers usually come to grief over the assumption that the importance of what they produce lies in the importance of what gets *said*.532

[534] Oh, God, if Kierkegaard had only carried through his "repetition" scheme, instead of sneaking it out like a fart in the course of abusing a harmless reviewer for not reading what he hadn't written! I'm not clear why his three stages are related only by transcendence, or why Hegel's logic of immanent mediation has to be rejected. But I'm sure he did, at that point, though he lost his grip on it soon afterward. (I've just been asked to write an afterword for a book of Margaret Laurence).533 It doesn't matter that the context is one more ow-oo about Regina: that's the right context, a myth with enough "existential" urgency to push it in a metaliterary direction, a *Vita Nuova* in reverse, as I've said.

[535] For some time now I've been scolding myself for not reading a lot of the "good books" on my shelves, or opening them and not having the guts to finish them. Then I take book after book from my shelves and find that I've read it carefully all through, with marginal comments that prove I have. What gives? Is senility just the flipside of human existence?

[536] Re across [par. 533]: the whole "existential" movement revolves around philosophical principles closely related to literature (Kierkegaard, Nietzsche, Sartre, Dostoievsky, Kafka). It's really a "metaliterary" movement unable to find a metaliterary or kerygmatic style.534 In S.K. "aesthetic" works signed with pseudonyms constitute all his valuable work: he struggled to get beyond it, but could produce only dialectical & rhetorical forms (he says this in his diary, but I can't find the refer-

ence).[535] The Sickness unto Death is a work of casuistry, as noted [par. 528]. There's still the notion that when rhetoric leans away from myth & moves close to dialectic it comes closer to "truth."

[537] Nietzsche is subtler: he knows more of the literary answers. There's a famous passage in William James' VRE [*The Varieties of Religious Experience*] (which would be an almost definitive book on its subject if it hadn't used those absurdly tendentious "healthy-minded" and "sick soul" categories) where he says that on coming out of nitrous oxide he was aware of parallel worlds, some so close as to be entirely recognizable.[536] The world of Jaynes' "hallucination" is one such world: a world where God speaks.[537] That's where the kerygmatic voice comes from: a hell of a good universe next door.[538] Or sometimes, just hell.

[538] My own kerygmatic anthology would include The Marriage of Heaven and Hell, some fables of Dostoevsky and Kafka, the opening of Buber's I and Thou, some Rimbaud & Holderlin. *Zarathustra* I should disqualify for trying too hard. This is a purely subjective list of no value: I made it because it shows that *no* kerygmatic canon will ever be drawn up: it would be impossible to find a committee to agree on the selections.

[539] Rug-weavers in Islamic countries are said to leave some flaw or loose thread in their design: being formal designs, I suppose they could achieve "perfection," which would be a closed pattern of magic, a defying of God. You have to leave a hole for Allah to look through & see what's going on. Similarly, holistic views of perfected art are an opaque & resisting surface of ego: think of all that tedious waste of time in which Henry James revised his novels, refusing to allow them their own lives. Well, refusing to allow *himself* a life: didn't he develop and change styles like everyone else? So he turned a row of novels into a logocentric canon.

[540] Heidegger says that while conventional metaphysics says being is essentia, & essentia is prior to existence, the statement "existence is prior to essence" is still a metaphysical statement.[539] Evidently he wants to go beyond metaphysics into a metametaphysics. He knows that what he's after is connected with poetry, and quotes Hölderlin and Nietzsche and writes poems of his own, but it's no good (at least as far as kerygma is concerned): God doesn't speak from *that* world. Open Buber's I and Thou & we hear the voice at once. It seems equally obvious to me that an "Antichrist" is still a figure in a Christian universe.

[541] Kierkegaard makes a remark in his Diary I should not have expected him to make: it turns on the assumption that we're born with a "soul" or vital consciousness, and that "spirit" takes much longer to develop, appearing as the child of the soul-body (here of course I'm reverting to me).[540] Young people are "psychic," full of soul & body, & shouldn't be exposed to the serious issues of Xy [Christianity] until at least their forties, when enough spirit may have developed to take it. The implication that his father was an obsessed old fool who warped & stunted his life by giving him the full blast at once in childhood is one he doesn't allow to emerge very often. This principle is one that could relate James' preposterous "healthy" & "sick" categories intelligibly.[541]

[542] It's curious the vogue for deconstruction in America today: there's something hysterical about it, something out of focus. My own view that it makes it possible for anybody to become a critic, or at any rate to produce critical articles, may be part of the point. It's curiously antithetical to the Zen Buddhist vogue at the other end of the intellectual society. Koans, parables, & the like, are designed to stop you talking all around the subject & looking for additional meanings. They don't, of course: they just add one more convention to literature and keep yacking about it. Still, it's interesting that a Zen master confronted with the logic of supplement would reach for his stick. Perhaps at the back of the deconstructive critical mind is some hazy analogy with atom-smashing: eventually we'll break down my gross accumulations of rhetoric into protons, hadrons, quarks. I think that's a false analogy.

[543] The Book of Job is profound enough as an Israelite drama, but it seems to be a story about an Edomite visited by north-west Arabians who carry on a discussion in an area of natural cosmology founded on *analogies* to the Deuteronomic code. That way, we can't question the failure of that code to function, and yet at the end God descends out of the whirlwind to talk to a bloody *Edomite*! That dimension is what makes Job the profoundest drama in the world. Note the sequence friends > Job > Elihu > God, and contrast the "still small voice" of Elijah's retreat [1 Kings 19:12], where the implications are still of a stinker-God.

[544] Nietzsche's three metamorphoses—camel, lion, child—make some sense.[542] One needs Blake's contrary-negation for him: a contrary-Antichrist, who is still, as the "Christ" part of the word reminds us, is [sic] essential to the Christian vision: it's the negation-Antichrist who would

be a Hitler. But when Nietzsche goes into his Antichrist routine he stops being a serious writer and becomes merely a "challenging" one. If challenged by a panther, says Ogden Nash, don't anther. Those dreary Teutonic metaphors about lions & tigers!—man in a state of *Herrnmoral* [*Herrenmoral*][543] is a weasel or ferret. Even Yeats, who had so much of that silliness in him, saw that. Nietzsche is very rewarding as a satirist, attacking the soft-mindedness & hypocrisies of bourgeois culture. But when Z. [Zarathustra] comes to "war & warriors"—well, that's his convention, so he starts to gibber about how the battle hallows the good cause & how woman is the relaxation of the warrior, & we realize that Nietzsche really asked for his proto-Nazi reputation.[544] The contrary *becomes* a negation if it persists in its contrariness—so does the other side.

[545] The terms word and spirit—the dividing and uniting aspects of human awareness—move in the direction of obliterating all the nonsense of either-or and God plus man. Is there *a* God or not? Can we get along with just man or do we have to have God too? Is God dead or alive? (Any God of whom that question can be asked is certainly dead; but the place of asking it may be his tomb & the time may be the last Sabbath. At that time & place resurrections are unpredictable.) My guess is that all this stupid nonsense comes from the conception of faith as simulated knowledge. Such faith *limits* hope instead of providing its hypostasis: it limits because it tries to define. Meanwhile, both word & spirit can be used either with or without any sense of the "supernatural."

[546] Without infinity of hope, we have only the accuser's record: human history is the record of the only animal in nature more repulsive than nature. We can hope for nothing in either man or nature: there has to be an apocalypse within man. I personally don't see why humanity still exists without some power that cares more about it than it does about itself, as history records nothing persistent or continuous except the impulse to self-destruction. But that's not an argument: the principle is that everything charitable makes for the elimination of the sacred-secular antithesis in Word & Spirit. Spirit (esprit, Geist) can be freely used with no suggestion of the "supernatural," but it doesn't eliminate such suggestions either.

[547] Hexagram 24: Fu, Return. ☳☷. It furthers one to go further, like.[545]

[548] The sense of unreality I feel about this book focused originally on the thinness of literary allusions: even things as deep in me as Shakespeare weren't getting in. Then there was a sense of too much archetype-spotting, in contrast to real argument. That extended to too much kerygma spotting in 4. Finally I'm back to the Introduction, where I don't even repeat my original confidence in the Bible as the only sacred book with a literary shape. Put that back in, you stupid bastard.[546]

[549] Five should stress that the ladder is not going from one world to another, but upward in the same world: hence the steps. Literary to kerygmatic expression may be involved. Six, on "feminist" imagery, should reinforce the reaction against the absurd gabble of "anything but that" coming from Zen, Tao & kindred fashions.

[550] The quotation from Samuel Butler shouldn't be where it is, but back in Three with the first Laforgue quote.[547] (I note I'm starting to use quote as a noun. Onset of senility.) Find out where Hegel's Ph. [*Phenomenology of Spirit*] switches from soul to spirit, & put in (if you can find it) that remarkable passage from S.K.'s diary about exposing oneself *late* to Xy [Christianity].[548]

[551] As for kerygma, start a new episode at the end of II of 4, on the "metaliterary" writers from Blake on, and the tendency of Romantic writers to be prophetic. Coleridge & the repetition of creation; droves of critics down to T.E. Hulme explaining they shouldn't do that; even Eliot, who seemed pro Hulme, still wants to "get beyond" poetry in the Quartets.[549]

[552] Despite the Sermon on the Mount, kerygma is not an identifiable style, and does not belong to criticism as a structure of knowledge. It's rather an aspect of the shaping experience of reading. Modern metaliterary writers do not claim any "thus saith the Lord" authority; but what they imitate has shifted from nature to Buber's "Thou."[550] That is, kerygma is the model for the metaliterary, never more so than when it's repudiated on an "anything but that" basis, as with Nietzsche & Mallarmé. (The demonic teacher is a major theme in Eight.)

[553] My present hunch is that I have to write about a hundred pages on each chapter of Part Two and then start cutting. I've got a hundred pages

on three of the chapters, and the feeling keeps nagging that there *are* only three chapters, following the Trinity rhythm rather than my two creations, two falls, & four heathen gods.[551] Naturally, I'm still kicking like a steer. There MUST be four bloody chapters: I just don't know enough, that's all.

[554] Well: at this rate Five winds up with the Paradiso, Hegel and Mutability Cantoes vision: the "Sabbath sight" of the third fits particularly well,[552] along with the twins figuration and metamorphosis themes, and Diana's cunt to connect with Six.[553] (The latter is the MND [*A Midsummer Night's Dream*] red & white cycle of the white goddess under the *real* Virgin.)

[555] Six may have to add a lot of beauty, including Poe's Domain of Arnheim & the locus amoenus passages from Baudelaire & elsewhere: in English they start with the Phoenix.[554]

[556] Six may then go on to include Castiglione's natural grace (and its ramifications in Butler & Yeats as well as Shakespeare) and the Aristotelian ethical ideal.[555] Jesus as a ballet dancer.

[557] Seven should include Biblical descent themes: (a) Joseph & Daniel, in the lower worlds of Egypt & Babylon-Persia (really Syria), dreaming and interpreting dreams, going through prisons, pits, dens & ordeals but emerging as just stewards. (b) Prophets of captivity: Jeremiah, 2 Isaiah, Ezekiel, with suffering servants & valleys of dry bones. (Here the captivity corresponds to the wilderness stage of the archetypal journey.) (c) descent narrative in Jonah, Job, Tobit (d) Samuel & the Witch of Endor (e) Psalms of deep waters, with deluge & leviathan links.[556]

[558] Then Seven should go on to the symbolism of eating the god, & to the Gospel of John as a continuous Eucharist.[557]

[559] Eight, if there is an eight, should survey (a) the Biblical deviants, Cain, Ishmael, Esau, and their Romantic cult, along with Lucifer (Praz, Romantic Agony)[558] (b) Classical gods in Shelley, Holderlin & Nietzsche (c) contrary Antichrists (Nietzsche) vs. negative ones (Hitler).[559] Yeats & his primary-antithetical setup; Stevens' fiction. Incidentally, Stevens says the great poems of heaven & hell have been written & the great poem of the earth has not.[560] Why? Because the heaven & hell poems are fictions

& it's harder to make a fiction of what seems to be "there." Yeats also & his "Vacillation."

[560] The Paradiso is one of the models for Five; the Purgatorio may be the central model for Eight. And yet that spiral is so typically Five; but then Eight always was a lower stage than Five. Anyway it's clear that Five as I have it is unfinished. Eight does seem purgatorial: Spenser's Faerie, Keats' vale of soul-making;[561] human life making moral sense and the authority of Five coming the other way.

[561] Three: insert a sentence on *pure* sound, catalogues, roll-call of names, Spenser's and Drayton's and Joyce's rivers: orgy of naming in FW [*Finnegans Wake*]; abnihilisation of the etym.[562] Euphuism maybe. It may also be in three that you have a reference to Vico & Schelling you should cut.[563]

[562] Just done another benediction job: I said knowledge was the food of the spirit: it had to be shared, & if hoarded would spoil.[564] There is a metaphorical identity link between food & knowledge: the spoiled hoard has its type in manna and its antitype in the parable of talents. Feeding of 5000 with miraculously stretched food—type Elijah's cruise [cruse] of oil [1 Kings 17:12–16]. Christ's body is a food vessel as well as a drinking one—that particular miracle is the only one all 4 Gospels have, and in the synoptics it's duplicated (4000 with *seven* loaves).[565] Link with my gradually emerging theory that the Gospel of John is a series of Eucharists.

[563] As Goethe would have said if he'd been a wiser man, Romanticism is life, Classicism death.[566] The classic is the verbal icon, symbolized by Winckelmann's corpse-statues.[567] The *im*perfect is our paradise.[568]

[564] I also said that whatever is genuinely inexhaustible must be benevolent (because the malevolent is an illusion and the neutral, or simply-there, hits a blank wall). At the same time there's a mystery behind knowledge we have to accept: it's not darkness but shadow. There's no knowledge of what's across death, of why we're born & die, of the purposes of God, of the future. In such areas we can have only illusions that restrict freedom and limit hope.

[565] The benediction itself said: "May the presence of God consecrate our studies and transmute their elements. May what we offer in igno-

rance be accepted in providence. May the reverence for God's creation, which all the arts and sciences express, grow in us and unite there with his will to create all things new." I transcribe this because I asked for help with it and feel I got it. It links with a lot of WP themes, or what ought to be themes, like the commissioning.[569]

[566] In my detective-story frenzies I've read Ngaio Marsh's *Light Thickens*, her last book.[570] Very so-so story, one of the large number set in a theatre, but the performance is of *Macbeth*, & she's quite eloquent about the unique compulsiveness of that play.[571] The reason I've given elsewhere: its convention is the Tudor mystique about the king as Messiah-figure, which lifts it out of the category of murder stories.[572] We say we can't "believe *in*" this convention any more, which is irrelevant. We can't believe *in* Dante's hell either. Literature is a mass of fallacies from that point of view. The myth is the ideology presented as imaginative possibility. That should go at the end of Three, with the gospel myth of the Passion holding the personal *plus* of the myth. I know what I mean: I haven't found the words yet.

[567] Ngaio Marsh is a kiwi, & this story has a Maori who uses the word *tapu* a good deal.[573] When I was in New Zealand[574] I noticed this word (usually "taboo") which identifies the holy and the forbidden ("Tapu Papiea" [Paipera] means the Bible). That's the metaphor represented by the angel with the flaming sword over Paradise, whom Blake says can be driven off by a prick [*The Marriage of Heaven and Hell*, pl. 14].

[568] I was talking to a friend about the blocks I have with this book, and he asked me if I had any major projects following it. I said no, and he suggested that that could be the trouble: the self-preservative instinct balks at the swan-song ritual. Maybe, though I have reasons for not thinking so. But, apart from a collection of already written essays, what do I have? I've always wanted to write "my own" book of *pensées*, not like Pascal's but more like Anatole France's *Jardin d'Epicure* or (I've just discovered) Connolly's Palinurus book.[575] Neither A.F. nor Connolly is a first-rate mind, so these are examples, not models. Do I have a first-rate mind? Perhaps in some respects I do, but I lack education (i.e. my range of interests is exceedingly narrow). And a book of that type depends on a pretty superior mind that wouldn't instantly start to date. (The model is Nietzsche's Gaya Scienza, probably). The disadvantage of this project is that it can't be planned.

[569] I notice that passages in Connolly's book that are for him fantasy, things he can't possibly "believe in," are far more profoundly true than his expressions of what he thinks he thinks. Similarly with Pascal, who says great things when the shitty bastard he lets take charge most of the time isn't listening, or at least isn't censoring.

[570] In *One* insert a couple of sentences about the inability of the educational bureaucracy to distinguish literature from the acceptable ideology, and the assumption that the only way to make literature "relevant" to the contemporary world is to obliterate it & substitute ideology.[576] My "Adventure" report.[577]

[571] Myth as *aition*, explaining the origin of something, often a name. It's both Biblical & Classical: Callimachus' *Aitia* & Ovid's *Fasti*.[578]

[572] Rilke has a poem *Wendung* (*Letzte Gedichte*), where he speaks of the internalizing of earlier impressions into an anima figure. The poem is dated Jan. 1914, a bit early for Jungian animas.[579] Important for *Six*, though it also has *Seven* connections.

[573] Ovid's House of Fame in Book 12 should be immensely important for the inner-life passages of *Seven* or *Eight*.[580] And while you're about it see what the perpetuum and deducite references in the opening lines amount to.[581]

[574] The main sticking point of my book is that I don't know what the Derrida people are talking about, and am too lazy & cowardly to find out. I *don't* know why "God is dead" should become (so ironically) a dogma; I don't know what's wrong with being "logocentric." My first tentative guess is that deconstruction is a Lenten criticism, where the Word wanders in the desert, most vulnerable to temptation, as Eliot says [*Burnt Norton*, ll. 98–9], never making contact with the Spirit. The contact with Spirit is like two gases that will burn combining to form the liquid water that won't.

[575] I suggested in San Francisco that there were so many critical schools because of an assumption that everyone employed on a university teaching staff ought to be a "productive" scholar, and the variety of schools provided a prefabricated series of models.[582] Many of these schools, such as feminism, are only temporary ideological trends: I note that even such

broken-winded old nags as Yvor Winters and F.R. Leavis are taken out of pasture. The whole notion of "productive" is an assembly-line notion that is now being outgrown. A scholar should take a *creative* interest in his subject, and what will make the "productive" compulsion less universal will be the rise in adult education.

[576] Re the Rilke reference [par. 572]: it seems to me that a relation of love entirely free of the sado-masochist cycle is simply not possible under the "selfish gene" conditions of human existence. A loving & happy companionship is possible, with the aid of a few illusions, but they leave one with a sense of the reality of love as something to be achieved in another level of existence, not the renewal in difference (revival in another form) but renewal in identity (resurrection). Certain other "emanation" factors come into play at that point. I never deliberately hurt Helen, but a lot of selfishness, as well as indolence & ineptness, got into our relations and cramped her style. I daresay she used me to cramp her own style, though that isn't my business. I think celibate orders are, by & large, a perversion, but one can see how they arose. Milton's "He for God only, she for God in him" [*Paradise Lost*, bk. 4, l. 299] was never intended as the model for husband-wife relations in *this* world. It's a quite accurate statement of the relation of Christ to his Bride or people. Before his fall, the first Adam would have had the authority of the second one in relation to Eve, and by extension to the unfallen Adamic family that never materialized.

[577] Joseph is a descent figure ("behold, this dreamer cometh" [Genesis 37:19]), but don't forget that Jacob's ladder-vision is also a dream. Yes, but it wasn't a wish-fulfilment, Freudian, self-aggrandizing dream. Egypt & Babylon are essentially dream-worlds: all heathenism is a dream; Job's Satan-dominated world is a dream.

[578] Eight has been held up for months because I don't know nothing. The grammar is correct. Boehme apparently thinks of God as Sieyes thought of the bourgeoisie: he's everything; he was originally nothing; his purpose is to be something.[583] The implication, which I've always accepted, is that God's aim is to be a bourgeois, the middle class of the middle world, which remains after upper & lower unrealities have vanished.

[579] But I want to make Eight my Bible of Hell, the essay that turns the whole Bible inside out into Milton's manifesto of freedom, that "converts" (i.e. reverses the thesis of) Nietzsche, identifying Christ with the affirmation of life & refusal to get torn up by women like Dionysus or the Christ of Gerontion. The "will to power" is a silly thesis, nearly as silly as identical recurrence. Man has far too much power now, & without wisdom & love the opening of the Western Gate would simply bring back the Flood. (The Deluge, like the snatching at the wrong tree, is the central myth of the *premature* act that brings about its own nemesis: the archetype of tragedy.)

[580] Whatever nothing is, it's the goal of time, which is why every surrender to time, like death, leads in the direction of nothingness. Is that why the *axis mundi* is so central; because it's the [*dead*?] pillar of the risen body set up as an emblem of resurrection, of refusal to surrender?[584] I've been wondering where my way & journey stuff went: "there" is always an illusion, the end of the promising rainbow.

[581] Apparently Annabelle [Annabel] Patterson has a book in which she suggests that the category of literature came into being through censorship: through the revelation of an aspect of writing that wasn't just acceptable ideology.[585]

[582] The premature act is not a violation of time: it's time's violation of eternity: the "now" that's a perversion of the real now. The "there" above [par. 580] is actually the perverted parallel in space, the locatable "here" which is, of course, always *a* there, just as the perverted now is always a then.

[583] The participating apocalypse is the ultimate detective story where the murderer is identified & cast out: the panoramic one is its catastasis.

[584] Eight, as I've always known, deals with the positive Enoch, the rebel angels as teachers of the arts. It's also the essay that incorporates a theory of tragedy, as Seven does of comedy. Genesis 6:3 means that God tolerates the heroic, but refuses to accept anything in it as genuinely divine. It's an imposing of limits parallel in the other myth to the creation of Eve (which of course the Nephilim have got anyway).[586]

[585] I've said that the canon of the Bible gives its imagery a context, & that I'm suggesting that all literature is potentially canonical, the Word of creative man telling a single story. I quoted Graves on it in EI,[587] and all the selective-trdn. [tradition] people assume it, picking a canon out of lit, and writing the rest off as apocryphal repetition. I want to make the canon big enough to find a place for every genuine piece of writing. I'm not a great 17th c. poet like Milton, or a great-prophetic artist of the 18th > 19th c. like Blake, but it's possible that I'm a great 20th c. reader, and this is the age of the reader.

[586] So I expand the categories of creation & criticism to Word & Spirit, what man creates & what man responds to. A work of literature is a "creation," because *the* creation itself is a mirror of consciousness, and, as Rilke says, we are always facing the creation: we can never look out from it as the animals do.[588] The spirit achieves its own "sense of an ending," or apocalyptic new creation, through the unconscious inner unification of all its responses, which I once said goes on in everyone.[589] "Interpretation," I suspect, is a bastard recreation in the service of an ideology.

[587] I talk as though there were only two persons in the Trinity: I want Eight to lead up to a glimpse of the Father as containing Mother and Son within his own body, no longer a transcendent authority figure but the creative power common to subject and object, consciousness-nature; in short, the third Adam. The spirit is residually female, the K'un respondent I've always felt was my particular area in the I Ching setup.[590]

[588] You've got Orpheus in 6 all right; but you should make more of him, looking at Book X in Ovid & linking Ovid's "metamorphosis" with O's sparagmos at the hands of women (note that it's not just women that tear Christ apart). Orpheus retains the magic power that *almost* extracts Eurydice from the lower world. (Eurydice : Persephone :: Orpheus : Dionysus).[591]

[589] So I'm looking at Rilke's Orpheus poems, some of which are immensely profound: II, i, for instance: breathing the invisible poem that interchanges subject & object in space (*Weltraum*). I'm enduring that hee-hawing jackass MacIntyre,[592] partly because he's a sobering caricature of me. *Don't ever let yourself sound like that.* Re the Vera business: note how frequently a young girl's death affects a poet with a sense of intolerable

pathos: Donne's Elizabeth Drury, Wordsworth, De Quincey, Poe, & any number of Germans, including Rilke, Hölderlin, Novalis . . . I suppose the century of tuberculosis had much to do with it; but Beatrice & Laura also show that surviving a young woman's death is a very central poetic theme.

[590] Don't show any tolerance for the pearl-in-oyster crap, that poetry is only profitable when it's pried loose from its metaphorical structure. That structure is an absolutely essential part of its poetry, except that there's a metamorphosis (agon > pathos > sparagmos > anagnorisis) between text and reader at the myth > kerygma stage. This should come into focus in Seven.

[591] Incidentally, the breathing in & out metaphor seems to be in Hölderlin: it isn't just Eureka, & you may have to look at it more carefully.593

[592] The adulation of Louis XIV & the like is an outgrowth of the convention that the poet's function is to celebrate the hero, *the poet's counterpart in action*.594 The Romantic recovery of this myth is one reason why it drops out.

[593] I think, with a modicum of that horrible obscene four-letter word (ugh) WORK, these four chapters will come off all right. Eight will simply extend the ascending ladder into evolutionary & other views that start with nature & end with man. The intensifying of consciousness bit & the four levels of time & space will fit into the end.

[594] *Now* what do I do?

[595] Well, first you finish the fucking book. The difference between Seven & Eight is a difference between Orc & Los. Seven is revolutionary upheaval & culbute, the rising of the repressed; Eight is about education in the largest sense, running from wisdom through a sequence of social models (myths) to participating apocalypse. Seven is where Nietzsche goes with his Oedipus & Dionysus complex. What I haven't got clear yet is the role of eating in Seven.

[596] In each essay we should have (a) the apocalyptic ascent & descent

(b) the ascent & descent of the demonic parody (c) the authoritarian ideology it's adapted to. In Five (a) is the descent of the Word & ascent of the Spirit (b) is the rise & fall of empires and (c) is the chain of being cosmos. In Six (a) is the descent of the Dove and ascent of the Virgin (b) is the sado-masochistic cycle of the patriarchal and white-goddess movements (c) is the father-mother control.

[597] In Seven (a) is the descent to the world of fantasy & dream and the ascent of liberated repression (b) is the descent to hell > death > excretion and the *culbute* uprising that—guess what—goes in a circle and (c) is the repressiveness that keeps both social & sexual life-principles alienated. In Eight (a) is the descent to the mothers & myths & the ascent of creative skill through education (b) is the descent to nothingness & the rise of self-destructive hysteria (c) is the dominating of education by time & memory (superstition or inorganic repetition). Here be bugs. But it *will* work out, just the same.

[598] There's something to be said for the god of the gaps:[595] when you're faced with the unknown you project into it, so "God" is the totality of nothingness first of all. That must be something of what Boehme was getting at. Also it links up with the mütter-mythe business in Faust and Morris' EP [*The Earthly Paradise*]. Wonder if anything decisive does happen after Faust makes that descent: it sounds as though Goethe had a genuine hunch but couldn't do more than just play around with it. In Shakespeare, as I've said, the word "nothing" relates to a loss of social function that for a public figure is a being far deeper than personal identity.[596]

[599] Schiller's ode sees joy as permeating the whole chain of being with a sense of "play," or sheer exuberance of existence at being in one's "natural place":

> Wollust ward dem Wurm gegeben
> Und der Cherub stets [steht] vor Gott.[597]

Not great poetry, but good rhetoric about a great poetic theme, & so more useful to a composer of a Choral Symphony than great poetry would have been.[598]

[600] Eight ends with a summary of Frye on education and Utopian social visions.[599] One minor point: the difficulty of teachers to get students in literature to accept the (partly historical) conventions involved, as compared with their readiness to accept them on television. Advertising is halfway between: its conventions may be accepted by a ten-year-old but must be greatly weakened by twenty if one is to retain any self-control at all in a consumerist society. (That's why it's so important to break the hold of the rhetoric of advertising as soon as possible.)

[601] Assimilation to the "selfish gene" is the demonic aspect of food *and* sex *and* power, the aspects of gluttony and lechery and pride. The basis of democracy is an utterly unquestioning acceptance of original sin, the certainty that everyone will abuse power if he gets a chance. Also that every organization capable of exerting social pressure becomes over-organized and presses too hard.

[602] Five: the very first page should include a great deal more: Yeats on the "philosophy" of Shelley; the fallacy of identifying thinking with conceptual thinking; logical contradiction vs. imgve. [imaginative] variety; early gurus like Heraclitus that project (because they lived a long time ago) not confused but commentary-engendering aphorisms; everybody, certainly every poet worth reading, has a rigorous structure or system of thought in his mind, though there's a fashion for saying he hasn't because of the fallacy above, etc. etc.

[603] Everyone knows with half his brain that the language of religion is myth and metaphor; with the other half we continue to use rhetorical adaptations of conceptual and dialectical language. Intro.[600]

[604] We need both languages, for one is "creative" and the other "critical": i.e., one presents and the other explains. Kerygma uses the language of presentation, but it isn't self-sufficient: the critical & explanatory ideological reserves have to be brought into action too. They are even in the Gospels (e.g. the parable of the sower & its silly commentary).[601]

[605] The fool hath said in his heart, there is no God [Psalm 53:1]. But every human being is a fool, and every human being has denied God in his heart. One may say other things later, but that is what one says first,

& that is what one continues to hold to, as the central principle of existence, through life. One reason is that the first *positive* feeling in life is "I am," which carries with it the sense "there is no other." An embryonic consciousness of God may begin with the sense of the reality of other people; next comes the sense of the inevitability of death, where the feeling "I shall be not" suggests "something other is & will be." For most people this other could only be nature; then comes the specifically vulnerable loss (often a parent, only Helen for me) suggesting "if she is not, what is?" Or, more related to myself: "if I am to be not, maybe I've got hold of the wrong I." Anyway, "God is dead" is a silly bloody remark; "God never was" would at least be intelligible.

[606] It's *Bergson* who talks about nothing, not Heidegger. *Creative Evolution.*[602] I'm still fascinated by the pun, the simple negative nothing (not anything) & the positive negative Nothing, or Nothingness. God made the world from nothing, so nothing is co-eternal with God. That's a pacifier for the devout to suck. God made the world from Nothing, so Nothing is co-eternal with God. Yeats wanted to call his play "Where There is Nothing, There is God." But if so, "Where there is God, there is Nothing."[603]

[607] Every great poet has a structure or system, but of metaphors, not of ideas. First page of Five: see above [par. 602]. Every reader has something correspondent, though only reading brings it into his consciousness.

[608] The bottom of the *axis mundi* is not in Jacob's brain or ours, but in the abyss. Nothing (the abyss) then becomes what is projected into it, the hell of heat without light, the cave of the Mothers and the myths. With the birth of light it begins to become a furnace and, as hell separates from it, a purgatorial furnace.

[609] As in all four chapters, there's an apocalyptic ascent from the deep, which is the process of creative or positive illusion, the power of love & imagination which is its own reality. The descent is to the mutter-mythe void. The demonic demonic, so to speak, is the real demonic horror of human psychoses: the mob in particular suggests a monstrous giant that isn't the unaided powers of human evil. Nietzsche is the great popularizer of the rebel angels as the teachers of arts & skills, or at least of what's in that area. Hell is the demonic cast-off.

[610] Negative illusion, where there's a reality behind it is Plato's *eikasia* that eventually turns into *pistis*.[604] The separation of the two forms of illusion is a tricky but very central theme. Because 7 is the descent into eikasia that doesn't go all the way to nothingness. The illusion concealing the reality is the narcissistic illusion or doppelganger. The Witch of Endor [1 Samuel 28] worked in a world where vague entities floated around, ready to claim any reality suggested to them, and was terrified when she suddenly saw real "gods" and, apparently, the real Samuel.

[611] Six and Seven have the Miltonic pattern of normal appetites, food & sex ("the savory pulp they chew" [*Paradise Lost*, bk. 4, l. 335] recalls the N.T.'s τρύγω [gather grapes] [Revelation: 14:18]), with the demonic perversions of greed & lust that cause all the cruelty & aggression in the world (because they're based on *excess*).

[612] *Eight* has to do with the interpenetrating of negative & positive illusion. At the negative end is the assumption of design, that flowers and birds are beautiful because God made them that way for the delectation of man. This is the "paranoid" attitude ridiculed in *Micromegas*: *Gravity's Rainbow* is one of the very few works of literature to deal with this theme seriously.[605] Yet it combines with creative illusion to form the paradisal model. This process forms the evolution of *praise*. (This theme has to be introduced in Six.)

[613] Five: this chapter is built around the concern of construction, of building a house or shelter for the god, so as to catch & localize him, keeping him surrounded by a *temenos*. The holy *place*, for Xy [Christianity], was destroyed by Jesus, when he identified the temple with his body, and the ladder or "way" to the higher world also with his body. At that point the place became the Word, no longer objective, but in the subject-object intermediate "here." It was a long time before Heidegger got around to saying that language was the *dwelling-house* of being,[606] in other words the constructive principle. Perhaps Eight is concerned partly with the next step, the reconstruction of the body itself into a spiritual form, which of course starts in Six. Six, of course, deals with the expanding of love from its sexual focus into the spiritual environment.

[614] The main thesis of this book is that literature forms a finite but unbounded universe. Its individual products are infinitely variable, but are recognizable as belonging to a fluctuating but identifiable "literary"

category. People resist this because (a) they want "taste" rather than knowledge (b) because they're afraid of being caught inside a critical jail or "system," specifically mine (c) because they are mainly publish-or-perish academics who are terrified of running out of subjects, overlooking the term "unbounded." Hence the popularity of "deconstruction." Finite, however, means only intelligible, not exhaustible. Deconstruction promises the unbounded without mentioning the finite, hence it can make sense but obliterates the idea of *total* sense.

[615] The Bible, so far as we can see, was intended to be a construct of (a) historical events in the past, very polemically slanted & deriving their significance from that fact (b) events in the future predicted on the analogy of the past (c) a structure of (ethical) doctrine for our guidance in the intervening present. It gradually dawns on us that there is no reality in any of this except verbal reality. What reality there is is what we make out of the words. So the Bible's reality turns out to be imaginative, a model for literature except that it doesn't stop there but suggests the recreating of our lives. (See also 176, top [par. 607]). It is as certain as anything of the kind can be that there was no conscious intention (whatever a conscious intention is) to construct a model of the literary or imaginative universe, but it did.

[616] Whenever a subject begins to look exhausted it moves to another level of comprehension. The great example here is physics after 1900. Criticism is not going to be exhausted, but most academic critics have a lurking fear that it is: look at the way they fall on every new poet or novelist like a school of piranhas.

[617] The Virgin Mary represents the expansion from sex into spiritual love: she's the mother of the Word but the bride of the Spirit.

[618] I think the main body of Ruth must belong in Six after all: I've considered putting her in Seven. But certain emphases: the redeeming of the land, the redeeming of the Moabite, the sense of a half-secret society spreading its roots: the rejuvenated Naomi who's a "mother" of David corresponding to the redemption of the black but comely bride in SS (*Solomon's* Song).[607]

[619] The real covenant (berith, diatheke)[608] is between Word & Spirit.

In the last words of Revelation the covenant is completed in the bride (here Jerusalem or humanity), when the Spirit & the Bride say come [22:17].

[620] Introduction: the central factors are text and reader, the modes of creation and criticism. The objective extreme, that the reader need only read his text, & the subjective extreme, that there are no texts and only readers' variations on a theme, are equally irresponsible fantasies. The Bible is a kind of laboratory model of created product and creative reading, where the two factors expand into Word & Spirit. Expand, because "Word," with its creation myths & its exodus-gospel, includes nature & history, and "Spirit" includes a community of readers & cannot be confined to the waking consciousness.

[621] The "publish or perish" syndrome created a variety of prefabricated formulas for enabling sterile scholars to become productive: they were aided by a recrudescence of the old myth-as-lie syndrome. I don't want to attack or dismiss any genuine development, but there is certainly going to be a text in my class,[609] however enormously flexible and approximate the "establishing" of that text is to be. Texts, starting with the Bible, expand in meaning because they mean first of all what they say, & because they mean that they can mean infinitely more. We've never believed that poets really do mean (start with meaning) what they say.

[622] Eight: there are negative illusions and creative illusions, but the negation enters into the creation and becomes part of it. That's why the "facts" of history and the "truths" of doctrine get screwed upon mythical & metaphorical language. The last line of Stevens' "Snow Man" says it all.[610]

[623] There are creation myths of extracting a bit of mud from the bottom of the sea: the rise of Atlantis in Shelley is the complete form of this, the growth of land at the end of Faust II perhaps an authoritative distortion of it.[611] The Tempest, based as it is on the post-flood archetype, is purgatorial.

[624] Check William Mueller (1959) on *The Prophetic Tradition in Modern Literature* (memory only): Biblical allusions in modern writers.[612]

[625] Introduction: I have never understood the association of maturity with the limiting of ambitions. The older I get, the more reckless my books get.

[626] It is obvious that reading is unified by the taste, experience & temperament of the reader: this is subjective unification. The question that has preoccupied me from the beginning is: are there objective factors of unification? Introduction, obviously.

[627] I don't want to leave the impression of moral wimpishness, and I wonder if I can get away without a conclusion putting all this on a basis of humane values? Values, like God, come first as creative assumptions, not last as judges.

[628] Eight should deal with the *urban*, as Six deals with the oasis & Seven with agricultural.

[629] Fantasy ranges from the formulaic to the creative. At the formulaic extreme are the "confessions" extorted from "witches" about kissing the devil's anus and such. The uniformity of these confessions proves nothing except that people who torture women are not creative or original people: a thesis that hardly needed proving. The imagination is *beneficent*: objects of genuine hatred are usually projected, assumed to be "there," though usually they are not.

[630] Introduction: it seems to me that many academics who have devoted themselves to literary criticism get bored or dissatisfied with the subject, feeling that it lacks the discipline of philosophy or history or the relevance of social science, & that it is parasitic on literature itself. I have constantly opposed these views, & tried to point out that man attaches himself to his society by his imagination, & lives by the model of a metaphorical vision. Re the above note: hatreds can be rationalized by pseudo-logic and a stupid major premise ("a heroic Germany must be Jew free"), but they always offend the imagination, & that's what must be suppressed.

[631] Introduction: what I have done amounts to knocking an icicle off the top of an iceberg: there is no effort here, for example, to deal seriously with the structure of novels deeply involved with the Bible, such as, say,

Wuthering Heights, Moby Dick, or *The Rainbow.* (Some Canadian critics have begun to do this with Margaret Laurence and Alice Munro.) There has been more critical interest in this area, though much of it is still allusive (significance of names and the like) rather than deeply structural.

[632] End of Six: I hope I am suggesting that these conventional metaphor-structures have a "logic" of their own consistent with their postulates, and are not a mish-mash of historical accidents.

[633] Six (I have most of this): Kant's formula makes the distinction that the more pedantic Freudians & feminists overlook: the distinction between an aesthetic object & a sexual object, a human admiration for a pretty girl from a male fantasy of entering her body. "Beauty" has become suspect because of its tendency to fall into approved ideological conventions, but it's really a vision of the universe as play, where flowers are not *just* sex organs designed to attract seed propagators (birds & insects), & still less artefacts designed by God for man to admire, but part of Pynchon's recreated paranoia.[613]

[634] "Seventy times seven" as (demonic) O.T. type (Lamech) and N.T. antitype, one revenge, the other forgiveness [Genesis 4:23–4; Matthew 18:22].

[635] Foucault (Order of Things, p. 298), in a statement about God that's admirable as far as it goes, quotes Nietzsche as saying that it's hard to get rid of God when we still believe in grammar.[614] I'd say, as all "good" words are part of the Word, we can't get rid of God except by misusing or perverting language. The latter is the unforgiveable sin against, not the Word, but the Spirit responding to it: unforgiveable because it cuts off the possibility of its own forgiveness.

[636] Cyrus (Isaiah 45[:3]) is promised the treasures of darkness and the hoards of secret places. Part of the buried-treasure world of heathen kingdoms.[615]

[637] Macho heroes depend on women & are curiously immature in relation to their mothers. Hercules (Omphale); Achilles (Thetis and the Scyros episode); Samson; Shakespeare's Coriolanus. Genesis 6:3 implies

that the "giants" correspond to Hesiod's age of heroes, & God is rejecting the divine-human mix of heroes. (I probably have this.)[616] Re the above [par. 635]: the only really godless society would be one like that created by Newspeak in the last sentence (I think) of 1984.[617] Consciousness, no less than the freedom that's part of it, creates a terrible responsibility. Adam's fall was a half-fall into the cycle of nature & mortality; the stupid giants at the bottom of Dante's hell fell still further.

[638] Part of the turn-around in Seven or Eight comes from the "revolutionary" discovery that the bourgeois capitalist system was founded on a socially approved form of theft, a.k.a. original sin, a.k.a. knowledge of good and evil. Mandeville's "private vices public benefits"[618] thesis was greeted with howls of fury, but by Adam Smith the principle that, in Hume's phrase, avarice is the spur of industry[619] was generally accepted. Hence socialist views tended to become associated with ideas of perfectibility, & developed the common view that production for use rather than profit was morally superior—which in principle it is. Balzac & Stendhal.

[639] This continues, or links with, my point about Dante on H3 & E1 [Henry III & Edward I]: H3 was a bad king who endowed schools & colleges, & E1 a good one who murdered Welsh & Scots & expelled the Jews.[620]

[640] Love is the consciousness of consciousness, the total awakening of which "self-consciousness" is the demonic parody.

[641] You left something very obvious out of Six: the kind of hierarchy of love represented by Spenser's Four Hymns, Sidney's "Leave me O Love" & Shakespeare's "Poor Soul" sonnets.[621]

[642] Seven: the apocalyptic descent into the dream-world of wish-fulfilment & the ascent is through recreation (revolution that stays). The demonic descent is to hell, and the ascent the rotating revolution that creates a new hell (Spenglerian or Viconian vision, perhaps). See the perversion note above [par. 611].

[643] Then comes the apocalyptic vision of integration of life & the

separation from death. The former has the metaphor of food (Eucharist in time; tree of life in eternity); the latter, shit. (Rabelais is for Eight).[622]

[644] Eight: computers travel at a speed the brain can't follow, but the unconscious can sometimes work out problems and visions with extraordinary speed—this is Butler's unconscious knowledge. The Biblical metaphor for this is the voice of God speaking to the prophet. (The prophet is the spirit trying to make sense of what he hears; he doesn't invariably get it right.) Jesus also says he does nothing except what he sees the Father do [John 5:19]: I haven't got this clear yet. But the final apocalypse, with God all in all, is a totality of life continually recreating itself in a Kierkegaardian repetition, the opposite of the ouroboros-recurrence of Nietzsche (perhaps that passage from *Comus* could be quoted).

[645] Anyway, the total journey is surely what concludes Eight. The rebel angels are teachers, not just devils: Cain is the cycle of empire but some of his progeny (not of course Lamech, who's in the demonic cycle) are artificers.[623] Hebrew doesn't distinguish smiths from carpenters except by the context: the Bible has a divine carpenter's son (the antitype of the mysterious Hiram) [Matthew 13:55; 1 Kings 5] and demonic smiths.

[646] Devils are purely human (Bunyan's valley), and the angelic-demonic is the buried spirits of man. From here one can construct Blake's Bible of Hell & what some French student calls *Le contre-bible Melville*.[624] And here's where Goethe's Mothers & Shirley go. If the human creature is symbolically female, the angelic spirit of power can be a Titanic Lilith, or the humanity responding to genius in Genesis 6:1–4.

[647] Moral ambiguity of nature (Wordsworth & Sade) based on close intertwining of creative & demonic descents.[625] Similarly with the doppelganger, who may be an evil spirit or Jungian shadow (Poe's William Wilson, etc.). Narcissus is deceptive, the male counterpart of the siren. The Biblical pattern is the first Adam of ordinary consciousness & the buried second one who plunges up out of death & hell.[626] The Resurrection comes from & through hell: that's all the "Bible of Hell" amounts to.

[648] Stendhal speaks of the despotism of public opinion in small towns

& provinces as a tyranny abhorrent to those coming from the "republic of Paris." Note that the term for those on the revolutionary side was *citoyen*. He says public opinion tyranny is what makes England & America so gloomy: I don't know how he accounts for London & New York.[627]

[649] The general argument of Seven-Eight is: Rousseau started the revolutionary drive toward incorporating nature (*ata* in the identification with reason; *ans* in the educational argument of *Emile*)[628] into the spirit of man. But the Biblical tradition had always warned against the evils inherent in nature, and the bottoms-up 19th c. thinkers repeated the ambivalence. Hence Wordsworth & the Marquis de Sade both appealed to "nature"; Schopenhauer recognized its dangers; Nietzsche recognized them and glorified them; Huxley warned against them. The strictly revolutionary position in Marx & Freud was "godless" because it saw only the incorporating of nature, & with that "revolution" acquired its other meaning of a change toward the same thing.[629]

[650] What Eight explores is the otherness which is not of nature: this starts with nothingness, within which myths gradually develop, and a will that strives not to assert or be a power but to identify itself with the "unconscious" or assimilated knowledge. "Inspiration" in the prophets means one of those intuitive jumps into speeded-up clarification that we're now building mechanical models for. I think most of the doppelganger argument, which climaxes in the second & first Adam, with the Spirit-Bride incorporated in the Word or second one, belongs in Eight. The sense of otherness gradually shifts from the Nothing else to the "je est un autre" of Rimbaud.[630] There must be a third Adam who is the Father.

[651] Seven will have to wind up with Nietzsche. He started with his conception of tragedy as the harnessing of the energy of Dionysus to Apollo; then Dionysus took over as the will to power. Like Blake (whom he resembles in the fact that his fame was almost entirely posthumous, counting his breakdown as the end of his life) he saw everything as a structure of myth & metaphor. Only he stayed on the Seven rotating level, though he carried it through consistently. He had to reject God: he had to accept a God of infinite recurrence as a life-principle (a "dying" god was for him a reviving one). He doesn't fall into the either-or trap completely: he works through to the apocalyptic life-death separation.[631]

I think I read somewhere (I probably got it wrong) that we actually see things upside-down before the mind corrects it: Nietzsche was perhaps the purest visionary on record.[632]

[652] The only thing that gives him away—and I haven't got the clue to that yet—is the unvarying contempt of women in his writing. Blake is disturbing enough on this, but at least his poetry is concerned with nameless shadowy females that are not women. The spirit *and the bride* say come [Revelation 22:17], and Nietzsche's self-transcending man is a male. Sublimating love through violence (will to *power*) won't work.

[653] I haven't said much about evolution yet, though I think a lot of it props up the old hierarchical chain of being on a temporal metaphor. But the old triad—an original spontaneous state buggered by consciousness and restored as *ludens* assimilated skill—has to be there somewhere. Nietzsche thought that what distinguishes man from the animals was not consciousness but *will* to power. There's an essential link here with Derrida's "logocentric" I have to get clear: they're totally different, but seem to agree on the verbal as part of the intermediate stage.

[654] One: a writer can write only what takes shape in his mind: but *why* certain themes & subjects do take shape at certain times is something my kind of mythical geography can sometimes explain.

[655] Six: the white goddess does *not* represent the hatred of either sex for the other, but the wasting of love.

[656] You have been making a mistake in thinking of Eight as going deeper than Seven. Eight is the deep part of Six, and Seven of Five. Los is below Orc, but I've been misled by that.

[657] Don't forget that Blake re-establishes the *old* four-level cosmos, though purified of authoritarianism and ideology.

[658] Creative mutability: Spenser has his version: it's dominated by lesser & greater metamorphosis, the latter of course symbolized by Trans-figuration & not resurrection. But becoming & change don't have to go in the direction of death. Wallace Stevens' Sunday Morning; Mallarmé's Cantique; Valéry's Cimitière [*Cimetière*] Marin.[633]

[659] A central symbol of criticism for me is Jacob wrestling with the angel, but I don't want this to be the frame-up that many modern wrestling matches are.

[660] I wonder if I'm going in the direction of saying: the objective is the verbal (or mathematical)? That would (a) separate the objectivity of the death-world from the real descent (b) integrate the theme of "nothing-ness." To the extent that the object becomes verbal, the subject becomes spiritual. Is that the kernel of reality in "deconstruction"? The word "logocentric" suggests the opposite, but perhaps the logocentric is the speaking subject going in the wrong direction, toward logos instead of spirit. The emphasis on écriture is paralleled in journeys to the code in *Endymion* and *Arthur Gordon Pym*. If I'm "right" in thinking that the truly objective is an epiphany (ecriture) of the verbal, I'm surely within sight of the end. Jacob (Hosea 12:3) starts as a usurper & ends up fighting with God (an "angel" would still be a messenger of the Word).

[661] Nietzsche again: the conception "Antichrist" means very little ex-cept in a context established by Christ. But why a dying god is a life-principle and a risen god a dead one I don't see, though I certainly understand why one would want a God who was the exact opposite of middle-class Christian morality.

[662] The secret of Prometheus was that the offspring of Zeus & Thetis would be greater than the father: Shelley uses this theme, though without Thetis. So Thetis was married off to Peleus, & the result was Achilles, who being just a hero, even though a divine & invulnerable one, was no threat to the Almighty Shit. That's the tragedy that parallels Genesis 6:1–4.

[663] Introduction: every member of a humanities department in every university is supposed to be a productive scholar, & no reasonable person will deny that a tremendous amount of overproduction, repeti-tion and straw-thrashing results. Hence one of the causes of the prolifer-ating of critical theories is to provide inexhaustible fields of critical enterprise. The struggle for a unified perspective on the whole subject seems to pose the threat of exhaustion. But there is little danger of that: whenever a subject approaches such a point it goes into a metamorpho-sis, as physics did after 1900 with the work of Planck & Einstein. Perhaps critical theory has done this since the *Anatomy* was published, but I am

not convinced of this. (See pp. 179–82 [pars. 617–34].) I address myself to the public, to undergraduates, & to graduates for whom the shades of the prison-house of language have not yet closed in. I am not opposed to any development in theory as such, only to the obfuscating of perspective.[634]

[664] (I thought I had this but I can't find it.)[635] The element of negative illusion gets into all literature: it's not really happening. But in serious literature (my stock example is the blinding of Gloucester) what isn't really happening reflects what does happen. So what is physically absent is spiritually present. (Because verbally present.)[636]

[665] Plato's divided line as a ladder: after the bottom is *eikasia*, negative illusion. Then comes the world of objective "reality" we're supposed to believe "in" (*pistis*). After that we move into an intelligible world full of ideology, where the objective is verbal & mathematical rather than physical, myth & metaphor assimilated to hierarchy, centralization, authority & ideological rationalizing. That's as far as Plato gets in practice. Above it is the total identity of Word & Spirit, the top (*klimax*) of the hierarchy where the hierarchy disappears and the ladder is kicked away. (I'd like this for Four, but the presence of the ladder metaphor indicates Part Two, perhaps Eight.) Not lower-half physical and upper-half intelligible, but a world with the two intertwined all the way up.

[666] "Many waters cannot quench love, neither can great floods drown it" [Song of Songs 8:7]. St. Augustine (natch) said that Noah's ark was a type of the Church [*City of God*, bk. 15, chap. 26]. The Bible says, or suggests here, that it's a type of love.

[667] Six & Eight add to traditional Christian categories: Six establishes the fact that the erotic is absolutely essential to Xy [Christianity]. Eight establishes a distinction between demonic & daimonic: the old identification of them is nonsense. The demonic is to be escaped from; the daimonic or creative is to be harnessed.

[668] Five & Seven establish that the emphasis on centralizing, authority, hierarchy, & the continuity of tradition are degenerate perversions— at least they are when the *kairos* moment comes for them to be outgrown. Seven stresses my "pre-revolutionary" point of keeping Socrates & Jesus alive and *not* collapsing into the cycle. Fifty years ago Marxists & Catho-

lics believed intensely in the four elements just listed: now there's a lot of restiveness about it.

[669] Eight: God's creation is involved in nothingness: when the conception of creation shifted from a divine product to a human process nothingness became the dark half, so to speak, of human creation. I don't need to make a point more difficult than that. In Mallarmé the white paper the poem is written on symbolizes this.[637] In rethinking 5–8 I must unify the theme better: divine product in daylight is still a human process in darkness. The latter doesn't follow or imitate the former: it *has* created it, arranged the rendezvous, as Stevens says [*Final Soliloquy of the Interior Paramour*, l. 12]. And what it creates below now keeps reshaping what is above. Look at Yeats' Unicorn from the Stars & its climactic "where there is nothing, there is God."[638] WS's Snow man, of course.[639]

[670] Blake knew what Los was: Demogorgon has a parallel role in Shelley, but I don't think Shelley knew what Demogorgon was. I'd like to confine Seven to the revolutionary reversal, the natural cycle of death and rebirth, the double, and the double Adam. Then Eight could take in nothingness, the paleolithic caves, the positive demonic, & the purgatorial progress. The Mut. Coes. [*Mutabilitie Cantos*] are Eight; Heart of Darkness might be Seven. Death & hell are mostly Seven: the Lucianic katabasis obviously is, because it's a *culbute*.[640] So in a way are my shit passages: they too reverse the hierarchical direction. I can contrast Swift's MOS [*The Mechanical Operation of the Spirit*] with Marvell's drop of dew without weighting the balance.[641] Besides, there's Rabelais, certainly a Seven figure.

[671] No: Seven is an Orc (Urizen) book & Eight a Los (Spectre) book. Yeats' US [*The Unicorn from the Stars*], which I just referred to, is about a mystic who gives up rebellion for vision & creation & finds his root in nothingness. That's Part One: the purgatorial journey is Part Two: its basis is the Exodus. Note (a) Yeats' comment (US) about the ouroboros shape of journeys[642] (b) Thibaudet's comment (I think) about Mallarmé going up a staircase from the wilderness of the Parnassians (who surely ought to be on a mountain) to the lush land of the symbolists.[643]

[672] Angels & manifestations: between a message from God and a Word of God there's a difference only of degree, not of kind.

[673] "This is one of the subtle ways in which Dante indicates that all spatial & temporal terms in Paradise are merely symbolical."[644] What a trained critic should say is: ". . . images in the Paradiso have reached their true metaphorical context." Having outgrown their spatial and temporal projections, that is.

[674] Seven: I can't rid myself of the notion that the cyclical dying god is something other than the descending & ascending Kore. There's no siren-betrayal or white-goddess sacrifice possible with a mother & maiden story; I think the whole resurrection story, as distinct from the renewal one, from Inanna to Shakespeare's Perdita, is actually female. Even though it includes the renewal one, as it obviously does. Eleusis means Advent, and a reaped ear of corn must have meant something more than simply a harvest, however important the food supply. Pericles four "fathers."[645]

[675] Kenosis is the N.T. antitype of the nothingness of God.[646]

[676] Seven: don't leave Blake's black girl out of the picture: the buried treasure is sometimes a sleeping beauty. The blackness is Proserpine in hell as well as SS [Song of Songs].[647]

[677] Eight: the conclusion of the whole book should be based on the stopping of the journey: all journeys are cycles (Yeats' US [*The Unicorn from the Stars*]: Roethke & Atwood;[648] methinks it is no journey:[649] the Way & the transforming of horizontal to vertical movement; the abolition of vertical movement. (At least for time {cf. Mike Joseph's comment on his Achamoth book};[650] but even space journeys are limited to the solar system if the speed of light remains a limit.)

[678] Introduction: the method may seem absurd or preposterous to critics who have not yet learned the primary language of their own discipline. But it can hardly be arrogant to say that it matters very little what pseudo-critics think they think. Some do not know the language of myth & metaphor; some know something about it but do not know how to use it. (Reverse direction to lead in to previous sentence better.) In metaphor there are innumerable essential distinctions that do not have to be made.[651]

[679] Gnostic book, p. 399: female must be made male to enter the

kingdom, starting with Mary: linked by editor to the form-male matter-female metaphor.[652]

[680] Four: the sacraments of religion may be "more" than symbolic, but the understanding of them must approach them symbolically before they can mean anything "more" than that. To try to decide at what point some sacramental kerygmatic essence enters that takes it "beyond" symbolism would be a dreary & futile exercise. It's an intensification of the symbolic, not a transcending of it.

[681] In Eight, in the Genesis 6:1–4 connection, remember there are goddess seducing males. Ishtar & Gilgamesh, Calypso & Odysseus, the moon & Endymion, etc.

[682] I've always known that "Byzantium" was central to the Eight vision: there the action goes up from the death-world. "S to B" [*Sailing to Byzantium*] is the same world looked at statically, as a chain of being structure.[653] Compare Blake's inversion of the Four Zoas & his final vision of them right side up, but without hierarchy.

[683] In conformity with your usual policy of leaving out all the obvious things that any fool would have the sense to put in first, you seem to have omitted the whole *locus amoenus* theme from 5 and 6.[654]

[684] Note that poetry is missing from the Seven Liberal Arts; also that we get secular counterparts of the dialogue of Word & Spirit in such fancies as "The Marriage of Philology & Mercury."[655] Perhaps footnote material.

[685] I think the Buber dialogue principle is the only one that breaks out of the Narcissus prison. If Word & Spirit are human doubles we're stuck.[656] Bloom on Shelley.[657]

[686] I've said this many times, of course, but still: all that crap about poetry making pseudo-statements in a world of science implies that there is no poetic thought, only conceptual thought. If only people knowing nothing about literature said this it would be bad enough, but it's literary critics (starting with a 1926 essay by I.A. Richards) who say it.[658]

[687] Lawrence's dark gods & Yeats's historical cycle are two things you've so far paid very little attention to. Though the latter at least was prominently featured in the graduate course.[659]

[688] The divine king is mythologically de jure only: but life can't assimilate *pure* myth, & a "king" will be a leader too. Since Napoleon's time at least we've realized that the pyramid shape is symbolic but that a *supreme* king or "dictator" fits only the army, society organized for death, and can rule only by martial law.[660]

[689] Buber again. Tat tvam asi: thou art the super-It.[661] Nuts.

[690] Eight: reincarnation does occur in the Bible, not as an indefinite series of rebirths, but as a process completing this life by another reversing its movement. Yeats was right after all: it's the completion of the ascending & descending movements. For once I could do with a prooftext: maybe Acts 1–2 does it.[662] In the paradisal vision Nothing is cast out. Perhaps the purgatorial & paradisal visions keep working together in this life, whether in another or not.

[691] In revising Seven, remember that a lot of people think sex is shit: here's where I could say more about Lawrence & his dark gods.

[692] Eight again: the paradisal vision is re-established, but without hierarchy. It's a vision of order but not of authority—except the spiritual authority that exists *only* in education.

[693] The end of the journey is interpenetration, or perhaps the hologram model.[663] It's the recognition scene of proclaiming word & responding spirit.

[694] I know I'm impatient to get a draft of the book finished, but that's no reason for invariably leaving out the central point. In Seven, in the double passage, you left out the Zoroaster passage in Shelley.[664]

[695] I think Four *still* needs an explanation of myth-metaphor *plus*. The plus may be (usually is) straight rhetorical ideology: *what* is the characteristic of genuine kerygma, which is to the first as eggs are to shit? Or *is*

there any real difference at all? My present argument says there isn't a definable difference, but something like the difference between Yeats' stare & glance may be involved.[665]

[696] Bleibtreu's *Parable of the Beast* has some extraordinary things: it connects Eucharist symbolism—transformation of the flesh—with genetic codes, makes memory a kind of trickster god, and talks about apparently voluntary creations of subspecies by discrimination, like Jews & their imitators, the Nazis.[666] Food-sharing, in southern integration, the most difficult thing—see my nausea passage in Seven.[667]

[697] The climax of Four, and the central point of the whole book, is: myth has ideology, rhetoric & authority on one side and kerygma or lifestyle alteration including primary concern on the other. I've got it in; the definitive writing out of it is something else, but the whole book turns and depends on it. See across [par. 694].

[698] Buber's it-world is what I mean by the there-world: the world of experience that one points to across a gap, not the world of what he calls relation and I call identity. If you say to me "Is there a God?" I say no, because I don't believe in God's thereness (I don't like the indefinite article, either: in fact it would intensify my answer to "of course not, stupid.")

[699] I suppose the difference between Buber & a Christian view is that in the latter the Word itself becomes a Thou, and thereby identifies the ultimate I (the Spirit) and the ultimate Thou (the Father: the embrace of Jerusalem 99).[668]

[700] There is no end to numbers, but one can get tired of counting. There is no end to the universe, but one can die and annihilate it. Perhaps that's the reason for death: to shake off infinity. Beckett's Murphy thought that the Resurrection was God overdoing things again.[669]

[701] My passage on trickster Gods in the O.T. is weak.[670] The God who wants Agag hacked up is an idol [1 Samuel 15], a human derivation of a God from nature, including human nature. All persecution & bigotry are forms of atheistic humanism, making God in the image of man. But what finally turns this around? That's another hinge of the book.

[702] It's a matter of simple prudence never to deny *a priori* the possibility of something there might conceivably be evidence for. The evidence could be validated, and one would have made a fool of oneself to no purpose. It's different with God: there there's evidence enough, but I don't see how it can be validated.

[703] Re over the page [par. 699]: the place where the Word turns from It to Thou is in the apocalypse, when a collection of things becomes a collection of relations or identities. My remarks on *symbol*, which belongs to this point, are also weak.

[704] Prescribed rituals are, *by themselves*, superstition or inorganic repetition. They become the basis of creative repetition only when a "secular" transformation takes place along with them. Except that "secular" really should be "spiritual."

[705] D.H. Lawrence: got involved in all sorts of fascist or mystical nonsense, but also got hold of a central primary concern: men must live with nature and if possible love it, and not merely dominate and exploit it.

[706] Censorship is an expression of weakness. Or confession.

[707] Expansion of the shit section: Swift's attitude is that if there is a ladder, we have to walk up it and not try to fly. Perhaps I could also refer again to the philosopher "seduced by his lower parts into a ditch." Swift's attitude is moral, even theological: the excremental vision in Rimbaud is even more ferocious, and is more simply an intensity of vision. But it's not a dead end in him, as the *Illuminations* show, and in one of them ("Matinée d'Ivresse") there's a glimpse of a ladder ("it began with every sort of crudity, its ends with angels of fire and ice" [ll. 23–4]). Nausea, as above [par. 696].

[708] The age of dialectical rigidity between capitalism and socialism, which Lenin took advantage of, ended in 1939 with the growth of fascism into its inevitable end of war. Nazism was closest to a type of anarchism or nihilism, and it spread ripples (I mean that attitude did) over the U.S. in the sixties, and over much of Africa & Latin America. The Soviet Union is trying to outgrow the Leninist dialectical rigidity,

and some elements in the U.S.A. are trying to outgrow its counterpart. But it's hard: Reagan is the great symbol of clinging to the great-power syndrome, which is why he sounds charismatic even when he's talking the most obvious nonsense.

[709] The Pope is in an even tougher spot, trying to maintain the Catholic dialectic even when it's disintegrating all around him, even among Catholics. I must feel insecure about a sentence when I put three evens in it.

[710] Did I get my detective story illustration into Eight?[671] Note that the Swift attitude is an attack on the premature apocalypse: trying to approach the panoramic apocalypse without bringing together all the aspects of [the] human condition, which we must do before we can really reach the participating stage.

[711] The shadow of a third book, dimly rising on the horizon as I complete the draft and begin the revision of WP, is something I must put out of mind for the present. Its main theme is an elaboration of the two notes over the page: the conception of kerygmatic dialectic founded on myth and taking over from Marxist dialectical materialism in the secular sphere [par. 708] and Newman-Thomist dialectical realism (I know it's out of date, but no successor is visible) in the sacred one [par. 709]. Not that the Catholic dialectic is the only Christian one: the exclusivity principle in Barth has to be transcended too. There's a part-whole oscillation involved: the exclusive "he who is not for me is against me" built up the Christian revolution; the inclusive "he who is not against me is for me" is the complementary principle.

[712] The Russians call the 1939–45 war the "Great Patriotic War": that's what I mean by a mythical title. But it's more comprehensive, more involving for the Russian people, and in every way that makes sense more true, than a simply historical or descriptive title would be.

[713] One function of poetry, or at least of the metaphors in poetry, is to reconstruct the pre-verbalized instant before recognition. When I recognize something to be *that*, it's an object in the s-o [subject–object] universe; before that it could be anything, usually something more humanized. See an excellent book, *Infinity and the Mind*, by Rudy Ruckert [Rucker], p. 146. And why should this world be reconstructed? I suppose

to set the actual in its context of infinite possibilities. Ruckert [Rucker] is talking about the parallel-worlds problem: I haven't the mathematics to follow him, but the metaphorical side of it interests me.[672]

[714] The shit section goes on to say that the excremental vision (and the vision of sex as partly excretion) is now a normal part of most writers' equipment (it was still "shocking" in Rimbaud's time) and is inevitably a part of the *axis mundi* total pattern. Marvell's drop of dew is metaphorically valid, but there's a wistful, longing-for-release element in it. I've missed something here, but I'll get it when I write it out, perhaps.[673]

[715] "God is perhaps not so much a region beyond knowledge as something prior to the sentences we speak." That's Foucault's *Order of Things* p. 298, what I should have quoted earlier instead of the Nietzsche nonsense he goes on with [par. 635].

[716] This may take me back to the Seattle intuition: Finnegans Wake is a kind of hypnagogic structure, words reverberating on themselves without pointing to objects (but not without *naming*, as in Mallarmé: see a previous note [par. 241]). This may be the hallucinatory verbal world within which God speaks.[674] At present, this could go in as an expansion of the nothing section in Eight.[675] It's also, more obviously, William James' blooming buzzing confusion.[676]

[717] In other words, the pre-recognition aspect of poetry is connected (a) with the magic of sound business in Three[677] (b) with the condensation-displacement restatement of my old centripetal-centrifugal point. Condensation is a movement toward metaphor and onomatopoeia; displacement of course is metonymic (*not* simile, as I used to say). There's a movement *within* condensation from pre-recognition (oracular) to recognition (funny).[678]

[718] Another thing I haven't got in the book that may belong there is the conception of the subdrama, an idea I got originally from Strindberg's Miss Julie. It has Biblical precedents: in fact narrative seems to be infinitely divisible, as matter is sometimes said to be. Only I need to expand the notion beyond the sub-drama.

[719] FW [*Finnegans Wake*] is not merely the epic (or sacred book) of

condensation, as perhaps War and Peace is of displacement, but raises the whole ambiguity of the social "body" as both one and many, which I've rather skimped.[679]

[720] In looking through the works of younger (thirties & forties) Canadian poets, it's very obvious how much of their work is poetry of protest, and how deeply they are outraged by cruelty & violence & ugliness. But they don't want any longer (as so many did in the 1930s) to be identified as "left-wing," say, or ideologically programmed in any way. They've matured to primary concern.

[721]

metaphorical	metonymic
centripetal	centrifugal
condensation	displacement
imagery	narrative
metaphor-cluster	myth
oracular magic	witty recognition
space-time	duration-time
figurative	realistic
dream space etc. etc.	subject-object space

[722] Reincarnation doesn't seem to be a functional *conception* in the Bible, except metaphorically (Nebuchadnezzar *is* Nero, etc.) but naturally it can't be kept out of literature, especially with the prestige of Virgil. Fielding's *Journey from This World to the Next*, some early stories of William Morris, and I think that extraordinary story of Gogol's.[680]

[723] Well, now, I think my condensation set-up gives the best explanation for Finnegans Wake on the market. Only I'd like to expand it to account for the myth-history shape too. One FW is enough, as Eliot said:[681] 95 percent of literature is ironic, but irony depends on the submerged "normal" model. This normal model is ultimately something *buried* in the mind: it has to be exhumed. Even myth (see table across) [par. 721] is displaced, though of course less so than history. All my "undisplaced" interpretations of works of fiction go in the direction of an apocalyptic metaphor-cluster, but can't go all the way as long as narrative is still present.

[724] That Canadian poetry article I wrote for David [Staines][682] had

something: what may seem totally introspective & withdrawn poetry may be nothing of the kind: the artist's antennae may be exploring not his private conflicts—oh hell, there is NO private imagery in poetry—but himself as representative of the fears & guilts of his society. In Canada these fears and guilts are mainly about the obliterating [of] (or attempting to obliterate) indigenous culture and the slaughter and torturing of (fur-bearing) animals.

[725] The imagination constructs its own cosmos, parallel to but different from the cosmos of description, argument & ideology. That cosmos has an axis mundi, of course.[683] It's easier for Dante & Milton to work in centuries when there were descriptive (scientific) parallels to the axis mundi, but not essential.

[726] There is nothing subjective in literature, no, repeat no, private associations or images or symbols. Strindberg's fear of being poisoned by his cooks started as a private neurosis, but as soon as it got mentioned in his plays we're into (a) contaminated and polluted food, a social problem (b) the great theme of nausea (c) a literary tradition going back to the Harpies in Virgil. We speak loosely of its being "essential" to know about Strindberg's goofiness, but it's not essential: it's interesting and valuable information, documenting what we could guess anyway, but there's a lot of such "essential" information about, say, Shakespeare that we don't have in spite of Caroline Spurgeon.[684] And we get along all right without it.

[727] Nothing objective either, of course, no actual people or settings. Critical interest has shifted from substance or content to the signs and symbols that express it, and yet some kind of content remains as the focus of a community. It's a spiritual substance, a shared love-feast or communion.

[728] What fascinated me about Spengler when I read him was the vision of every historical phenomenon being a symbol of all the other phenomena contemporary with it. Every age presents a symbolically interlocking group of phenomena: I suppose that's what the word "culture" means. I reacted against that, because of the over-dominance of that dimension of history, but it really means that the narrative of history can be halted at any moment and looked at as a thematic stasis.

[729] The reality of the cosmos constructed by myth and metaphor is in its articulation of primary concern: its postulates start with the hypothetical "what if" and end with the existential "seeing that."

[730] The poetic cosmos has a lot to do with the creative paranoia of Pynchon's *Gravity's Rainbow*, a contemporary statement of original sin as a condition we cannot live without and yet want to get rid of.

[731] The nub sentence of the whole book: what difference does God make in human life? has still to be articulated. Original sin means that there is no way of separating means from ends, good from bad, vision from history, without God. I'm writing in Russia at the moment,[685] and in churches or cathedrals still functioning as such, listening to the liturgy and the murmured responses from the dense crowds, I can only feel that in 70 years the essential principles of Christianity have been compromised far less than the principles of Leninism. Lenin hated religion because the church of his day was inseparable from the Czarist regime, but the same perversion overtook his revolution, as yesterday's radical became today's bureaucrat (if, after Stalin, any radicals survived to do so).

[732] There's a lot of straight rhetoric & ideology in the Bible: I shouldn't try to deny that when it's true. But its unity is held together by its inner poetic structure of myth and metaphor. That unity is there, and how it got there will perhaps always be something of a mystery. The mystery has to do with canonicity, not with history or doctrine, and, in its larger aspect, with Shelley's one great poem.[686]

[733] Kerygma, in short, is metapoetics, not rhetoric or dialectic. Its basis is hope, or hypothesis; it moves through the substance of hope and through creativity (elenchos, the realizing of the unrealized) to its goal in love.

[734] The birds hymned the dawn, and the Beloved,
　　Who is the dawn, awoke.
　　　　And the birds ended their song,
　And the lover died in the dawn for his Beloved.

Ramon Lull: Blanquerna[687]

[735] No one-man Bible is possible, because the limitations of the one

man would show through: for example, FW [*Finnegans Wake*] with its endless whining about Joyce's poverty and neglect. Besides, the real argument for going on from the poetic to the kerygmatic is that poetic unity is an end in itself & blocks off advance: all we have to do is read the Bible & we'll know everything. The crisis of GC was its demonstration that the overall unity broke up into millions of unities.

[736] The movements I've been calling "anti-intellectual" are not just that: they are Kierkegaard's demonic "dread of the good":[688] that is, they are simply sin. It doesn't follow that their victims are necessarily good people, only that original sin may at any time become the driving force of an ideology.

[737] Quote from Foucault on p. 201 [par. 635]: the *content*, which may be "mama" or, as in Paul, "abba,"[689] is not the important thing, except as indicating primary concern.

[738] Further on the one-man Bible: he'd be conditioned by history, and the Bible being a product of canonicity and consensus, is capable of Heilsgeschichte.

[739]

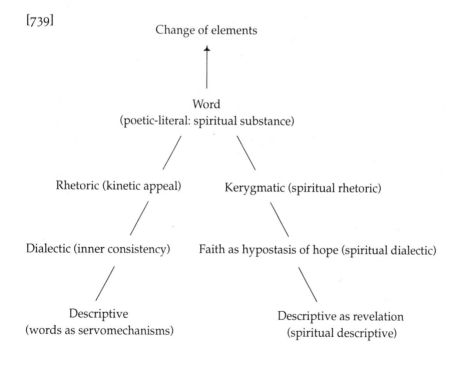

Change of elements

Word
(poetic-literal: spiritual substance)

Rhetoric (kinetic appeal)   Kerygmatic (spiritual rhetoric)

Dialectic (inner consistency)   Faith as hypostasis of hope (spiritual dialectic)

Descriptive   Descriptive as revelation
(words as servomechanisms)   (spiritual descriptive)

[740] At the top mythology consolidates into *the* myth, which [is] a change of elements involving (a) spiritual substance (b) I-Thou dialogue (c) Heilsgeschichte. Spirit, Father, Word.

[741] Fn. [Footnote] Intro. [Introduction]. Some writers in Canada describe me as a "thematic" critic, with the implication that that is the wrong kind of critic to be. But it is only "thematic" criticism, of whatever kind, that actually discovers anything about literature.

[742] Fn. to John Prologue as a separate poem: cf. G.R.S. Mead, *The Gnostic John the Baptizer*, 1924.[690]

[743] Fn. to Canadian reference: add Margaret Atwood's poem with the same title as Roethke's.[691]

[744] Fn. in Four: there is also a rhetoric within the poetic, a poet's habitual idiom of language. Hopkins calls this "Parnassian."

[745] My next book has the central theme of education and Utopia. The axiom that a Utopia is really a projection of a theory of education has been borne out so often I don't need to query it: just find examples of it. I have four papers, on More, on Castiglione, on Butler's Life and Habit, & on William Morris,[692] to draw on, along with a lot of intuitions about Plato and the symposium form of dialogue. My present question is whether it belongs to the *Great Code* series.

[746] I also feel that my circle of arts, the conception of painting as essentially a "cave" or unborn art, my hazy intuition about music as one of the verbal languages, also belongs. I used to get excited about this ever since I was setting and marking essays on More's Utopia and thinking about the encyclopaedic visions of Elyot, Spenser, etc. Also the greatest form for prose being the Utopia (Greville on Sidney).[693] Some of this of course I've gone over. I'd like to make the central metaphor the centre-circumference interchange and the whole-part interaction.

[747] We're still not out of the silly antithesis of either individual or society, and don't seem to realize how preposterous the Atlas Shrugged and Looking Backward versions of it are.[694] It's no good complaining that our students are conservative: where are they to go? The gang-of-

four dynamic in the sixties couldn't have been sillier. Yet I hear people saying in effect: it doesn't matter what students say & do as long as they're not conservative. Why the hell shouldn't they be conservative? Do we fill up our day-care playgrounds with dangerous obstacle courses so they'll be sure to break their necks?

[748] The image of shaking dice in Mallarmé goes back to the *juec d'amor* in William of Poitiers, except that the sexual innuendo (allegory) is more explicit in the earlier writer.[695] I don't even know if it's in Mallarmé or not.

[749] Things to think about in Seven: the world of the dead as a potential culbute; the substitute interrex as a reminder of the Golden Age or reign of Saturn;[696] the world of identity in Atlantis or underground as the pre-metaphorical world of Homer & the Bible[697] (at present cut out of Four; perhaps it fits better in Eight). Power without words is certainly Eight.[698] Detective stories shouldn't be split between the two chapters.[699] The pre-Homeric cipher-world must have links with my Seattle epiphany—whatever happened to the St. Clair one?[700] Maybe that belongs in the Utopia book.

[750] The real demonic descents are in Eight: perhaps I've left out the demonic descent in Seven, which is into *exile*, the descent of Cain repeating that of Adam. Death is a deeper exile. Ghosts are revenants, spirits trying to come home.

[751] I cut out the primitive cult (18th c.) in Seven, but maybe it's part of the Seattle epiphany and the cave archetype. If the demonic descent of Seven is into exile, surely the cave is *home*.

[752] Three: the pictorial analogies connect with the fact that a work of literature does not talk or *say* anything: it's a "silent" presentation like a picture.[701]

[753] I have just had an itchy and uncomfortable eczema skin eruption all over me. I suspect a partly "psychosomatic" factor: I'm the most irritable and irascible of men; I'm aware of the folly of expressing this in front of innocent people, so the irritability comes out in this form. To compare small things with great: were Job's boils his body's protest

against his patience? If so, something in him agreed with his wife [Job 2:9–10].

[754] In Luke 1 an angel comes to Zechariah & tells him Elizabeth will have a son. He says: "How shall this be? She's too old." The angel says: "All that will be taken care of, but you'll be struck dumb for doubting." In Luke 2 an angel comes to Mary and tells her she'll have a son. She says "How shall this be? I'm a virgin." Gabriel says only "All that will be taken care of." Mary had Gabriel, who was a decent soul; poor Zechariah was stuck with a heavenly asshole.

[755] I cut, reluctantly, Ted Roethke & the Canadians from 8: they could go in footnotes.[702]

[756] June, 1989. The massacre of the students in Tiananmin [Tiananmen] Square and the utter complacency of the senility squad about it, their confidence that all they have to do is to keep repeating the big lie, has definitely established Marxism, from Lenin on, as what Blake calls the Synagogue of Satan.[703] Nobody can support a Marxist political movement anywhere now without being, on the Burke principle, not just a mistaken man but a bad man.[704] Gorbachev's glasnost looks better, but even it is imposed from the top down.

[757] The creatures in China cannot "reform" anything, because to reform is to introduce the unpredictable, and they've proved they can't deal with that. They can only repress: that's all they know, and they will devote their entire energies to repression until their devils call for them. Their reforms or bourgeois revisions were forced out of them by the fact that the preposterous Marxist economy doesn't work. But forced & involuntary modifications, which don't come from any sort of vision, can lead only to chaos and anarchy, the other side of tyranny. Gorbachev is going back to the old pre-war game of disarmament conferences because, like the Americans, his economy won't stand the terrible military drain it's been getting, but whether his treatment of Georgia or Uzbekistan or the Baltic states will be any better is a quite different question.

[758] There's no doubt that the vast majority of people want peace and freedom and an open critical society: that's superficially closer to what

the Americans have, but America is not all that reassuring a model. I'm writing this out because I'd like to work on another big book. *Words with Power*, like its predecessor, dealt with everything under the sun except the relation of words to power: it's my "excluded initiative" in another context.

[759] A polarized or adversarial position is *not* a dialectical one: Lenin's notion that it has hung like a cloud of poison gas over this foul century. "Words with power" includes a situation in which power is a demonic parody of words, and dialectical materialism means opposed powers but has no philosophical basis or affinities. Curious how the Tiananmin [Tiananmen] massacre repeats the Shelleyan *Revolt of Islam* situation.

[760] I'm very pleased about the publicity given to the pederasty of Newfoundland priests:[705] however horrible it is to be accused of such practices when one is innocent of them, there seems no question of that here. Another corner of hell, that is, of abuse and arbitrary power, has been opened up to public scrutiny and, more important, superior authority. Priests have been buggering their choir-boys since the days of St. Paul, but they were always able to hush it up and refuse any jurisdiction but their own. They could only reform it themselves if they wanted to, and it was seldom they wanted to. In Voltaire's day it was an assumption that a young man visiting Rome was unlikely to return with his arsehole intact. The United Church, realizing that every religious body had a "gay" issue, brought the question into the open and got viciously slanged for doing so. Maybe they'll get some credit now for courage and foresight, but I doubt it.

[761] July 14/89.[706] The same ambivalence about the French Revolution that there was in the days of Fox and Burke. In my student days it was assumed that Bastille Day was the opening day of a new era, and that the terror was not really even regrettable, because it was so essential an incident in an evolving drama. There is a historical process, but tracing it brings me around to that silly man DeWitt's "evolution of the unintended" in another context.[707] Everything dramatic in history is bungled—well, there are some completed ones, like the Spanish Armada, but the rule holds—the historical process is never contained in the drama of history. Historical literature shows this negatively: the greatest historical novel, *War and Peace*, shows how utterly chaotic & haphazard the

productions of the historical dramatist Napoleon turned out to be. The historical process is guided by the arts & sciences.

[762] I'm moving in the direction of the third book here. The motive power or efficient cause of primary concern is democracy, the will of the majority. But of course an unconditioned popular will is as bad as any other unconditioned will. The telos or formal cause at which it aims is liberalism, as manifested or epiphanized in the liberal arts and sciences. Majority rule, it's always said, should be balanced by minority right, but minority right is ancillary to the one central and primary minority right, the right of culture. We pay an attention to the indigenous peoples now that we never paid a century ago, because we have a clearer idea of the importance of our culture. And our culture, which is essentially pluralistic, *is* our identity.

[763] But why liberal rather than a liberal-conservative dialectic, as in Mill? Because the conservative impulse is enshrined already in majority will, and is given form and direction only outside that will, in the counter-environment of culture. Not only is the popular will wrong as often as right, but when it doesn't have a liberal goal it's *always* wrong. For one thing, it's always directed & manipulated. If this directing force is the polarizing power-dialectic outside the social contract, as with Lenin, the eventual result is, first, tyranny, then anarchy and chaos. The last quarter-century has seen a growing sense of the importance of reconstituting the contract, including the contract with nature.

[764] What has this to do with the Bible? Well, the above is about the social contract, and the Bible consists of testaments (diatheke, not syntheke).[708] The testament is a "will" drawn up by a God who is *not* going to die. This is the figure even in *A Tale of a Tub*.[709] But God leaves man to figure it out much as though he were dying.

[765] What I have so far is:
   Natural and Revealed Communities.
   Historical Process and Historical Drama.
   Contract and Testament.
   Dynamic and goal: the educational contract.

[766] The crystallizing drop of the imagination is what causes the chaos

of events to take a symmetrical shape, and symmetry means something taken out of history. This I dreampt [*Antony and Cleopatra*, 5.2.94, folio ed.], July 14/89.

[767] I said of Bolingbroke that situations change, and the leader does what fits the new situation, not what's consistent with what he did before.[710] The fact that hypocrisy is the central political virtue makes some people very cynical. The Catholic Church maintains that it has preserved both consistent continuity and adaptability—that's Newman's point—but it's not easy for anyone outside the Church to believe that. (Nor necessary for anyone inside it to believe it, whatever is officially said.)

[768] (I've got this elsewhere)[711] Seven contracts in the Torah: with Adam, with Noah, with Abraham, Isaac & Jacob, with Moses (burning bush) & with Israel (Mt. Sinai, Deuteronomy). No contracts as such in the N.T.: only the events of Incarnation, Resurrection, Ascension, and Pentecost, with the explanations of what they mean. I suppose the restoration of Israel in the prophets, corresponding to the N.T. Second Coming, is a future contract. That's the eighth eye, the eternal Sunday.

[769] The human race, in its infinite stupidity, always assumes that the greatest men—Alexander, Caesar, Napoleon, Lenin—are those who have managed temporarily to give the illusion of having turned the historical process into a historical drama. This raises the thorny question of the role of leadership: Carlyle's hero crap.

[770] The book seems to be a phenomenology mountain, and this business of process and drama (i.e. the incarnating of myth) in history probably comes at or near the beginning. Obviously we need charismatic figures at a certain phase of the process—not impossibly at all phases—but my feeling that the pyramid model just won't do anymore still stands. In the Biblical contracts of course God is the top of the pyramid.

[771] What I'm aiming for is not any goal of absolute knowledge but the assimilating of action to vision: the "democratic" driving force compelled to take form in a "liberal" structure. After which I move cautiously in the direction of Utopias and model states. The ark isn't the church, as Augustine thought [*City of God*, bk. 15, chap. 26], but the church could be an ark at a certain point in time. The Toynbee picture would help here.

[772] My big books are like lakes or oceans, and my "parerga," as Sparshott calls them,[712] rivers flowing into them. My Shakespeare criticism didn't flow into WP—that was mainly a Blake & Romantic book—but I think this book will be full of Shakespeare. Historical process vs. drama are [is] the theme of the history plays; Montaigne's Utopian paradoxes come into T [*The Tempest*]. Even the two-world structure of MND [*A Midsummer Night's Dream*] seems to belong. In studying Shakespeare I constantly have the illusion of a definitive comprehension of the play and a definitive rendering of it in critical language. Half my brain knows that this is nonsense; the other half knows that there's some reality there, if we think in terms of wordless possession rather than verbal translation.

[773] Historical process & drama form the lower part of the mountain, the educational contract the middle section; the great Platonic forms, republic and symposium, emerge above them. It's a *very* Christian book, I'm afraid: I never did understand the Deuteronomic side of Judaism.

[774] Regarding things like silly reviews of me: what is important about free speech in a democracy is not only that everyone has a right to express an opinion, however ill-considered, but that fools should have full liberty to speak so that they can be recognized to be fools.[713]

[775] Romantic Esauism, the restoring of the heir who is "rightful" according to human expectations of what is right, is contemporary with the human reversal of the chain of being. Also with Napoleon, the first of the two men in the modern world (the other was Lenin) who squeezed the historical process into a historical drama. (Napoleon attacked Russia from outside, & Lenin from inside.) The focus of this is Carlyle, the exponent of the Great Man theory of history, the opposite (really) of the Biblical "judge," or hero as instrument of God. Shaw has a less coherent Great Man theory, though he tries to turn it into a Great Woman theory.[714]

[776] I've been reading Bruce Elder's *Image & Identity*,[715] a preposterous book in many ways, but useful in others. Just as I find French easier to follow when it's spoken with an English accent, so I find philosophy more useful when it's expounded by an amateur. Elder's book tries to set a study of Canadian film in a philosophical framework derived from George Grant (himself an amateur, perhaps) and the Armour-Trott book.[716]

[777] Recently a woman sought naturalization as a Canadian, & made a great to-do about being horrified to discover that Canada was a monarchy. (It can hardly have been a discovery.) Such people are exhibitionists of conscience: they seek out issues so that they can parade down the street with their beautiful consciences naked.

[778] "Natural law an appeal to oral tradition": Innis's Idea File, 83.[717]

[779] Don't overlook the ladder image in the Fall of Hyperion.[718]

[780] Did the Virgin Birth happen or didn't it? Answer, yes or no. In the spiritual world, which we enter through myth, there are no yeses or noes and all either-or questions are wrongly put. The past historical event is not important to me, so it didn't happen for me; it's important for you, so it did happen for you. This is insane, of course: therefore it's what we must live by.

[781] The top of the ladder in Five is a vision of *order*, of which hierarchy and authority are degenerations. The authority that emancipates instead of oppressing is involved here. The top of the ladder in Six is the hierogamy or sacred marriage between the Bridegroom who is both individual & universal humanity and the Bride who is both responding humanity and redeemed nature. The free-style speculations about sex life in the spiritual world remind us that we pass from the symbolic hierogamy to a world where the difference between loving one and loving many no longer exists and where the present conception of "person" is no longer applicable.[719]

[782] The *bottom* of the ladder in Seven is the treasure, the pearl of great price, again a symbol of something below it essential to one's identity. In the shit passage I need to introduce the cycle-dialectic contrast. Food & drink are the central symbols of union with nature; shitting is the central image of separating the excrementitious husk from the spiritual kernel.[720]

[783] End of Six: excrete the shit (about fifteen pages at the end) and focus the climax on hierogamy with its three aspects (1) Bridegroom as redeemer & Bride as community (*all* of it, niggers & Moabites & women)[721] (2) Bridegroom as king (royal metaphor or community as individual) and Bride as the inner vision of paradisal nature (Beulah)

(3) Bridegroom as conscious love & Bride as beauty (Plato; Kant's CJ [*Critique of Judgment*]).[722]

[784] End of Five: Merging of time & space into real present & real presence, eternal & infinite as here & now, Spenser's "Sabbath sight" which is also a vision of plenitude (tzabaoth) or "allness."[723]

[785] So Five is the Vita Contempliva; Six the Vita Activa. Five is the freedom of movement actualized in a freedom of thought, presented under the paradox of immobility. Six is the existential metaphor or identification of which sex is the primitive metaphorical kernel. Love-beauty merger is methexis < mimesis.[724]

[786] Fucking is for fucking's sake. Beauty, in the Critique of Judgment, is purposiveness without purpose. Nature says: fucking has the purpose of begetting children & perpetuating the species. Every genuine fuck, even when fertile, cheats silly nature. I don't mean all this, but the hunch is worth recording. Sublimation goes up the other way, toward the sense of the sex partner as *person* or individual. Children are loved as part of the community: the love for them has an educational factor.[725]

[787] Valery's *cimitière* [*cimetière*] *marin* is a perfect evocation of the end of 5, with all its paradoxical images of death (graveyard) "oceanic" loss of identity (sea) and Zeno's vision of a motionless universe.[726] The jeune parque is the corresponding Six vision of a conscious (naturans) life.

[788] Eight descends either to the world of *real* death & nothing *or* to the negating of nothing that starts creation.

[789] The second coming expands the first: it doesn't follow it in time. Seven incorporates the enlarged knowledge of the future in the lower world early, and it should become a central point toward the end. The Second Coming is not a future event, but the enlarging of the first one from ideology to authentic myth. Not that the gospels aren't authentic myth, but Revelation is the authentic antitype, and the "magisterium" damn well ain't.

[790] "Lead kindly light" is a hymn I have a peculiar dislike for. Not because it's doggerel in shaky grammar—it could be that and still be a memorable or even great hymn. But choosing and seeing one's path is not pride: it's what God wants us to do. Otherwise we get the dangers of

spiritual gravitation. The whole point of Newman's journey over crag and torrent was that the R.C. Church was at the bottom, ready to end the journey. I suspect that Newman never *really* wanted to become an R.C., but once he got into this "lead Thou me on" routine he couldn't avoid falling into it.727

[791] Five note: I pass over Plotinus and his Jacob's ladder of emanation downward and inspiration upward. Also, re. Davies' Orchestra, the word mnesteron means both "suitors" and "recalling to mind."728 Also, the O.T. type of the 144000 celibates [Revelation 14:1–4] is Deuteronomy 20 on the holy war.

[792] How we ought to act, how we ought to know, how we ought to feel: these give us the Platonic triad, the good, the true, the beautiful. These form Kant's three critiques. Over the three is the form of the fourth: how we ought to make: man's role as creator. Faith is not assent to the probably untrue: it's man making himself in the image of God. To what extent can man do this, if he's in a state of total depravity and is wholly dependent on grace? Well, God does not become God until he also becomes Man. Grace *is* incarnation. It's [Its] product is resurrection, or liberation. Only I wish Kant hadn't talked about Judgment (Urteilskraft): when did man suddenly become a judge?

[793] The history of my aesthetic responses over the years has taught me that it's silly to confine the beautiful to the functional: that's one of the many things wrong with all arguments from design. Also it justifies Kant's formula.729

[794] Watch out for the fallacy of premature consensus: nothing sensible ever gets said or done except by an individual, so it's no good holding a conference to determine a consensus. The consensus emerges much later, and secretly. God's purposes in regard to the world are deeper and more secret still.

[795] Note the poem to Anna Flaxman in one of Blake's letters, where Jacob's ladder descends on Blake's cottage (Felpham) in a spiral.730

[796] Nothing in Plato's Menexenus makes any sense, but note the remark (238A) that woman imitates earth, not earth woman731 (who ever said it did?).

[797] Philo also notes the Heshbon-reasoning connexion and says Potiphar was a eunuch.[732]

[798] Yeats' cat & moon poem comes from Plutarch. Isis & Osiris, 376.[733]

[799] I'm haunted constantly by the feeling that I don't know anything; then I read scholarly books & wonder if my hunches & guesses are really so inferior to their knowledge. Now I'm wondering if I could explore the Great Doodle. Erikson says little boys make tower structures & little girls enclosure ones.[734] Islamic countries have the minaret & the mosque; Christian ones the bell-tower & the basilica; Toronto the C.N. tower & the retractable Skydome. I've written about the axis mundi & only hinted at the G.D. [Great Doodle]. I am not a historian: I'm an architect of the spiritual world. I should start with the female or group aspect of God, the Schekinah. The "mankind" synecdoche affects all the spiritual world. The feminists keep yapping about Sophia, but I don't know what they know about her. Maybe God's intelligence is a group of emanations of wisdom.

[800] Dianoia, theme, and the innumerable variations of narrative or mythos it can contain. Themes are the lively stones of the temple [1 Peter 2:5].

[801] The Father is the origin lost in time, recreated in the Son or Word, the world revealed as verbal "between" the subjective & the objective. The Spirit is the Sophia or emanation of the revealed world, the power that inspires us to create.

[802] That skit of Borges had something: the Goldberg theme played at the end of the quest or conspectus of variations is not the same thing as the original theme.[735]

[803] The theme, dianoia, can have an infinite number of mythoi or variations. There's no reason why there couldn't be a female gospel just as there are minor variations to a major theme.

[804] I've been trying to read Kelber's book on the oral & written gospel[736]—wonder why the orality people write so badly. I suppose my two forms of rhetoric, with myth intervening, correspond to the oral tradi-

tion, the written gospel, & the recreated oral tradition (kerygma) for the reader who has got past the Ascension & has entered the spiritual world that's beyond both speech & writing.

[805] I've so often been asked: but can't you do anything creative like writing poetry or fiction? My creative powers, I've said, have to do with professional rhetoric, on both sides of myth-metaphor. To carry this farther I'd need a distinction between specific (Biblical) and general kerygma. Though that wouldn't help if the latter were just inspirational. It would have to be something part of specific kerygma though not its precise context. A lot of kerygma in the Bible is faked anyway: the "still small voice" [1 Kings 19:12], for example.

[806] Opus Perhaps Posthumous: Working Title: Quintessence of Dust. Four Essays.

[807] Theme: I'm not pitting (subjective) imagination against (objective) reality, but two kinds of reality, spiritual and physical, against each other. The s-o [subject–object] distinction disappears in the spiritual world.

[808] One: Prelude-Impromptu: starts off with that loud flash I got at Zagreb: the ideal of spontaneity, where the moment of composition and the moment of performance are the same.[737] I've written a fair amount about this, down to the Tempest as an imitation of an improvised knocked-together commedia dell'arte. Writing brings a special dimension: in Mallarmé, one could almost say, the white paper sheet with "nothing" written on it comes first.[738] The real point about ars celare artum is to present the product of a unified mind, the product being its own unity.[739]

[809] A recent reviewer talked about WP as though I were pitting the (subjective) imagination against an (objective) reality, thus preserving the s-o [subject–object] split.[740] What I'm really saying is so different I'd better start a new page for it.

[810] Man lives in two real worlds, one spiritual, the other natural, physical, or psychic. In the spiritual world God exists in us and we in him: a paradox that only metaphorical language can begin to express. In this world nature exists in us and we in it, but here the centralizing

principle, or ego, is constantly trying to isolate itself. The spirit interpenetrates with its world but never violates: our interpenetration makes war, as Heraclitus said, the centre of all activity,[741] because it's always withdrawing to objectify.

[811] The second essay is the reason why this series may come to nothing before my death. It uses books on pop-science about the bootstrap theory, the implicate order, the hologram metaphor, the wild pendulum, & the like, to show how the inner dynamic of science increasingly drives it to describe the physical world as an analogy of the spiritual one.[742]

[812] The third essay faces what I've never really faced before: What does Heilsgeschichte history tell us? I noted that although scholars know the conception, they never apply it consistently, but make the gospels as distorted a version of Weltgeschichte as possible.

[813] The fourth essay (not yet quite separated from the third) is the great doodle itself, the cosmic cunt. Perhaps the difference is that the journeyer is always symbolically male; the stations he stops at are symbolically female. This seems to make the feminists awfully mad, but if it makes sense they'll have to lump it.

[814] One: even the illiterate formulaic poet is producing a mythos of a dianoia, a variation of a theme. This conception of mythos as theme hasn't come up yet—oh, fuck, I mean as variation. That leads to a kind of integrating of myths around a theme I've never seriously looked at before. The theme here would have to be a super-motif. Of course the theme has no existence except in its variations.

[815] (I think I have this elsewhere but want to get it out of my mind.) One form of displacement is a distortion caused by anxiety that turns the theme into allegory. The Ancient Mariner is a profound & haunting story of man's alienation from nature (the murdered albatross) followed by the spontaneous re-identification with her. This gets twisted into the Ancient Mariner's becoming an itinerant member of the Society for the Preservation of the Albatross stopping the one of three most likely to shoot them (no previous evidence for this). Even Coleridge had an idea he'd goofed.

[816] Oral formulaic poetry exists wholly in time: writing is a primarily spatial concept. In Mallarmé you start with a sheet of blank paper with nothing on it.[743] The minute you write the word "nothing" on it poetry begins.

[817] In the spiritual world everything interpenetrates without violation; nature "allows of penetration less," & hence is a constantly aggressive & competitive world.[744] I don't know about the vacuum axiom:[745] perhaps the spiritual world doesn't know the distinction of full & empty.

[818] Quintessence and dust; Quarks or pinpoints; Quest and Cycle: Quiet Consummation.[746]

[819] The statement "if the common people got to know this they would make the wrong use of it" is always translatable into: "if other people got to know what we know, or think we know, we'd lose power." That's common in Catholic attitudes; when I see it in occult literature I know that only pseudo-knowledge is involved, as is also mainly true of Catholic doctrines.

[820] Lenin's error was in thinking that cultural entities (Lithuania, Georgia, etc) weren't important: they were part of the old history people would readily throw away as they jumped into their new role as workers of the world. A small tactical error, but enough to destroy the whole Leninist dream, which so nearly conquered the world.

[821] Every people is *the* chosen people: that's what a translated Bible means.

———

[822] I wonder if I could be permitted to write my *Twilight* book, not as evidence of my own alleged wisdom but as a "next time" (Henry James) book, putting my spiritual case more forcefully yet, and addressed to still more readers.[747] I wonder about a "Century of Meditations": if there isn't time for that, perhaps a "theme with variations," where after 32–3 meditations a central theme is repeated. Some of the meditations might be fictional, like my early efforts.[748]

[823] Thus: God exists in us and we in him, the metaphor of Paul where part and whole keep interchanging, might be the second announcement of the theme, while "we exist in nature and nature exists in us" could be the opening statement.

[824] Perhaps what I'm after is a series of gigantic "commissionings." It is, after all, a statement as trivial as the Diabelli waltz—I mean the nature one.

[825] Yes, I will pray for inspiration to complete another book, closer to "Power" than ever before. As long as I don't confuse power with dogmatic emphasis. The Spirit will translate what I ask for. Buber says the real devil doesn't deny or defy God: he just never makes up his mind.[749]

[826] What Paul meant by the Spirit rephrasing the prayers is [Romans 8:27–8], I think, that every petition has an ego-centered or selfish core in it—in this case the desire to be thought of as a wise man or great writer, confounding my hostile & indifferent critics. The Spirit purifies the prayer for God, but perhaps not necessarily for me: I've always had a hunch that the ego supplied an essential *sprone* or spur.

[827] The metaphors applied to God: king, ruler, sovereign, lord, master, are inevitable, and yet they *are* metaphors, and drawn from the wrong kind of human social organization. Even though they include liberty ("whose service is perfect freedom")[750] and equality (all are equal before God). There's an illusory quality about both liberty and equality until they are solidly linked to fraternity: the interpenetrating of the Christ-nature within all of us.